ABRAHAM ON TRIAL

A B R A H A M

O N   T R I A L

T H E   S O C I A L   L E G A C Y

O F   B I B L I C A L   M Y T H

Carol Delaney

PRINCETON UNIVERSITY PRESS · PRINCETON AND OXFORD

Second printing, and first paperback printing, 2000

Paperback ISBN 0-691-07050-4

The Library of Congress has cataloged the cloth edition of this book as follows

Delaney, Carol Lowery, 1940–
Abraham on trial : the social legacy of biblical myth / Carol Delaney.
p. cm.
Includes bibliographical references and index.
ISBN 0-691-05985-3 (hardcover : alk. paper)
1. Isaac (Biblical patriarch)—Sacrifice. 2. Child sacrifice—
Religious aspects—Comparative studies. 3. Abraham (Biblical patriarch)
4. Bible. O.T. Genesis XXII, 1–19—Criticism, interpretation, etc.—
History. 5. Koran. Surat al-Ṣāffāt—Criticism, interpretation,
etc.—History. 6. Fatherhood—Religious aspects—Comparative studies.
7. Gender. 8. Ishmael (Biblical figure). I. Title.
BS1238.S24D44   1998
222′.11068—dc21   98-12174

"The Story of Abraham" by Alicia Ostriker, which originally appeared
in 5 A.M. 2, no. 3 (1990), is reprinted with the permission of the author;
"Sarah's Choice" by Eleanor Wilmer, which originally appeared in Sarah's Choice,
The Phoenix Poets Series (Chicago: University of Chicago Press, 1989),
pp. 21–24, is reprinted with the permission of the author.

Frontispiece and part title pages: Detail of a Rembrandt etching of
Abraham and Isaac, from a private collection.

This book has been composed in Sabon

The paper used in this publication meets the minimum requirements
of ANSI/NISO Z39.48-1992 (R1997) (Permanence of Paper)

www.pup.princeton.edu

Printed in the United States of America

3   5   7   9   10   8   6   4   2

To my mother,

my daughter, and

my grandsons

and to all those without whose care

and protection none of us

would be here

To see what the writer makes
of Abraham is often to see most clearly
what the writer is trying to say.

S. SANDMEL, 1956:29

Contents

Illustrations

Acknowledgments

$\mathbf{B}$ECAUSE of the wide range this
book traverses, I have relied upon numerous people for help in finding my
way in different discourses and reference systems. First, I wish to thank
members of the family and all the participants in the California trial—the
attorneys, the judge, the psychiatrist, the translator, and the jurors. John
Sullivan, a friend and a public defender in California, shared information
and expertise and read drafts of the trial chapter. When she was a student
at Harvard Law School, Megan Muir, now a Seattle attorney, discussed
legal material with me and researched important documents in the law
school library. When I was daunted by writing something so different
from my usual subjects, Marcia Yudkin helped me over a writer's block.
Paul Rock, professor of criminology at the London School of Economics,
was an excellent critic of the trial chapter. His own work on trials and
courts so closely paralleled my own that I felt less alone.

Without leave from Stanford and a research fellowship at Harvard Divinity School in 1992–93 the research for the chapters on archaeology
and religious commentary would have taken much longer. I am exceedingly grateful for the opportunity to return to a place where I had studied
(1973–76) and worked as assistant director of the Center for the Study of
World Religions (1985–87) and where I knew the library well. The fac-
ulty, students, and staff were, as usual, interested, stimulating, and help-
ful. I especially thank Professor JoAnn Hackett for generously sharing her
knowledge of the ancient Near East, for numerous references, and for
informative, delightful discussions.

Several former graduate students at Harvard Divinity School need special note. Denise Buell, now assistant professor at Williams College,
helped enormously with her mastery of Hebrew, Greek, and Latin and
her deep knowledge of Judaism and Christianity during what is called the
"intertestamental" period. Similar thanks are owed to Gene McAfee, a
tutor at Lowell House, Harvard. Larry Wills, a professor at the Episcopal
Divinity School, shared his enthusiasm and knowledge of Greek and early
Christian society. The other research associates—Rosalind Shaw, Tal

Ilan, Hyun-kyung Chung, and Stephanie Jamison—provided stimulating discussions and conviviality during a long, cold, and lonely winter.

Tal Ilan showed me how to negotiate the labyrinthine system of rabbinic reference. Later, Howard Eilberg-Schwartz, formerly assistant professor of Jewish studies at Stanford, read a draft and corrected some dates and misrepresentations. Bob Gregg, the dean of Memorial Church at Stanford University and an expert on early Christianity, read a draft of the Christian chapter and encouraged my nonapologetic critique. The Muslim chapter was helpfully commented on by Gordon Newby, Bill Beeman, Saba Mahmood, and a number of respondents at the meetings of the American Academy of Religion, 1995, where I presented a summary.

Diane Jonte-Pace of Santa Clara University, whose expertise is in the field of psychoanalysis and religion, graciously read the Freud chapters. I also received comments and suggestions from Judith Van Herik, professor of religious studies at Penn State, who has, herself, written eloquently about Freud, femininity, and faith. Graduate students in my seminar, "Religion," helped me clarify my critique of Freud, and Bill Maurer, now assistant professor at the University of California, Irvine, helped me see that one chapter should become two.

I am also indebted to Sandra Razieli, who, during her fieldwork in Jerusalem, alerted me to some uses of the Abraham story and took the photograph of the Dome of the Rock; to Shari Seider, whose work among Orthodox Jews in Argentina provided insightful discussions about Judaism and nationalism; and to Stefan Helmreich who helped me think about the title and chapter headings. In the last stages, I benefited greatly from the comments of the reviewers, Bill Beeman, Jorunn Buckley, Gillian Feeley-Harnik, and Gordon Newby, who kindly revealed themselves to me, enabling us to discuss further their proposed revisions. Mary Murrell, my editor at Princeton, suffered through the whole process, providing inspiration, incisive criticism, and numerous clippings and references. Marsha Kunin did a superb job of copyediting the final manuscript. I have tried to accommodate their suggestions, but the mind truly does have a mind of its own and I could not always find the proper place for them. There is much that has been left out—otherwise the manuscript could easily have grown to a book for each chapter.

A fellowship at the Center for Advanced Study in the Behavioral Sciences (1996–97), partly funded by a grant from the Andrew W. Mellon Foundation, allowed me time to complete the book, which had languished due to a heavy teaching load. The interest and enthusiasm of the other fellows provided the fuel to get on with it and get it done. I am especially grateful to those who read and commented on drafts of chapters: Gillian Feeley-Harnik, Martin Green, Susan Okin, Paul Rock, and the Family and Children group. I wish also to thank several members of the Center staff: Patrick Goebel, the computer wizard, taught me how to operate my new computer and was there when I or it got stuck; Kathleen Much edited the penultimate draft; and Virginia MacDonald helped with some of the word processing.

Finally, I wish to thank my daughter, Elizabeth Quaratiello, who is, herself, a gifted writer and editor. Her reading of an early draft helped with the subsequent ones. She also contributed by giving birth to her first child, my first grandchild. During the hard work of writing, they were a most delightful distraction and helped me keep some needed perspective. Stephen poignantly kept in front of me the insanity of a system that has made a virtue out of the willingness to sacrifice a child.

ABRAHAM ON TRIAL

1. And it came to pass after these things, that God did tempt Abraham, and said unto him, Abraham: and he said, Behold here I am.

2. And he said, Take now thy son, thine only son Isaac, whom thou lovest, and get thee into the land of Moriah; and offer him there for a burnt offering upon one of the mountains which I will tell thee of.

3. And Abraham rose up early in the morning, and saddled his ass, and took two of his young men with him, and Isaac his son, and clave the wood for the burnt offering, and rose up, and went unto the place of which God had told him.

4. Then on the third day Abraham lifted up his eyes, and saw the place afar off.

5. And Abraham said unto his young men, Abide ye here with the ass; and I and the lad will go yonder and worship, and come again to you.

6. And Abraham took the wood of the burnt offering, and laid it upon Isaac his son; and he took the fire in his hand, and a knife; and they went both of them together.

7. And Isaac spake unto Abraham his father, and said, My father: and he said, here am I, my son. And he said, Behold the fire and the wood: but where is the lamb for a burnt offering?

8. And Abraham said, My son, God will provide himself a lamb for a burnt offering: so they went both of them together.

9. And they came to the place which God had told him of; and Abraham built an altar there, and laid the wood in order, and bound Isaac his son, and laid him on the altar upon the wood.

10. And Abraham stretched forth his hand, and took the knife to slay his son.

11. And the angel of the Lord called unto him out of heaven, and said, Abraham, Abraham: and he said, Here am I.

12. And he said, Lay not thine hand upon the lad, neither do thou anything unto him: for now I know that thou fearest God, seeing thou hast not withheld thy son, thine only son from me.

13. And Abraham lifted up his eyes, and looked, and behold behind him a ram caught in a thicket by his horns: and Abraham went and took the ram, and offered him up for a burnt offering in the stead of his son.

14. And Abraham called the name of that place Jehovah jireh: as it is said to this day, In the mount of the Lord it shall be seen.

15. And the angel of the Lord called unto Abraham out of heaven a second time;

16. And said, By myself have I sworn, saith the Lord, for because thou has done this thing and has not withheld thy son, thine only son:

17. That in blessing I will bless thee, and in multiplying I will multiply thy seed

as the stars of heaven, and as the sand which is upon the seashore; and thy seed shall possess the gate of his enemies;

18. And in thy seed shall all the nations of the earth be blessed because thou has obeyed my voice.

19. So Abraham returned unto his young men, and they rose up and went together to Beersheba; and Abraham dwelt at Beersheba.

20. And it came to pass after these things, that it was told Abraham, saying, Behold, Milcah, she hath also born children unto thy brother Nahor;

21. Huz his firstborn, and Buz his brother, and Kemuel the father of Aram,

22. And Chesed, and Hazor, and Pildash, and Jidlaph, and Bethuel.

23. And Bethuel begat Rebekah: these eight Milcah did bear to Nahor, Abraham's brother.

24. And his concubine, whose name was Reumah, she bare also Tebah, and Gaham, and Thahash, and Maachah.

Introduction

━━━━━

IN THE BEGINNING of the last decade of the twentieth century, in that most modern of places, California, a tragedy of Biblical proportions unfolded with the morning newspaper:

Father Sacrificed Child. God Told Him To.

So accustomed are we to horrendous tales of domestic violence that this headline might seem only a bizarre twist on the ordinary. People who read about the incident over their morning coffee noted it, registered a reaction, and turned the page, muttering, "The man must be crazy." In this way, the man was defined, the deed was labeled, and the whole thing could be put out of mind. A year later, when Cristos Valenti came to trial, only one of the jurors remembered the newspaper story.[1]

Yet once upon a time, God asked another father to sacrifice his child. For *his* willingness to obey God's command, Abraham became the model of faith at the foundation of the three monotheistic (Abrahamic) religions: Judaism, Christianity, and Islam.[2] His story has been inscribed on the hearts and minds of billions of people for millennia. Even today, Abraham's devotion is revered and his example extolled in countless sermons and in the secular media. With that cultural model readily available, it is not so surprising that Cristos Valenti felt he must obey God's command. Yet for his willingness to comply with God's request, Cristos Valenti was brought to trial.

This book puts the Abraham story on trial. The contemporary case, to be discussed in chapter 2, helps bring the Abraham story emotionally closer and raises several issues that recur throughout the book. But it could not raise the most important question, the question that motivated this book and the years of research that have gone into it: Why is the willingness to sacrifice one's child *the* quintessential model of faith, why not the passionate protection of the child? What would be the shape of our society had *that* been the supreme model of faith and commitment? By critically examining the Abraham story, I think we can catch a glimpse.

If it is true, as Shalom Spiegel suggests, that the "story of Abraham renews itself in every time of crisis" (Spiegel, 1969, back cover), then the time has come to take another look. The crisis of society today is about values, about the very values that, I think, are epitomized by the Abraham story—not just faith and sacrifice, but also the nature of authority; the basis and structure of the family, its gender definitions and roles; and which children, under what circumstances, shall be deemed acceptable and be provided for. My purpose is not to reinvigorate these values but to challenge them at their foundation.

The story of Abraham, some will say, is just a story about something that happened (or might have happened) long ago. They feel it has little to do with their lives or their faith, and thus they do not usually imagine that it has any bearing on contemporary life. What they forget is that the story of Abraham, like that of Jesus, was powerful enough to change the course of human history.[3] It is clear that the story of Abraham is not just one story among others; it is "central to the nervous system of Judaism and Christianity" (Goldin in Spiegel, 1969:xvii). It is also central to Islam. Insofar as it has shaped the three religious traditions, their ethical values, and their views of social relations, it has shaped the realities we live by. Even if we are not believers, any of us raised in a culture influenced by Judaism, Christianity, or Islam has been affected by the values, attitudes, and structures exemplified by the story.

My interpretation of the Abraham story attempts to uncover the set of assumptions that make the story possible; it is a way to get behind the story. Traditional exegeses proceed out from the story, and move quickly to conventional contexts for interpretation, namely sacrifice and faith, contexts that predetermine possible lines of interpretation. For example, if the story is viewed in the context of the theories and meanings of sacrifice, then the questions put to it will be how and in what ways does it conform to, deviate from, or shed light on known sacrificial practices? Related, surely, is whether the story represents the end of the supposed practice of child sacrifice and the institution of animal sacrifice. But even if child sacrifice was practiced in the ancient Near East, a discussion of which will occupy chapters 3 and 4, such interpretations fail to recognize that Abraham is revered not for putting an end to the practice but for his willingness to go through with it. *That* is what establishes him as the father of faith. *That* is what I find so terrifying. The story is not about substitution, symbolic or otherwise, but about a new morality; it represents not the end of the practice of child sacrifice but the beginning of a new order.

Interpretations that focus on Abraham's faith argue that to demonstrate his absolute, unswerving faith he had to be willing to sacrifice the thing he loved most in the world—the son he waited so long to have, the very child his God had promised. The paradoxical aspect reveals, to some, the mystery of God and the power of faith; one must simply make a leap of faith and believe.[4] I am suspicious of these types of interpretations and think there is another, less mysterious question that, perhaps because it is so simple, has been overlooked.

Neither religious commentators nor lawyers in the contemporary trial asked the question that has nagged me: what allowed Abraham (and Cristos) to assume the child was *his* to sacrifice? At first blush, the question seems meaningless. God asked him. But could or would the all-knowing God ask only one parent for the child, knowing that a child belongs to both mother and father or, perhaps, to neither? The story, however, conveys the impression that the child belonged to Abraham in a way he did not belong to Sarah.[5]

The focus on fatherhood pervades Genesis; one need only think of all the *begats* and the emphasis on the patrilineage, to realize that this is the case. But if so, on what basis were children attributed to their fathers? To say that the child belongs to the father because of patriarchy, a usual response, explains nothing, because *patriarchy* means the power of fathers; such an answer is circular and only defers the question. What we need to ask is: what is it about fathers or fatherhood that conveys such power?

My interpretation turns on the meaning of paternity and shows how the definition and assumptions about paternity made it possible for Abraham (and perhaps Cristos) to think that the child was his to sacrifice. The meanings are integral to the story; it does not make sense without them. Moreover, the same meanings have been carried over and reinforced by ancient as well as modern, religious as well as secular, interpretations; the meanings have been assumed, not examined. Drawing on anthropological studies of kinship and gender, I argue that neither the role nor the power of the father is a given in nature and the order of things, but that both are intimately connected to a particular *theory* of procreation, a theory that is, in turn, connected to a cosmological/metaphysical system.

Paternity has not meant just the recognition of a biological relationship between a man and a specific child, nor the social role built on that recognition; paternity has meant *the primary, creative, engendering* role. In the Bible (and in the popular imagination) it is symbolized by the word "seed." Identity, whether of plant or of person, is imagined as a matter of seed; in human terms it is bequeathed by the father. The soul, also, was imagined as transmitted via seed. The child belongs to the father because it *is* his seed. Women, in contrast, have been imagined as the nurturing medium in which the seed is planted rather than as co-creators; they foster its growth and bring it forth, but do not provide its essential identity. The very notion of paternity, therefore, already embodies *author*ity and power and provides the rationale for a particular constellation of the family and the structure of relations within it. This notion of paternity is integral to the story of Abraham, for it is all about his "seed."

The seemingly simple word *seed* is anything but simple or neutral. By evoking associations with agriculture and the natural world, the image naturalizes a structure of power relations as it also conceals it (see Yanagisako and Delaney, 1995). Represented as seed and soil, male and female roles have been differentially valued and hierarchically ordered. This theory of procreation, common to both the ancient Hebrews and the ancient Greeks, has been the dominant folk theory in the West for millennia, shaping popular images and sentiments of gender.[6]

From today's perspective, this theory of procreation is obviously erroneous. Today we believe that both male and female contribute the same kind of thing to the identity of a child, namely genes, and that each contributes half the genetic endowment, half the seed, so to speak. Women, of course, contribute much more—by way of nurture to the fetus in utero, by giving birth, and often by providing additional nurture and care during its early life—but women are still popularly associated only with the nurturing, not the creative aspects. The modern, biogenetic understanding of reproduction is relatively recent, known only to certain of the world's peoples, and it tends to be confined explicitly to biomedical discourses. Yet notions of paternity and maternity were culturally constructed long before the development of biology and genetics, and these older notions are still being perpetuated by popular images and sentiments about gender and by the social arrangements, especially the family, that continue to affect the way men and women are thought about.

The meanings of paternity and maternity were not originally based on biological theory, and they do not simply change in response to changes in biological theory. They are rooted far deeper and their extent is far wider than the discourse and domain of reproduction; ultimately they are rooted in a cosmological system, in this case the monotheistic world view that is elaborated somewhat differently in Judaism, Christianity, and Islam. The foundational story of Abraham is central to these belief systems as well as to the societies influenced, and the social arrangements legitimated, by them.

For believers, the story has a central place both theologically and ritually in each of the religions. Jews recite Genesis 22 annually at the new year services of Rosh Hashanah; it is also included as part of the daily morning prayers of the devout. Christians think the story prefigures the Crucifixion, when God the Father sacrificed his only begotten son; a recitation of Genesis 22 is traditionally part of the services during Easter week. Muhammad's mission was to recall the people to the one true religion given in the beginning to Abraham. Each year Muslims dramatically

reenact the event on the most sacred day of the Muslim calendar—the
Feast of the Sacrifice—that occurs at the end of the rituals of the *Hajj*. On
that day, whether in Mecca or at home, each male head of household
sacrifices a ram (or substitute) in place of the intended child. And every
male child can imagine that, but for the grace of God, there might he be.
Told year after year, generation after generation, the story has continued
to make an impact on the minds and emotions of people who are, as
promised, countless "as the stars of heaven and as the sand which is upon
the seashore" (Gen. 22:17).

The Abraham story overflows the boundaries of religious communities. As one of the most common religious themes depicted in painting
and also well represented in literature, sculpture, and music, it has become part of the cultural mainstream. In the space of two weeks in November 1992, just when I was beginning work on this book, the story was
the subject of (1) an art exhibit in Berkeley, California; (2) a sermon delivered by a minister in Little Rock Arkansas, and directed at Bill Clinton,
who was sitting in the first pew the Sunday after his election to the presi-
dency; and (3) a *Peanuts* cartoon just before Thanksgiving.

As a way of protesting the Vietnam war, Bob Dylan wrote a song
("Highway 61 Revisited") that imagined Abraham questioning God's
order. Perhaps he was aware of the practice of using the story of Abraham
to legitimate war, as was Wilfred Owen in his famous poem against the
"fathers" sending the "sons" off to World War I. Leonard Cohen wrote
a song called "The Sacrifice of Isaac." When George Segal was commis-
sioned to make a sculpture commemorating the deaths of the students at
Kent State, he chose the theme of Abraham and Isaac. And when Kent
State rejected it on the grounds that it was too inflammatory, Princeton
University bought it and placed it near the chapel on campus (see fig. 1).
The story was the subtext of President Carter's book about the Middle
East, *The Blood of Abraham*; more recently of a novel, *The Sacrifice of
Isaac*, by Neil Gordon, about the ambivalent legacy of the Holocaust; as
well as of Woody Allen's film *Crimes and Misdemeanors*.[7] On Easter
Sunday and Monday 1994, in the midst of my writing, a miniseries en-
titled *Abraham* was shown on television. I mention each of these uses of
the story—and there are many more—primarily to make the point that
the story is very much alive in contemporary American culture.

I approach the story of Abraham as an anthropologist viewing it not
purely as a religious text but also as a cultural text, for no matter how
divinely inspired it may have been, it is an artifact of human culture. My
goal, however, is not to recover the particular time and place of Abraham. The story was transmitted orally and edited repeatedly for hundreds
of years before it ever reached its canonical form; therefore "any interpretation which substantively depends on relating the text to an historical

FIG. 1. Sculpture by George Segal, *Abraham and Isaac*.
Princeton University. Photo by author.

context must itself be forever tentative and hypothetical" (Moberly, 1988:312). At the same time, I do not mean to imply that it can be totally taken out of its context, for the opposite hermeneutical tendency often assumes that it is, therefore, timeless and represents "the human condition" or universal human psychology. That approach is equally misleading.

Regardless of its provenance, the story does not merely reflect a particular culture and society; it also incorporates a vision of society, indeed, a vision of the cosmos that has animated numerous cultures over considerable time. To connect it only to a particular time and locale would be to lose sight of that fact. Too often we forget the way that events themselves are transformed in relation to mythic structures of interpretation (see Mintz, 1984; McNeill, 1986; Sahlins, 1981; Samuel and Thompson, 1990). People continue to derive their identity, orient their lives, and interpret the meaning of life from the patterns first charted by the story.

> Scriptures are not only a record of the past but a prophecy, a foreshadowing and foretelling of what will come to pass. And if that is the case, text and personal experience are not two autonomous domains. On the contrary, they are reciprocally enlightening; even as the immediate event helps to make the age-old sacred text intelligible, so in turn the text reveals the fundamental significance of the recent event or experience. (Goldin in Spiegel, 1969:xvi)

Religious myth has social implications; conversely social events (are made to) speak to religious themes. In this way is woven the moral fabric that helps people make sense of their lives. We can never recapture the living quality of the culture of the biblical writers, but we can investigate their vision of the world and its legacy. We can ask about the role of the Abraham story in that vision. And we can ask if this vision is one we wish to perpetuate.

GUIDE TO READERS

First a caveat and then a *brief* on how the book will proceed. Although questions I put to the material are contemporary, this does not mean that I expect people who lived thousands of years ago to have had the same ideas we do, or to have acted according to values we cherish. Quite the contrary. New questions can expose assumptions of the past, and can show that those assumptions were not naturally given or inevitable, but part of a culturally constituted universe. By asking new questions of well-known stories, stories that we continue to tell ourselves and, perhaps more important, our children, we may gain new insight into their meanings. Such questioning does, however, make some people nervous. Directed to foundational stories, the questions are felt by some as if they are threats to the foundations of a house, for they begin to unsettle the edifice built upon it. But for those of us concerned with dismantling patriarchy, it is important to understand the power of this most patriarchal of stories.

Using anthropological and historical methods, I scrutinize material from several disciplines: archaeology, biblical and religious studies, and psychoanalysis. Each begins from different premises—different assumptions are made, different questions are asked, and different styles of interpretation prevail. Because of these differences it is not easy to move from one to the other; the distinctions are important and their blurring too often leads to distortions, errors, and anachronisms. For this reason, the material from each discipline is treated in a separate section—each focusing on the questions, subjects, arguments, and evidence that characterize it; each section also tends to partake of the discursive style of that discipline. Despite the differences, I demonstrate that the same assumptions about gender, kinship, and procreation pervade them all. These assumptions form the backdrop for interpretations; they are the things that go without saying; they underlie and unite a seeming variety of interpretations and contemporary social practices. By turning our attention to these assumptions, we begin to glimpse the outlines of a powerful myth we live by—its destructive legacy as well as the possibilities for constructive change.

The chapters are not meant to form an argument built up layer upon layer; instead they should be imagined as different facets of the same basic argument. Each has a different slant; each adds light to the cumulative power of the whole. Chapter 1 is the case for the prosecution. It outlines my argument: (a) it discusses the relevance of anthropology, the importance of the study of kinship and origin myths; (b) it elaborates the notion that paternity and maternity are cultural constructions rather than reflections of natural roles; and (c) it discusses the power of language and what happens when we try to change it. After the first chapter, the reader may move to any of the subsequent chapters. Chapter 2 is an account of the trial in California of Cristos Valenti, who sacrificed his child because God told him to do so. His story is not the same as that of Abraham if for no other reason than that Cristos had the model of Abraham before him. It is not so much because one is secular and the other sacred or because, in Cristo's case, the child was killed whereas Abraham's God intervened in time; Cristos Valenti's story unfolds within a context already shaped by the values inherent in the Abraham story. His rationale depends on these values and his defense rests on them. The emotional power of Valenti's story helps to focus a number of moral issues, but it never challenges the model on which it is based: Abraham is never put on trial.

The second section (chapters 3 and 4) addresses the common belief that the story is meant to mitigate a more ancient practice of child sacrifice by the substitution of a ram. I discuss the evolutionary assumptions embedded in such views and the archaeological evidence for and against the practice. Like the archaeological evidence, the evidence in the Bible is generally considered later both narratively and chronologically than the Abraham story. Although the sacrifice of children may have occurred at some time in the circum-Mediterranean world, the Abraham story cannot be seen as the mitigation of such a practice. In addition, I question whether the story should even be interpreted in the context of theories of sacrifice.

The third section (chapters 5 through 7) is devoted to exegeses of the meaning and place of the story in each of the three religious traditions and to the kinds of debates that have arisen in each. In an attempt to preserve the integrity of each tradition, each will be treated separately. At the same time, I undermine the religious "defenses" by showing that all of them rest on similar assumptions about paternity and gender that, in turn, are integral to the theological meaning.

Psychoanalytic theory has also grappled with the relationship between gender, kinship, and religion. In the fourth section (chapters 8 and 9) I challenge Freud's theory of the Oedipus complex as foundational not only for individual psychology but also for society as a whole, that is, as the foundation story wherein "religion, morals, society and art converge" (Freud, SE 13:156). Why did Freud focus only on the son's desires and acts without considering those of the father? In the Oedipus story, why did he ignore Laius's homicidal impulse? In *Moses and Monotheism*, why did Freud fabricate a story of the symbolic "sons" killing the "father" rather than using the story *in* the biblical text of the father willing to kill the son? His proposal of Oedipus as the myth we live by eclipsed that of Abraham; Freud's blindness allowed the story of Abraham and its values to persist unchecked.

Finally, in chapter 10, I briefly discuss how the story of Abraham has bequeathed a moral legacy in which we have been taught not to question the authority of "fathers," even though, in the process, we betray children. Contemporary examples illustrate the ways in which the sacrifice and betrayal of children has been institutionalized. One can point to the dreadful conditions in which most children in the world are living. Children are abused at the hands of their parents, most frequently fathers or their surrogates, and by priests—the very "fathers" who stand in for God and whose mission it is to protect children. One can also include war and point out that "children" are sent off to fight old men's battles and that the U.S. military budget vastly exceeds that of welfare. The recent welfare debate itself shows how the "fathers" (of state) exercised their power to determine the fate of a whole generation of children.

The story of Abraham is not causative in any direct sense. But because it exemplifies and legitimates a hierarchical structure of authority, a specific form of family, definitions of gender, and the value of obedience that are simultaneously the fountainhead of faith and the bedrock of society, it has created an environment that has made it seem sacrilegious to question these issues.

As Abraham takes the knife to slay his son, God calls out: "Because thou hast done this thing, and hast *not* withheld thy son, thine only son: I will bless thee, and I will multiply thy seed as the stars of heaven and as the sand upon the seashore, and thy seed shall possess the gate of his enemies. And in thy seed shall all the nations of the earth be blessed, because thou hast obeyed my voice" (Gen. 22:16–19).[8]

Like that knife eternally poised in mid-air, several questions should be held in the mind of the reader. Why is the willingness to sacrifice the child the model of faith? What is the function of obedience? Why so little attention to the betrayal of the child? Whose voice counts? Like another sacrificed by his father, did Abraham's son cry out at the critical moment: "Father, father, why hast thou forsaken me?" Why have we eulogized their submission?

This book puts on trial the story often referred to as "Abraham's trial"—a reference both to God's testing of him and his own suffering. The question before us is whether we should perpetuate the story and the lessons it has taught. In the next chapter I present my general argument. In the following sections, evidence from several very different perspectives is brought forth. Attend to the kinds of questions that have been asked, and to the silences. Consider whether and how well the evidence supports my argument. You the reader must consider the verdict.

PART ONE

Abraham on Trial

CHAPTER ONE

Abraham on Trial: Case for
the Prosecution

For CULTURES influenced by Judaism, Christianity, and Islam, Abraham is symbolically the first patriarch. As Abram, his name meant something like "exalted father" or "the father is exalted," and as Abraham, it meant "father of nations." His story begins what are aptly called the "patriarchal narratives." What better place, then, to begin an investigation of patriarchy?

Although feminists have long been concerned with patriarchy, no feminist theorist, as of this writing, has focused directly on Abraham.[1] Some feminist interpreters of the Bible have included the story of Abraham along with those of other biblical figures as if it were merely one story among others. A few have skirted it in their discussions of Sarah, Abraham's wife, or Hagar, her handmaid, his concubine (e.g., Teubal, 1984, 1990; Trible, 1984), but all have failed to recognize the centrality and the social weight of the story in Genesis 22.

The desire of some feminist interpreters to resurrect the voices of ancient women is important as no expression of their feelings exists in the text. Indeed, that is where I began. Although the Abraham story has bothered me since childhood, I began a serious investigation of it only after becoming a mother. It was easy then to imagine how Sarah might have felt when she discovered that her child was missing and learned what had happened. Imagining her reaction, however, could only register her pathos and her exclusion; it could not directly challenge the story, for, given the way the text is constructed, she can only react. I wanted to know why the story was constructed that way. I wanted to know why the foundational story is centered on a father, his son, and a male-imaged god. Is their gender merely accidental, or is it precisely the point?

When I told people I intended to analyze the story in terms of gender, most did not understand what that could mean. "But it is not about women," some said, as if only women have gender. "The story of Abraham," others countered, "is about religion, about spirituality. What can it possibly have to do with gender?" Gender may seem irrelevant to those concerned with drawing out the spiritual message of the story, which, they further presume, could be addressed to anyone. But does the story have the same meaning for women, or is it inextricably entangled with meanings of masculinity, particularly fatherhood?

Gender *is* precisely the point. The religious content cannot be separated from notions of gender and notions of generativity, especially paternity. The importance of paternity has been missed by most scholars because they have misunderstood what it means; they have assumed that it means merely the recognition of the biological relationship between a man and a given child.[2] That is not so surprising—most people in the West assume that kin terms *mean* the biological relations that are established through sexual reproduction.

Rather than reflecting natural facts, the meanings of father and mother, paternity and maternity emerge relative to a *theory* of procreation. In this theory, the male role is construed as the creative one: he is the one who "begets" and by means of his "seed" imparts the life-giving essence that defines a child. The female role is to nurture the seed-child implanted in her and to give birth. I have elsewhere (Delaney, 1986, 1991) called this a *monogenetic* theory, as the *principle* of creation comes from only one source. Symbolically, it is the human analogue of divine, monotheistic creation. The life-giving abilities attributed to men allied them with God, and women became associated with what was created by God, namely the Earth.

The power to create life implies the concomitant power to destroy. God both creates and destroys; if he chooses, he has the right to destroy what he has created. Indeed, that is a pervasive threat in Genesis and in the Hebrew Bible more generally, as well as in the Qur'an. Men, with the help of God, were thought to bestow life; analogously they were also given power over it. That is what the story of Abraham enacts. God speaks to Abraham, Abraham speaks to Isaac. He does not tell Sarah where he is going or what he is about to do; he does not need to. Isaac is his, Isaac is Abraham's seed. The transaction is between Abraham and God on the one side and between Abraham and Isaac on the other. The story is about the deal these three struck: by relinquishing some of his power to God, Abraham received it back a thousandfold. When he submits to God's will, God's will flows through him and becomes identical with his; male authority is invested with sacred power.[3]

God is symbolically masculine, imagined foremost as Creator; his divinity could easily be imagined as a denaturalized and reified male-paternal generativity.[4] In the natural world that he created, that creativity

is channeled through males and becomes part of the definition of masculinity. The religious aspects of the story lend an aura that naturalizes patriarchal power; it is seen as part of the natural order, an order that is,
however, ordained by God. In other words, patriarchy is not just a secular social order, but an order at once sacred and secular, a point often
missed in numerous social analyses, including feminist ones, that have
focused on economics and/or politics and relegated religion to a peripheral or residual category. Regardless of the religious identities or affilia-
tions of the analysts, there is a tendency to see religion as a reflex of
social-structural arrangements or as a personal choice having to do primarily with one's spiritual concerns. There are, of course, notable exceptions, for instance the tradition beginning with Weber.

Gender is clearly not a peripheral or subsidiary aspect of the story, or
of theology more generally, but an integral part of the theological meaning, and vice versa. Expressing the opinion of many who are opposed to
female ordination, Michael Novak, a contemporary Catholic thinker and
editor of the journal *Crisis*, says, "sex differentiation is not simply a trivial detail, to be discarded or altered without concern for consequences;
it is essential to the story of salvation. Fundamental. Foundational"
(Novak, 1993:29). Recent unprecedented changes in reproduction, such
as chemical birth control and new reproductive technologies, not to mention surrogacy and legalized abortion, have begun to erode traditional
meanings of gender and family. These changes strike at the heart of religious authority and portend the erosion of theological meanings and
structures. It is no wonder that these are the issues at the center of contemporary religious and social debate.

This threat to religious authority is a crisis unlike any other. In the past
the story of Abraham was offered to encourage people to keep the faith of
Abraham; today the crisis seems to be about that kind of faith and about
the values that are integral to the story: a particular definition of family
and "family values," gender definitions and roles that derive from an
outmoded theory of procreation, and a hierarchical social order that
stresses authority and obedience. The struggle is between those who believe that the traditional definitions and values should be upheld at all
costs and those, like myself, who feel that they are part of the problem.
Today, both liberals and conservatives who speak about the "social crisis" focus on the breakdown of religious values as well as on the so-called
breakdown of the family. Furthermore, they often imply that it is father-
absence rather than the lack of emotional and financial support (as well
as day care, health care, education, and opportunities) for the mothers
that is the cause of juvenile crime, teenage pregnancy, drugs, and gangs.
Such politicians and social scientists reinforce gender (as well as racial
and class) stereotypes when they imply that "mothers can't control the

kids," as if only fathers can instill moral values, demand respect, and provide appropriate discipline. Rather than accept that the "family as we know it" is not (and perhaps never really was) the norm, they call for a reinvigoration of the supposedly natural and traditional family. Instead of thinking of creative ways for helping people raise and support their/ our children, they impose impossible demands on those who do not conform. At such a juncture, it is useful to return to the foundation story, not to ascertain its truth or falsity (as if that were possible) but to better grasp what it presupposes and implies.

ORIGIN MYTHS

When anthropologists study other cultures they usually include a study of the foundational stories or origin myths of that culture, for a myth "is a sacred narrative explaining how the world and man came to be in their present form" (Dundes, 1984:1). Anthropologists look to origin myths to learn something about a people's conception of the world, of nature, of time and history, of male and female, of social organization, within which the identity of a specific group is situated. And given such conceptions, they ask what kinds of values and attitudes are implied by such a vision. In other words, anthropologists, at least since Malinowski, have tended to assume that "an intimate connection exists between the word, ethos, and sacred tales of a people on the one hand, and their ritual acts, moral deeds, their social organization and even their practical activities on the other" (Malinowski, 1954:96). Yet they do not apply this wisdom to their own culture. Fewer than a handful have turned their attention to Genesis, the preeminent origin myth of Western culture, to consider its structuring function.[5] Ironically, just at the time when a number of "master narratives" are being challenged, the religious narrative remains relatively untouched.[6]

Myths of origin may not point to "real, true" historical origins, but they are important *representations* of origins: they provide a framework within which people situate and interpret their lives; they affect people's identity and orientation in that world; and most important, they provide answers to the questions "Who are we? Where do we come from? Where are we going?" Jews, Christians, and Muslims have been able to say, "We are the children of Abraham."

For centuries, however, these children have been fighting over the patrimony, both theologically and in everyday life. Who is the true "seed" of Abraham and who will inherit the promises? That biblical myth still affects social life was tragically illustrated by the massacre in Hebron on 25 February 1994 at the Cave of the Patriarchs, allegedly the tomb of Abraham. The area continues to be one of the most fought-over places in

Israel. I often think that if these "children" would just look up from their battles, they might see that their common father is the source not just of their unity but also of their strife.

THE STORY OF ABRAHAM

Regardless of whether he ever lived, Abraham is considered the person through whom a new conception of the divine entered human society. According to tradition, the new conception was not just of a new god or gods, but of the one and only God. Although that conception entered history at a particular time, it was projected back to the beginning; a vision not just of the way things are but of the way things always had been, a picture "of the way things in sheer actuality are" (Geertz, 1973: 89). There could be no stories about struggles between the gods for preeminence, as in some of the neighboring Near Eastern traditions; the new conception of God rendered them senseless. There could be only a story of recognition, that is, of acknowledging and submitting to the one true God. Abraham is imagined as the vehicle for revealing God's splendor to the world.[7]

Although the Bible begins with Creation, the narrative of Western cultural origins begins with Abraham. The creation of the world, of humans, of plants and animals, of language and its dispersion, and the Great Flood—that is, events of supposedly universal significance—take only eleven of the fifty chapters in Genesis. "The break between Primeval History and the story of the Patriarchs is sharper than is immediately apparent" (Speiser, 1964:liii). The primeval history has many parallels with material from other ancient Near Eastern cultures, for example, the order of Creation, and the stories of Cain and Abel and of the Flood.[8] But the story of Abraham is unique. It is with Abraham that Jewish, Christian, and Muslim religious traditions have their beginnings; it is the center of gravity, the pivotal story. A number of scholars believe that the Biblical editors borrowed much of the primeval material from their Near Eastern neighbors, reinterpreted it according to their guiding vision of the one and only God, and used it as a frame for the patriarchal narratives that begin with Abraham.

Abraham's story begins when he first obeys the call from God to "Go forth from your country and your kindred and your father's house to the land that I will show you" (Gen. 12:1). During his migration he is subjected to a number of tests or trials of faith.[9] One of them concerns the covenant God made with Abraham (Gen. 17), the sign of which is engraved on male flesh: circumcision. "The last trial," the one that established him as the father of faith, was the one in which he was instructed: "Take your son, your only son Isaac, whom you love, and go to the land of Moriah, and offer him there as a burnt offering upon one of the mountains of which I shall tell you" (Gen. 22:2). Abraham had so much faith in his God that he was willing to sacrifice his son when that God commanded.

That is the story at the foundation of the three monotheistic religions. The story is performative, for it is Abraham's action that gave shape and substantive reality to the God to whom the action was directed.[10] Abraham's action established his faith as well as the traditions of faith it set in motion. But the meaning and explanation of the act has been the subject of considerable debate for millennia. At the same time only certain kinds of questions have been asked, and certain voices given expression. For example, if Abraham had wanted to prove his devotion and obedience, why didn't he offer to sacrifice himself? Speaking for him, some people assume that, of course, he would have been willing to sacrifice himself in order to save his son. However, if he had been willing to go that far (and that is purely conjecture on their part), why didn't he do *anything* to save his son? Why didn't he argue with God as he did when Ishmael was to be banished, or as he did to try to save Sodom and Gomorrah from destruction? Instead, he was silent.

Continuing the line of this argument, some go on to say that if Abraham had sacrificed himself, it would not have been the ultimate sacrifice, for he had to sacrifice the thing he loved the most. Yet it is one thing to relinquish something one values or to do without it; it is quite another to extinguish the life of a human being. The former sense of sacrifice is illustrated by the story of the two women (1 Kings 3:16–28), each of whom claimed the same infant as her own. Solomon judged that the one willing to relinquish the child, rather than letting it be divided in two, was the real mother. The primary value was the protection, not the possession, of the child. The sacrifice is the mother's; she protects the child even as she lets him go. Although this story illustrates a model of love and sacrifice different from that in the Abraham story, it has not been used to challenge it. Significantly, *it is not the foundational story.*[11] The conflation and rationalization by commentators of the different meanings of sacrifice obscures important implications and is, for me, the proverbial slippery slope.

A far more important question is never, or rarely, asked: *Is Isaac his to sacrifice?* What gives Abraham the right to take Isaac? To sacrifice him without consulting Sarah? (Or, in the Muslim version, Hagar?) Why is she excluded from this most important communication from God? One must ask either (a) why would God have asked only Abraham, or (b) what were the assumptions of the biblical writers about paternal rights that allowed them to portray the story this way, that allowed them to ignore the mother? Such questions must have seemed beside the point;

one does not question God. Commentaries begin with God's command. They take it at face value and do not see the exclusion of Sarah (or Hagar) as problematic.[12] Although theologians routinely give voice to Abraham (and even to God) in their interpretations, the voices of the mother and child have been muted. The mother and child have little place in the discourse, as the focus is on God and Abraham. As we shall see, mother and child also had little place in the modern courtroom. We need to think not only of the processes of their exclusion but also of the implications such processes have for interpretations. In this case it blinded subsequent interpreters from asking what allowed the biblical writers to portray the story as if Abraham had an unquestioned right to take the child.

If the child was thought to belong to Abraham in a way that he did not belong to Sarah or Hagar, then we need to know the reason. Those who pass off the question as reflecting patriarchy imply that patriarchy is self-explanatory and assume that patriarchal organization was already established and was/is separable from the beliefs that construct and support it; they overlook the possibility that patriarchy is conceptually and institutionally established on the basis of certain meanings and practices. The very word *patriarchy* includes a notion of father and so, too, does Abraham's name. That fathers are exalted is not a bad *description* of patriarchy, but we need to go further and ask *why*.

We need to ask why fatherhood is so important. Much of Abraham's story is taken up with his desire to have a son; only a son will fulfill God's promise that he would be a "father of nations." But why a son rather than a daughter? And why is the father exalted above the mother? When I asked myself these questions, gender and generativity began to seem central to the story, and terms that I had taken for granted, namely *father* and *mother*, began to seem less transparent. Instead, I became aware that the terms relate to and derive from the way procreation is understood, that is, to a specific *theory* of procreation. I had to ask what theory of procreation is embedded in the Abraham story, and what were the culturally perceived roles of male and female in the process. These questions, normally passed over by traditional as well as feminist scholarship, marked the turning point in my research.

The Relevance of the Anthropological
study of Kinship

My questions pushed me in the direction of anthropology, which had been involved with issues of procreation, kinship, and religion since its inception in the nineteenth century. Indeed, type of kinship system and type of religion were often seen to go hand-in-hand and arrayed in evolutionary sequence (e.g., Bachofen, 1861; Durkheim, 1915; Morgan, 1870, 1877; Engels, 1884). Like these early anthropological theorists, I, too, believe there are integral connections between kinship, procreation, gender, and religion, but unlike them, I do not imagine the different integrations as stages on an evolutionary ladder. Instead, I imagine them as different cultural systems. The differences in our theoretical stances involve different assumptions about kinship and the nature of language. As I have dealt with these issues at greater length elsewhere (Delaney, 1986, 1991) I will not elaborate them here. Kinship theory is an extraordinarily complex topic and what follows is admittedly an oversimplification.

The traditional patriarchal family, according to these nineteenth-century theorists, was the bedrock of society; it was the real, true, and proper form because it was ordained by the Bible. But the biblical basis was being undermined from within and without. The idea that the Bible was a pastiche of stories from various times and places, pieced together by a few editors, cast doubt on the idea that it was the direct, literal word of God. Archaeological discoveries revealed ancient, sophisticated civilizations not mentioned in the Bible, and anthropological discoveries of contemporary "primitives" who had different notions of kinship, family, and religion raised questions about the basis of their own family systems. From another angle, women were challenging the system by demanding rights in marriage and the right to divorce. All these considerations prompted the theorists to seek a *natural* foundation for the family. As they did so, however, they incorporated a number of biblical assumptions about family and kinship into their theories.[13]

They became obsessed with origins—of family, marriage, religion, and the human species itself.[14] They thought an investigation of origins (where or what they had come from) would provide some insight into who they were and what they had become. Like them, I, too, am concerned with origins, but unlike them I am concerned with people's *representations* of their origins, not for information these might "really" provide about the past, but about what they can reveal about the present—the concepts and values that underpin a people's view of themselves and their world.

Debates in the nineteenth century raged over whether human society was always patriarchally organized (as the Bible portrays it) or whether it had gone through various stages of cultural evolution beginning with primitive promiscuity or a matriarchal order and then simply switching to patriarchy with the "discovery" of paternity.[15] Like their predecessors, most people today, if they think about it at all, probably assume that these are the only alternatives. Behind this assumption, however, is a prior one: that kinship is always and everywhere rooted in the natural facts of procreation. Most people today, like the theorists of the nine-teenth century (e.g., Bachofen, Durkheim, Engels, Freud, Marx, Morgan, and Smith), tend to assume that kin terms reflect biological relations and that, at the very least, the mother is always known. This idea fostered theoretical speculations that the original organization of society was ma-triarchal.[16] For some of these theorists, the so-called "discovery" of pater-nity marked a great leap forward in human cultural evolution. Peoples who had achieved it were therefore considered intellectually superior. The family, as depicted in the Bible, could then be viewed as an advance over what they construed as primitive forms of social organization.

> The progress from the maternal to the paternal conception of man forms the most important turning point in the history of the relation between the sexes. The mother's connection with a child is based on a material relation-ship, it is accessible to sense perception and remains always a *natural* truth. But the father as begetter presents an entirely different aspect. The triumph of paternity brings with it the liberation of the spirit from the manifesta-tions of nature. . . . Maternity pertains to the physical side of man, the only thing he shares with the animals: whereas the paternal-spiritual principle belongs to him alone. . . . Triumphant paternity partakes of the heavenly light, while childbearing motherhood is bound up with the earth that bears all things. (Bachofen, [1861]1973:109–10)

Similar ideas, perhaps without the same flair, can be found in the work of thinkers such as Morgan, Marx, Engels, and Freud. Morgan was an American lawyer who initiated the anthropological study of kinship after coming into contact with the Iroquois in upper New York state. He soon became aware that they had a kinship system quite at variance from the one with which he was familiar. In order to make sense of the discrep-ancy, he began an exhaustive study first of other Native American peoples and then, by means of questionnaires sent out with missionaries and ex-plorers, of numerous peoples around the world. He learned that there is a great variety of kinship terminology systems. The variety is not just a matter of different languages; the terms are structurally different—they do not always refer to the same sets of people. The explanation of these differences became the basis of the anthropological study of kinship; but to this day there is no consensus among anthropologists about the basis of kinship.[17]

Because Morgan assumed that his own (English) kin terms, such as *mother*, *father*, *son*, *daughter*, *aunt*, and *uncle* represented the true and accurate outflow of the streams of blood (Morgan, 1871:486), Morgan called kinship systems of this type *descriptive*. When he and other theo-rists came across peoples who had very different sets of kin terms, they were thrown into a quandary. Especially puzzling were what Morgan called *classificatory* systems, in which one term was used to classify a number of people, for example, one term for all the women in the generation above me. Because of his assumption that kinship was necessarily about blood relations produced by heterosexual intercourse and legitimated by marriage, he leaped to several interrelated but erroneous conclusions. Either these others must be practicing different forms of marriage that implied they did not understand the real, true facts of procreation (namely paternity, as maternity was assumed to be self-evident) and thus could be stashed on a lower rung of the evolutionary ladder, or that the terms had survived from a prior time when people lacked that knowledge.[18]

Morgan's work had a great impact on Marx and Engels, for whom the so-called discovery of paternity marked "the world historical defeat of the female sex" (Engels, [1884]1972:120). As we shall see in chapter 8, Freud believed that the "discovery" of paternity was a great intellectual and cultural advance, and he, too, associated the achievement with males. The associations between fatherhood and the spiritual realm and between motherhood and nature have hardly disappeared, but it is clear, in the quotation from Bachofen, that paternity has meant far more than merely a recognition of a biological relationship.

THE MEANING OF PATERNITY (AND MATERNITY)

The discovery of peoples who seemed to get along quite well without a concept of paternity sparked a protracted debate referred to as the Virgin Birth debate after the title of a pivotal paper by Edmund Leach (1967).[19] In that paper, he equated the Christian doctrine of the Virgin Birth with beliefs of the Trobriand Islanders (and others) that pregnancy occurred because of actions by spirits rather than as the occasional but necessary outcome of heterosexual intercourse. I have taken issue (Delaney, 1986) with his assumption that these beliefs are equivalent, primarily because the Trobriand women (a) were hardly virgins, and (b) did not consider their conceptions unique events in world history, as the Virgin Birth is considered by believing Christians. Instead, their notions of conception described the normal everyday way the process was assumed to occur. The debate over these issues represents deep and continuing divisions in anthropology, the social sciences, and Western thought more generally. The issue concerns theories about the nature of language (whether it is reflective or constitutive of reality) and whether there is one form or multiple forms of knowledge and truth (see Rosaldo, 1989).

Of course, sense perception tells us that babies come from the bodies of women. But sense perception tells us nothing about the meaning of that

observation, nor does it tell us about how a baby is thought to be related
to the woman out of whose body it comes. To know that, we need to
know what people say about what babies are made of and who or what
contributes to their coming into being. In some places babies are considered reincarnations of gods or spirits, and the "mother" is imagined as
merely the incubator for the baby, who comes from a god, a spirit, or an
ancestor; in these cases, there is, according to Ashley-Montagu (1937) a
physical relationship but not a biological one. It is not, therefore, a natural conclusion to assume that all peoples believe that the woman who
bears a child is biologically related to it, for that demands, as a prior
condition, a theory of biology.

The main point I wish to make here is that not even *mother* is self-
evident. All that one can assert is that a child comes out of the body of a
specific woman. *Mother* is a term relative to a specific theory of procreation; although we have presumed there is a biological connection between
mother and child, we have imagined that connection differently from the
one through the father, namely that the mother is the nurturer of the seed
implanted by the father, the primary agent. Genetic theory has hardly
eroded these popular images. As the meanings of *mother* are today being
fragmented and challenged by new reproductive technologies and surrogacy, we might learn something from these "primitive" others.

What about paternity? Is it only the recognition that heterosexual intercourse is/was necessary for pregnancy to occur? That is what most
people assume. They do not imagine that there can be a number of conceptual possibilities for the male role—all of which have been documented ethnographically in a variety of societies. For example:

  1. In Trobriand (and Australian aboriginal) society the male may merely
  open the passage for a fetus/child to come by other means—in which case
  intercourse is necessary for pregnancy to occur but does not imply any
  notion of biological relatedness—and in some instances, sexual intercourse
  is expendable.
  2. Again, in the Trobriands and elsewhere, repeated intercourse can be
  imagined as the act whereby the male feeds, or provides the nurture for, the
  fetus.[20]
  3. In China and some African societies, the male contributes a particular
  substance such as bones.
  4. Or in the folk theory of our own society, the male is imagined as the
  primary, engendering, creative agent.

Only the last is what has been meant by paternity. It is tempting to add
something like "in Abrahamic societies" or "in the West." But that would
completely miss the point I am trying to make. It is not that "paternity"
is some kind of Platonic idea that each culture can fill in as it pleases, but

that there is no way to think about it outside of this construction.[21] Because the contemporary meaning of paternity in the West is often reduced to its purely physiological or genetic sense, we lose sight that its wider meaning, illustrated by so many phrases, images, and laws, has constructed the male role as the life-giving role. It is this ability that symbolically allies men with divine creativity.

What has been so difficult for most Westerners to grasp is that the lack of a concept of paternity does not mean there is no role for the male in relation to a woman and the children she bears. It does mean that their roles and relationships are conceptualized differently, and that means that gender and procreation are also conceptualized differently. Conceptually, we have linked together physiological difference, sexual intercourse, pregnancy, and kinship, and the social consequences thought to result from them, such as marriage and the provisioning of the domestic group, because we think they go together naturally. These connections do not necessarily obtain elsewhere.

In Trobriand society, for example, they are constructed differently. All the men in the generation above my own would be called *tama*, but that does not mean they are all my fathers. There is no concept *father*. Nevertheless, a man will do a considerable amount of child care and express deep affection toward a child of the woman he lives with without the idea that it *belongs* to him, without the idea that it is his "flesh and blood." He feeds the child and helps to shape it, but the child is a reincarnation of a matrilineal ancestor. The child, whether male or female, is constituted from matrilineal flesh and blood as well as spirit (see Malinowski, 1929; Weiner, 1976, 1978; Montagu, 1983); the child belongs to, and inherits from, the matrilineal clan. In societies influenced by the monotheistic traditions, a person's soul is thought to be given by God, but through men. Children belong to their fathers and inherit their names, status, and property from their fathers.

To his credit, Malinowski, who brought the celebrated case of the Trobrianders to public attention, tried to show the *conceptual* basis of paternity. He said "the term 'father,' as I use it here, must be taken not as having the various legal, moral and biological implications that it holds for us, but in a sense entirely specific to the society with which we are dealing" (Malinowski, [1929]1982:4). He also recognized the intimate connection between the notion of paternity and Christianity: "The whole Christian morality . . . is strongly associated with the institution of a patrilineal and patriarchal family, with the father as *progenitor* and master of the household" (ibid., 159, emphasis added). Furthermore, "a religion whose dogmatic essence is based on the sacredness of the father to son relationship, and whose morals stand or fall by a strong patriarchal family, must obviously proceed by confirming the paternal relation, by show-ing that it has a *natural* foundation" (ibid., emphasis added).

Yet Malinowski did not take his insights to their logical conclusion to point out that there are not different meanings of the terms or concepts *mother* and *father*, instead there are different concepts of the male and female roles in the process of procreation and child rearing; clearly, if a spirit, god, or totem is thought to be involved, the roles are not limited to just male and female. The number and description of procreative roles are imagined differently in each culture and in each are linked to more gen-eral beliefs about coming-into-being.

Although Malinowski recognized that the Trobrianders had a different system, he believed there was a true doctrine of procreation. He confessed that in order to test the firmness of their beliefs he became "aggressively an advocate of the *truer* physiological doctrine of procreation" (ibid.: 158 emphasis added). Fortunately, Malinowski, unlike most other theo-rists, was quite explicit about what he meant by that. He "advanced the embryological view of the simile of a *seed* being planted in the *soil* and the plant growing out of the *seed*" (Malinowski, [1948]1954:223, emphasis added). The natives were understandably curious and "asked whether that was the white man's way of doing it" (ibid.).

Malinowski, unwittingly perhaps, had presented the millennia-old Western folk theory of procreation. From our perspective framed by the science of genetics, it is just as erroneous as the theory he was trying to refute. To reiterate, *maternity* and *paternity*, *mother* and *father* do not merely reflect biological relationships, they are concepts that derive their meaning from cultural understandings about the process of coming-into-being at both human and cosmological levels. It should be obvious that these cultural understandings vary. This brings us back to Genesis.

GENESIS AND GENDER

Although it may never be possible to know exactly what the theory of procreation was in Abraham's time, or at the time of the Biblical editors, there are clues in the text. In Genesis, especially, there are numerous ref-erences to *seed*, whether of plants, humans, or Abraham. For example, in reference to plants: "the herb yielding seed and the fruit tree yield-ing fruit after his kind, whose seed is in itself" (Gen. 1:11); or to humans: "let us make our father drink wine, and we will lie with him that we may preserve the seed of our father" (Gen. 19:32); or to Abraham: "All the land which thou seest, to thee will I give it and to thy seed forever" (Gen. 14:15).

The emphasis on seed can be immediately grasped, especially if one has a Hebrew, Greek, Latin, or King James version of the Bible, for the word (*zeraͨ, sperma, semine, seed*, respectively) occurs many more times in Genesis than elsewhere. The Revised Standard Version (RSV) of the Bible, in an attempt to use nonsexist language, translates *seed* as children or progeny. Although the ancient writers may also have meant children or progeny, children were, nevertheless, imagined as the product of seed and only men had seed.[22] This issue raises serious questions about efforts to make the biblical text contemporary and relevant. Attempts to make the language more inclusive may make some women feel more comfortable, but they simultaneously conceal the reasons for their exclusion in the first place. My position here is very close to that described by the Swedish biblical scholar Anders Hultgård, who wrote, "By projecting the modern image of a genderless and sublimated God back into the biblical times, it becomes possible to reinterpret a massively patriarchal body of text in more 'favorable' directions. This appears to me to be but an attempt to save the Bible as the canon of church and synagogue" (Hultgård, 1991: 35). Salvage attempts to change the language imply that gender had nothing to do with the theological concepts or spiritual message.

Implicit in the linguistic changes are assumptions both about language and about the meaning or message of the text. Those arguing for the inclusive changes appear to be saying that the real, underlying meaning has nothing to do with gender, that words such as *seed* are merely accidents of history. They might also be implying that the gendered meanings embodied in *seed* can be extended to women without changing the entire system of beliefs, practices, and institutional structure. Something similar is going on among those who think the image of God the *Father* is accidental, not integral, to the concept; some suggest replacing it with "Mother/Father God." It seems to me that this would further reify and reinforce the very meanings that are under question. In contrast are those who believe that meaning is not separable from the words in which it is expressed; words, they argue, do not reflect meaning but construct it.[23] God, or at least the ancient Hebrews, clearly had a constructivist understanding of language—after all, God created with the word. From a constructivist stance, the language of procreation creates the way it is thought about and the roles that men and women (and possibly God) play in it. It is not so easy to dismiss a theory of procreation as merely bad biology and assume that everything else can remain the same. Instead, one becomes aware of how deeply implicated are notions of procreation in gender definitions and theological conceptions.

Religious people and biblical commentators have long discussed *who* is the seed of Abraham, but they have not thought to examine *what* is seed. As we shall see in chapter 6, they have focused on which group (Jews, Christians, or Muslims) is meant. Because they have not even noticed the gendered aspects of the concept of *seed*, they have totally missed the social and theological implications embedded in the belief that only men produce seed. In order to address this issue, we must get a more contextualized understanding of seed and its implications.

Genesis is preoccupied with the interrelated notions of seed, paternity, and patriliny: who begat whom. Only men produce seed and only men have the power to transmit the line. The line was conceptually eternal if each man had a son; thus the focus on fathers and their sons. The language of seed conveys an image of women as the material in which the seed is planted; like the earth, they provide the nurture that builds up the physical body. Not surprisingly, women were and are defined in terms of barrenness or fertility, words that are also applied to soil. The issue of barrenness is emphasized more in Genesis than elsewhere in the Bible; Sarah, Abraham's wife, is the first woman to whom the term *barren* is applied. Men's procreative ability is defined in terms of potency—the power to bring things into being. This power symbolically, at least, allies men with God; *Yahweh*, linguistically, appears to come from a root that means the power to call into being (a son), to create (Cross, 1973:66). The sign of God's covenant with Abraham, circumcision, was carved on the organ felt to be the fountain of generativity, the vehicle for the transmission of seed.

These images of seed are not confined only to the ancient past but continue up to the present day. They are deeply ingrained, even unconscious. A most graphic representation of this belief appeared in *Time* magazine (15 August 1994) in an article about the biological basis of gender. The illustration portrayed a man sowing seed—which looked like tiny sperm—into the ground; there was no comparable image of woman or of ova, instead the idea conveyed is that women are like the undifferentiated soil. When we use the word *inseminate* we convey, however subliminally, that the male put the seed in; and this concept is implicit in the phrase "she's having his baby." This belief was horribly illustrated by the statements in the 1990s of Muslim Bosnian women who had been raped by Serbian soldiers: they said they did not want to have a *Serbian* baby. The horror of the rape is compounded by their assumption that the child's identity is bestowed by the man. In an episode of a popular television show, a woman learns that it is not her fault she has not become pregnant. She says to her husband: "You're the one who couldn't get the seed planted."[24] David Koresh, the Waco cult leader, like Elijah Muhammad, seemed to have had little difficulty convincing a number of women and girls to carry his divine seed. The night of the tragedy, Koresh's ex-wife was interviewed on television and said: "He thought he was God. His children were God's seed. How could they die? He believes they will be resurrected and will come back to repopulate the earth."

Nor is this language confined only to the context of procreation. We speak of seminal ideas and pregnant thoughts. A seminal idea is creative and, as several people have told me, "starts a whole new line of thinking"; a pregnant one is merely potential. Women may have seminal ideas, but the language implies that creative thinking is masculine in character. The controversial Korean feminist theologian, Hyun-kyung Chung, told me that Christian missionaries to her country imagine themselves planting the seminal word in the barren soil, figuring her country not only as female but also as empty, as having nothing of its own to contribute. And a seminary is that place where the divine word is implanted and nurtured.

Seed has been used theologically. Indeed, procreative imagery for conceptualizing the divine has been used for over two millennia.[25] Seed is the essence of the father, and his child is of the same essence. Because the seed "belongs" to the man, so too does the child belong to him in a way it does not belong to the mother. In addition to being of the same essence as the father, a male child additionally has the ability to reproduce that essence. Father and son *are* one. This is the Christian definition of God. In this theory of procreation I have outlined, mother and child are not one, they are not of the same essence, the same seed, even though they are literally of one and the same body for the period of pregnancy. In this theory of procreation, women cannot provide the image for God. Jesus was known by the term *Monogenes*, which meant "only begotten, begotten of the father." Mary provided the physical body, but she was not co-Creator.

In Genesis, the awareness of the identity between father and son is related to the issue of succession. But rather than a struggle among the gods over succession, as occurs in some other ancient Near Eastern texts, the issue is worked out through humans: who shall be chosen to carry on the divinely ordained line? The fact that the male child possesses the same generative power as the father, and will grow up to take the place of the father, also raises the issue of authority. An ethic of obedience would help to keep sons in line. Abraham's obedience to God is the model for the son's obedience to the father.

Devora Steinmetz, a Jewish theologian who has written a book about fathers and sons in Genesis, claims that "the son represents (for the father) both the ultimate promise and the ultimate threat, immortality and death" (Steinmetz, 1991:29). Neither she nor anyone else makes the same kind of argument about mothers and daughters, reinforcing the idea that they are not considered related in the same way as fathers and sons. She goes on to say that "Isaac can serve as the substitute for Abraham's act of self-dedication to God because he is in essence identical with Abraham."

But only, of course, within a specific *theory* of procreation in which a man identifies with his seed.

The Canadian psychologist David Bakan has also seen a connnection between paternity and the story of the near-sacrifice of Isaac. The Bible, especially Genesis, represents for him the crisis precipitated by the discovery of paternity. "The essence of Judaism and Christianity," he asserts, "is the management of an infanticidal impulse" provoked by that discovery, "and a *binding* on the father against acting out the impulse" (Bakan, 1974:208, emphasis added). He sees in the *Akedah* (the term used by Jews for the story of the "binding" of Isaac) redemptive possibilities—the symbolic substitution is a means to mitigate and control these tendencies. But it seems to me that the substitution also perpetuates the idea that the child is the *appropriate* sacrifice.

Both Steinmetz and Bakan believe these social consequences follow naturally upon the "discovery" of paternity, which they see as true and inevitable. Neither of them understands that paternity is not merely the *discovery* of a physiological relation of a man to a specific child, but the *construction*, indeed the invention, of that relationship. If paternity were merely the recognition of a biological relationship, then similar issues would presumably confront mothers.

Steinmetz and Bakan, like so many others, assume that paternity means merely the recognition that sexual intercourse is necessary for pregnancy, a recognition that they presume automatically implies that the male has a physiological relation to the child.[26] They misunderstand the meaning and implications of paternity, for they never consider that there are a number of other conceptual possibilities for the male role. They never considered that it is a notion constructed in relation to an entire system of the world, not just the "discovery" of a biological relationship. Nor did they understand that the female role of *mother* is *simultaneously* constructed and relative to the notion of *father*. The female capacity to bring forth children would have a different meaning if conceptualized in the absence of the male role, or if the male role were imagined as secondary. In the theory I have been discussing, the female role has been understood as secondary, receptive, and nurturing; it associates women with nature, with what was created *by* God. God has no female partner in the monotheistic religions, instead Nature (the Creation) is symbolically female. Nature is in a dependent, subordinate position to God; so too have women been imagined in relation to men.

Gender, I believe, must be situated and understood within this wider cosmological framework. In the "monogenetic theory" of procreation, the principle of creation is symbolically masculine. Projected onto the cosmic plane, it came to be felt as inherent in the structure of the universe. Monogenesis and monotheism are, I suggest, two aspects of the same symbolic universe manifested somewhat differently in Judaism, Christianity, and Islam, and each is inherently, not accidentally, patriarchal.

At the center is the story of Abraham. So too is gender and generativity. Although gender may have something to do with procreation, procreation is not just about sex, biology, and the natural. Instead, procreation has been imagined as the vehicle for channeling divine creativity to earth. And ever since Abraham, it is men who embody the power to do so. That is the basis of patriarchy.[27] These beliefs form the common ground of assumptions over which a variety of interpretations tread, yet few have taken the opportunity to look at what is directly beneath their feet.

From here, the reader may dig into the two chapters that present the archaeological and biblical evidence for and against the practice of child sacrifice in the ancient Near East, or leap ahead to the section devoted to religious interpretations. The following chapter, in contrast, presents the quandary in which a contemporary court found itself when confronted by a modern version of the story. In that trial, just as in the original and its voluminous commentary, the child disappears. The focus of concern and center of gravity is on the father and on the strange conjunction of insanity and faith. Cristos Valenti never admitted to murder; he claimed that what he did was a sacrifice ordained by God. That was his explanation, his excuse. In that sense the story of Abraham served as his alibi.

CHAPTER TWO

Abraham as Alibi? A Trial
in California

T HE EVENING was just passing into
darkness, the first stars were becoming visible. Cristos Valenti took his
youngest child, his most beloved child, with him in his truck. He often took
her with him to visit friends and she liked to accompany him. They drove to
the place he had been directed to—to the place in the park where all the trees
are. They got out of the truck. He took her hand and together they walked
into the park. It was dark and quiet. She held on to his hand more tightly.
"Don't be afraid," he said, trying to allay her fears. "We are going to meet
God." "I don't know anyone named God." "You will meet him soon," was
the answer and they walked on in silence. When they arrived at the place
God had appointed, her father told her to lie down on the grass. "Start
praying the Our Father, Our Father who art in Heaven," he said as he took
the knife and took her life.

He sat next to her body and prayed for several minutes. When he looked
up, he saw her star shining brightly in the night sky; he saw two stars moving
closer together. He knew then he had fulfilled her destiny, he knew he had
done the right thing. He picked her up and took her home. When his oldest
daughter opened the door she saw her father holding the child, like a *pieta*.
"Call the police," he said. "I have given her to God."

This is a true story. It happened on 6 January 1990, in California.[1] The
above statement was taken from the verbatim report given to the police
that evening. The same story was repeated when the case came to trial
more than a year later. I attended the trial and have interviewed the participants—the jurors, the judge, the district attorney, the public defender,
the psychiatrists, the minister, and members of the family. Except for a
story in the newspapers the day after the event, it did not appear in the
media again.

As soon as I saw the newspaper headline, I knew I had to follow the case. I had long been interested in the story of Abraham,[2] and I thought the case might provide a new perspective on the biblical story that it, superficially at least, so closely resembled. This chapter examines the issues as they emerged in the courtroom, in the living rooms of the jurors and the family, in the judge's chambers, in the psychiatrist's office, and in the church.[3]

The mystery lies in the radical disjunction between the horrible nature of the deed and its supposed religious motivations. How could one make sense of it? That was the job of both the district attorney and the public defender assigned to the case. They conducted their own investigations, trying to put together pieces of the puzzle that baffled family and friends, as well as the legal system. They talked to members of the family and neighbors, they searched the defendant's medical records, they interviewed the minister of the family's church—all for some clues to the mystery. Unlike a typical murder mystery, the body was present and its identity known; the perpetrator was also known, and the weapon was surrendered. About these basic facts, there was no doubt or difference of opinion. For the attorneys, this was the first time in their careers that both sides agreed on the basic facts, but the stories they would tell to connect these facts would be quite different.

The disjunction between the deed and its religious motivation raises the issue of how a secular court can deal with such a case. Whether it was murder or sacrifice can hardly be decided in court, as sacrifice is not a category recognized by the law. Today, the law circumscribes the intervention of religion in secular affairs, but this obscures its origin. We have forgotten, according to legal scholar Harold Berman, that "without the fear of purgatory and the hope of the Last Judgment, the Western legal tradition could not have come into being" (Berman, 1983:558).

In contemporary America, the word *sacrifice* means giving up things, doing without; alternatively, it is thought of as something only pagans, witches, satanists, or primitives do.[4] The only permissible religious sacrifice is a symbolic one, the Eucharist, celebrated in the Catholic, and some Protestent, churches. Whether it is a sacrifice or merely a commemoration of the Last Supper is a sectarian debate that has become more vigorous recently because of the issue of women's ordination (as, traditionally, only men could perform blood sacrifices).

Given the secular nature of American society and the supposed separation of religion and state, sacrifice was not a possible plea; the deliberate killing of a child could only be called murder; the deed was already defined.[5] The legal question could only be, what kind of murder. Was it murder in the first or second degree, or could it be considered manslaughter, even though it was clearly not accidental? Was there malice involved? Was it the result of insanity? Several jurors thought that such an act was crazy by definition; they didn't need a psychiatrist to tell them that.

Day after day we sat in the room watching Cristos Valenti. We became familiar with the visible details of his person, and these became signs for much more. Every morning, before the court was called to order, we witnessed a touching scene. Very discreetly, a clean shirt was passed from the family to Cristos's lawyer, and a soiled one made the reverse transit. His self-presentation was clean as well as serene. He sat very still throughout the proceedings and did not fidget. More than one juror commented on his very white, soft hands. "His hands were so white, I could hardly keep my eyes off them."[6] Another juror noted: "They give me the creeps. How could such baby soft hands have done what they did?"

We became more than observers, however; we became unwitting participants in the unfolding drama. "It felt like you became a witness to a crime, and you wish you hadn't seen it," said one of the jurors. In a time and space separated from everyday life, the ritual was more like a morality play, observed one of the psychiatrists. And each of us had a role to play.[7] The essential characters were the judge, the attorneys, the jurors, and, of course, the defendant; the supporting cast consisted of the court stenographer, the bailiff, and the translator. These participants were on the other side of the rail, separating them from the observers. Although all these people are unique individuals, I refer to them only by the roles they played, that is, *juror, judge,* and so on. I do, however, distinguish between the attorneys and the sex of the jurors, when relevant. In order to preserve the anonymity of family members and jurors, I do not use their names, nor do I make up names, which would add unnecessary clutter. In this telling of the story, their views, but not their identities, are important.

The audience was meager. In addition to Cristos's father and mother, who came every day, and a changing number of his siblings, there was only the minister from an evangelical Baptist church that Cristos had recently been attending, and me. Occasionally, a friend of one of the attorneys dropped in for a brief period. It was an intimate group. One could not disappear in the crowd. As the days wore on, the feeling that we were all in it together intensified.

Because of the intimacy of the place and the size of the group, I quickly became known to everyone. During the recesses, the family, the jurors, and I were all in the hall together. As the judge commented, "We try to protect jurors from outside influences in court, and then out in the hall they get them all." Jurors could not discuss the case with me, but when I asked if they would be willing to talk with me when it was over, all but one consented.

VOICES

They wanted the story told; they wanted their voices to reach beyond the jury room; this may be why they were happy to talk with me. I have had the benefit of hearing these voices, all these different opinions, about what happened and why. The story I tell, however, is my version, my interpretation. I include their voices, but ultimately I am the one choosing; there is no way around it. Nevertheless, my interests do not totally affect the telling. Nor would the issue of veracity have been solved by a verbatim account of the proceedings, which would have filled more than a thousand pages, and would not have included my observations or those of the participants; the quality of voice and facial expression; my interviews; or the initial written reports made by the public defender, the police, and the psychiatrist.[8] I am also a witness, if not to the deed, to its retelling and evaluation in a court of law. The collective burden, the desire to tell it, weighs on me.

Jurors felt strongly that because they would be making a decision that would affect a man's life, they ought to be able to ask questions. They could not, and the judge told them that they "must not make any independent investigation of the facts of the law or consider or discuss facts as to which there is no evidence. This means, for example, that you must not on your own visit the scene, conduct experiments, or consult reference works or persons for additional information." Their job, the judge instructed them, was to "determine the facts from the evidence received in the trial and not from any other source. A fact means something that is proved directly or circumstantially by the evidence. Second, whether or not you agree with the law, you must apply the law that I state to you, to the facts, as you determine them, and in this way arrive at your verdict." Witnesses, too, are held to the questions asked; they cannot just give their own story. This became most poignant, as we shall see, when Cristos's wife, the mother of the child, took the stand.

The question of voice takes on a whole new meaning in this case because it turns on whether one particular voice, namely God's, can actually speak. Because Cristos heard voices, especially the voice of God, the plea of insanity was entered. Hearing voices is taken as a sign of insanity. Do we believe that? What if it *was* the voice of God? Do we allow for the possibility? If not, why not? Is there any way to tell? Did Cristos gain a voice by allowing God to speak through him?[9] What did Cristos want to say? The question of voice became pertinent with regard to the motive for the crime. "How could you *want* to kill your child unless you're mental?" asked Cristos. "I did not want to kill her, I loved her." He loved her so much that sometimes his other children complained. And she, in turn, adored him. This was not a child who irritated him or angered him. "Whenever he'd be working around the house, she was with him all the time. He liked her very much. . . . He was a nice man, really, with the children," said one of his closest neighbors.

No one in their right mind would want to kill their child, but if you do kill your child, that, according to Cristos, does not necessarily mean you are either evil or insane. Yet those are the only alternatives the legal system acknowledges. "How can you say no to God? Everything is his. We all belong to Him. It was an order directly to me from God; God asked me for her. You can't back out. I had no choice. The master of the universe commanded it. He could end all this in the next microsecond. You don't say no to God."

We cannot easily dismiss these words as those of a crazy man since similar sentiments appear with some frequency in the news and from the pulpit. "When the Father tells you to do something, you don't argue with Him. . . . You don't need to know why," (Rev. Brian Cox from his church in Truro, Virginia, quoted in *The Nation*, August 1991). I don't know whether Cristos heard similar things from his minister, but it is not out of the question. This rhetoric, applied to contemporary issues, is becoming common and acceptable. Anti-abortionists have claimed that God tells them to obstruct a particular clinic. David Koresh claimed an inside line to God and on 3 March 1993, he informed the police that he was not ready to come out of the compound because, "God is telling me to wait." Further along the continuum, Presidents Reagan and Bush occasionally said that God guided them in certain decisions. And recently, Patrick Buchanan, a Republican candidate for president of the United States, claimed to "have God's own word on how America can be healed again," (*San Francisco Examiner*, 10 September 1995). What is harder to understand is why so few challenge them on the extraordinary arrogance of their claims.

We all hear voices—usually negative ones. But most of us attribute them to our own conscience, our own thoughts and fears internalized, perhaps, from figures of authority—the superego, according to Freud. Voices like these can be destructive; they can paralyze one's thoughts and one's actions. Normally, however, we can distinguish between these kinds of voices and the kind that Cristos heard. When we "hear" voices, they are in our heads, they are silent—whereas Cristos experienced the voice he heard as sound, as seeming to come from outside himself. The psychiatrists called Cristo's experience an *auditory hallucination*.

In court, one of the psychiatrists gave a minilecture explaining two fairly common kinds of auditory hallucinations: (1) those that deprecate, that call one bad names; and (2) those that give commands, that tell one to do something. Cristos heard the latter, but he had also heard the former in other contexts.

God had spoken to Cristos before, but on January 6, late in the afternoon, God's voice was clear when He told him to offer one of the children, the "little one," the one Cristos loved most. Cristos was outside painting the house, and he nearly fell off the ladder. According to his cousin, Cristos first began hearing voices about five months before the day of the event. Cristos could not quite make out what they said, and it hurt him to try to think about it. His cousin said, "he saw things, he heard voices, people telling him to do things; they took over his mind. He saw a little white light when he was alone and then God would talk to him. Once, when God was speaking to him, he fell down and got somewhat delirious. He was scared and we took him to the hospital." At the hospital, he underwent psychiatric observation, but the doctors, with their tests, could discover nothing wrong with him.

Sometime before Christmas, he heard the voices again. This time he was in church. Cristos responded audibly, "I don't belong here. I am Judas. I am Judas." He went out into the street speaking incoherently and shaking his fist at the sky. The next moment, he was on his knees praying the "Our Father." Later, he went to visit his sister-in-law, begging her forgiveness. "But you have done nothing wrong," she said. Again he was taken to the hospital for observation; again he was released. The doctors could find nothing specifically wrong with him, but he may not have received a complete evaluation, because he was poor, without health insurance, the father of six, and temporarily out of work.

All members of the family and a number of friends and neighbors described him as a happy person, often playing with this child, singing when he got a bit drunk. He was not a mean man and never hit the children. After hearing the voices, he became withdrawn, morose. "He seemed to be trying to fight something in his mind and was afraid he would have to give in."

SEARCH FOR AUTHORITY

One psychiatrist said that, when someone begins to deteriorate mentally, he or she often searches for some authority: the church, the pope, some kind of higher power. Cristos had given up drinking about eight months prior to the event and had been going to Alcoholics Anonymous (hereafter AA). The philosophy of AA includes the admission of one's guilt, and step 3 of the program encourages members to surrender themselves to a higher power. A juror who had some familiarity with AA felt that part of its method (and cure) was to try to shift a person's dependence on alcohol to a dependence on AA or on God. Perhaps this became somewhat blurred in Cristos's mind. It would have been interesting to know what was said at the meetings he attended, yet no one from AA was called as a witness. Nor was his wife's statement that "he had been sentenced to death at AA," followed up on. She did not mean that someone was going to kill him, but that if he kept drinking he would surely die. But he may have taken it literally, as a judgment on his life. Regardless, this judgment must have had some effect on his state of mind. Several doctors concurred that withdrawal would not have caused him to hear voices; one even said that alcohol may have masked his psychotic symptoms. Perhaps the abstinence enabled him to see his life more clearly, and he felt guilty about his inability to live up to his own and his culture's ideals of masculinity. It is difficult to know for sure, but his feelings of guilt seemed to be strong.

Cristos had long been a reader of the Bible, and his wife said he had quite a bit of knowledge and wisdom about it. Yet he had been brought up in the Catholic Church, which discourages individual interpretations of the Bible and individual relations with God. Revelation and authority are mediated through an intensely institutional, bureaucratic, and hierarchical system from the pope down to the local parish priest. According to his wife, Cristos had found God, in a new sense, at AA. And at about the same time, he began going to what he called a "Pentecostal" church. Although the minister of the church would not characterize it quite that way, it clearly had charismatic, evangelical aspects. It was the minister of that church who attended the trial, not the family's Catholic priest.

On Christmas Eve, the little one, the one he would kill a few days later, was a star in the Christmas pageant. Maybe Cristos wanted to make her one forever. That seemed to be behind his thinking, because that was the reason he gave the police: "God needed her, to put her in a star."

On the fateful day, January 6, Epiphany, the night the wise men saw the star showing the way to Jesus' birthplace, that is what he did. The day began like any other—some of the older children went to school or work; he puttered around the house and had lunch with the little girl. Off and on he read the Bible. No one knows precisely which stories he had been reading. At one point he remarked to his wife that Gabriel was telling someone to make a sacrifice. In the afternoon he went outside to paint the doors. That is when the voice came; he knew then that he must sacrifice one of the children. He tried to allude to the topic, in a fairly general way, to test his wife's feelings on the subject. She said, "That's crazy, you must be misunderstanding. God is not bad, he wouldn't ask for a child. There used to be animal sacrifices, but not humans." "But I saw it in the Bible, to make a sacrifice. . . ." Her abrupt dismissal silenced him. He stopped talking about it.

He had dinner with the family and made a special Jell-O that the "little one" had asked for. Then he read to her from the Bible, explaining the pictures. The others who were at home went in to watch TV half-heartedly, and they soon dozed off. Some of the jurors wondered how Mary, the mother of the child, could possibly have fallen asleep given the discussions earlier in the day. They felt that she was at least partly to blame for what happened. They did not know that she cleaned houses every day and was exhausted. It was just after she dozed off that Cristos took the child with him in his truck.

On two occasions, outside of court and in his office, I spoke with one of the psychiatrists for several hours. In court, he gave his medical opinion: the voices were auditory hallucinations. In his office, I was able to ask a question that he was not asked in court: "Do you think God can talk to people?" to which he responded, "A lot of people make that claim, but, for me, the evidence for the existence of God is marginal. The claim that God can speak directly to people presupposes a worldview in which God most certainly exists. If there is doubt on that score, then it follows that there must be doubt about whether or not he speaks to mortals."

Not all people are so logical, however, and many people hold contradictory beliefs. There are also plenty of people who go to church, but do not really ever think about what they mean by God and do not puzzle over the philosophical issue of the existence of God. They take it for granted as one of those things that goes without saying. Those who make claims about God publicly are not usually asked to give an argument for the existence of God.

Most people are not trained to think through an ethical issue or to work out their own position on it. It is hard work, as the jurors discovered. Thrown together in a small room, twelve strangers—males and females of different ages and from diverse socioeconomic, educational, ethnic, and religious backgrounds and life experiences—were sequestered until they were able to reach a verdict.[10] They had to thrash out their views of what had happened and, given that, come to an agreement on the verdict. But in order to reach a decision they had to expose their most personal moral beliefs to the scrutiny and judgment of the others. "Emotionally, we had to take off our clothes and get naked," said one.

Several times they almost came to blows. Another commented, "It is a good thing they don't allow murder weapons in the jury room, I thought J was going to kill S." It became apparent that making a decision was neither obvious nor easy. None of them was really prepared for the experience. "This was a lot more than we bargained for, but I realized it was no free ride, no mental free ride." Although the deliberations were difficult, most of the jurors felt, in the end, that their service had been worthwhile and extremely educational. Differences of opinion, they soon realized, were not easily resolved by reason alone, because they entailed different values, different notions of what a person is, of what motivates people, and even of what kind of world we live in. They talked about God and religion, about voices and authority, about fatherhood, motherhood, sacrifice, love, and family—not to mention about crime and punishment. Most of us rarely have a chance to spend hours talking about such topics, stating our opinions, trying to back them up, and trying to convince others to adopt our point of view.

Certain voices began to dominate, but they were not always male. One woman said she was impressed by the men: "They were quite emotional and that was wonderful to see. They didn't dominate, at least not in a raised-voice kind of way, maybe in length of time." But others felt that certain men did raise their voices, and even the bailiff heard them.

One of the more assertive jurors, who called himself an agnostic, told me, "If there is a God, then yes, I guess he could speak directly to people, but I don't think it happens on a regular basis on this planet." An equally assertive woman said: "Very few chosen people have experienced that—I don't think even a priest or the pope—you have to be an extra special person. People like that Oral Roberts who say, "If I don't make a million dollars, I'll die,' are using it [the idea that God speaks to them] just to make money." She had her own system for classifying religions: "There are Catholics, Evangelicals (well, Episcopalians), Jews, Greeks, Protestants, and Lutherans—they're religions. But the Baptists—the Bakkers and the Swaggarts—they're just out to make money."

Another woman felt quite strongly that she had been given personal direction by God. At a critical time in her life she searched for some guidance and, in her hour of need, God did come. "God can speak to people sometimes; I get premonitions about things, like a flash." One of the men agreed, "Yes, it's possible, why not? But that doesn't mean I think God is necessarily a Being—like you or me—but something else, something bigger." He was convinced that Cristos believed God had spoken to him. But another man was adamant in his belief that God, whether or not he exists, cannot speak to people. "People use it as an excuse, it makes them feel better to have God on their side. It made Cristos feel easier about killing his child, if it was God who told him to."

One of the alternate jurors was a nurse. She said that some of her elderly and dying patients had auditory hallucinations, but not one of them had ever said that God spoke to them. And "you would think that might be just the time." Instead, they have said things like, "I am at peace," "I feel close to my Maker." For her, a patient's claim that God spoke to him or her would indicate mental illness. And she added, "When one is under the influence of mental illness, it doesn't much matter whether the voice is God's or the devil's." That was the position of most of the jurors, but one or two said it would make a difference. "If Cristos thought it was the devil, I would have thought him a wicked man, but since it was God's voice, it makes him kind of holy."[11] On the other hand, she said, "God wouldn't ask such craziness. If God had asked me to do such a thing, I would have said: why me? what's so special about me? why do I have to prove something?"

She would have argued with God and would have resisted. In the biblical story, Abraham argued with God about trying to spare the few good men of Sodom and Gomorrah. Yet when it came to his own beloved son, he never murmured, never argued. He acquiesced without a word. So, too, did Cristos. According to the psychiatrist, "There was not even a question, no conflict in mind; it only became so later under questioning."

Another of the women said that her first impulse would have been to protect the child, even though she does not have one. She went on to describe a situation in which she was in charge of her younger siblings. They had all gone to a movie and on the way home five men tried to get in the car. When she saw her little sister sleeping in the back seat, she "stepped on the pedal and took off, leaving two bodies on the ground. . . . [T]he impulse was so strong to protect the children that if I hit them [the men] then I hit them." They were not killed. "The whole idea that God would ask for a child to be sacrificed is simply nuts." She had thought Abraham was first told to sacrifice the lamb, and so she had wondered why he took his child instead. She thought Cristos was as confused as Abraham, but in the course of the trial she realized that she had had the story mixed up and wondered whether that was what she had been taught in Catholic Sunday School. "But if Cristos heard the voice of the devil, I would have thought he belonged to a cult." She and a couple of the others first thought maybe he did belong to some kind of Satanic cult. "Occasionally you hear such things about cults, that supposedly human sacrifice is performed." She also confided that when the other jurors heard that I was an anthropologist some of them thought I must be interested in ritual sacrifice. Others thought I was observing interpersonal dynamics among the jurors. On such slender threads of evidence, we weave elaborate stories.

Connecting what Cristos did with ritual sacrifice is a common enough conceptual move; it is the same move that scholars of the Bible make when interpreting the story of Abraham. Yet a ritual sacrifice would, by its very nature, be a regular, even if rare, occurrence, for that is what *ritual* means. Cristos was following a pattern established by Abraham, but ritual sacrifice is not an appropriate arena for interpreting the Abraham story, although it is just where most interpretive efforts have focused. It is also important to remember that the most important sacrifice in the Christian world was a one-time event and, therefore, hardly ritual.

What has been ritualized, instead, is the symbolic repetition, or the memory, of that event.

Cristos claimed that his deed, too, was unique and in response to a direct command from God. It was not about following a ritual but about following orders—from God. For him, clearly, the voice mattered. Not so for many of the jurors. For them, it was just a voice. It made no difference whether the voice was God's or the devil's.

The judge, however, thought differently. Although this was his first murder case and his first insanity case, he had seen lots of people who claimed to have had communications from all kinds of voices. "Just go take a look at the LPS roster."[12] Speaking with him in his chambers a few weeks after the trial, I was impressed by his open mind and his willingness to tolerate ambiguity. He said, "Throughout human history there have been phenomena that are not easily explained in our common framework of explanation." He cited the belief in beings from outer space as an example. "In the 1950s there were all kinds of reports of flying saucers. Most people don't believe it happens, but a few wonder." He left open a space for that wonder, that uncertainty—a good quality in a judge, I thought. The more I thought about it, the more I thought Cristos Valenti had been well served by the justice system. He had had an excellent public defender, whom a number of the jurors thought was an expensive private lawyer. Cristos had also had a thoughtful psychiatrist and an open-minded judge. The judge told me that I had witnessed an excellent trial, meaning that all had played their parts to perfection and that the procedure had been smoothly accomplished. "You don't see many like that," he said.

He took a long time pondering whether it would make a difference if the voice had been from the devil, not from God. Finally he said, "Yes, it does make a difference. There is something more sympathetic about a person who says it is God, not the devil, who is telling him what to do. It casts the perpetrator in a better light. . . . But it is a two-edged sword because if you do evil at the command of God, it almost seems hypocritical. It is easier to understand if evil things are done at the command of evil. Then there is not such a contradiction, not such a paradox." It was just that paradox that exercised Kierkegaard in *Fear and Trembling*, his book on the story of Abraham. When I asked the judge about the story of Abraham, he said he could not help but make the connection, the parallel was so strong. "But," he said, his association with it "goes back more than forty years. I thought it was gruesome at the time and found it very difficult as a child, in Sunday School."

Neither the prosecutor nor the public defender called Cristos's minister to the stand. He might have provided valuable information about Cristos's character, religious involvement, and background; he might have been able to recall the contexts in which he had discussed the Abraham story and/or sacrifice. When I interviewed him at his church, he told me that he did not think Cristos was insane, even though he claimed to hear voices. He had trusted Cristos to drive the church's school bus. The minister also said that God had not told Cristos to do it, that another voice had. "He was driving toward the park—right over there," he pointed. "He heard another voice that said: take the child back to her mother. He was going to turn around, but too many cars came along and he couldn't. He was going to obey that voice, but then the other voice said: take her, take her." How the minister knew all this, he did not say.

The minister is the only one who gave any indication that Cristos struggled between good and evil, between the voice of God and the voice of the devil. But which is which? In both Jewish midrash and Muslim legend, to be dealt with in chapters 5 and 7 the voice of ethical reason is expressed by the figure of the devil, who says to Abraham something like: "How could you possibly think of killing your precious son? This is the son God said would make you the father of many nations." The point of both midrash and legend is that the devil is trying to tempt Abraham away from his duty to God by arousing his compassion for his son. Abraham's duty was to follow God's command. But in the twentieth century, the minister felt that the voice telling Cristos to do the deed could not possibly have been God's.

The minister's view was made clear in the next sentence: "If he'd turned around, then it would have been like the Abraham story." In other words, Cristos's story would have (should have) had the same ending. Stories, for the minister, were models, if followed exactly. What he failed to recognize was that it was not Abraham who averted the sacrifice, but God. Cristos, too, was following a command from God, not the biblical model, and his God did not tell him to stop.

During the autumn prior to the fateful event, the church's Bible study group had studied Genesis 22. The minister could not remember whether Cristos had been there, but other members of the family were. The minister read to me some of the Christian commentary he had used in the group, some of which construes Abraham's sacrifice as a trial run for the Crucifixion. "Abraham laid the wood on Isaac as the cross was put on Jesus." The minister connected this to Noah getting wood for the Ark and went on to explain that the word for "*tar pitch*, that which sealed Noah's ark, is also the word for the blood of Jesus protecting us from the evil of the world, the outside."

There was a huge, crudely constructed wooden cross in the vestibule of the church. I asked him about it. He was obviously pleased; he had made it. "We used that at Easter time; a child was fastened to it throughout the service. People were very moved." In physically representing the Crucifixion, the central act of Christianity, the sacrifice that atoned for sins, he had made it present and visible. (Recall, too, that Genesis 22 is recited during the services of Easter week.) Returning to Cristos, the minister said, "God has no need for sacrifices any more. Jesus is the sacrifice. In Old Testament times animal sacrifices were made. However, a lot of it was simply due to the fact that all meat that was to be eaten had to be brought to the altar to be sacrificed. People don't know that," he said. But he went on to talk of other sacrifices that were performed to cleanse people so that they could enter into the presence of the Lord. "But now, those who love Jesus are saved. They do not need to make sacrifices, they need to love God." How? He then alluded to Gospel passages (Matt. 10:37; Luke 14:26) that say, in effect: If you love your wife, mother, daughter, son more than me, you are not worthy of my love. These Gospel passages have always disturbed me. The message is the same as the one in the story of Abraham. The love of God takes precedence and is often represented as conflicting with love of family. But why shouldn't love of God be shown *through* caring relationships with family and fellows?

Why should the minister or anyone else assume that God always wants the same thing? Nevertheless, the most common response was that Cristos would have been following God's orders if he had followed the Abraham story more exactly. How do they know? How can they presume to know the mind of God?

Cristos seemed to believe that he was following God's orders, that he was being obedient to God. That is why he felt he had done the right thing, even though it conflicted with human law and ethical norms. "He was a man at peace with himself and his Maker," was the impression of the police who questioned him the night of the event. He surely gave that impression in court. He scarcely moved throughout the long, grueling hours of the trial; his facial expression did not change, and he kept his hands folded on the table.

The psychiatrist said that Catholics of his generation, and he included himself as well as Cristos, were brought up by nuns, priests, and parents who stressed obedience. "You were taught that the ultimate expression of goodness was to do what parents, father, cardinal, pope wanted. If you do what you are told you will always be saved; that was the important message."

Several jurors corroborated this view. One woman said she had divorced the Catholic Church when she was eleven, and that leaving the church was as difficult as leaving a marriage. But the church had betrayed her. She had gone to Catholic school and church. She had missed mass a couple of times and went to the priest to confess. But, instead of absolving her, he raged at her, "You don't deserve to be in Catholic school," and told her to get a transfer to public school. "I said I was sorry, but he didn't forgive me. I realized then I had a choice: either I am damned forever, this is not my church, or, if I remained, I would go crazy." She decided that it was not her church and left it; that difficult decision caused psychological pain that is still with her thirty years later. "It takes a lot of work to undo the harmful stuff; it's scary because it pervades everything. A lot of it you are just not aware of until something happens. You are not always being tested on a day-to-day basis." But when her test came, she resisted, she did not acquiesce.

A nun to whom she confided this incident did even more damage. "I trusted her but she screwed up my mind even more than the priest because she said: I want you to forget everything that happened; pretend it never happened and don't tell anyone." The nun wanted her to deny what had happened as well as her feelings about it; the nun did not support her. "I still didn't get absolution and I felt like a sinner; it meant eternal damnation." That event had a major impact on her life; after that she couldn't trust nuns or priests. "That was a crazy thing to do to a young child." She decided that *her* God would not be like that. She came to the conclusion that God does not make these rules, that men do. "All my life it was inculcated in me to uphold men and their values." She was betrayed by the very people she'd been brought up to trust, who represented authority as well as love. But in her hour of need, they had betrayed her.

It was precisely on the dictum of obedience to a higher authority that Cristos Valenti made his defense. He knew it was against human morality, but how could you not obey God, "the Boss of everything?" That was the position the public defender argued. He also argued that Cristos's belief in a higher power overrode malice, a necessary condition for murder in the first degree.

TRIAL BY JURY[13]

There is religious precedent for a jury of twelve, and that is the number in modern American jury trials.[14] The jury selected for Cristos's trial consisted of six men, six women, and two alternates, both of whom were women. All but one of the women, including the alternates, had been raised Catholic, and the one exception had often gone to mass with her Catholic friends. Most of them were not, at the time of the trial, practicing Catholics. The religious background of the men was more varied; only one was Catholic. One, born in Europe, claimed he had been brought up without any religious training because his father was so against it. "Religion is what caused my father to emigrate to the United States." Another man, who was an avowed agnostic, said his wife calls him a heathen. One was Baptist, and two were Methodist.

Fourteen people with such different backgrounds, such varied histories and life experiences were brought together as peers not only of each other but also of the accused. The notion of a trial by peers begins with the Magna Carta, but surprisingly, the U.S. Constitution mentions only a trial by an impartial jury. According to the judge's instructions, this means, "You must not be influenced by pity for a defendant or by prejudice against him. You must not be biased against the defendant because he has been arrested for this offense, charged with a crime and brought to trial. You must not be influenced by mere sentiment, conjecture, sympathy, passion, prejudice, public opinion, or public feeling." Yet it seems unreasonable, contrary to human nature, even perverse, to ask jurors to suppress their human feelings.

This view of rationality and objectivity has been revered in Western tradition as a whole, not only in its legal tradition.[15] As we shall see in chapter 5, Abraham is revered because he suppressed his compassion for his son and was willing to kill him in order to do God's will. The ability to suppress human feeling is also the quality desired in jurors. But isn't human compassion more appropriate?

The popular belief that one should be tried by one's peers—consisting, at least partially, of people of the same ethnicity, race, sex, religion, and class—may make more sense than the norm of impartiality. Popular sentiment recognizes that these cultural issues do make a difference. According to the American Heritage Dictionary, "A peer is one who has equal standing with another as in rank, class, or age." Although a trial of peers may seem more just than a trial by an impartial jury, can there ever really be a jury of peers at a murder trial?

The most significant impediment is the obvious power discrepancy. The decision of the jury affects the life of the defendant, whereas the latter has no power over them—so they can hardly be considered peers in power or rank. One juror felt it was inequitable that the jurors all spoke English well, whereas Cristos needed an interpreter. Three of the jurors, however, were from the same ethnic group and spoke the language he did. Although one of the jurors was retired, none of the others was unemployed, as the defendant had been for some time. The incomes of the working jurors ranged from about thirty thousand dollars to a high of ninety thousand. Clearly, they were not peers in class or income. All the jurors had more education than the defendant. All but one of the jurors had children. The defendant was forty-seven; the ages of the jurors ranged from thirty-four to sixty-nine but most were in their late forties or early fifties. The religious background of the defendant was well represented among the jurors.

The closest peer was a man who was the same age and of the same ethnic group, had been brought up Catholic, had been in jail for domestic violence, and had been a drinker, like the defendant. "I've been there," he said. He had to use up his vacation time in order to be on the jury. Others missed several weeks of work, without pay. The court paid only five dollars a day—hardly enough to cover transportation and lunch. Some jurors' employers absorbed the costs. But the burden of fulfilling their civic duty fell, not surprisingly, on the very people who could least afford it.

When the jurors were given a brief description of the case, only one recalled having seen it in the newspaper more than a year earlier. Although four of them had been jurors in civil cases, none had ever sat on a murder trial. "Most of us didn't know what it meant to be a juror. I got some pamphlets and read up on it," one of the men told me, when I interviewed him after the trial. One of the women, who had recently moved to the area and was taking a self-imposed extended break from work, was happy she had the time to fully throw herself into the trial and to be able to give it her undivided attention. Not all of them were as diligent or took it so seriously. One woman admitted that she had almost faked an excuse to get out of jury duty because it was going to interrupt her professional life. But in the middle of the jury selection, she decided it was an opportunity to see the workings of the court and the mechanics of the law.[16] She also felt that destiny was involved, because her birthday fell on the same day that the murder was committed. Another juror turned forty-seven the day the jury was selected. Several other jurors mentioned personal connections to dates, names, or places associated with the case. Was this a tacit acknowledgement that they, too, believed in some external power moving their fate?

Most admitted that they were pretty naive and had little idea about what would be demanded of them intellectually and emotionally. They went into the trial thinking of themselves as observers called upon to make a rational decision based on evidence and facts. They did not expect that the trial would have a powerful emotional effect that would change their lives.[17] "It was an extraordinary learning experience compressed into the space of a couple of weeks." Although some of the explanations by the lawyers and psychiatrists were like lectures, the jurors were especially referring to how much they learned about themselves and about human nature.

All but two of the jurors knew the story of Abraham and were aware of the parallels. One of the men said, "You remember what you are taught, and it affects the way you think." Another of the men told me that it was after he had heard the Abraham story (the sacrifice part) that he stopped being religious. He also told me that children usually hear this story when they are very young, as he did, in Sunday School or in catechism class, before they are really able to understand or question it. In that way it becomes part of their cultural and psychological landscape. And I thought that this might be related to the widespread assumption that because the story takes place in the mists of time, it has no present effect. I wondered also about the way one's own early history can become intertwined with what one is taught about the early history of the (human) race. A few of the jurors, nevertheless, felt uncomfortable when Abraham was mentioned in court. Religion had its place—in church— and the two do not mix. The importation of a Biblical story into the courtroom seemed to muddy the distinctions, confound the categories.[18] Regardless of whether the Abraham story directly affected their decision, their views and feelings about religion were very much a part of their deliberations.

FRAMING A TRIAL

A trial is framed in a number of ways—spatially, temporally, procedurally—and the frame determines, to a large extent, what can take place; it allocates power, classifies people, and determines who has the right to speak and when, and what kinds of speech and action are legitimate.

This California courtroom was relatively new. It was paneled in fine pale oak, was well lit, and had comfortable padded seats arranged in rows along either side of a center aisle—like church. Several jurors and other participants remarked that the structure of the room and the ritual reminded them very much of church. A juror remarked, "there is no incense, no communion, but it is male dominated, the judge has his own altar, and they could be speaking Latin because it is a language all their own" (see also Nicholls, 1993). They would be interested to know that, traditionally, courthouses *were* built to look like churches. The translator was reminded of church by the judge on his high altar, the jury off to the side like a choir, and the chancel rail separating the legitimate participants from the congregation. For me, it was more the sepulchral, hushed atmosphere and the way the process was set apart from ordinary life—in a kind of sacred space and time—that made me think of church.[19]

As soon as I entered, another analogy struck me. Which side should I sit on? Was it like a wedding, where you sit on either the bride's side or the groom's? Would it make a difference? The side I chose would be obvious to all, as there were so few of us. I sat on the side of the family, mostly to be less conspicuous. Did others think, therefore, that I was sympathetic to the accused? The jurors didn't make that assumption, but the family did, and that, no doubt, made them more open in talking with me. I realized only later how quickly and unwittingly a course can be shaped.

COURT PROCEDURE

Court proceedings, as any viewer of Court TV is aware, are highly ritualized, very much like church ritual.[20] A trial occurs in a special place and time; there is a definite beginning and end to each day of hearings and to the trial as a whole. There is a precise order to the proceedings, and each person, from the judge to the bailiff, has a role to play. The language is highly stylized, as is the behavior and order of deference. Yet, as Rosaldo reminds us, it is important to remember that "rituals serve as vehicles for processes that occur both before and after the period of their performance" (Rosaldo, 1989:20), that is, by the structures and values that operate outside the specific ritual event.

The jury filed in past the railing that separates the official area from the spectators, and they took their seats on the right-hand side. The bailiff said, "Please rise," and we all stood up. I almost expected to hear processional music. The judge, in flowing black robes, entered through a private door and took his place on the bench. I learned later, when I interviewed him, that the door through which he entered led to "secret" corridors and offices, his chambers and those of the other judges—that is, to a whole area of the court normally invisible and inaccessible to an outsider. The term *bench* is hardly accurate, as it describes a very high, raised platform not unlike an altar, where, according to the jurors, the judge seemed to be performing his own rituals, which seemed to be attuned more to his private computer and phone than to the trial. "Perhaps the danger that unregulated contact with the public may profane the sacred aura of judges helps to explain why, even in secular republics, they retain more of the trappings of traditional authority than any other branch of the government" (Scott, 1990:13). The judge, wrapped in his black robes, sat up there alone with the symbols of his power behind him—the U.S. and California flags, and the seal of the state.

We were told to be seated. Then the judge summarized what was about to happen. "*The People v. Cristos Valenti*, accused of murder, a felony, number 187 of the penal code. He killed X, a human being, with a knife (exhibit A), and has entered a plea of not guilty by reason of insanity." We learned that there would be two phases to the trial. The first phase, the guilt phase, would determine the kind of crime he had committed—whether, for example, it was murder in the first degree or manslaughter. The second phase would determine whether he was insane at the time the crime was committed. The second phase was more critical because whatever was decided during the first could be mitigated by insanity.

The judge told the jurors the procedure: there would be opening statements by the attorneys; then, in the guilt phase, evidence would be presented by the attorney for the state. The defense would then present its evidence, and the prosecuting attorney (the district attorney) would have an opportunity for rebuttal. Finally, each would make a closing argument. In the insanity phase the burden was on the defense.

> Jurors are to determine the facts developed by evidence and come to a verdict. In considering the facts think about what weight to give them, about the credibility of the witnesses—standards here are the manner or demeanor, character of testimony, extent of ability to recollect and communicate, character of witness, veracity, interest, bias, prejudice, and contradictions, and to distinguish between correct evidence and circumstantial evidence. Attorneys' statements are not evidence. It is not your job to determine the law; the judge will instruct on the law and about the rules of evidence and the conduct of the trial. It is better not to take notes.[21]

THE GUILT PHASE: WAS IT MURDER OR SACRIFICE?

After summarizing the story and events of 6 January 1990, the prosecutor concluded his opening remarks, saying: "Cristos Valenti planned and executed the plan knowing it was wrong and had the disapproval of the family; he made a choice, a deadly choice. There is only one conclusion. Cristos Valenti killed his daughter; it is a case of murder in the first degree."

The job of the defense was more difficult. The crime is heinous and most of us are repulsed when we hear of it. People said things like: "The guy should be hanged or at least be put away for five hundred years. There is no reason to keep this person around; I would have gone for the death penalty." The grand jury, meeting before the trial, had determined that the death penalty was not an option in this case.

The public defender told the jury that a "trial is a struggle between two directors over who controls the script." The essential facts were known and agreed upon, but each attorney constructed a somewhat different story to explain them. For the district attorney the "script begins and ends on January 6th," whereas for the public defender, that day was placed in a wider context that included not just the extenuating circumstances and the events leading up to the killing, but also the ancient biblical story of Abraham.

The attorneys may struggle over the script, but its parameters are quite narrowly drawn. Given the way a trial is framed, certain things are not and cannot be considered. I felt that there was something very similar between the structure of the trial and the structure of the biblical story. What neither of the attorneys included, or could include, was the mother's story. Her feelings, her loss, her betrayal were irrelevant. She was permitted to focus only on the deed and on her husband. Her story had no place in the trial; even less was there a place for the dead child. No one spoke *for* her. The district attorney argues the State's case, the public defender defends the accused; no one, including the mother, was permitted to argue for the child. According to criminologist Paul Rock, "Victims have no standing in law" (Rock, 1993:169ff.); it is the State that is the metaphysical victim, which is why the case is mounted as *The People v. Cristos Valenti*.

The public defender began by denying that it was a clear-cut case of first degree murder. According to him, there was no malice—a rather archaic word, but crucial, as the definition of first degree murder must include evidence of "malice aforethought."

Murder in the second degree is "also the unlawful killing of a human being with malice aforethought when there is manifested an intention unlawfully to kill a human being but the evidence is insufficient to establish deliberation and premeditation" (CALJIC 8.30 of the Penal Code 187). Where there is doubt about whether the murder is first or second degree "you must give the defendant the benefit of that doubt and return a verdict fixing the murder as of the second degree" (CALJIC 8.71). Murder and manslaughter are distinguished by the idea that murder *requires* malice, whereas manslaughter does not.

Voluntary manslaughter is an intentional killing without malice aforethought. There is no malice "if the killing occurred upon a sudden quarrel or heat of passion or in the honest but unreasonable belief in the necessity to defend oneself against imminent peril to life or great bodily harm" (CALJIC 8.40).[22] Finally, a killing is unlawful if it is neither justifiable nor excusable. The specific definitions vary somewhat from state to state, and the judge said that there is some debate about definitions of degree of homicide in the appellate court. He also informed me that the Supreme Court was considering several cases in order to clarify the definition of manslaughter. A more uniform but detailed classification of homicide would be useful, as none of them seemed to quite fit the case at hand.

The public defender went on to say that murder in the first or second degree and manslaughter are all *intentional* killings. He digressed somewhat to give a brief history of the reasons for the distinction. When California became a state in 1850, laws about crimes and punishments were passed, but by 1856 they were already not working very well. People recognized that there were different kinds of killings, that there are different degrees of blameworthiness or moral culpability when a crime is committed in the heat of passion or as the result of premeditated deliberation.[23] He stressed that *deliberate* does not mean on purpose, that that is what *intention* is meant to cover.

Here *deliberate* means that there were deliberations about the pros and cons of an action, as you will deliberate in coming to your decision. There is no dispute that this was an intentional killing, but of what kind? Is this a case of cold-blooded murder or an almost unspeakable tragedy that befell a family and a man who loved his daughter and a daughter who loved her Daddy? Was it the result of a tragic mental illness or a cold blooded execution? What has the ring of truth to it?

This was the only time Cristos was seen looking directly at the jury—and it tore at the heart. Several people had tears in their eyes.

The pivotal difference between murder and manslaughter is malice. And it was difficult to see malice in this case. The defense attorney painted a picture of Cristos as a quiet, respectful, unassuming, and religious man who went to mass. Not native-born, he struggled to make a living and bring up his family of six children (five girls and one boy). With his own efforts he had built a small but tidy house. He did a lot of carpentry, had added another room to the house, and continued to improve it and keep it in good repair. He worked as a carpenter but had been laid off about eight months before the event. He tried to eke out a living repairing tires in his backyard until neighbors complained of the noise. They described him as a good husband and a good father who never struck or spanked the children. Several of his children were called to the witness stand. They had not seen him since the event. Despite their tears and anger at him, they all testified that he "was a good father, was always there, did a lot of family things, was not strict and didn't hit them."

He did, however, go out drinking with the guys, as was customary among his peers. Although his drinking created some domestic discord, he didn't turn mean when drunk, but happy. He used to sing along with the band that occasionally played in one of the local bars. His drinking buddies, a couple of whom took the witness stand, said that he was law abiding, believed in the police, gave good advice, and did not hassle women. One of them revealed that his nickname was *Christ*, and his sister later confirmed this.[24]

In 1981 (ten years earlier) he ran into an old friend who had stopped drinking and found God. Cristos was impressed and went with him to his church; he, too, gave up drinking for more than a year. Then he had a relapse and continued to drink on and off until about six months before the killing. But just before he quit again he got involved in a bar fight, sustained head injuries, and was taken to the hospital. Doctors could find nothing wrong with him but superficial trauma. He was also arrested for driving under the influence, and the judge ordered him to AA. This was about 5 to 6 months before January 6. The public defender recounted a number of strange events that occurred during the fall—the two hospitalizations, his bizarre behavior in church and outside, and especially the fact that he heard voices.

The act Cristos committed, according to the public defender, was not a malicious killing, but the result of severe mental illness. The jury did not buy it, at least not in this phase of the trial. Fairly quickly, they returned a verdict of murder in the first degree. The public defender was stunned; he had thought manslaughter would be the obvious choice because there had been no malice. Their verdict, however, seemed to reflect the jury's feelings about the heinous character of the deed, rather than the intentions of the defendant. That marked the end of the first phase, but the trial was not over. This was not the final verdict.

The Insanity Defense

We had a one-week recess before the second phase, the insanity phase, began. The task of the public defender was now much more difficult; he had to convince the jury that his client was insane at the time he committed the crime. He was insane, according to the public defender, because he heard the voice of God, he obeyed God's order, and he made a sacrifice. Curiously, the argument turned on Cristos's unwavering belief that what he had done was a sacrifice. He had to be proved insane *because* of his religious beliefs. How did Cristos know the voice was God's? But, so too, how did Abraham? If we think Cristos was insane because he heard God speaking to him, why, then, don't we think Abraham was insane? Conversely, if we believe Abraham heard the voice of God, why don't we believe Cristos? Complicating these issues are the more basic questions: do we think God can speak to humans, and, ultimately, do we believe there is a God?

The public defender seemed to believe Cristos; he gave a very moving and convincing performance. He told us that Cristos Valenti "believed absolutely that God commanded that he make a sacrifice. Like Abraham, he didn't tell his wife; he felt he had no choice. Since the master of the universe commanded it, it could not be wrong. God had ordained this act, yet Cristos knew it was against the law and that it would upset his family. Like Abraham, he knew he had to sacrifice the one he loved the most; it was his destiny and hers. She would become a star—God had a plan for her." When Cristos was asked: "What God, the God of what religion, told you to do it?" he said, "The God of all of them, and none of them," a theologically correct and sophisticated answer.

When Cristos was asked whether he would do it again, if God asked him, he answered yes. Since he had nothing to gain by that answer and everything to lose, his answer was evidence for both the psychiatrist and the public defender that he was not feigning mental illness. They felt that it demonstrated the severity of his mental illness, as well as the sincerity of his defense.

A long verbatim account of the testimony Cristos gave to the police the night of the event was entered into the record. It had been videotaped, and we watched portions of it in the courtroom. We were thrown back in time to the night of the event, brought emotionally closer to it. The purpose of the questioning was to test Cristos's basic level of functioning. Questions were asked about vital statistics—age, date and place of birth, address, phone number, social security number, license number, things that seemed so trivial in proportion to the magnitude of the event. More relevant perhaps were the names, ages, and dates of birth of his children and his own siblings. But since he was one of ten children, that was quite a task, especially because most of them also had children (his nieces and nephews), and he was asked about them as well. The entire process was long and monotonous. I doubt many so-called sane people could have responded as well as Cristos; indeed, some jurors were surprised that a person could be labeled insane and still function so well. The district attorney had picked up on this and had argued that, because Cristos functioned quite well, he must be sane and that, therefore, the act was first degree murder. And it *was* difficult to see him as insane—he seemed normal with regard to everyday functions. Even in regard to the sacrifice, he presented his case and his reasons in a calm, clear way. He clearly believed that God had told him to do it. *That* is what was considered insane; the psychiatrist said he suffered from a religious delusion.

At one point, near the beginning of the questioning, the police asked the following series of questions.

POLICE: How many children do you have?
CRISTOS: Well, I have five left.
POLICE: How many in total?
CRISTOS: There were six, five are left.
POLICE: How were there six?
CRISTOS: Don't you know why I'm here?

He must have begun to wonder just who was crazy. Although there were some questions he couldn't answer because he didn't know or couldn't remember, throughout the entire process, he never referred to what he had done as anything but an offering, a gift to God, a sacrifice in accordance with God's command.

But why that child? Why didn't he sacrifice his son, his only son? That would have followed biblical precedent. Perhaps that question is like asking, as did a juror, "Why didn't he stay his hand, like Abraham?" But Abraham did not stay his hand, God did. Maybe this time God decided not to; perhaps this time he needed more proof of obedience, of love. Although the Bible emphasizes sons, especially firstborn sons, in the one case in which a daughter is involved (Judg. 11), she is sacrificed.[25]

According to his son, who visited him in jail soon after the event, Cristos was in the backyard painting when God asked him for a sacrifice. "He was confused by God's request and went inside to read the bible about sacrifices. . . . God told him to sacrifice the person he loved the most . . . and that was when he knew it would be the little one. . . . He said he couldn't sacrifice himself. He did not feel guilty about her. When God came into his life," said his son, "he followed God's orders."

THE LAW

The court-appointed psychologist questioned Cristos about the law.

> PSYCHOLOGIST: Why are laws necessary?
> CRISTOS: Laws are for everybody because there's a lot of trouble around out there.
> PSYCHOLOGIST: Thou shalt not kill, what about that law?
> CRISTOS: That's God's commandment.
> PSYCHOLOGIST: Did you break that law?
> CRISTOS: Yes and no. I did break it because the Bible says that, but I didn't break it because God told me to.

Which is the law? That which is written or that which is given by the Giver of Law? What is the ultimate authority—tradition or conscience, a mediated relation with God or a personal one? This is no simple question: it is at the heart of the Catholic-Protestant split. Cristos embodied that split in his own life, as he left the Catholic Church and moved to a charismatic, Pentecostal Church.

The debate about written versus higher law enters into interpretations of the Abraham story. Abraham was before the law, before the written code given to Moses, so he could be said to be above the law, a law unto himself, abiding by the law given directly by God. He had a special relationship with God; he is one of the few people in the Bible with whom God speaks. As we shall see in chapter 6, Luther argued that Abraham was justified by faith alone. Since his personal relationship with God was unmediated by law or tradition, Abraham has been imagined as a quintessentially Protestant figure! God singles him out for his mission. Yet it is precisely the fact that Cristos had a special, singular relationship with God that today marks him, not as the friend of God, as Abraham was known, but as a psychotic.

The claim to a higher law is also a recognition that temporal, secular state law is made by humans and therefore fallible. The claim to a higher law is a claim of transcendence over human authority. Yet notions of God, regardless of whether he exists, are also humanly constructed, though this rarely enters into the arguments. In a secular court of law, there can be no higher law. Conscientious objectors claim to follow a law higher than secular, civil law; they claim to follow their consciences. But it could also be argued that they are actually following biblical law, specifically the Mosaic commandment not to kill, which is in conflict with the power of the state to command killing in war.

The claim to be following a higher law has, of course, been used by a number of people and groups in addition to conscientious objectors.[26] Yet even if we accept Cristos's claim that he was following a higher law, one that allowed him to abrogate human and even biblical law, there is still a question that has not been asked. What made him think he had the right to take the child? This may seem a nonquestion, because he claims God told him, that he acted on God's authority. And we have a whole tradition spanning at least two thousand years that tells us that everything belongs to God and He can do what He wants. This is what Cristos said throughout. But if there had been no model, he could not have made such a claim. This is when my own feeling about Cristos began to change. Even though Cristos was not physically elsewhere when the crime was committed, his mind was. He was preoccupied by notions of biblical sacrifice, and he understood his motivations and the deed in that sacred context. In that sense, the story of Abraham served as an alibi, an excuse.

The ideas that inspired his action did not begin with him. He was following in Abraham's footsteps, in the tradition that Abraham initiated. Cristos inherited a venerable tradition in which sacrifice, or the willingness to sacrifice, is central. Even though Judaism teaches that, with Abraham, God put an end to human sacrifice, and Christianity teaches that the sacrificial death of Jesus atoned for all time the sin of the world, the tradition has also taught that you must love God more than money, fame, and even your family, and that, if called upon, you must be willing to sacrifice what you most love.[27] That idea is at the heart of Judaism, Christianity, and Islam. It is the standard of faith. And it is that standard, that model, that I am calling into question.

Taking a person' s life is quite different from relinquishing something precious, yet both can be defined as sacrifice. The conflation is dangerous, but it is traditionally promoted in interpretations of the Abraham story. In the modern courtroom, a sacrificial killing is not a legitimate option. Although Abraham did not, in the end, sacrifice Isaac, he did not question the legitimacy of the demand. He did not ask, "By what right can one sacrifice the life of another?"

What made Cristos Valenti assume he was an instrument of God's will in this case? The child was not *his* to sacrifice. Despite the fact that in his belief system everyone belongs to God, in the human world, the child also belongs as much to the mother as to the father if, indeed, it belongs to anyone. Yet paternal privilege is deeply rooted in the Bible and in our culture.[28] Like Abraham, Cristos did not think he had to get permission from the mother; he assumed he had a right to take the child by himself. The assumption is built into the story. It is so much a part of it that commentators have not felt it was worth mentioning.

WHAT THE STRUCTURE EXCLUDES

Where is the mother; where was Sarah or Hagar? The most dramatic moment of the trial came when the district attorney called Cristos's wife, Mary, the mother of their child, to the stand. She was a handsome, tastefully dressed woman who carried herself with dignity. The jurors were clearly impressed. She was shy about her ability to speak English and had requested an interpreter. That added to the drama, or at least to the tension, for the drama never really materialized, despite the poignancy of her testimony. She was never really allowed to give her story, to tell her feelings, so focused were the questioning and cross-examination on the event and her husband.[29] "There was so much I wanted to say at the trial, but my feelings were trapped inside me," she said later.

Mary wanted to give some expression to her anguish and her sorrow; she felt that her feelings should be considered, but they were not. She told me she wanted to cry out: "How could you [Cristos] have done this? Why? Why? Why?" She wanted some answer to the mystery, something that would help to ease her emotional unrest. Her emotional turmoil contrasted sharply with her husband's calmness, and this reveals the craziness of conventional associations regarding the irrational versus the rational. She wanted the court to know of the effects of his deed on her and the children, and about their nightmares. It was her daughter, the child she had carried in her womb, given birth to, and suckled. What about the effect of that loss on *her* life and on that of the other children? When I spoke with her some time after the trial, she told me she wished she had never gone to the court. "I was very confused after the trial."

The court seemed to ignore her claims or interests in the child. Her rights as well as her perceptions were silenced by the very structure of the court and the trial. She expected to be able to present her side and to have her feelings vindicated, but instead she had to focus on the deed and on her husband.[30] The procedure focuses on the deed, the specific event. The jury is instructed to focus on what is said, not on what is left unsaid. Mary could not ask any questions, she could not make her claims. She was as peripheral in the court as in the event and as Sarah was in the Abraham story. There was no room for her; it was not her story. Had she shown undue emotion, her testimony would have been discredited, "just like a woman." But isn't it more perverse to think she should have been calm, rational "just like a man" under these circumstances? Yet that is the expected and respected courtroom behavior; she had been well groomed by the lawyer.

We learned that she had been married to Cristos for twenty-six years and had given birth to nine children, of whom six lived and now only five remained. Enough tragedy for one woman. She had wanted to stop having children when she was twenty-nine, but he persisted. The little one was born when she was forty. We learned her version of the fateful day and what happened when she woke up from her nap and found them missing. "I felt desperate and ran out into the street screaming. I begged God that nothing had happened to my little girl. I woke up our daughter and together we took the car and went searching for the truck. . . . I drove through red lights. . . . I don't know why the police didn't stop me." When she got to the place where AA met, all was dark; no one was there. She went to her mother-in-law's house, and her sister-in-law went out with her to look for Cristos. When she finally returned home she saw the street closed off by police cars, lights flashing, and yellow tape surrounding the house. She swooned. "I knew something had happened to the baby; I thought she hurt herself, that there had been an accident. I never imagined what had happened."

The police would not let her into the house. They told her the baby had been hurt. They took her to the hospital, but only for a minute before they whisked her off to the police station. I felt that this was cruel and barbaric. She did not get to see her daughter or to stay with her. My shock at their insensitivity seemed to give her permission to register again her anger and her grief. With tears in her eyes and halting breath, she said: "I never saw her until the funeral parlor, and then I couldn't believe it was she, it was so unreal."

From the police station, the son that had accompanied her called the hospital. When he burst out crying, she knew something dreadful had happened. "She didn't make it, she died," he said. Repeating it in court, she also cried.

With such swiftness that we gasped, the questions switched to the mundane, as if to brush these emotions aside, as if to say they do not belong in the court of law, they are irrelevant to the case at hand. It affected me and the jurors as exceedingly cruel, and it did not work to the advantage of the district attorney. When I talked to him later, he realized that in this story, as in the biblical one, the child is left out. No one is an advocate for the child. "No one thought about her; we dismissed her, she [was] dead." He became pensive for some time.

From the emotions tearing at her heart, Mary was asked to think back to a time before the event. Then surprising news: Cristos had wanted to get out of his obligations to support the family. He did not want a divorce, only to be relieved of his responsibility for the children. We learned that he had driven their car through the fence around the yard and run into the house waving a piece of paper and demanding that she sign it. "He said he no longer wanted any responsibility, that I and the daughters could cope. I asked him, 'What about the baby? She's our own, you have to help her along. How can you say you don't want any responsibility? Ever since the first child you already had responsibility.'"[31]

"If you don't do it, I'll knock the house down," he threatened. "Give me time to get the children out," she said, without signing the paper. They went to a neighbor's house, but he didn't do anything further. So there *was* an ulterior motive, maybe. The district attorney brought it up and then dropped this tantalizing bit of evidence. The public defender changed the subject. Why didn't the district attorney press this? When I talked to the lawyers, both said something to the effect that lots of people threaten divorce, but don't really mean it. "There is not enough to go on." I am not so sure. He had no job, his unemployment compensation was about to run out; the pressure was mounting. Because the other children were mostly grown up, he may have viewed the little one as holding him back or holding him to his responsibility. Yet, if that had been the motive, Mary said she would feel even worse. "That is no reason to kill a child, that is not enough of a reason."

He could have just walked away, as so many fathers do, but he was probably not prepared to do that. His family and his familiarity with the area were supports for him. Without intellectual, psychological, or financial resources, where would he go? He may have felt trapped. The resolution he chose may have been the desperate act of a desperate man. The desperation may have pushed him over the edge. Who knows? Perhaps it does not matter, as he began to hear voices.

The whole trial is focused on him; he is the center of attention. The wife and child are excluded from consideration by the presumptions of law and the structure of court procedure. One is silenced by death and no one speaks for her. Her death should have been present in the courtroom, instead it was all but ignored. The mother was used merely as a witness, an accessory, not to the crime but to the main story, which centered on him.

The child is invisible and the mother's story has no legal weight; so, too, is her suffering ignored. After the "accident," which is how Mary refers to the killing of her daughter, her son slept in the same room with her to calm and protect her. It has taken a toll on all of them, especially the oldest girl (who was twenty-five at the time). She was the one, in addition to Cristos, who looked after the "little one." "She has no confidence in men, she doesn't want to get married, she just wants to be with her mother, but I don't want that to happen." Mary understands her daughter's desire yet hopes that she will be able to move on with her life. But she has no money to pay for the psychiatric help she needs for herself and her children. She is also responsible for her husband's hospital bills, and her house may be taken away. These affronts add to what she has suffered.[32] With one blow, Mary lost her husband and her daughter, and she is not compensated. No wonder she feels as if she is the accused.

DELIBERATION

The end of the trial approached. All the witnesses had been called and the experts had given their opinions. The attorneys had a last chance to persuade the jury of their version of the facts. The district attorney asked them to focus on January 6th, whereas the public defender asked again whether it was "a cold blooded murder or an almost unspeakable tragedy as a result of mental illness? What has the ring of truth to it?" Everything turned, of course, on the legal understanding of insanity. That was not a word used by the psychiatrists, who preferred the term *mental illness*. Most of the jurors had the common image of an insane person as out of control, not in touch with reality. Yet here they were confronted with a man who looked normal, who sat still and didn't fidget or roll his eyes or drool. His answers seemed rational.

According to police testimony, witnesses, and even the psychiatrists, Cristos was a man who was able to function quite well; he could plan normal everyday activities and carry them out. It was difficult to square that with insanity. The jury was to decide about the day on which the event occurred, so it was irrelevant that he seemed sane now. Still they wanted some empirical evidence that he was not sane; it would have made their task easier. The public defender used their expectations to his advantage, to prepare them for the district attorney's position: "Even though the psychiatrists and psychologist agreed that he had a mental illness, the district attorney will say when you hear the legal definition of insanity, you will find him sane."

The legal definition of *insanity* is not the same as the definition of *mental illness*, of which there are a number of different kinds. The judge instructed them: "A person is legally insane when by reason of mental disease or mental defect he was incapable of knowing or understanding the nature and quality of his act *or* incapable of distinguishing right from wrong at the time of the commission of the crime. The defendant has the burden of proving his legal insanity at the time of the commission of the crime by a preponderance of the evidence" (CALJIC 4). This is a clear statement of the M'Naughten rule, over which there has been some debate.[33] At issue is whether one needs both "prongs" of the definition or only one to judge a person insane—it is a case of either/or, or both/and. The judge further explained that a moral wrong is one that is in violation of general standards of morality.

During the deliberations, the one question the jury asked the judge to clarify was whether both prongs or only one was necessary to consider Cristos insane. The judge wrote: "In order to find the defendant sane, you must find that at the time of the commission of the crime he was capable of distinguishing between legal right and wrong with respect to the act, *and* you must find he was capable of distinguishing between moral right and wrong with respect to the act." The judge was following the ruling in Skinner.

Cristos Valenti clearly knew he had committed a legal wrong, otherwise he would not have asked his daughter to call the police. He also said as much in the first interview with the police. But with regard to moral wrong, the ground was murky. He knew that what he had done went against the general standard of morality and even against the biblical commandment "Thou shall not kill." He told the psychologist, "Well, you could look at it as wrong because it is against the commandment, but I saw it as doing what God wanted me to do. He calls the shots, if it's a toss between what is said in the Bible and what God tells me, I do what God says." Thus he was actually capable of *distinguishing* between moral right and wrong, if distinguishing is the salient term. What made this side of the scale more difficult was, of course, his belief that because God had commanded it, it could not be morally wrong.

If the jury found him sane, would they also be saying that God could be ignored? An insanity verdict, ironically, allows for belief in God and the possibility that they, the jurors, could not be the ultimate judges. Perhaps a verdict of not guilty by reason of insanity is our way of showing mercy. "The defence of insanity was, properly understood, only a way of extending mercy to some whose sickness led us to wish to forgive them their acts—that was all: a means of extending mercy when we sympathised with what would otherwise be a crime" (Morris, 1992:113).[34]

"He had no remorse at the time, but felt calm. He must have thought, I am returning her to God, maker of the universe, he'll put her on a star. He wasn't thinking, when I stab her, she will be dead." The public defender made the further point that if Cristos had not been insane at the time, he could not and would not have done it. "How could he? He loved her." He showed no anger, no hostility, no vengefulness during all of the questioning.

The psychiatrist said Cristos's mental illness was not as severe as some he had seen, but it was as debilitating. He said he had talked with other people who had murdered their children, siblings, parents, but in those cases "the quality of evil was unredeemed by insanity."

The district attorney then asked whether the psychiatrist would have a different opinion if Cristos belonged to a religious cult in which sacrifice was acceptable practice. "Then he wouldn't be crazy."

JUDGMENT

"Judging is nothing less than the wielding of power over life and death through language."[35]

The jury got the case at noon on Thursday. They deliberated all that afternoon and returned again on Friday. I arrived at the courthouse at 11 A.M.; the jury was still sequestered. Cristos's family (mother, father, siblings) were all there. So, too, was the minister, who sat off by himself. I talked with one of Cristos's sisters. She said that the family, meaning their family of origin, did not like the minister. "He performed the funeral. We are all Catholic, but he did the funeral." Nor did she like the idea that he would report to Mary about their testimony and their behavior. The sister also told me that she had seen a change in Cristos over the fall. They had been very close, but he had become more distant. He used to sing and tell jokes, but he had become morose. "He used to come over to our parents' house and just sit without talking." That was when she told me that he was sometimes called Christ.

While we were sitting there, the jurors came out for a break. Their faces revealed the stress. Gone was the lightness and conviviality of the group. They went their separate ways to the toilet, or stood alone. They had to pass the family. How did that affect them? They did not talk with me. Some faces were dark with what appeared to be suppressed rage or maybe just frustration. It appeared they were struggling, not just with a decision but with each other. Later I learned that three of them had walked into the jury room and declared, "Obviously he is insane, there is not much to discuss." Even if some jurors agreed with them, such a preemptory move was sure to anger other jurors. The judge's instructions made it clear that their behavior was inappropriate. At lunchtime it was evident they were still struggling. I learned later that by that time a few more had gone over to the side of insanity, several were straddling the fence, and at least two were adamant that Cristos was sane and therefore guilty of murder.

By the afternoon break their faces seemed calmer, some rapprochement had been effected, they were approaching a resolution—but what would it be? Their decision turned on the M'Naughten rule, the only issue they asked the judge to restate. At 4:50 we were called back into the courtroom. The jury had reached a decision. They seemed relaxed. But the tension mounted. Would they affirm the verdict of murder in the first degree reached in the first phase of the trial, or would they cancel that out by deciding that the defendant was insane at the time of the killing?

It was Friday, it was almost five o'clock. The public defender announced that he could not stay afterward to talk with the jury, as was his normal custom, because he had to pick up his four-year-old daughter. Their faces registered this information—that all this time he had been defending a man who had killed his four-year-old daughter.

The foreperson of the jury (a woman) handed a piece of paper to the bailiff who handed it to the female clerk who handed it to the judge, who slowly and carefully unfolded it and silently read it. Then he handed it back down to the clerk. She stood up and began slowly: "The State of California, . . . Section . . ." and finally just before we might explode with tension, she said: "The jury finds the defendant, Cristos Valenti, was insane on the day of January 6, 1990."

VERDICT, BUT NO CONCLUSION

When the judge rephrased it and announced to the court that Cristos Valenti was thereby acquitted of murder, the jury was noticeably shocked. Somehow the word *acquitted* had not entered their minds as they struggled with the question of insanity. Many of them told me later that when they heard that word, they felt betrayed. They had assumed he would be put away for a long time and now they were not sure. Even though he was acquitted, he was not free to walk out of the courtroom; he would be assigned to a mental hospital instead of a jail. Just to be sure, several of the jurors decided to attend the hearing when the decision about his placement would be made. Nevertheless, with this verdict and this kind of placement, he will be eligible for release every six months.

The verdict of "not guilty by reason of insanity" may be a way of showing mercy, but in this case, anyway, and however much below the surface, it was also a way of affirming paternal power (*patria potestas*), a man's right to determine the fate of his child unilaterally, that is, without consulting the mother. He was never asked: by what right did you take the child without discussing it with her mother? And the question never came up in court. It was a crime of omission on two counts.

The trial was over. The family cried, I cried, the public defender cried. The district attorney was noticeably angry and stalked out, agreeing along the way to meet with jurors outside the courthouse. It would be closed in a few minutes. As the jurors filed out, one of them asked me about the nature of my project, for he had made a bet with another juror. When I told him it was about religion and the Abraham story, he said he had lost. He had thought I was there observing interactions among the jurors.

The trial was over but people's lives go on. More than a year after the trial, two years after the killing, I met with Mary again. I didn't know it, but it was the eve of what would have been her daughter's sixth birthday. Mary had just come from the cemetery, where she had laid flowers. She told me about the continuing effects of the "accident." She and the children continue to have nightmares, and they are terrified that if Cristos is released from the mental hospital, he will come back and kill again. Their story and their lives are private and they bear the consequences alone.

EPILOGUE

As one part of my research on Abraham, I attended a meeting of a small Jewish study group at Stanford University on the day scheduled for a discussion of Genesis 22. The group consisted of a rabbi, some students, and a few professional people from the area. By extraordinary coincidence it was the morning after the conclusion of the trial, a coincidence that made my participation more than academic. I had wanted to know how contemporary Jews were interpreting the story; now I also wanted to know how they would react to the story of the trial.

We were not allowed to take notes, because the use of pencils or pens is forbidden to Jews on the Sabbath.[36] Commentaries were distributed to each member of the group; a few were in Hebrew; most were in English or English translated from the Spanish, French, or German. Each participant, in turn, read the commentary he or she was assigned; by the end of the meeting we were able to perceive something of the whole through the

different facets revealed in each text. Although each commentary was a
Jewish interpretation, and strictly within Jewish tradition, each had a
slightly different light to shine on the story.

At the end of the meeting, I asked them how they would respond if they
heard about a similar story occurring today; and I told them about the
trial I had just witnessed. The majority opinion was, "God would not ask
us to do something contrary to Scripture." They thought the man had
gotten it all wrong, that he must be crazy. The rabbi, however, raised the
question I had in mind: "How can you presume to know the mind of
God?" The first response is bound by tradition and is within the law; the
other could be considered more theologically based, and in the spirit of
Abraham, who was before, and therefore above, the law.

PART TWO

Archaeological and

Biblical Evidence

CHAPTER THREE

Child Sacrifice: Practice
or Symbol?

ONE of the most common attempts
to interpret Genesis 22 is as an injunction against the practice of child
sacrifice. This interpretation was given to me by lay people, by a number
of ministers, and by a highly educated rabbi in a very sophisticated congregation. This kind of response finds support in numerous religious and
scholarly publications. For example, the popular *Interpreter's Bible*
states that the "story of the proposed sacrifice of Isaac would not have
been told except to discourage a custom which already existed" (Interpreter's Bible, 1952, 1:1009). The *Encyclopedia Judaica* says the following: "The original intent of the narrative has been understood by the
critics either as an etiological legend explaining why the custom of child
sacrifice was modified in a certain sanctuary by the substitution of a ram
(Gunkel) or as a protest against human sacrifice" (Encyclopedia Judaica,
2:480–81).

Despite the commonality of this type of interpretation, there are historical, anthropological, and theological reasons why such interpretations
are untenable. Because it is so common, it is necessary to challenge it
before moving ahead. This chapter focuses on the archaeological-histori-
cal evidence for and against the practice of child sacrifice in the ancient
Near East and chapter 4 will take up the passages in the Bible that have
been thought to refer to such a practice. Regardless of whether the practice ever existed in that part of the world, the evidence used to support
these assumptions points to a period later than the story of Abraham, and
thus may have little relevance for the Abraham story. Unlike most other
theorists, I don't think sacrifice—whether human or animal, ritual practice or theoretical discourse—is the most appropriate context for the interpretation of the story. Just because (animal) sacrifice as a ritual practice
became important in the Israelite cult and is discussed in later books of

the Pentateuch, it does not mean it is the appropriate context for the interpretation of the Abraham story, especially since there is so little mention
of sacrifice prior to the Abraham story, and no mention of the practice of
child sacrifice. *Sacrifice* is an important category of religious analysis and
is applicable to a fairly wide range of societies including that of the ancient Israelites. Although it may be appropriate for interpreting animal
sacrifices that were a central part of the cultic practice, it is an enormous
leap to suggest that they were a substitution for ritual child sacrifice, and
even more so to suggest that this is the background of the Abraham story.
Even if incidents of child sacrifice did occur, the notion of ritual child
sacrifice as a religious obligation and unitary phenomenon is, I believe, a
concoction of biblical scholars who constructed it from various fragments and allusions. It seems similar to the construction of "totemism"
among anthropologists who, from supposed beliefs about the soul among
Australian aborigines and from bits and pieces of their ritual practices,
fabricated "totemism" as a specific *religion* relative to a specific rung of
the social evolutionary ladder. But it does not and did not ever exist in
fact.[1] I am not presumptuous enough to assert that child sacrifice never
existed, although I am dubious that it was ever a cultic ritual. If it existed
in the Near East, I believe it was late, sporadic, and symbolic of patriarchal power. But let us turn to the interpretations.

PROBLEMS WITH THE ETIOLOGICAL EXPLANATION

The etiological explanation assumes that human (or child) sacrifice had
been practiced before Abraham's time. There is, of course, no mention of
it in Genesis before the story of Abraham and, except for that story, it is
not mentioned again in Genesis. If the Abraham story was meant to pro-
hibit the practice, one would think the biblical writers would have portrayed it as common. Instead, the preceding stories are about sexual relations and sexual transgressions. In subsequent books of the Bible the
theme of sexuality often occurs in relation to other supposed references to
the sacrifice of children; this association has not received the attention it
warrants and will be taken up in chapter 4. Finally, if the story was meant
to demonstrate that child sacrifice was "modified" by the substitution of
a lamb, it implies that child sacrifice preceded animal sacrifice.

   Yet the story itself shows that animal sacrifice was presupposed. In the
most poignant sentence in the whole story, Isaac asks Abraham: "Father,
Behold the fire and the wood: but where is the lamb for the burnt offering?" Isaac, anyway, knew that the expected sacrifice was an animal.
Nevertheless, even animal sacrifice is rarely mentioned before Genesis 22;
there is the precedent of Abel's offering (Gen. 4:4), and though sacrifice

may have been the intention, it is not specifically mentioned. The only clear mention of an animal sacrifice before Genesis 22 is that offered by Noah in thanksgiving for the safe delivery of the Ark unto dry land (Gen. 8:20).[2]

Far more important, an etiological tale seems unlikely as the foundation story of three world religions. The etiological interpretation diminishes the theological importance of the story. A prohibition against child sacrifice, if that is what it was, is merely negative, rather than a positive constitution of the new faith. "The Akedah in its final form is not an attempt to combat existing practice, but is itself the product of a religious attitude" (Sarna, 1966:162). That religious attitude understands the story as a unique event and a "test of faith." Religious interpretations will be the subject of chapters 5 through 7.

EVOLUTIONARY ASSUMPTIONS

Etiological explanations generally incorporate assumptions about cultural evolution that are untenable. The notion that animal sacrifice substitutes for, or modifies, the practice of human sacrifice reflects just such an evolutionary bias—that is, an assumption that the more ancient the group, the more barbaric it was, and that, obviously, the most barbaric must have practiced human sacrifice.[3] Shalom Spiegel, for all the merits of *The Last Trial*, his fine book on this story, perpetuates such a view. "The ancients can accept the rigors of sacrifice as they offer up their first born to the gods. . . . It is only inch by inch that laws were mellowed and humanized. [In the story of Abraham is the] remembrance of the transition to animal from human sacrifice—a religious and moral achievement which in folk memory was associated with Abraham's name, the father of the new faith" (Spiegel, 1969:63–4). This statement implies that the ancients were not quite human, that human sacrifice preceded that of animal sacrifice, and that the religion of Abraham is, therefore, a moral and cultural advance. That is, of course, what we have been taught to believe.

Yet human sacrifice, when it is found, is found not in primitive or pastoral societies but in urban, highly sophisticated, and civilized ones. My use of *civilized*, in this context, does not mean morally advanced, or the preordained goal of cultural evolution; I mean merely to indicate a society characterized by certain complex forms of social organization, artistic and, often, literary achievement, as well as religious institutions involving temples and priests. This was not part of the culture generally ascribed to Abraham, which is portrayed as seminomadic, pastoral, and tribally organized.[4] Of course, whether Abraham lived at all is an open question; he may have been a real person, an eponymous ancestor of a particular group, a legendary, mythic hero, or a fictional character. Regardless, there is no indication in the biblical narrative that child sacrifice was practiced before or at the time of Abraham. All allusions to the practice occur not only after Abraham but after the patriarchal narratives, that is, much later in the narrative of the Israelites.

HISTORICAL ISSUES

The use of material occurring later in the biblical story (e.g., Exodus, Leviticus, Judges, Ezekiel) for explaining narratively earlier material is therefore already ideological for it incorporates theoretical assumptions that are not often articulated explicitly. It is not that I necessarily object to these interpretations, but the presuppositions need to be stated. In this case, such usage assumes that the narrative chronology can be dispensed with. Simply put, the problem is this: is the text a historical document and does it reflect or refer to historical traditions? If so, how? Or is it meant primarily to be an inspirational, even allegorical, story? These basic assumptions need not be mutually exclusive, for even allegorical stories reflect assumptions about what is considered "natural," the things that "go without saying." Nevertheless, they do affect the way one approaches the text. Different assumptions engender different projects and different modes of interpretation. To paraphrase Sandmel, the way one thinks about the story of Abraham indicates how one thinks about the biblical text.

Most scholars today assume the historicity of the text but debate the history that it reflects. Do the patriarchal narratives reflect authentic traditions of an early period, or are they retrojections that thinly disguise the preoccupations at the time the biblical texts were gathered together? The latter, of course, depends upon an acceptance of the documentary hypothesis, a theory first developed in the eighteenth century, that the Bible is composed of different strands from different places and times. Although "fundamentalists" and some others reject the documentary hypothesis, it is, today, a common assumption among biblical scholars and an increasing number of lay people. They no longer believe that the Pentateuch or Torah (the first five books of the Hebrew Bible—those that are most relevant for this discussion) is a seamless story that was composed by, or revealed to, Moses as had been the accepted tradition for generations.

The "documents" from which the Bible is thought to be composed are, in the documentary hypothesis, assumed to represent the various strands that have been detected in the text. These have been labeled E, J, P, and

D, and they are thought to have been woven together and edited by R. J refers to the Yahwist strand which means that the term for God in the text is *Yahweh* (sometimes translated as *Jehovah*).[5] J is generally conceded to be the oldest strand, written during the time of the Monarchy, sometime in the tenth to ninth century B.C., though Friedman (1987:87) makes J and E roughly contemporaneous.[6] In any case, that does not mean that the traditions recorded in J are necessarily older than those in E (Wenham, 1980). In the E strand the term used for God is *Elohim*, a plural form of *El*, a common Canaanite word for god. All of Genesis 22 except for a few lines is usually attributed to E. P stands for Priestly and is so named because the concerns of which the P strand treats are those of a priestly caste; D stands for Deuteronomy and is felt to have been written by someone close to the court of King Josiah. R is for Redactor(s), that is, for the editors who put the whole thing together into the text we have received.

Although the biblical text does not always form a seamless coherent story (for example, there are two different versions of the creation of humans), nevertheless, it is assumed that the editor(s) have spliced the various strands together according to some kind of guiding frame. The detective work that has gone into unraveling the different sources is fascinating but a different kind of study (see Friedman, 1987, for one of the best and most readable accounts). Most scholars assume there has been an enormous amount of splicing, but they do not really tell us just how they think the process actually occurred.

The questions to be asked about the story in Genesis 22 are: (1) Does it reflect or echo an ancient barbaric practice that the substitution is meant to supersede? This is, as we have seen, the common etiological, evolutionary position. (2) Or does it reflect contemporary practices projected backwards and, if so, are the practices those of vile others or of their fellow countrymen? (3) Does the Abraham story possibly represent the first introduction of the *idea* of child sacrifice—an idea later put into practice by some people? Surely, it has been a very powerful idea in the history of religious thought, particularly in Judaism, Christianity, and Islam.

Exegesis over the past hundred years or so has vacillated among several positions: (a) that the stories are literally true and describe the origins of the Israelites, (b) that, properly interpreted, they can provide a glimpse into these early origins, or (c) following Wellhausen, that the stories of the patriarchs "reflected the times of the later writers and not an older period in Israel's history" (Van Seters, 1975:7).

Biblical archaeology, though not confined to any of these positions, is, nevertheless, the result of acting on the belief that the stories incorporate or point to real events of real people in real places. Biblical archaeologists

were perhaps inspired by Schliemann's discovery of Troy and its trea-
sures. Schliemann openly admitted that his discovery was the outcome of
pursuing his belief that the Greek myths reflected real events and places,
albeit transformed and dramatized.[7] Some scholars harbored similar beliefs about the biblical text and began, in earnest, to explore the Holy
Land archaeologically.[8] Rather than "artifical creations of Israelite
scribes of the Divided Monarchy or tales told by imaginative rhapsodists
around Israelite campfires during the centuries following their occupation
of the country . . . archaeological discoveries of the past generation have
. . . [provided] the rapid accumulation of data supporting the substantial
historicity of patriarchal traditions" (Albright, 1950:3). Eventually, these
were dated by a number of scholars to sometime between the early and
middle second millenium (e.g., Albright, 1950; Bright, 1959; Glueck,
1955; Wright, 1960).

    In 1975 John Van Seters challenged the view that the "patriarchal tra-
ditions" must belong to the second millenium and proposed the startling
idea that they referred to the period of the Exile, that is around 600 B.C.
Other scholars are more cautious and recognize that even though one
does not need to accept a second millenium date, one is not forced to
accept such a late date. A return to an early date for the patriarchal narratives has, however, been proposed by a number of British scholars (Millard and Wiseman, 1980). Regardless of when the stories were written
down, they argue that the stories contain authentic traditions from the
early second millenium (Wenham, 1980; Wiseman, 1980) and specifically to the Middle Bronze I period, circa 2000–1800 B.C. (Bimson,
1980).[9]

    An important theoretical issue that is not well addressed in any of the
commentaries is a discussion and rationale of what historical material the
story *must* reflect. An old story can be recast in new garb as is so often
done in opera and film, for example. We need more information about
the criteria by which these scholars have determined what aspects or
items are essential and what are substitutable. Debates about the dating
of the patriarchal narratives will undoubtedly continue for some time, yet
regardless of their outcome, if such there can ever be, there is little or no
evidence to support an attribution of the practice of child sacrifice to an
early date or to the area from which Abraham is said to come. Because
this is such an important issue, it is important to consider the evidence.

THE EVIDENCE

Evidence for the practice of child sacrifice has been based on either physical, archaeological remains or epigraphical material, written material
explicitly referring to the practice. Mythological material is often in-

cluded, uncritically, in the latter category. Freewheeling comparisons from different times, places, and cultural traditions can only indicate that such a practice is possible; they can hardly be used as evidence that it did occur at one time in the land of Israel. Such comparisons might provide insight into evaluating a possible occurrence, but, clearly, the most reliable evidence would be from cultures that are related temporally and geographically.

Most scholars discuss the story of Abraham in relation to Israel; a few have also given attention to Mesopotamia and the cultural background whence Abraham allegedly migrated with his father.[10] Fewer have focused on Haran (alternatively Harran), the town they are said to have migrated to and dwelled in for a long time before Abraham left for the land of Canaan. Although there is no evidence for the practice of child sacrifice in Haran, it is here that Abraham's new faith emerged. Haran was strategically located and could very well have been the cauldron in which new ideas were forged.

Haran

Haran is a real place located in upper Mesopotamia in the Balikh valley off a tributary of the Euphrates. Today Haran, also known by its Turkish name, *Altın Başak* (Golden Wheat), is a small village in eastern Turkey very near the Syrian border. Extrabiblical references to Haran have been found in Cappadocian texts from the twentieth and nineteenth centuries · B.C., and from the Mari texts of the eighteenth century B.C. Although there has been speculation about whether contemporary Haran is the same place as ancient Haran, most scholars now believe it is, making it one of the oldest continuously inhabited places in the Near East. Because it is still occupied, archaeological excavation has been confined primarily to the upper, Islamic levels, although a few exploratory soundings have revealed very early material evidence of habitation.[11]

Haran was a major stopping place on the trade routes connecting East and West, from Iran (perhaps even India) and Mesopotamia to Anatolia (and perhaps on to Greece), and North and South, from the Black Sea to Syria-Palestine (and perhaps into Egypt). In this ancient melting pot, stories, beliefs, and customs—not only relating to heroes and gods but also to kinship, affiliation, gender, and procreation—would have been exchanged along with goods, and these would have been carried home again with the traders. Recent scholarship has noted the similarity between the Akedah and some stories in early Vedic literature (Shulman, 1993; also Turner to Delaney, 1975, discussing work by Ramanujan). A conclusion would be that the Akedah must, therefore, reflect universal human psychology or a stage in its development.

Anthropologists are suspicious of such claims. Even though themes similar to the Akedah may be present in the myths of several contiguous cultures stretching from India to Greece, they are surely not universal. The myths of a father killing his son often have something to do with the male sexual organ (castration or circumcision), as well as struggles over succession; one can imagine that beliefs about masculinity-paterniɔy spread across this area and were absorbed differently in different cultures depending on the circumstances.

Rather than taking sexuality, gender, and procreation for granted, we need to ask: what notions of the person (male and female), of affiliation (kinship), and of procreation are embedded in the texts, and in what ways are they similar across these varied cultures? Because Western scholars tend to believe that kinship is natural and biological, we have often tended to assume equivalence between ancient terms and our own, and to project our own meanings back onto ancient peoples. Biblical (and literary) scholars would do well to familiarize themselves with the anthropological literature on kinship. The problem with assessing ancient terms is compounded because there is hardly any corroborating sociological material.[12]

Some scholars of the Bible have speculated on the relevance of Hurrian custom and belief for patriarchal narratives. The Hurrians, a non-Semitic people, settled in the area around Haran at the end of the third millenium B.C. and "may have been responsible for the sudden emergence of high urban civilization in that region" (Foster, 1989:143). Hurrian marriage and adoption contracts, such as those found at Nuzi (a site in what is now Iraq), indicate a kinship system different from that found in the Bible, incorporating, therefore, different notions of affiliation, descent, and procreation. Speiser (1963, 1964:92) thought they revealed a kind of "fratriarchal system" that conforms to a certain kind of matrilineal system, and Jay (1992:94–111), possibly influenced by Smith (1903), attempted to show that remnants of a matrilineal descent system exist in the biblical text.[13] Children may be distinguished by their mothers in a polygynous society, but that hardly denies the overarching patriarchal, patrilineal structure. It is quite possible that the biblical stories were a response to another type of kinship system, and incorporated some elements of it, but that does not mean that the system was matrilineal, even less that it was matriarchal. (For problems with this concept, see chapter 1.) Because most of these theorists tend to assume that kinship is, self-evidently, about biology and blood relations, they also assume that notions of affiliation, descent, and inheritance must follow the flow of either patrilineal or matrilineal blood.

Although an explicit connection between Haran and Ur is made in Genesis, it does not disclose the religious connection between them.

FIG. 2. Beehive-domed houses in Haran, allegedly Abraham's home,
now a village in southeastern Turkey. Photo by author.

Archaeologically informed historians have suggested that temples to the
same deities existed in both places, even though the specific deities may
have changed over time. For example, Haran was, allegedly, the site of a
temple to the moon god Sin, apparently the "daughter" of the "mother"
temple in Ur (Parrot, 1968).[14]

Regardless of the enigmatic points of interest regarding Haran's past,
it is a pivotal place in the story of Abraham. Although Haran is, today, a
dusty village of beehive-domed houses (see fig. 2) not far from the Turkish
city of Urfa, the inhabitants are quite aware of its religious and archaeological significance. Stories and traditions about the figure of Abraham are found in both Jewish and Muslim texts and have become part of
the folklore there (see chapters 5 and 7). The area is now considered pro-
pitious for those seeking relief from problems associated with barrenness,
pregnancy, and childbirth.

Mesopotamia

Without specifying a date for Abraham, Philo of Alexandria, one of the
earliest commentators writing on the story of Abraham, notes in his *De
Abrahamo* that "in Babylonia and Mesopotamia and with the nations of

the Chaldeans with whom he was brought up and lived the greater part
of his life the custom of child slaughter does not obtain" (Philo of Alexandria, [20 B.C.–A.D. 50] 1959, vol. 6:93). His opinion is supported by
a number of twentieth century scholars who have investigated this topic
(de Vaux, 1961; Mosca, 1975; Cartun, 1975; and Day, 1989). Roland de
Vaux, for example, notes that "the theory of human sacrifice is scarcely
tenable for Oriental cultures other than of Israel, but it has been asserted
that even Israel practiced it" (Vaux, 1961:442), and he concludes that it
was introduced into Israel quite late. The Akkadian words that have been
translated as *sacrifice*, he contends, referred to libations—of water, beer,
and wine—or to a meal that included all kinds of food but without any
mention of blood (ibid.: 433). Furthermore, he claims that the ritual use
and meaning of blood was minimal or nonexistent. He does note possible
evidence for an offering in times of danger but claims that not even animal sacrifice took place; instead a substitution made of a reed-and-mud
model of an animal was offered and then destroyed (ibid.:434).

Some people assume that the royal tombs at Ur, uncovered in the excavations by Leonard Woolley between 1922 and 1934, which contained
the remains of several royal personages and their retinues, were clear indication that human sacrifice was practiced. The "standard interpretation
now is that these were not human sacrifices but funeral gifts for the de-
parted" (Cartun, 1975:18; see also Vaux, 1961:441). That distinction
may be stretching the point; nevertheless, there was no evidence of violence.[15] "The search for corroborative evidence from Mesopotamian
texts has so far turned up only blind alleys, as far as human sacrifice is
concerned" (Cartun, 1975:18; cf. Mosca, 1975; Day, 1989).

Although the scholarly consensus appears to be that human sacrifice
was not practiced in Mesopotamia, Green (1975) claims that it was and
even distinguishes between northern Mesopotamia where he claims residential sacrifice was performed, and southern Mesopotamia where he believes human sacrifice was practiced as part of a temple cult. Residential
sacrifice refers to the idea that children were sacrificed at the construction
of a house, and it is true that skeletons of children have been found in the
foundations of houses. Without additional evidence, it is difficult to ascertain whether these were actually child sacrifices or merely burials after
the fact. With respect to a temple cult, the evidence he marshals is primarily glyphic: seal stones that portray "shackled individuals conducted by
guards and put to death in the presence of seated deities" (Green, 1975:
192). Whether this represented the execution of criminals, prisoners of
war, or sacrificial victims is, again, difficult to assess without textual evidence. But texts are problematic, as they do not necessarily reflect reality;
just as often they construct a vision of it, and they are especially unreliable
when referring to the practices of a "repugnant other."[16]

Even if one considers these events—whether the extraordinary burial of an entire royal retinue, or the execution of prisoners—human sacrifice, they are quite different from ritual sacrifice of children, especially of the firstborn son. Yet it is these alleged practices that are most relevant to the Hebrew Bible, in general, and to Genesis 22, in particular.

Canaan

When we turn to Canaan, the evidence for child sacrifice is hardly more substantive. The popular image of lascivious, barbaric, and child-sacrificing Canaanites has been abstracted from the Bible itself and embellished over the centuries by believing Jews and Christians. Ironically, the identity of Canaan appears to evaporate on closer scrutiny. Often, it is assumed to be the name that refers to the land of Palestine before the establishment of Israel. Others associate it more specifically with Ugarit (also known as Ras Shamra) and the Ugaritic texts found there. Ugarit was apparently a city in the early second millenium with its golden period in the Late Bronze Age (1350–1150 B.C.). There *is* a Ugaritic myth about the god El killing his son, a myth that appears to have analogies to a Hurrian myth about Kumarbi and to the Greek myths about Uranus, Kronos, and Zeus. In each of these the theme of succession is strong—the son is seen as a threat to the father or an oracle says as much. The theme of paternity and authority is quite clear in these stories, but they are not so much concerned with religious concepts and practices related to sacrifice.

Canaanite is also used to refer to a set of languages that includes Hebrew, Moabite, Ammonite, Phoenician, and Edomite, among others, but Ugaritic is not a Canaanite language![17] The Phoenicians apparently did call themselves Canaanites, and Phoenicia became a named place about the same time as Israel, around 1000 B.C. Phoenicia established a colony in Carthage, a city on the coast of North Africa, and it is from Carthage that most of the supposed archaeological evidence for child sacrifice comes.

Carthage

Although Carthage was founded sometime around 750 B.C., the archaeological "evidence" relating to child sacrifice occurs later, with most of it concentrated from 400–146 B.C., the year Carthage was destroyed. Therefore this material is, by any account, much later than the Abraham story. Excavations of Carthage have unearthed hundreds of urns filled with the charred bones of small children and small animals, such as lambs, as well as amulets, beads, and perhaps toys. Projecting from the density of the material excavated to date, Stager and Wolff "estimate that as many as 20,000 urns may have been deposited there between 400 and 200 B.C." (Stager and Wolff, 1984:32, see also Stager, 1982:158). They note that in the later period the percentage of infant bones versus animal bones actually increases, which overturns, for them, the evolutionary argument in which animal sacrifice is supposed to replace that of human sacrifice.

The human bones are those from stillborn or newborn babies, and they state that it is very difficult to distinguish between the two. If they are the former, the burial could not possibly be considered the result of sacrifice, as the baby would have been born dead. If not stillborn, it is still possible that the baby died within the first few days of life. The neonate bones, however, were often found together with those of a somewhat older child (one to four years old).[18] Stager and Wolff assumed that they must have come from the same family, "since this range is the natural birth interval that can be expected in families not practicing prenatal forms of birth control" (ibid.: 49). Nevertheless, they give no reason for assuming that these families were not practicing birth control, nor any convincing reason why the children must have been from the same family. Clearly they were unaware of the substantial scholarly literature on premodern knowledge and forms of contraception (e.g., Noonan, 1965; Musallam, 1983; and Riddle, 1992). And they quickly discounted the possibility "that disease or some other disaster would have affected only the two youngest children" (Stager and Wolff, 1984:39), without considering that the most dangerous period (because of disease, accident, or lack of care) for children is from birth to about four years. Instead, they interpret the finds as follows: if the child who was the intended sacrifice died before the sacrifice occurred, the parents would offer the next oldest child (ibid.:49).

Stager may be right that these urns and bones are the remains of a grisly practice of child sacrifice, but the evidence is not unequivocal.[19] His interpretation has, in part, been affected by classical references to the practice, some of which explicitly cite Carthage. All of these references can be found in the six-page appendix compiled by Day (1989).

Classical References

The earliest classical reference is supposedly a fragment of Sophocles' *Andromeda* (fifth century B.C.), which states: "There is amongst the barbarians a law which from olden times prescribes the offering of a human sacrifice to Kronos" (Day, 1989:87). Other authors often cited are: (1) Diodorus Siculus, who wrote in the first century B.C. but refers to instances of child sacrifice, also offered to Kronos, that are supposed to have taken place in Carthage in 406 B.C.; (2) Tertullian, a Church Father who lived sometime between A.D. 160 and 225 in Carthage, also refers to the practice of child sacrifice in earlier times (curiously, however, he notes that "between murder and sacrifice by parents—oh! the difference is great!" [*Apology* 2–4, cited in Stager and Wolff, 1984:33]);[20] and (3) Philo of Byblos, who wrote in the first century but allegedly quotes a much earlier Phoenician scribe Sanchuniathon (also cited as Sakkunyaton[21]) but is nevertheless preserved only in Eusebius's *Preparation for the Gospel* composed in the fourth and fifth centuries. Uranus, reports Eusebius, had several sons, including one Elus who is also Kronos whom he tried to destroy; Kronos, however, waylays his father and emasculates him. "But on the occurrence of a pestilence and mortality Kronos *offers his only begotten son as a whole burnt offering* to his father Uranus, and *circumcises* himself, compelling his allies (the Eloim) to do the same" (Eusebius, 1903:29, emphasis added). Whether the parallel to the biblical story was original or Eusebius's doing, the interrelated themes of sacrifice and circumcision are not difficult to miss. The question remains, however, as to whether the theme is about sacrifice or about the power and authority of fatherhood.

The references, in any case, occur over a period of about eight hundred years; none of them is an eyewitness account and only one (Sophocles') is contemporary with the events of which they write. The reports appear to be so similar that it is also possible that rather than being multiple accounts, as they are often presumed to be, each writer—or at least several of them—simply transmitted, and perhaps embellished, the same story. Then the question arises as to whether it was simply a story, or whether it refers to something that really happened and, if so, whether it ever became a ritual practice. Nevertheless, Stager believes that "even if we dismiss the classical literary evidence for child sacrifice as ancient slanders spread by foreign antagonists who wanted to discredit the Carthaginians, the growing body of archaeological and epigraphic evidence, provided by the Carthaginians themselves, strongly suggests that the classical and biblical writers knew what they were talking about" (Stager, 1984:38). He means, not just the burial urns, but also inscriptions on stelae that have to do with vows, and he cites a recurrent phrase "Life for life, blood for blood, a lamb as a substitute" (Stager and Wolff, 1984:40), which, according to Weinfeld, is "reminiscent of the biblical talio formula" (Weinfeld, 1972:135). Stager and Wolff assert that there can "be little doubt that the burnt animal burials at Carthage are animal substitutes for child sacrifices" (Stager and Wolff, 1984:40). But why should we not interpret the passage and the sacrifice as a propitiation, made with the *hope* that the child will live?

Day (1989:8, n.23) cites a similar but more extended inscription taken from Eissfeldt that comes from Algeria and is dated circa A.D. 200. "Prosperity and salvation! To the holy lord Saturn a great nocturnal sacrifice—breath for breath, blood for blood, life for life, for the salvation of Concessa—on account of a vision and a vow Felix and Diodora have offered a sacrifice *molchomor* with willing hearts, a lamb as substitute" (Eissfeldt, 1935:3–4). Levenson goes even further, stating that the vow "suggests that the daughter had become ill. Presumably, the parents, crediting Saturn with her recovery, wished to present him with an equivalent of the child who, had she died, would have become his" (Levenson, 1993:23). Let me suggest an alternative: there is no reason to suspect that the child had been ill; her parents may have offered a sacrifice so that the god would not take their daughter. Perhaps they had a vision that she would become ill if they did not perform the sacrifice.

This alternative interpretation was suggested to me in 1975 by an encounter in Urfa, a city close to Haran in eastern Turkey, where stories and practices related to Abraham still abound. There I met a pregnant woman who told me she had been unable to conceive for a long time. A few years earlier she had made a sacrifice (of a lamb or sheep) at a shrine dedicated to Abraham, where such offerings are thought to be especially effective. After that sacrifice she had become pregnant, but the child died. When I met her, she had come to make another sacrifice, with the hope that the child she was pregnant with would live.[22] In other words, it is possible to read the ancient inscriptions not as references to substitute sacrifices, not as animals in place of children, but as propitiatory sacrifices, requests for a healthy child.[23] I am not arguing for one interpretation over the other, but I am suggesting that there is more than one way to read the current evidence.

The Carthaginian material is often used to illuminate biblical references regardless of the fact that, even if such a practice existed, it was hundreds of years later than the biblical stories and perhaps as much as a millennium later than the story of Abraham. We should also consider how biblical references have conditioned our interpretations of the material from Carthage. Because of the cultural similarity between the Phoenician and Punic worlds, it has been assumed that similar rites must have been practiced in the "mother" country, Phoenicia, or more popularly, Canaan, and from there infiltrated Israel.[24] (But perhaps it was the reverse.)

The assumption of the existence of human/child sacrifice in Canaan has been derived primarily from the Bible and not from any explicit evidence, either archaeological or historical, from ancient Canaan. There are mythological fragments that include a story of the father-god El killing his son. El was a common word for God among the "Canaanites"; it was associated with the north and, in the plural form *elohim*, it is the word used for God by the patriarchs. *Yahweh*, in contrast, is the name used for God from the Mosaic and southern traditions.

Frank Cross, the eminent Harvard biblical scholar, thinks that the Canaanite El is best characterized by the word *patriarch*. Sitting at the head of the assembly of the gods, he is judge, lawmaker, creator, king, and father. El did not come by his position easily; there were many struggles for succession, similar to those fought by Kronos and Zeus in Greek mythology. The struggle was for patriarchal authority (Cross, 1973:43). The myths of Kronos, Zeus, and El are what he calls *succession myths*.

Cross sees an echo of the succession motif in the story of Abraham, but the struggles (between the gods) have been excluded. In the Bible, God was there from the beginning; he created the world and established his order. Although Genesis is not about the succession of the gods, it is all about succession: about which son will inherit, about who is the proper heir and transmitter of the sacred line. The struggle has been transferred from gods to men. In the story of Abraham, the issue of the succession concerns Ishmael versus Isaac. The story is not ostensibly about the father's jealousy of the son, as is the case in the Greek and Canaanite myths, but it is about obedience; the beloved son is the obedient son. The story concerns the issue of paternal authority and power. There is a problem comparing myth with biblical story, for the latter claims to be, and many people believe it is, the story of real, historical people and practices, whereas myth concerns the antics of the gods; and though these may reflect human practice, they may be purely imaginative.

The heritage in which the Canaanites have been constructed as "the repugnant other" obscures the fact that ethnically, linguistically, socially, and, no doubt, religiously, they were close relatives of the Israelites. According to Vaux (1961:438) "Canaanite sacrifices do not seem to be materially different from those which were offered to Yahweh," but they do appear to contrast with those of other neighboring peoples. That "which distinguishes Israelite and Canaanite rituals from those of other Semitic peoples is that, when an animal is sacrificed, the victim or at least part of it, is burnt upon an altar" (ibid.:440). Because the practice of human/ child sacrifice is often assumed for the Canaanites, the question arises as to whether it was also practiced in Israel. The idea that it may have been practiced in Israel touches some very sensitive nerves. This may explain the circuitous route from the periphery to the center—from other cultures to Israelite culture—that scholarship on this issue has taken.

Israel

It is becoming more and more difficult to maintain the view that the Abraham story reflects, and thus is a survivor of, an even more ancient practice by barbaric others, as Frank Moore Cross implied when he saw in Genesis 22 an echo of the human sacrifice supposedly made to Kronos (El) and the myth whereby El sacrificed his own children (Cross, 1973:26). Instead, some scholars are beginning to conclude that the practice was centered in the land of Israel itself (Mosca, 1975; Green, 1975; Day, 1989; Levenson, 1993) and that the story of Abraham and the "sacrifice" of Isaac was constructed in a context where child sacrifice was being practiced either by the Canaanites or the Israelites, or by both. These scholars focus on biblical passages that imply sacrifice to Molech or those that stress the idea that the firstborn belongs to Yahweh. These alleged practices, often used in the interpretation of the Abraham story, are the subject of the next chapter.

CHAPTER FOUR

Child Sacrifice in the Bible

I N THE BIBLE there is textual evidence of the occasional sacrifice of children. The story of the sacrifice of Jephthah's daughter in fulfillment of a vow (Judg. 11), often compared with the Greek story of Agamemnon's sacrifice of Iphigenia, is the most obvious. There are a number of other cases, but whether they should be placed on a continuum with the Abraham story is questionable.[1] They demonstrate that human sacrifice was a possibility, but can they be used as evidence that such a practice was widespread during the time of Abraham? First, these stories are very much later in the biblical narrative than the story of Abraham. Second, in each case the child *was* sacrificed, whereas in Genesis 22 it is not. Third, the sacrifices differ in motivation. More important, however, these stories are not foundational, as is the story of Abraham.

In general, the debates about the practice of child sacrifice in Israel have focused on passages regarding: (a) the worship of Molech, (b) the dedication of the firstborn, and (c) the relevance of circumcision. Sexuality in the service of procreation is prominent in these contexts, especially as it relates to issues of legitimacy, yet it is hardly ever taken into account. I suggest that it is the *theory* of procreation that relates and illuminates these seemingly unrelated issues.

Once the male is imagined as creator/author of a child, the question arises as to which child belongs to which man. A man's anxiety would be most severe over the firstborn, because the woman may have been pregnant when he married her or had sex with her. The anxiety is also greatest regarding a son, because in this theory of procreation, only a son is imagined as able to pass down the lineage via his seed. The emphasis on making sure that the line passes to the "right" son is hard to miss in Genesis. Insecurity over paternity might help to explain the ambivalence over the firstborn; it would be expedient to pass over the firstborn son or, conceivably, to sacrifice him. Before resuming this discussion, let us turn to the issue of Molech.

SACRIFICES TO MOLECH

The ambiguity of passages, such as the following, have given rise to considerable debate. "And thou shalt not let any of thy seed pass through the fire to Molech, neither shall thou profane the name of thy God" (Lev. 18:21; see also Lev. 20:2, 3, 4, 5; 2 Kings 23:10; Jer. 32:35). Although the term *Molech* appears only eight times in the Hebrew Bible, five of them are in the Holiness Code of Leviticus—that is, Leviticus 17–26 (Mosca, 1975:121–2). Debates have ranged around several questions: (1) is Molech a deity or a kind of sacrifice? (2) if he is a deity, is he Canaanite or Israelite and, most important perhaps, (3) does passing through the fire mean a purification ritual or a burnt offering? That is, does it refer to child sacrifice?[2]

"Until 1935 it was universally believed that when the Old Testament speaks of Molech it is referring to a god. Scholars certainly differed on the question of the identity of the god and the nature of his cult, but there was nevertheless unanimous agreement that a god was intended" (Day, 1989: 4). In 1935 Eissfeldt threw a wrench into the works by proposing that the word (*molek*) was a "term for a type of sacrifice, just as *mlk* (*molk*) in Punic is a sacrificial term" (ibid.). Day, a lecturer on the Old Testament at Oxford, challenges this view and has reverted to the older view. He asserts, that although it is true that *molk* is a sacrificial term in Punic texts, there is little reason to assume that it means the same thing in Hebrew texts (cf. Weinfeld, 1972, 1978; Smith, 1975). Nor does he believe that the Israelites merely misunderstood the term and personified it.[3] In a short, concise, and scholarly book, Day claims, instead, that Molech *was* a god and that he was an Israelite god. Molech, for Day, was an underground deity whose abode was crevices and underground caves in the valley of Hinnom, not far from the center of the Israelite cult in Jerusalem. The worship of Molech, he believes, included the sacrifice of children at the *tophet*—a word that is taken to mean the place, perhaps a kind of pyre—on which they were burned (see Day, 1989:24ff., for discussion of various attempts to translate the word). In the Bible, *tophet* is used only in relation to the valley of Hinnom, not elsewhere. Even if this deity and the practices associated with him had been taken over from the Canaanites, Day believes that the cult was part of Israelite religious practice. In other words, he implies that there were (at least) two major deities—Yahweh and Molech—that were the focus of human devotion. The Molech cult may not have been official, but he claims it was popular among some of the people, especially among the ruling class, who turned to it in attempts to avert disaster (ibid.:62).

Day differs from scholars who "have concluded that, although Molech may have been a foreign god in origin, those who worshipped him equated him with Yahweh" (ibid.:65, see note 121). Some people accept this equation because of the (rare) associations of Yahweh with human sacrifice (such as Genesis 22) and because of the dedication of the first-born (see below), both of which, Day argues, are not the same as the sacrifices of children supposedly offered to Molech. He thinks it highly unlikely that people confused the two, partly because Yahweh is not mentioned in connection with the *tophet*s in the valley of Hinnom. He alerted me to the very interesting and thought-provoking suggestion that *Gehenna*, the term for Hell in Jewish literature, is derived from the Aramaic name for Hinnom. Gehenna is usually associated with fire and "the only fires that are certainly attested in connection with the valley of Hinnom are those associated with the sacrifices offered to the god Molech" (ibid.: 53). Without too much imagination, one can see how the *tophet* may have developed into the popular notion of Hell, as the underworld, with the devil (formerly, Molech) presiding over the fires.

Despite the protests in the Hebrew Bible against the cult of Molech, Day thinks the people did not see their worship of Molech as incompatible with the worship of Yahweh, nor did it necessarily imply their faithlessness (ibid.:68–9). They simply had different kinds of worship for different purposes, even though both may have involved child sacrifice. The sacrifices to Molech, Day claims, were children—both sons and daughters—and therefore should not be associated or equated with the dedication of the firstborn, who were always sons. He thinks these were different rites, established by different religious motivations, and that they should not be conflated (cf. Weinfeld, 1972).

Levenson, a professor of Jewish Studies at Harvard Divinity School, disagrees. He traces what he purports is the transformation of child sacrifice in Judaism and Christianity, and sees the types of sacrifice above, as well as a number of others (e.g., Jephthah's daughter; Mesha), as part of the same continuum. Not only does he place these biblical examples on a continuum, he assumes a comparative method: "without reference to ancient myths associated with child sacrifice, certain biblical narratives about the origins and character of the people of Israel and of the Church cannot be properly understood" (Levenson, 1993:37). Because his book is likely to receive a fair amount of attention among scholars, it is important to point out some of the flaws in his principal assumptions.

That similar practices can have very different motivations and meanings was made very clear by one of the foremost anthropologists in this century, Franz Boas, and it is a point that most anthropologists learn at the beginning of their studies. Rather than comparing all these various myths and fragments, we need to explore the function the story has in the Bible and in the religious traditions of Judaism, Christianity, and Islam.

Levenson's argument is basically psychological, for in order to make his argument, he must assume psychological continuity, even fixity, over time and geographical area, perhaps even a universal human psychology. But if one assumes a basic human psychology, as Freud and his followers do, how then does one explain the diversity of myths and practices? The mediating, even constitutive, role of culture is disregarded in Levenson's analysis, just as it is in Freud's. Levenson does not consider the interrelations between a culture's myths and stories and its people's psychology; that is, rather than assuming that myths, stories, and practices reflect universal human psychological needs and desires, one could assume that these needs and desires are themselves shaped by a culture's stories and myths. As Mary Douglas succinctly put it: "Psychological explanations cannot of their nature account for what is culturally distinctive" (Douglas, 1966:121). Not only does Levenson assume a certain fixity in human psychology but, as we shall see, he takes for granted that the meanings of gender are stable and self-evident.

He collapses Molech worship, the sacrifice of Jephthah's daughter in honor of a vow, Mesha's killing of his son to avert defeat, and Abraham's intention to sacrifice Isaac into a more general theme that he calls "the death and resurrection of the beloved son." Immediately, problems emerge: there is a difference between a daughter and a son, between a "beloved son" and a firstborn son (Isaac, after all, was not the firstborn son of Abraham), between an actual sacrifice of a child and an animal substituted for one, and between a sacrifice to fulfill a prior vow and the motivation of Abraham. In addition, in a chapter entitled "YHWH vs. Molech," Levenson speaks very little about Molech but suggests that, "to understand the nature and extent of the cult of Molech," we must turn to the "largest body of data on the grisly practice" (Levenson, 1993:20), namely to Carthage. Not only is he taking the contested material at Carthage as fact and repeating all the usual anachronisms, but he is assimilating the practice of offering *children* to Molech with the notion of the sacrifice of the firstborn son as it appears in the Bible (e.g., Exod. 13.2; 22:29–30). He does recognize some of the difficulties, but he says, nevertheless: "Lest the two practices be too sharply disengaged, however, the obvious point should be restated: both involve child sacrifice, and both seem to have had some frequency in ancient Israel" (ibid.:18). It is not at all clear to me what relevance material from Carthage, even if it is true, has for Israel. Levenson argues backward, both temporally and in significance, from Carthage to Israel, rather than beginning with what is clearly the most important story, the foundation story, of the three Abrahamic religions—the Abraham story. He further undermines the significance of this story when he refers to it as "the wrenching *little* narrative that is the aqedah" (ibid.:23, emphasis mine).

This *little* narrative, unlike any of the others, was, or at least is considered to be, a turning point in the world's orientation. But rather than beginning with that and moving out, Levenson collects bits and pieces of information and rituals from various places in an attempt to support his claim for the common motif or theme. Problems with creating such a typology—namely, who is creating the theme and the typology and for what purposes—have been noted ever since Frazer's *Golden Bough*. Even if we were to accept Levenson's typology, only one of the three explicit biblical examples he gives comes close to that theme—the one found in Genesis 22—and even there, the construal as death and resurrection is really stretching the point.

MOLECH AND SEXUALITY

A more fruitful approach, at least regarding "sacrifices" to Molech, might begin with the recognition that the biblical injunctions against this practice are in the midst of a discussion of sexual behavior. Much of the Holiness code and all the references to Molech are preceded or followed by discussions of who may engage in what kind of sexual practices with whom. Giving one's seed to Molech is analogous to playing the whore/harlot with Molech (Lev. 20:5), and immediately after this passage there is a discussion of adultery and other profane unions. Two scholars, according to Day, have supposed "that it was the children of sacred prostitutes who were offered up to Molech" (Day, 1989:23). Others, notably Weinfeld (1972:142; 1978:412), not so literal-minded, have noted the association between sacrifice and prohibited sexual behavior, but such suggestions have been ridiculed by Smith (1975:478).

Day, however, thinks the sexual context of the prohibitions is important and suggests that it is precisely because "the Molech cult is thought of metaphorically as an adulterous one *vis à vis* Yahweh" (Day, 1989: 23). He notes that "the ease with which the Old Testament slips from speaking of literal adultery to spiritual adultery is well known (cf. Jer. 3.1, 2, 6, 8–9)" (ibid.); that is, each context illuminates and reinforces the meaning of the other. Although Day recognizes the sexual context and connotations, he does not recognize the assumptions about, and implications for, gender that are embedded in these allusions. The warning, "do not give any of your seed to Molech," is addressed, at least figuratively, to men, whereas "whoring after other gods" implies promiscuous behavior on the part of women.[4] At issue is the fate of "seed." It is as wrong for men to give it away to whores or to Molech as it is for women to play the whore and bring alien seed into the pure community. In either case, the purity of God's chosen is sullied; the message was meant to keep the lines pure, and that demanded something of both men and women. The injunctions were also used figuratively. Israel was sometimes imagined as the "bride" of God; if "she" went whoring after other gods, "her" stain would have to be scrubbed out by, in today's vernacular, ethnic cleansing. Sexuality and gender are used for conceptualizing theological ideas and spiritual relations, but it is sexuality and gender as constructed in relation to a particular theory of procreation, as is made clear in the following passage: "The ultimate purpose of biblical genealogies was to establish the superior strain of the line through which the biblical way of life was transmitted from generation to generation. In other words, *the integrity of the mission was to be safeguarded in transmission, the purity of the content protected by the quality of the container*" (Speiser, 1964: 93–4 emphasis added). In Speiser's interpretation, the male is construed as the transmitter of the valuable content, the female is figured as the container. The pivot, of course, is Abraham, because it is through his seed that the pure line really begins. This issue, cast in a different light, is, I believe, intimately related to the issue of the "sacrifice of the first born." None of the interpreters have considered the sexual and gendered components.

SACRIFICE OR DEDICATION OF THE FIRSTBORN SON?

The presence of child sacrifice in Israel is also deduced from biblical passages such as: "Sanctify unto me all the first-born, whatsoever openeth the womb among the children of Israel, both of man and of beast. It is mine." (Exod. 13:2) This and other passages like it have sometimes been interpreted as indications that perhaps children were once sacrificed, presumably to Yahweh himself.

Although the passage does not specify sons, that is the way it is usually interpreted. Clearly, not all firstborn children are sons. Conceivably a woman could have several daughters before a son; does that mean they were not counted? The word used, *bekhor*, is a masculine noun and could conceivably be inclusive of gender in the way that *man* has functioned in English, or it could be more like the Turkish *çocuk*, which means both child and son; *kız* is the Turkish word for girl or daughter.[5] *Bekhor*, however, has traditionally been understood to be gender specific, to mean firstborn males. I have no argument with traditional interpretations that assume, I believe correctly, that the referent was sons; but interpreters have not been explicit about *why* it is sons who are considered the appropriate sacrifice, and why firstborn sons.

Interpretations often assume that "because of his favored status, the first born is considered the most desirable sacrifice to the deity where

human sacrifice was practiced" (*Encyclopedia Judaica*, 1971:1306).
They do not say why the firstborn is the favored status, nor consider that
its status may have become elevated *because* of sacrifice. One cannot simply assume that the firstborn was already favored—that is exactly what
needs to be proved.

Curiously, Freud suggested that the favored position was that of the
youngest son, and that it was natural because "protected by his mother's
love, [he] could profit by his father's advancing years and replace him
after his death" (Freud, 1939:103). Levenson suggests that *beloved son*
is meant symbolically rather than literally, but he still presumes a status
that reflects the concepts and significance of primogeniture. He is distinguished from other interpreters only by the idea that the status can be
assigned at the discretion of the father (Levenson, 1993:69). Because
"primogeniture is a persistent and widespread institution whose legal,
social and religious features were reflected in the norms of ancient Israelite society" (*Encyclopedia Judaica*, 1979:1306), it is assumed to have
been the norm in Abraham's society.

Regardless of which son, neither Freud nor Levenson nor any of the
other interpreters considers the question: Why sons? What is it about
sons that makes them special? It is far too easy to say simply that sons are
valuable in a patriarchal society; one needs to ask why.[6] And one also
needs to make explicit one's assumptions about the foundations of patriarchal society, that is, whether one assumes it is a natural formation or
the result of specific concepts, practices, and institutions. Even if there
was a tendency toward male dominance, patriarchy is an ideology in
which the notion of *father* is integral. It may be true that the principle of
primogeniture *became* the norm in Israelite society, but there seems no
justification for assuming that was the case in Abraham's society. Any
perceptive reader of Genesis recognizes that *all* of the firstborn sons are
passed over, whether for blessing, favor, or inheritance, beginning with
Cain (see Delaney, 1977; Syren, 1993). Levenson may be right that this is
not simply a matter of God favoring or choosing the younger over the
elder, but that does not mean he is right in concluding that God "*reversed*
the order of the two and assigned the one he favored the status of the first
born" (Levenson, 1993:69, emphasis added).

If one believes that the documents are humanly constructed, it is not a
question of *God choosing* but of the motives of the writers for showing
that God passed over the firstborn. Levenson does not consider that. Instead, he reads into the patriarchal stories motives that derive from the
law/lore of a later (at least later narrative) time. His prior assumption is
that the status of the firstborn is of greater importance, even if of less
fixity—that is, he gives the father the power to *assign* that status (ibid.,
1993:69). Because he does not question the concept of paternity and its

integral relation to a *theory* of procreation, he does not consider the possibility that some of the textual ambiguity and ambivalence about the firstborn son might represent a conflict with other notions of procreation, or might be related to a transitional period during which notions of paternity and its implications were being socially assimilated. That is, he does not consider the possibility that the story of Abraham represents the establishment of the *concept* of paternity and its powerful implications. In that case, then, the passing over of the firstborn, as well as the favoring of the second or younger, could be seen as representing two sides of the same thing, representing the insecurity a man might have over the paternity of a particular child. A more nuanced reading can be found in Syren's *The Forsaken First-Born: a Study of a Recurrent Motif in the Patriarchal Narratives* (1993), which Levenson does not cite. Syren argues, basically, that the patriarchs stand in for God, their choices really signal God's choice of who is deemed appropriate heir. He thinks the motif highlights the whole idea of divine election. He still does not address the issue of gender: why fathers and sons?

In connection with the sacrifice of the firstborn son, the following biblical passage is often cited: "Thou shalt not delay to offer the first of thy fruits and of thy liquors: the first born of thy sons shalt thou give unto me. Likewise shalt thou do with thine oxen and with thy sheep; seven days it shall be with his dam; on the eighth day thou shalt give it to me." (Exod. 22:29). I want to explore several issues in relation to this passage: (1) the analogy established between fruits and liquors (assumed to be the press from grapes) on the one side, and sons and animals on the other, (2) the equivalence of the animal and human offering, and (3) the significance of the eighth day.

Fruits and Seeds

Regarding the equation between fruit offerings and animal offerings, the allusion to the story of Cain and Abel is hard to miss. In that story, Cain offered the fruits of the soil and Abel the firstling of the flock; without any reason given, God is shown to prefer the animal offering over the fruits. The different valuation has often been thought to represent the "conflict between the pastoral and the agricultural ways of life" (Speiser, 1964:31; see also Pritchard, 1950; and Wolkstein and Kramer, 1983; but for an opposing opinion see Sarna, 1966:28).[7] Exegesis has also focused on what is assumed to be the paltry quality of Cain's offering in comparison with Abel's. One presentation seems to be more an offering, the other a sacrifice; one involves gifts from one's abundance, the other involves the destruction of life; one is a gift from the soil, the other of blood.

The conflation between these different types of offerings may conceal a theological/political agenda. We must consider the possible motivations of the ancients as well as of the modern expositors who have usually placed offerings of grain, animals, and humans along a sacrificial continuum in which the differences lie in their unequal value rather than in different motivations and conceptual systems. Fruit, cereals, and the soil have often been associated with women and with devotion to female figures (Kraemer, 1988; DuBois, 1988), whereas blood sacrifice is primarily associated with patriliny (Jay, 1992),[8] yet here and in other passages a conflation has been made between fruit and seed and child, as, for example in Micah's question: "With what shall I approach the Lord, Do homage to God on high? Shall I give my first-born for my transgression? The *fruit* of my body for my sins?" (Mic. 6:6–7). Clearly the man is imagining the child as the fruit of *his* body, the fruit of his seed (cf. discussion between Weinfeld and Smith cited above). Might the conflation between fruit and seed be an attempt to co-opt, encompass, and thereby appear to supersede, not a different means of subsistence, but a different socioreligious system, just as, later, Christianity rhetorically attempts to do with Judaism?

HUMAN AND ANIMAL

In the Exodus passage we are discussing (Exod. 22:29, and in the earlier one [Exod. 13:2]), the human offering (sacrifice?) is named first; the animal offering (sacrifice?) is not a substitute for the son, nor the son for the animal: they are presented as analogous and both are required.[9] In Exodus, more explicit references to the killing of the firstborn are found, but they are not ritual sacrifices; instead, they are a sign of God's punishment. They occur in relation to what God did to the firstborn of the Egyptians: "At midnight, the Lord smote all the first born in the land of Egypt, from the first born of Pharaoh who sat on his throne to the first born of the captive who was in the dungeon, and all the first born of the cattle" (Exod. 12:29). This was God's punishment meted out to Pharaoh because, although Pharaoh had witnessed the power of Moses' God, he refused to submit. His heart had hardened, and so God punished him by killing all the firstborn Egyptian males—both human and beast.[10] Yet it was not just Pharaoh who suffered. So, too, did all the innocent firstborn of other Egyptians, as well as their animals. Israel was sometimes conceptualized as God's firstborn son (e.g., Exod. 4:22–3), and when "he" was not being a proper son, showing proper respect for his "father," there were threats of punishment and destruction, similar to those meted out to the Egyptians.

In Exodus 13:13 and 13:15, however, there is a shift: "And every first-ling of an ass thou shalt redeem with a lamb; and if though wilt not redeem it, then thou shalt break his neck: and all the firstborn of man among thy children shalt thou redeem" (Exod. 13:13). This does not say the firstborn is redeemed with a lamb; instead the passage is followed by a reference to the exodus: "the Lord slew all the firstborn in the land of Egypt, both the firstborn of man, and the firstborn of beast: *therefore* I sacrifice to the Lord all that openeth the matrix, being males; but all the firstborn of my children I redeem" (Exod. 13:15). The Israelite God does not oppose the killing of children in general, but only the killing of certain ones. This passage implies that the redemption of the firstborn of Israel came on the backs of the slaughter of the innocent children of Egypt.

Circumcision, Sacrifice, and the Eighth Day

Let us look again at the passage above: why is the eighth day the one on which the offerings should be made, rather than, say, the fourth or the sixteenth or the thirtieth? The traditional explanation is that the eighth day is significant because it is, in Jewish tradition, the day on which circumcision is performed. The traditional explanation analogizing circumcision with sacrifice merely begs the question, however, for we need to ask why circumcision is performed on the eighth day and, more to the point, why circumcision?

Circumcision

The practice of circumcision was instituted with Abraham. It was the sign of the covenant God made with Abraham, a promise—engraved on the flesh of the male sexual organ—that he would be a father of nations.

> And I will make thee exceedingly fruitful, and I will make nations of thee, and kings shall come out of thee. And I will establish my covenant between me and thee and thy seed after thee in their generations for an everlasting covenant, to be a God unto thee, and to thy seed after thee. And I will give unto thee, and to thy seed after thee, the land wherein thou art a stranger, all the land of Canaan, for an everlasting possession, and I will be their God. (Gen 17:5–8)

The context of circumcision is fruitfulness and procreation, not sacrifice. After Abraham was circumcised, God promised him Isaac, the one through whom his promises would flow. There is no mention of blood in the account of Abraham's circumcision, but some people have clearly imagined the flow of blood as the symbolic "ink" in which the covenant was signed, no doubt because the blood of sacrifice has, traditionally, been considered the means of communication between God and men. Levenson, for example, suggests that it is specifically blood that is important in the ritual; he relates it to the blood of the paschal lamb, which redeemed the firstborn sons of the Israelites as God smote the firstborn sons of the Egyptians. "The blood of circumcision functions within the larger redacted story of Moses and Pharaoh as a prototype of the blood of the lamb" (Levenson, 1993:50–1). God instructed the Israelites to sacrifice a lamb and to daub the lintels and doorposts of their houses with its blood, "and when I see the blood, I will pass over you" (Exod. 12:13). In other words, it is the blood, in this case of the lamb, that is salvific. As we shall see, this line becomes important in midrashim about the "sacrifice" of Isaac. But is it the blood of the lamb or that of the Egyptian firstborn that substitutes for the firstborn of the Israelites? Abraham's relation to circumcision has disappeared in Levenson's interpretation.

Levenson then suggests that circumcision might be considered along with the paschal lamb, the later dedication of the firstborn to Levitical service, and the much later practice of *pidyon haben*, the redemption of the first born with monetary payment as "a sublimation for child sacrifice in ancient Israelite religious practice" (Levenson, 1993:51).[11] But, if so, all of these substitutions or sublimations imply that "the impulse to sacrifice the first-born son remained potent" (ibid.:52); they also imply that the impulse to sacrifice the firstborn son is a natural desire. Levenson is in good company, for this has been a common interpretation among those with a psychological, even Freudian, orientation, as we shall see in chapter 9. Such a position was also discernible in the statement made by a New York rabbi, in a widely read column in the Sunday *New York Times Magazine*, 13 March 1994. Rabbi Joshua Hammerman claimed that the rite of circumcision ritualizes the jealousy and murderous wishes of a father toward the son. He implied that those feelings are natural. Neither he nor Levenson nor Freud considered the way the meaning of paternity and the rite of circumcision may foster those feelings.

More is going on with regard to circumcision than merely the spilling of blood. When circumcision is first mentioned, in Genesis 17, the context is not sacrifice but fatherhood and generativity. The sign of the covenant is inscribed only on males, and on the very member that is imagined as the "fountain of life," or at least the means through which life is transmitted (Speiser, 1964; Delaney, 1977). It is "a cut on the male sex organ: a partial castration analogous to an offering, which in return will bring God's blessing upon *the organ that ensures the transmission of life and thereby the survival of the Hebrew people*" (Soler, 1977:25, emphasis mine). This may be a good representation of ancient Hebrew beliefs, but Soler does

not use contemporary knowledge (that both male and female are necessary for the transmission of life) to challenge the system. Unfortunately,
and like so many others, he seems unaware that the perpetuation of such
notions perpetuates a particular view of gender and procreation that de-
values the female role.

Eilberg-Schwartz, an eminent scholar of ancient Judaism, begins with
the question that few have asked: why is the covenant signed on the
penis? If blood is really the crucial issue, surely the cutting of another part
of the body would provide the necessary flow of blood.[12] In a rich and
ethnographically inspired chapter, "The Fruitful Cut: Circumcision and
Israel's Symbolic Language of Fertility, Descent and Gender," Eilberg-
Schwartz (1990) shows a variety of ways in which circumcision is associated with fruitfulness and notions of descent, namely the patrilineage,
and the ways in which the symbolic language of the Bible draws numerous analogies between fruit/agriculture and human generativity. Especially significant are the biblical references to uncircumcised trees and
how pruning makes them more fruitful: "Cutting away the foreskin is like
pruning a fruit tree. Both acts of cutting remove unwanted excess and
both increase the desired yield. One might say that when Israelites cir-
cumcise their male children, they are pruning the fruit trees of God"
(ibid.:152).

There are other references to uncircumcised organs—hearts, ears, and
lips—which are closed up and unable to perform their God-ordained
task. Similarly, says Eilberg-Schwartz, circumcision "enables the penis to
more effectively discharge its divinely allotted task . . . to impregnate
women and produce offspring" (ibid.:149). It is questionable whether
circumcision really enables the penis to perform better, but the Israelites
may have thought so. In any case, such performance is associated more
with manhood and virility than with infancy. In cultures where circumcision is practiced—not just in pagan cultures, but also, as we shall see in
chapter 7, in Islamic cultures—it is not usually performed on infants but
as a puberty or initiation ritual. The question that remains, then, is why
Jews perform it on the eighth day.

The Eighth Day

After Abraham was circumcised, God said to him: "he that is eight days
old shall be circumcised" (Gen. 17:12; see also Lev. 12:3). The eighth day
is also the day on which the firstborn shall be given to God—"both of
man and of beast, it is mine" (Exod. 13:2). Scholarly exegesis often makes
a connection between circumcision and sacrifice, since both involve the
eighth day. Eilberg-Schwartz departs from this tradition and associates

the significance of the eighth day to issues of birth and menstrual blood rather than sacrifice: "after the birth of a male child a woman is in a state of impurity as severe as when she has her menstrual period" (Eilberg-Schwartz, 1990:174), that is, for seven days and these days, in turn, are associated in Leviticus, with circumcision: "If a woman has conceived *seed*, and born a man child . . . in the eighth day the flesh of his foreskin shall be circumcised" (Leviticus 12:2–3, emphasis added). Eilberg-Schwartz notes that a woman's impurity during this time means that she contaminates anything she touches, thus one "can infer from these rules that during the seven days following a birth, a male infant is also unclean and would contaminate any man who performed the circumcision" (Eilberg-Schwartz, 1990). This is clearly a place where Mary Douglas's critique (1966) of "medical materialism" (the idea that proscriptions like those in Leviticus were built on a firm knowledge of health) is appropriate. From the standpoint of health, it is far more likely that a man touching an infant would be the contaminating party, not the infant, but as Douglas cogently argues, notions of pollution are related to a symbolic system, and not to hygiene.

Women's blood is considered "filthy, socially disruptive, and contaminating . . . women's blood is symbolically associated with death," whereas male blood "is clean, unifying, and symbolic of God's covenant" (Eilberg-Schwartz, 1990:174). He goes on to say that the rite of circumcision "marks the passage from the impurity of being born of woman to the purity of life in a community of men" (ibid.:175). Israelite circumcision was, in his view, a rite symbolizing not manhood and virility but fertility. Fertility, however, was not merely the result of the natural process of maturation; instead, "a boy's procreative powers were granted by God as a privilege for having been born into Abraham's line" (ibid.:176; cf. Jay, 1992).

But perhaps there is a price to pay for this privilege, and perhaps the line between circumcision as symbolic of sacrifice and circumcision as symbolic of fertility is not as distinct as Eilberg-Schwartz draws it. If the child is considered the fruit of the organ that is imagined as the pure channel through which God's chosen people come, then anxiety over paternity and legitimacy remain. Recall Speiser's comment that "the integrity of the mission was to be safeguarded in transmission, the purity of the content protected by the quality of the container" (Speiser, 1964:93–4). Circumcision could, then, be seen as *pars pro toto*, a part of the child for the whole of the child; it could symbolize the sacrifice of the child, or the idea of the sacrifice of the child created by the anxiety generated by the notions of paternity and the problem of illegitimacy. At the same time, circumcision would also symbolize that, despite these anxieties, the child is accepted.

Although this interpretation is attractive, it is problematic because the institution of circumcision occurs *before* the demand that Abraham sacrifice his son, *before* Isaac is even born. In the chronology of the narrative, circumcision could hardly be seen as a substitute for sacrifice. Indeed, the issue of the sacrifice of the firstborn does not occur until Exodus (and later Leviticus). In this context it is well to recall that Isaac was not the firstborn. Rather than a substitute for sacrifice, circumcision, like sacrifice, can be imagined as an integral part of the ideology of paternal power—marking the organ of (pro)creation and all those who belong to the patrilineage.

After Abraham is circumcised, God tells him he will be exceedingly fruitful, yet he must remember that creative, even procreative, power ultimately rests with God. Through submission to God, the father becomes the channel through which God's creative power flows to earth. Although circumcision may draw attention to procreative power, it simultaneously represents the "cutting" of it, in recognition of the fact that the power of the father derives from God.

The emphasis on the eighth day may relate to a similar emphasis in ancient Greek society. The eighth day was the day on which a father could exercise his *patria potestas* (paternal power)—his right to accept or reject a child. In Israelite society, the rite of circumcision appears to recognize the power of the father as it is transmitted from God by means of the male organ. In the Greek example, the father alone has that power, whereas in Israelite society, the father has that power through the grace of God. Abraham is the means for the transmission of that idea and that power. Those who refuse to recognize God's power, and submit to it, will be punished, for they have abrogated to the self that which is rightfully God's. The power of the father is, of course, reinforced, with the full weight of God behind it.

Eilberg-Schwartz demonstrates the close associations between notions of male procreativity and notions of circumcision, and he details the gendered nature of the associations, but he does not further develop his analysis to ask what makes the associations possible. Neither he nor Speiser, and certainly not Levenson, have examined the *theory* of procreation—the cultural construction of the roles of male and female in the process of "coming-into-being." It is clear from Genesis and other books in the Hebrew Bible (and the New Testament, for that matter) that the male is imagined as the "pro-creator," that is, the one who engenders. The female, in contrast, is imagined as the nurturer. Her role is important, to be sure, but it is of a very different nature and value.

Genesis, then, can be seen as the legitimating document for this theory of procreation, for Genesis, in particular, is concerned with genealogy, paternity, patriline, and the right "seed," through which God's line will continue (see fig. 3). But if the concepts of *seed* and *genealogy* are intimately related to theological conceptions, then a gender analysis does not merely point this out, it strikes a serious blow to these conceptions.

Is Genesis 22 an Injunction Against the Practice of Child Sacrifice?

The idea of the sacrifice of children plays a number of roles in the Hebrew Bible. One problem I have with the use of these other examples to explain Genesis 22 is that they are narratively later than the story of Abraham, and thus the context is quite different. Abraham's story is the initial story and, therefore, unlikely to be the representation of an injunction against the practice. In the Bible, the Abraham story is the first instance of such an idea or practice—and it was an idea powerful enough to found a new notion of god and faith. Perhaps it was heuristic, a device to communicate a particular kind of faith and fear of god; then, perhaps at a later time, it was taken literally. Or perhaps it symbolized the construction of paternity with monogenesis and monotheism as two aspects of one theosocial system.

Let us imagine, for a moment, that the story was, as some have imagined, a late invention inserted to combat contemporary practices among the Canaanites and perhaps also among the Israelites themselves—constructed, that is, in competition with those who practiced such a rite. By showing that the Israelites would be willing to go to such lengths to prove their love of their God, they could also show that their God was better because he did not demand follow-through. This is an ingenious explanation, but it does not alleviate the implications inherent in Abraham's willingness to kill his son. Because, if he was willing, how does that make him different from, or better than, his neighbors who, supposedly, were also willing, and did go through with the sacrifice? How, in other words, does this make Abraham unique? For it is his *willingness* to do it that makes him Father of Faith, not the fact that God put an end to the practice. And God blessed him *because* he did not withhold his son (Gen 22:16–8). If the story was meant as a prohibition or modification of the practice of human sacrifice, God could have said as much, or the biblical authors could have represented him making such an injunction.

Although the story is often interpreted in the context of a discourse on sacrificial rituals, especially blood sacrifice, this is not, I believe, the most appropriate context. Ritual is something that involves a community, something that is done regularly—this is what makes it a *ritual*. But the Akedah is considered a unique event in the Hebrew Bible, just as the

CHILDREN OF ABRAHAM

FIG. 3. (Above) Genealogical chart: The Children of Abraham. English version of *Fils d'Abraham*. Belgium: Brepols Publishers. (Below) Details showing the index of sects and the schematic of the tree.

LIST OF COMMUNITIES

† Adventists	† Dawudis	† Lollards	✶ Presbyterians
† Aglipayans	† Disciples of Montfavet	† Lutherans	† Priscillianists
☾ Ahmadiya	✡ Dönmehs	☾ Mandaeans	† Quakers
☾ Alawites	† Dolcinists	† Manichaeans	† Raskolniks
† Anabaptists	† Doukhobors	† Mariavites	† Reorganized Church of J.C. of latter Day Saints
† Anglicans	☾ Druses	† Maronites	✡ Sabbateans
† Antoinists	✡ Essenes	† Mar Thoma Syrian Church	✡ Sadducees
† Arians	† Ethiopians	† Mennonites	✡ Salvation Army
† Armenians	† Exclusive Brethren	† Methodists	✡ Samaritans
† Arminians	✡ Falashas	† Moravians	☾ Seveners
☾ Azalis	✡ Frankists	† Mormons	† Seventh-day Adventists
☾ Azraqis	† Friends of Man	☾ Mustalis	☾ Shi'is
☾ Babis	† Gnostics	† Nestorians	☾ Sikhs
☾ Baha'is	☾ Hafizis	† Nestorian Church of Trichur	☾ Sulaymanis
† Baptists	✡ Hasidaeans	✶ New Apostolics	☾ Sunnis
† Bogomils	✡ Hasidim	☾ Nizaris	† Syrian Anglicans
✶ Calixtines	☾ Hinschites	☾ Nusayris	† Syrian Catholics
† Calvinists	† Hutterian Brethren	† Old Apostolics	† Syro-Malabarese
† Caodaists	☾ Ibadis	† Old Believers	† Syro-Malankarese
† Cathari	☾ Imamis	† Old Catholics	† Taborites
† Catholics	† Invingites	† Old Episcopalian Church	☾ Tayyibis
† Catholic Armenians	☾ Islam	† Open Brethren	† The Living Church
† Catholic Copts	☾ Ismailis	† Orthodox	☾ Twelvers
† Catholic Ethiopians	† Jacobites	† Palaiolmerologites	† Uniates (Byzantine and Melkite)
† Chaldeans	† Jehovah's Witnesses	† Palmarists	✶ Unification Church
✶ Children of God	✡ Judaism	† Paulicians	† Unitarians
† Christian Scientists	✡ Karaites	† Pentecostals	† Utraquists
† Christianity	☾ Karmatians	✡ Pharisees	† Waldensians
† Church of Anjur-Thozhiyur	☾ Kharijites	† Pietists	☾ Yezidis
✶ Congregationalists	✡ Khazars	† Plymouth Brethren	☾ Zaydis
† Copts	† Kimbanguists	† Pneumatcmachians	✡ Zealots
† Darbyites	† Little Church	† Polish National Catholic Church	

Crucifixion is in the New Testament. Rather than interpreting the story within the context and discourse of sacrifice, as have most commentators, we need to begin with the story. The story of Abraham is not about the end of a practice but about the beginning of a new faith, symbolized by Abraham's submission to a higher authority, even if it means the sacrifice of his son. The faith traditions, to which we now turn, have recognized the religious and theological significance of the story. In the following three chapters, I discuss a range of interpretations of the Abraham story in each tradition, some of the debates that have arisen about it, and the variety of ways in which it pervades people's lives.

PART THREE

Religious Defenses and

Their Silences

Religious Defenses: Prolegomenon

R EGARDLESS of whether the story of Abraham represents the end of the practice of child sacrifice, religious interpreters have had to valorize Abraham's willingness to offer up his child. For this is the theological point of the story, the foundation stone of the new kind of faith. The next three chapters are discussions of Jewish, Christian, and Muslim interpretations of the story. Interpretations migrate from religious tradition to religious tradition, and from religious to secular culture, yet despite the fact that these religions share so much, they are mutually exclusive. Adherents of each tradition consider their own tradition distinct and complete in itself, and assume a direct connection and inspiration from Abraham, without any intermediary.

Aside from those who believe that the Bible (or the Qur'an) is the direct word of God, interpreters generally assume that, no matter how divinely inspired the stories may be, they are ultimately human constructions elaborated in relation, as well as in opposition, to what was culturally accepted, including notions of human coming-into-being. The stories may incorporate aspects of the society from which they originated, but they also project a *vision* of society as the authors wished it to be. The stories are, in short, ideological, for they incorporate and project the ideas, values, and aspirations of a particular group.

Interpretations are dually situated. They come after the fact and are affected by the background assumptions, preoccupations, and knowledge available, and by the commitments, aims, and position of the interpreter. Most commentary has been situated within a specific religious tradition, each with its own emphases and concerns. These will be taken up in each chapter. Yet some of the concepts—obvious ones, such as God, father, and sacrifice, but also those of Creation and time—are shared. Interpretations proceed from these background assumptions, which have been molded by the tradition they comment on. Because they are taken for granted, however, and imagined as part of reality, these concepts have been held as separate and separable from the stories that constitute them.

Until quite recently, most commentary has been written by men, for only men have been empowered to study and interpret sacred texts. They have not questioned the ways in which power is vested in their gender and how this may have influenced the questions and concerns that have shaped their commentary. Since the nineteenth century when Elizabeth Cady Stanton and a circle of women compiled *The Woman's Bible*, feminists have been raising new questions about biblical stories. For the past twenty-five years or so, with the increase in the admission of women to seminaries and divinity schools, and the appointments of women to teaching positions in them, feminist analyses have achieved a hearing and been accorded the respect they deserve; in some places they have become a permanent part of the curriculum. Similar attention has increasingly been directed to Qur'anic texts.

Feminist interpretations vary as much as the people who make them. Some feminists wish to point out gaps or oversights in previous interpretations, others attempt to fill in the gaps and rewrite the story, still others assume there is another, perhaps truer, story outside the narrative. Some are committed to the traditions that they simultaneously criticize, whereas others have become disillusioned. Regardless, all of us take the religious traditions and their histories seriously, for we are all aware of the impact these have had on the lives of ordinary men and women and the societies in which we live. In turn, our efforts are making an impact on theology, religious texts, rituals, personnel, and society at large. Without the examples of the many women who have been engaged in the work of feminist interpretation, I might not have had the courage to write this book.

Unlike many other interpreters, I do not argue from the perspective of a single tradition, even though I was born and raised in a culture heavily affected by Christianity. In addition, I have analyzed the story for what it reveals about gender; I do not assume that I know what men and women are, or were, in the time of Abraham (whenever that may have been).

Traditional, as well as feminist, exegetes of Genesis 22 do not question God's command. They take that for granted. All simply proceed from the text, assuming that, because God asks Abraham, that is all there is to it. None of them has asked: Why did God ask only Abraham and not both parents? Or, cast in human terms, what gave Abraham the right to take the child without asking his mother? Would God ask only Abraham if He knew that the child belonged to the mother as much as to the father?

If God is omniscient as well as just, then, clearly, he could not be confined to the ancient and now outmoded theory of procreation in which the child belonged to the man because he was the father's seed. If seed comes from two sources (a combination of both ovum and sperm, each gender contributing half the seed as we now believe, then God could not have asked Abraham, alone, for the child, for the child was not his alone. (If God had asked him alone, then interpretations would have to provide a rationale, but they have not.) Nor, of course, would Abraham have had the right, unilaterally, to take the child. Rather than an act of great faith, it would have been a heinous crime—kidnapping with the intention to kill.

What I am striving to point out is that the concept of God and the story of Abraham are mutually constitutive; together they constitute a notion of creativity expressed at both the divine and human levels, which by its very nature is authoritative and gendered. He who is *author* has authority and the power to command obedience. The story expresses the nature of fatherhood and the hierarchical order of patriarchal authority.

In addition to these common features, others become important in each tradition. For example, in Judaism, Abraham's faith is felt to ransom all future generations from God's wrath, and the story is invoked when the community is threatened. The sacrifice story is felt to be related to, and interpreted in the context of, circumcision and the redemption of the firstborn. In Christianity, the story prefigures the Crucifixion. It also represents the idea of faith above works, and it became connected with the Protestant ideal. In Islam, the story of Abraham is so powerful that Muhammad not only recalls people to that original faith but often seems to walk in Abraham's footsteps. The "sacrifice" establishes a "blood" brotherhood. All three traditions struggle over the patrimony; who is the rightful heir of the promises, who *is* the seed of Abraham? As their battle over religious patrimony has become more deadly in recent years, it is even more important to return to this foundational story.

My purpose in these chapters is threefold: (1) to discuss the meaning and place of the story in each tradition, (2) to examine a range of interpretations in each, and (3) to point out the common assumptions about gender and their theological implications. Simultaneously, the gender analysis undermines all of them.

FIG. 4. Marc Chagall, *The Sacrifice of Isaac* (1960–66).
Musée National Message Biblique Marc Chagall, Nice, France.
© 1998 Artists Rights Society (ARS), New York / ADAGP, Paris.

CHAPTER FIVE

Jewish Traditions

IN JEWISH TRADITION, the story in Genesis 22 is referred to as the *Akedah*, a word that refers to the binding of Isaac.[1] This form of the word appears nowhere else in the Bible. The use of the word *to bind*, which is from the same root as that used to tie up animals for sacrifice, implies that the intention was sacrifice. And the type of sacrifice was ʿolah, a whole burnt offering.[2] Throughout the ages, the story has traditionally been understood as a command from God to Abraham to sacrifice his son. It celebrates obedience to authority in return for the protection and favor of a mightier power.

The Akedah story, placed in the middle of Genesis, in the midst of other stories, is not mentioned again in the Hebrew Bible/Old Testament. The dearth of references to it should not lead one to assume that it is therefore of little consequence, but, rather, should be taken as a sign of its uniqueness.[3]

The Akedah stands as a banner or beacon to all future generations (Genesis Rabbah, 55:1), for it holds up a model of faith that has affected not only Jews but Christians and Muslims as well. Abraham did not hesitate, did not argue, did not waver in his intention to follow God's will. The story is austere in the extreme; there are no irrelevant details and no descriptions of Abraham's or Isaac's emotional state.[4] Yet it is these very gaps and silences that resound with the questions that have called forth the voluminous commentary, including this one. Before turning to Jewish interpretations, I will explain briefly the sources of Jewish tradition about the story.

Sources of Jewish Tradition about
the Story of Abraham

Genesis is, of course, the primary source of Jewish tradition about the story, but it is only the beginning. Commentary on the story is vast and derives from a number of sources; all have been influential for Jewish thought. *Tradition*, here, ought not be taken in the sense of a coherent, fixed, canonical set of interpretations, meanings, and practices, but instead as a reference to the variety of Jewish commentary—all of which is, or was at some time, part of Jewish tradition. The multiplicity of interpretations derives from the multiplicity of sources held as legitimate and valid; these, in turn, derive from works of individuals or of groups (like academies), namely, the *tannaim* and *amoraim* who were devoted to the translation, interpretation and codification of biblical texts, legal material, and legends. In addition there are a few noncanonical but biblical-type books, namely 2 and 4 Maccabees and Jubilees.

Dating of these sources is difficult because the actual, extant written texts are, in most cases, not the original; the "original," whatever that may have been, is also assumed to incorporate layer upon layer of (mostly oral) accretions from earlier times. For rabbinic literature, it is not really appropriate to speak of an original text, because oral traditions had a long history before being committed to writing. In any case, whatever may have been original would take on new meanings when inserted into a new context.

The earliest commentary on the story might be found *within* the biblical text itself, in lines 15 through 18, according to R. W. L. Moberly (1988). These lines have long been recognized as late additions to what is basically a complete story by line 14.[5] As a late interpolation, these lines are commonly treated as secondary or inferior (ibid.:313). They are attributed to the J source, although the rest of the story is assumed to be from the E tradition;[6] yet even this classification is not definitive, as references to Yahweh occur in lines 11 and 14. Although a number of scholars have noticed the anomaly, Moberly claims that few have pondered them at length. That is a moot point, however. R. J. Daly has argued that even though the divine blessings promised to Abraham are mentioned in several places, "this is the *only* one in which these blessings are explicitly presented as a reward of a *particular* virtuous act on the part of Abraham" (Daly, 1977:47). (In my opinion Abraham's acts in Genesis 15 and 17 could also be interpreted in this way.) Nevertheless, Daly links this notion of reward to what he considers a principal theological tenet of Judaism, namely "the idea of justification by works of obedience to the Law" (ibid.). In these lines, God says, "because thou hast done this thing,

and hast not witheld thy son, thine only son," he swears upon himself
that he will keep his promise of the blessings of seed and nation. And this
is, ultimately, Moberly's conclusion. Moberly emphasizes that elsewhere
in Genesis the blessings have been a unilateral and unconditional offer
from God to man (Moberly, 1988:318), whereas in these verses "human
obedience . . . can be taken up by God and become a motivating factor in
his purposes towards man" (ibid.:321). This is a profound theological
shift, for the promises depend no longer only on God but on Abraham's
obedience. And that is, surely, what is emphasized in later Jewish interpretations and uses of the story.

Another, perhaps not insignificant, point is that, although other promises to Abraham from God have mentioned seed and land, in these verses
only seed (and the nations that will spring from that seed) is mentioned.
The emphasis is further enhanced by the fact that, although the images of
both stars and sand have occurred previously to describe the number of
descendants, they have been used separately; in Genesis 22 they are used
in conjunction. Finally, it is in this passage that God speaks, for the last
time, to Abraham.[7]

Given the multiplicity of sources and the system of citations, the reader
will benefit, as I have, from a key. The few explanatory paragraphs that
follow are meant to be such a key and should make the discussion and
further exploration more accessible.

Among the the earliest sources about the story are (1) *De Abrahamo*,
written by Philo of Alexandria, who lived from 20 B.C. to A.D. 5,[8] and
(2) Josephus, a first-century Jewish historian and general living in Rome,
who retells the biblical story in narrative form in his *Jewish Antiquities*.
His telling includes a number of details not in the biblical version but
which may not have been his own invention. (3) Pseudo Philo's *Liber
Antiquitatum Biblicarum*, apparently contemporary with the Gospels, is
the source of a number of unusual views about the story. Both Jubilees
(4) and 4 Maccabees (5) develop the theme of Isaac as a protomartyr.
Jubilees is felt by most scholars to be a fairly early work (between 500 and
100 B.C., with most favoring a date circa 200 B.C.[9]), as it appears to have
been an influence on the community at Qumran. A number of documents
found there seem to depend on it. *Four Maccabees* is thought to have been
written between A.D. 30 and 40, possibly in Antioch. (6) The Targums are
another important source of information. The verbal form, *tirgem* means
to explain or teach, but when it is used as a noun it means translation.
Today it is generally used to refer to the translations (and there are several) of the Bible into Aramaic. The extant versions are Targum Onkelos,
thought to date from second century A.D.; the Palestinian Targums, including Neofiti and Genizah fragments which are thought to date from
the third or fourth century A.D.; and finally Pseudo Jonathan, which is felt

to be quite late, perhaps the seventh or eighth century A.D. All of the dates are provisional and all of the Targums, regardless of date, are presumed to incorporate earlier material.

In addition to these individuals, books, and translations, there were also sages referred to as *tannaim* and *amoraim*, who were active after the destruction of the temple in Jerusalem A.D. 70. They gathered, codified, and commented on much of traditional law (*midrash halakhah*) and lore (*midrash aggadah*). The difference between these types of exegesis concerns different orientations: the *halakhah* concerns laws derived from the biblical text and custom,[10] whereas *aggadah* is concerned more with the specific content—the words, phrases, figures of speech, and message of the biblical stories. *Midrash*, originally a general term that meant to search or seek in the Bible for God's truths, came to refer to works other than the legal material, especially homilies, stories, and *aggadah* commentaries on the Bible.

There were five generations of *tannaim*, and their work, known collectively as the Mishnah, came to an end around A.D. 200. At the completion of the Mishnah, another group known as *amoraim* continued, for several generations, the work of collecting, compiling, and commenting, now also on the comments of the *tannaim*. Some of them worked in Palestine, others were in Babylonia, and their work resulted in the Jerusalem or Palestinian Talmud and the Babylonian Talmud, dated to the fourth and fifth centuries, respectively.[11]

Each generation of sages passed down its wisdom and traditions to the next. These transmissions were imagined genealogically, even though they were not necessarily between a father and son—that is, the idea of male generativity and patriarchal succession had both physical and mental expressions. "He who teaches Torah to his companion's son is considered by scripture as if he had sired him" Sanhedrin 19B (Babylonian Talmud, cited in Goldberg, 1987:107). Goldberg argues that the "Perpetuity of *seed*, and the perpetuity of the Torah are closely associated" (ibid.:112, emphasis added).[12]

In addition to the legal material, there is a vast amount of exegetical commentary on the Pentateuch (the five books attributed to Moses). This midrashic work covers a range of types from exegeses, homilies, and sermons, to *aggadot*. The latter take off from the biblical text with great poetic license; they leap in fanciful twists and turns with the purpose of exciting interest and dive straight for the heart. Although these stories may diverge from the more conventional interpretations, they are often the ones most remembered.

One of the earliest midrashic works is Genesis Rabbah or Bereshit Rabbah, dated to the period of the classical Palestinian *amoraim* (A.D. 400–500), although some scholars believe there was a proto-Genesis Rabbah in existence early in the third century. Genesis Rabbah (often cited as Gen. Rab.) is a verse-by-verse interpretation of, and commentary on, the book of Genesis.

Midrashic activity continued into the Middle Ages with commentaries on other books of the Bible and, later, anthologies of these. This activity was supplemented by poetic and liturgical works, and no doubt the style of, and talent for, midrash continues in the work of contemporary Jewish storytellers. It would be impossible to mention, let alone discuss, all of the sources informing modern Jewish consciousness, and that is not my purpose here; most modern Jews are, perhaps, even more familiar with the medieval commentaries by Rashi, the great rabbi in twelfth-century France, and Ramban, also known as Nachmanides, in Christian Spain. These include and comment on some of the earlier traditions, at the same time adding opinions of their own. I will note them when appropriate. Today, there are several excellent and readable works that are compilations of these ancient traditions, and they are presented in continuous narrative form. One is Louis Ginzberg's *Legends of the Jews* in nine volumes; and one that specifically focuses on the *Akedah* is Shalom Spiegel's *The Last Trial: On the Legends and Lore of the Command to Abraham to Offer Isaac as a Sacrifice: The Akedah*.[13]

"AND GOD TRIED ABRAHAM"

Why did God try Abraham in the first place? Some translations use the word *tested*, but that conjurs an image of an examination; others use *tempted*, but that is even more problematic for modern readers, as it is usually associated with Satan rather than God. In a couple of Jewish as well as Muslim commentaries on the story, Satan does try to tempt Abraham away from his duty (see below). *Tried* relates to Abraham's ordeal, which is most often referred to as his *trial*; it also continues the theme of this book. Because God knew that Abraham's faith (*emunah*) was steadfast, why did he taunt and torture him in this way? One early tradition, which continues to the present, has it that God tests only the righteous (Gen. Rab. 55:2).[14] This tradition has puzzled Jews for a long time, and some of the earliest commentaries insert reasons for the test that purport to take the onus off of God.

The angels, or Satan, or the evil Prince Mastema in Jubilees 17, ask God to punish Abraham because he gave a huge banquet to celebrate Isaac's weaning and forgot to make a sacrifice (Gen. Rab. 55:4). Targum Pseudo Jonathan, Genesis Rabbah, and Rashi include a story wherein the test comes as a result of competitive boasting between Ishmael (son of Abraham with Hagar) and Isaac. Ishmael tells Isaac that he, Ishmael, is the one who ought to inherit because he is the firstborn.[15] Isaac retorts that Ishmael is only the son of a handmaid, whereas he, Isaac is the legitimate son. Ishmael then goes on to prove his worthiness by saying that he was circumcised when he was thirteen and thus at an age when he could have resisted but, instead, consciously chose to submit to his father's will.[16] Isaac was only eight days old and could neither resist nor consciously submit. Isaac responds by saying that even if God should ask for all of his members, he would give them all willingly, whereupon God takes him at his word.[17] In these interpretations, however, the motive of trying Abraham is lost.

More conventionally, this trial of Abraham is thought to be the ultimate trial, the last of ten, a tradition that is referred to in the title of Spiegel's book, *The Last Trial*.[18] None of the previous trials or tests of faith were quite enough to prove Abraham's obedience or to satisfy God. "Since the time of God's first call to him in Haran, no experience of his proved that his devotion to God was unconditional and boundless, not influenced by the many glorious promises he received or the wealth he achieved" (Sarna, 1989:393).

Another opinion is that God did not really put him to a test at all; it puts the onus on Abraham's misunderstanding. "What, do you think I meant for you to slay him? No! I said only to take him up. . . . and now I say take him down" (Gen. Rab. 56:8). Following this line of thought, a modern Jewish thinker suggests that God must sometimes mislead man because, if everything were clear, people would be like automatons and the most timid would be the most pious. God wants only the free to be his (Rosenzweig, 1971); Abraham's freedom, however, is conditional upon the total submission of his will to God.

The very fact of the test, a test God knew Abraham would pass, disturbed medieval thinkers as well. Rashi repeats the midrash above and Maimonides interprets this part of the story as "a test case of the extreme limits of the love and fear of God" (from Maimonides, *Guide to the Perplexed*, cited in *Encyclopedia Judaica*), which Shlomo Riskin, formerly a New York rabbi and now chief rabbi of Efrat and dean of the Ohr Tora institutions, has interpreted to mean that "Abraham was asked to do what all subsequent generations of Jews . . . would be asked to do" (Riskin, 1983:31). "The paradox in Jewish history," he notes elsewhere, "is that, had we not been willing to sacrifice our children for God, we would never have survived as a God-inspired and God-committed nation" (ibid., 1994). My question which, as we shall see, echoes that of a number of modern Israelis is: Is nationhood worth more than one's children?

If the point of the story was to prove Abraham's faith and obedience, why not have him sacrifice himself? Apparently, that would not be enough, for, as Sarna asserts (1989:393), Abraham would be willing to sacrifice himself in order to save his son and therefore the motive would be mixed. (Surely, it is easy to imagine that the motive is mixed in the sacrifice of his son; see, for example, Abramovitch, 1994:122.) In any case, if he had been willing to sacrifice himself to save his son, why does he do nothing at all to try to save him? Why doesn't he argue with God, as he did when trying to save Ishmael from banishment and Sodom from destruction? A moment of hesitation on Abraham's part is registered only in Genesis Rabbah (55:7), when he stalls and asks two questions of God. He feigns confusion and asks, "Which son?" When God says, "Whom thou lovest," Abraham queries: "Is there a limit to the affections?" Second, he asks God how he can perform the sacrifice, since he is not a priest. In this instant, God makes him a priest and says, "Thou art a priest forever."

Abraham is, nevertheless, revered not because of any heroic arguing with God on behalf of his son but precisely because he "concedes nothing to the tie of relationship, but his whole weight is thrown into the scale on the side of acceptability with God . . . he did not incline partly to the boy and partly to piety, but devoted his whole soul through and through to holiness and disregarded the claims of their common blood" (Philo, 1959:97). This theme, articulated several centuries earlier than the rabbinic commentary cited above, constitutes another powerful and continuing strand in both Jewish and Christian thought. Curiously these were the same terms, though with emphasis reversed, that the district attorney used at the trial of Cristos Valenti—"If he had stopped at the first cut, had thrown his weight on the side of the child, the child would be alive today." The sentiments expressed by Cristos, in contrast, followed more closely the ancient, religious model. That model—to be able to detach oneself from affective ties, not to let emotions get in the way of duty—is not just a model about the love of God; it has also been a model used to define masculinity.

Abraham is a heroic figure *because* he was able to cut that affective tie. As Abraham "suppressed his compassion in order to perform Thy will with a perfect heart," so God is asked to let his compassion suppress his anger when it is set against the children of Israel. These lines from Genesis Rabbah (56:10) and Leviticus Rabbah (29:9) are inserted into a prayer of supplication during the services of Rosh Hashanah; they petition God to remember the Akedah and to turn away his wrath. So, too, does the line from Targum Neofiti (1992:119), "Remember today the Binding of Isaac with mercy unto his seed."

The analogy between God and Abraham doesn't quite work because of the reversal of what is being stressed. Abraham must overcome his compassion whereas God must overcome his anger. Today, it strikes a discordant note, for it is a reversal in the emotional qualities more commonly associated with humans (anger) and God (compassion). Yet it directs attention to the idea that God is a jealous God. Far more troubling is the implication that it is good as well as necessary for Abraham to be able to overcome his compassion in order to do God's will. Why isn't compassion, especially love of one's child and fellow humans, stressed rather than suppressed? Why can't Abraham's love of God be shown by his unconditional love for his child? Why should there be a conflict between them? Why must loyalty to God be proven at the expense of one's child rather than expressed *through* one's love and care for one's family and fellows?

The prayer also implies that humans can chide God to act compassionately. When God is about to wreak his vengeance upon them, they can call out and tell him to remember the Akedah in a way that makes them equivalent to counselors of God. By this prayer they can bind God to his promise to Abraham.

Despite the general belief that the sacrifice was not completed, it counts *as if* it had been. Because of Abraham's willingness and, as we shall see, Isaac's submission, it counts as a perfect sacrifice. Abraham's perfect obedience, the "willingness of the founding father to sacrifice his son as proof of his devotion to God created an inexhaustible store of spiritual credit upon which future generations may draw" (Sarna, 1989:394; see also Milgrom, 1988:151).

The whole theme of obedience and disobedience characterizes the relation between God and humans in Genesis, beginning with Adam. Abraham's perfect obedience can be interpreted as making up for, redeeming, Adam's disobedience (see Chaim Lewis, 1973). The result is that obedience comes to be seen as an expression of love—at least in hierarchical relations. As Abraham shows his love of God by his obedience, so too does Isaac show his love of his father by his obedience. But what kind of love is that? Why *is* obedience valued so highly? Might not *disobedience* to such a command be a more appropriate response? These issues will be taken up later. Here, it is important to stress that, in Jewish tradition, Abraham's obedience is precisely why the Akedah comes to have a redemptive quality that allows it to function, for Jews, in a way somewhat analogous to Jesus' Crucifixion.

Whether the Akedah story had that meaning and served that function before the advent of Christianity, and thus served as a model for the theology of the Crucifixion, or whether it took on these meanings and functions in response to Christian theology is a vexing question of deep theological and historical significance; it will be addressed in the next chapter.[19] Here, I wish to bring out more of the Jewish associations and understandings of the Akedah, so that I can refer to them when I turn to the Christian material.

If Isaac is considered an expiatory offering, one might expect the Akedah to be associated more with the holy day of Yom Kippur, the Day of Atonement, but it is not.[20] Today, and for centuries, the Akedah is commemorated on Rosh Hashanah, the New Year. Rosh Hashanah falls in the autumn month of Tishri when, according to one tradition, all great events allegedly occurred—the creation of the world, and the birth and death of the patriarchs—and it is, therefore, suitably the time of Abraham's heroic deed. Rosh Hashanah is a "Day of Remembrance, a day for the blowing of the *shofar* (ram's horn); a holy convocation, as a memorial for the departure from Egypt" (from Rosh Hashanah Service). Although there is mention of the Exodus, Rosh Hashanah focuses more on the Akedah. Genesis 22 is recited in its entirety during the service, and other reminders are cited throughout. The shofar, a vital element of Rosh Hashanah, symbolizes, among other things, the horn of the ram sacrificed in Isaac's stead, a ram that, in midrash, was created on the evening of the sixth day of Creation and was waiting in the wings, so to speak, until its grand performance at the Akedah. The sounding of the shofar also represents a clarion call, reminding people of God's rule over his creation, and it is a reminder that the shofar will sound again in the last days, when the dead are resurrected. The sound of the shofar is also said to have accompanied God's revelation to Moses on Sinai; thus it links the beginning and the end of time, Abraham and Moses, and, implicitly, Rosh Hashanah and Passover.

Rosh Hashanah may not always have been the holiday to which the Akedah was attached, and some (e.g., Davies, 1979, Levenson, 1991; Sandmel, 1956; Segal, 1984) believe it was, at one time, associated with Passover. Passover falls in the spring, the time of new beginnings and new life and thus, also, a suitable time for the New Year. The Mishnah records the rivalry between sages over whether Tishri or Nisan should be the new year, and thus to which of these months the same great events should be attributed (Spiegel, 1969:54–5). For some Jewish groups, according to Rosenberg, "the connection of the offering of Isaac with the Passover was more important than the observance of the holiday as a memorial of the exodus from Egypt"(Rosenberg, 1965:386). Segal acknowledges that the book of Jubilees "does contain an explicit connection between the sacrifice of Isaac (or Akedah, loosely speaking) and the Passover" (Segal, [1984]1987:114). This is important for (some) Christians who argue for the coincidence of Passover and Easter, the Akedah and the Crucifixion.

Jubilees, a book concerned with the Jewish calendar, attempts to prove the patriarchal origin of certain feasts (here *patriarchal* refers to the patriarchs). Jubilees retells the biblical story from the beginning of the world; it is told by an angel of God to Moses on Sinai, expressing thereby the long-held belief that God revealed the Torah to Moses. Each chapter of

Jubilees begins with a statement of the month and day, situating the events of which it tells at a particular time. The Akedah is placed so as to fall at "the precise time of the precise day when the paschal lambs for Passover are slaughtered in the Temple" (Daly, 1977:55). As we shall see in the next chapter, some Christians have used the calendrical system of the book of Jubilees to confirm that Jesus was the Messiah. Perhaps the Akedah and Passover became linked in Jewish imagination because the theme of the redemption of the first born is common to both (Swetnam, 1981:39).

The sacrificial feast of the paschal lamb that commemorates the passing over of Israel's firstborn became associated not just with the ram offered in Isaac's place, but with Isaac himself.[21] When God is set to destroy the firstborn of the Egyptians, Jews are instructed to spread blood on the lintels of their doors as a sign to God of their identity so that, "When I see the blood, I will pass over you" (Exod. 12:13), and when he saw that blood, he is thought to have seen the blood of the binding of Isaac, the blood that protects the Jews. This tradition is said to derive from the Mekilta d Rabbi Ishmael (7:78–82), thought to be a fourth-century text (Swetnam, 1981:67).

"The saving virtue of the Passover lamb proceeded from the merits of that first lamb, the son of Abraham, who offered himself on the altar" (Vermes, [1961]1973:215). It seems as unreasonable to claim that there is no relation between the Akedah and Passover as it would to assert that there is no relation between the two great holy days of Rosh Hashanah and Passover.[22] In addition, there are other associations to the Akedah that may or may not be related to either of the holidays; these include associations regarding Moriah, the "blood of Isaac," and the "ashes of Isaac."

MORIAH, THE BLOOD OF ISAAC,
AND THE ASHES OF ISAAC

Although the location of Moriah is unknown, symbolically it has been identified with the Temple Mount in Jerusalem since at least the beginning of the first century and probably earlier. Today, the Temple Mount is covered by a Muslim mosque, the Dome of the Rock (see chapter 7), the rock from which Muhammad ascended to Heaven for a vision of God. Early Muslim tradition implies that it is the site where the sacrifice of Abraham's son allegedly took place, before that tradition moved to Mecca. In any case, it is no wonder (some) Jews want it back, and no wonder (some) Muslims refuse.

Moriah is also, in other traditions, associated with Sinai. In one midrash, Sinai is said to have broken away from Moriah as a piece of dough broken off from the rest (Schoeps, 1946:388, n. 12). Sinai, however important, never became a major shrine, but Moriah, equated with the Temple Mount, did. A modern interpretation reasons that it is because, at Sinai, God comes to man, whereas, at Moriah, a man and his son express willingness to commit themselves, body and soul, to God (Riskin, 1983). Others assert that Sinai could not have happened without Moriah, that theologically the events at Moriah preceded and prepared the way for those at Sinai (Milgrom, 1987; 1988:159).

Isaac's status as sacrificial victim, in combination with the idea that there can be no expiation without the shedding of blood (Talmud, Yoma 5a), may have led to the idea that Isaac was an expiatory offering and to the *aggadic* tradition that his blood *was* shed. Abraham was so zealous in proving his devotion that when the angel called out forbidding him to lay a hand upon the lad, Abraham is thought to have begged to let him bring forth at least a drop of blood (Gen. Rab. 56:7). But the angel said, "Don't do anything to him." A more elaborate *aggadah* says Isaac gave one-fourth of his blood (see Spiegel, 1969:47–9). Because that was the amount thought to keep a person alive, it would have been sufficient to stand in for Isaac—it would be as if he were sacrificed. This midrash implies, of course, that Abraham not only laid his hand on Isaac but that he slashed him with the knife (see Davies, 1989:59).

Isaac was afraid he might flinch at the sight of the knife and asked his father to bind him tightly so that he would not resist and thereby render the offering unfit (Targum Neofiti and Pseudo Jonathan). As noted earlier, the word for *binding* is exactly the word used to refer to the binding of the lambs for the Tamid sacrificial offering at the Temple—offerings that were, unlike the paschal lambs, whole burnt offerings. These offerings were made morning and night, and, in midrash, are thought to be in memory of the Akedah. Here, it is clear that ritual sacrifice is not the context for interpreting the Abraham story but that the Abraham story is the context for interpreting sacrifice. Some rabbis have wondered why daily sacrifices in the Temple were necessary if Isaac's sacrifice atoned for all time, but one scholar suggests that they are "perpetual reminders of Isaac's self-oblation" (Vermes, 1961:209).

It will be immediately apparent to the perceptive reader that, in some of the midrashic traditions, the focus on Abraham and his piety dramatically shifted to Isaac as the perfect sacrifice. Suddenly it is Isaac who is thought to have offered himself on the altar. Some scholars, notably Davies and Chilton (1978), believe this shift in focus could only have occurred after the destruction of the Temple and in response to Christian theology.

The connection with the Tamid offering may also have led to the tradition of the "ashes of Isaac," a tradition that implies Isaac was consumed as a burnt offering. The petition "O, do thou regard the ashes of Father Isaac heaped upon the top of the altar, and deal with thy children according to the Mercy attribute" (Spiegel, 1969:38–42) is part of a prayer at Rosh Hashanah. Yet perhaps it is only *as though* the ashes of Isaac were spread on top of the altar, or perhaps it was the ashes of a ram named Isaac who was substituted in Isaac's place (ibid.:40–1). In the Middle Ages a custom arose of putting ashes on one's head on fast days that were called for in times of distress. This custom did not spring up in the Middle Ages, but was known at least in the first generation of the *amoraim* (ibid.:42).[23]

An unusual midrash (ibid.:35) portrays the rabbis discussing the proper order of events in preparation of the altar for sacrifice: first the fire is laid, then wood, and finally the victim. As there is no mention of laying the fire in Genesis 22, but only that of laying of the wood (Gen. 22:9), they assume the fire had already been laid. Therefore, they reason that Abraham would not have to lay a hand on Isaac to slay him, in that he is already the perfect sacrifice, already consumed by fire. If that were the case, the ashes of Isaac would have "stored up *merit* for atonement generation after generation" (ibid.:27).[24]

Mostly, when it is believed that Isaac was slain, it is also believed that he was revived immediately, restored to life by the "dew of resurrection." In this way the Akedah comes to be associated with the idea of resurrection (ibid.:29), which may be why the ashes of Isaac are referred to in the *aggadah* about the prayers of Benediction for the dead (ibid.:32–7).[25]

Beyond the fact of whether or not Isaac was sacrificed, commentators also discuss whether he would have been a perfect sacrifice if he had not himself been a willing victim. The free consent of the victim, as emphasized in Pseudo Philo, is what makes Isaac's sacrifice "the sacrifice *par excellence*, whose lasting benefits would be felt for all time" (Vermes, [1961]1973:206).

Early on, some thinkers were clearly disturbed by the idea that Isaac should be sacrificed without his prior knowledge or consent. A few even wondered aloud how Abraham could bind a man of thirty-seven without his consent (Gen. Rab. 56:8).[26] When Isaac asked the most poignant question: "My father . . . Behold the fire and the wood, but where is the lamb for a burnt offering?" (Gen. 22:7), midrash amplifies Abraham's answer and lets Isaac know what is going to happen. "God will provide himself the lamb, O my son; and if not, thou art for a burnt offering" (Gen. Rab. 56:4). Josephus says that "Isaac received these words with joy" (Josephus, *Jewish Antiquities*, 1961:115), and he goes on to say that even "were this the resolution of his father alone, it would have been impious to disobey" (ibid.,). Isaac has become the willing victim in accordance with his father's wishes; the motives of the two coincide. Some of this Jewish concern may have found its way into the community of those who would become Muslim, for in the Qur'an Abraham says: "My son, I see in a dream that I shall sacrifice thee; consider, what thinkest thou?" (Sura 37:102) And his son replies: "My father, do as thou art bidden; thou shall find me, God willing, one of the steadfast" (ibid.).

In an attempt to get Abraham to desist from fulfilling his duty, Genesis Rabbah (56:4) has Satan speaking the words of commonsense morality. He tries to talk Abraham out of doing this terrible thing. He says something like, "What has happened to you, old man? Have you gone crazy? How can you even think of doing such a thing? How do you know it is God? Maybe tomorrow he will change his mind and call you a murderer." But Abraham resists. The temptation that Satan offers him, namely, to turn away from following God's order, becomes a prominent part of a Muslim ritual—the stoning of Satan—during the Hajj.

Satan is asking a very important question: How *did* Abraham know it was God who was asking? How did Cristos Valenti know it was God? Why do we believe it in one case and not the other? Why should we just take it on faith that God spoke to Abraham? Curiously, these questions have not been very central in the commentary. One of the few to raise them was Kant in a late and quite obscure little book, *The Conflict of the Faculties*.

> If God should really speak to man, man could still never *know* that it was God speaking. It is quite impossible for man to apprehend the infinite by his senses, distinguish it from sensible beings, and *recognize* it as such. But in some cases man can be sure the voice he hears is *not* God's; for if the voice commands him to do something contrary to the moral law, then no matter how majestic the apparition may be, and no matter how it may seem to surpass the whole of nature, he must consider it an illusion (Kant, [1798]1979:115).

Kant's voice in this case is not unlike that of Satan; he is taking the voice of reason and of human morality. Kant felt that in these circumstances, Abraham should have said a resounding "No." Kant does not let him off the hook as does Kierkegaard in *Fear and Trembling*. Kierkegaard allows Abraham to suspend the ethical—that standard of morality that applies to us all; for Kierkegaard, Abraham is above the law because of his faith. His faith "is a paradox which is capable of transforming a murder into a holy act well-pleasing to God" (Kierkegaard, [1843]1941:64).[27] Today, as we have seen, such faith is considered a sign of madness.

When it became clear that Satan was getting nowhere with Abraham, he approached Isaac and told him what was about to happen. But like father, like son: Isaac said, "I accept my fate." Satan then went to tell Sarah what her husband was about to do, whereupon Sarah cried out in anguish and died of a broken heart. This may have been one way to explain Sarah's death in Genesis 23.

Numerous commentaries interpret Genesis 22:8, "and they went both of them together," as an indication that they, both Abraham and Isaac, were of one mind and went with quiet hearts, resolved to do God's will. "The one who slaughters does not hesitate, and he who is being slaughtered stretches out his neck" (Neofiti, 118; cf. Gen. Rab. 56:4).

Although the dominant tradition is that Isaac was not sacrificed, the fact that Abraham returned alone gave rise to speculation. "So *Abraham* returned unto his young men, and they rose up and went together to Beersheba and Abraham dwelt at Beersheba" (Gen. 22:19, my emphasis). Where is Isaac? This question may have motivated traditions that Isaac was sacrificed or merely reinforced those already in existence. Genesis 22 ends with a recitation of the lineage established not through Isaac but through Abraham's brother Nahor; it is as if Isaac had ceased to exist.

Spiegel (1969:4–5) discusses several midrashim that attempt to account for Isaac's absence. One relates that Isaac was whisked away to Paradise for three years to recover from his wounds and await his marriage to Rebecca. Although there was no Torah at the time of Abraham, it figures anachronistically in several midrashim. One is that he was taken to the house of Shem to study Torah. According to a related midrash, this was the pretext Abraham used with Sarah in order to take Isaac away with him.[28] Abraham is said to have told Sarah that Isaac was too old to be spending so much time with her, that it was time he went to school to study Torah. Had Abraham used this excuse, he would have been a liar. Another midrash has Isaac confronting his father on Moriah: "So this is the Torah I was to learn at school?" (cf. ibid.:49; Graves and Patai, 1966: 174–5; Ginzberg, 1909). This is one of the few suggestions that Isaac rebelled—that for a moment, at least, he was not the willing victim.

Regardless of whether Isaac was sacrificed, tradition designates him the perfect, expiatory sacrifice that accrued merit for all generations. "The Akedah became in Jewish thought the supreme example of self-sacrifice in obedience to God's will and the symbol of Jewish martyrdom throughout the ages" (*Encyclopedia Judaica*, 1979, vol. 2:480). Whose *self*-sacrifice? Over time it seems that Abraham's submission to God and Isaac's submission to his father, Abraham's willingness to sacrifice his son and his son's willingness to be sacrificed, have been conflated, have come to represent the same thing. It is, however, a dangerous conflation, because it conceals both the hierarchical structure of the relationship and the dimension of (paternal) power. As we shall see, a number of contemporary Israeli Jews are rebelling against the model; they condemn the father and refuse to identify with the submissive, self-sacrificing son. But they have not yet analyzed the relevance of gender.

THE AKEDAH AS MODEL

The story of Abraham has served as a model of the man of faith for millennia, and it has been used to fortify and inspire others.[29] It is, according to Wineman, an archetype, not in the sense of a universal pattern but in the sense of "the presence of an older literary source which resounds in a later work" (Wineman, 1977:6). The most famous and probably the earliest example of this is in 4 Maccabees, which takes up and repeats a story from 2 Maccabees of Eleazar and the woman and her seven sons. In 4 Maccabees, their trials are associated with the Akedah. The stories relate to a time of persecutions under the Seleucid Antiochus IV (167–4 B.C.), during which the Jews were asked to eat the meat from Roman sacrifices. Eleazar refused to do so; bound and scourged, he wanted to set a good example for other Jews. "O children of Abraham you must die nobly for piety's sake" (4 Macc. 6:23). He also asked God to consider him a sacrificial victim: "Make my blood their purification and take my life as a ransom for theirs" (4 Macc. 6:29–30). This is an early, pre-Christian notion of vicarious expiatory sacrifice.

An important concern of the Hellenistic author(s) of 4 Maccabees, noted by a number of commentators, appears to have been the mastery of reason over the passions, so that Abraham's readiness to sacrifice Isaac becomes the model of the victory of reason over parental love. Usually reason is identified with masculinity and passion with femininity; that is why it is even more striking that the same sentiment is put in the mouth of the woman who saw her seven sons tortured to death and then followed them. "Not even her affections for her young caused the mother, whose soul was like Abraham's, to waver" (4 Macc. 14:20).

A midrash has the mother of seven making the following retort: "Go tell Father Abraham not to puff up his heart, if he made an Akedah of one son, I made an Akedah of seven" (Lam. Rab. cited in Spiegel, 1969:16). Once the Akedah became the supreme model of faith, subsequent faithful would be expected to model themselves upon it. Thus, rather than trying to develop a different model of faith, some women adopted the model and strove to fulfill it. Abraham's stoic heroism is more valued than the compassion of weeping women. In order to be considered faithful, a woman must become like a man: "she took her womanly thoughts and fired them with manly spirit" (2 Macc. 7:21).

The model was again consciously invoked in the Middle Ages, during the persecution of European Jews by the Crusaders—in 1096 at Mainz, Speyer, Worms, Cologne, Trier, and elsewhere (see Marcus, 1982), and again in 1146.[30] Jews were again asked to relinquish their religion and convert, and when they refused they were tortured. Rather than convert or be tortured, a great number of them are said to have killed their children and themselves—"everyone of them like the Akedah of Isaac, son of Abraham" (Spiegel, 1969:25). This response to the Crusaders' persecutions was primarily the response of the Ashkenazi Jews of central Europe.[31] Spiegel's well-known book on the legends and lore surrounding the Akedah are meant primarily to prepare the reader to understand the allusions to these terrible days in a poem by a twelfth-century rabbi, Ephraim of Bonn. In the poem, the Akedah was the model for their acts: "Both the sacrificer and the victims saw as the crowning act of their role the performance of the Fathers Abraham and Isaac" (Spiegel, 1969:25). Yet the poem, as well as the acts it commemorates, implies that Isaac was, in fact, sacrificed.

The theme of substitution, however, was also current in the Middle Ages. The ram substituted in Isaac's place was considered the preeminent substitution. The traditional explanation that the lamb substitution was meant to symbolize both the end of human sacrifice and the institution of animal sacrifice was dealt with in chapter 2. In a rite called *kapporah*, practiced in Geonic times (seventh to eleventh centuries) among Jews of Eastern Europe, a cock was swung three times around the head while the donor recited: "This be my vicarious offering, my atonement. This cock shall meet death, but I shall find a long and pleasant life of peace" (*Encyclopedia Judaica*, 10:756).[32] In the fourteenth century, children took palm-leaf baskets planted with seeds of various kinds and swung them around their heads, saying: "This be in lieu of me; this is my substitute and my exchange," and then threw them into the river (ibid.). Yet no matter how many substitutions are made, no matter how the child, especially the firstborn, is redeemed, the message is that the child is the appropriate sacrifice, a message that is epitomized in the central event of Christianity.

Spiegel's book is primarily a compendium of the traditions related to the Akedah as they inform the interpretation of the medieval persecutions; he is not so concerned with the legacy of those interpretations—how they shaped the psychological and moral outlook of the community for subsequent generations. This *is* the concern of Allan Mintz (1984); he argues that the Askhenazi Jews identified with and used the story of the Akedah to symbolize and explain their suffering but that they used it in a very new way. Nowhere in the Talmud or Jewish tradition is human sacrifice encouraged or enjoined as a religious obligation. Martyrdom at the hands of others, the willingness to be killed for the "Sanctification of the Name," that is, for the sake of God, had been a perennial theme since the times of the Maccabees. But that is quite a different matter from the consensual decision undertaken by the medieval community to commit homicide and suicide for the glory of God.

During the medieval persecutions, a different theological idea emerged in relation to suffering, an idea that has persisted in certain forms to this day. Previously suffering, especially of such catastrophic proportions, was interpreted as punishment, primarily for disobedience. But because of the nature of the destruction at Mainz, Speyer, and Worms and the confidence of that generation in their piety and observances, they had to find an alternative explanation. "The solution was to adopt the concept of 'afflictions from love'" (Mintz, 1984:6), a concept that saw the "suffering of exemplary righteous individuals as a sign of divine favor. This is an idea that goes back to Abraham's trial in the Akedah and to the doctrine among the Rabbis of 'chastisement out of love.' The idea holds that, paradoxically, God tests the faith of those he knows to be already faithful. The trial is an indication of worthiness, not punishment, and its purpose is to strengthen further those who are already strong" (ibid.:91–2). This was not a new theme in Jewish tradition, but Mintz claims this was the first time it was "mobilized as the dominant explanation for a historical catastrophe" (ibid.:92) and applied not to an individual but to collective misfortune. Destruction could be unhinged from sin, and martyrdom could be transfigured into a triumphant religious act. The present sacrifice could be understood as fulfilling what had preceded or prefigured it.[33]

Mintz's interest focuses on the way the actual events came to be symbolized in the discrepancy between the historical record and collective memory or, as he puts it, in the "transactions of the literary imagination with history" (Mintz, 1984:102). His goal is not like that of historians and archaeologists, who try to uncover from the layers of literary and mythologized material some kind of "historical actuality" (ibid.:90). Instead, he is concerned with the poetic transformations of the events that have left their mark on the emotions and morals of people, in this case the survivors and their descendants ever after, for about eight hundred years. Of all the possibilities available from the biblical text to represent the catastrophe at the hands of the Crusaders, it was the Akedah that captured the attention of the medieval poets. Indeed, a new genre of *piyyut* (a kind of hymn that was recited in the synagogue) became known as *Akedah*. By drawing an analogy between contemporary events and the trial of Abraham, the poets helped to collapse the distance between the suffering of the medieval faithful and that of Abraham as well as to give meaning and a sense of grandeur to it. The "events on Mount Moriah continued to structure perceptions and influence behavior. The choice of analogy imparted both a biblical sanction and a sense of election to the martyrs of Mainz" (Roskies, 1984:43).

At the same time, Mintz thinks the comparison was perverse. Their faithful performance of the deed could be seen as a claim to moral superiority over Abraham and thus an expression of pride that was inappropriate. He notes that the point of the Akedah was "to signal the supersession of human sacrifice . . . that what counts in God's eyes is the *readiness* to sacrifice one's firstborn, not the deed itself" (Mintz, 1984:91). He might have gone further and asked why even the readiness to so do should be considered virtuous.

Yet perhaps perversity can also be seen in the interpretation of their trial as an "opportunity given by God . . . a kind of spiritual compliment to the generation" (ibid.:92), which precluded any complaint, reproach, or rebellion on the part of the people against God. As Isaac had to be made into a willing victim, so too did these medieval Jews: "there was not a whisper of complaint" (ibid.:92). Mintz also points out that the Akedah could not fully encompass the triumphant emotional quality expressed in the poems about the medieval catastrophe. In the poems, the contemporary events and the murders and suicides were symbolically assimilated into the Tamid sacrifices. These were the daily animal sacrifices offered at the Temple before its destruction, and, as we have seen, the Akedah has sometimes been associated with them. Nevertheless, the exuberance of the detailed depictions of blood, bones, and dismembered bodies in the medieval poems went far beyond the actual events and called for some explanation. Mintz claims these elaborations were not a perverse expression of an obsession with blood, but a desire to understand their sacrifices as (perhaps more than) comparable. There *is* something perverse, however, in describing in minute detail the way children were slaughtered at the hands of their own fathers and mothers and then describing the outcome of the slaughter as a marriage in which the mingling of blood was the final consummation or union with God. Because that *was* the understanding, Mintz entitled the chapter about these persecutions "Medieval Consummations." Yet this conflation is not as bizarre as one may think. When we come to the Muslim material, we shall see how the story of the Akedah, as well as the actual bloody slaughter of a ram, is inserted into the marriage ritual in Morocco.

HOLOCAUST

The Akedah has also figured in some Jewish interpretations of the Holocaust. What follows should be understood as no more than an outsider's gleanings from scholars with far greater competency to discuss these matters; yet to ignore this world-shattering event would be irresponsible.

First, it is important to point out that the term *holocaust* is the Greek translation, rendered into English, of the Hebrew ʿolah. The word alludes to "going up" in flames, and it has traditionally been taken to refer to a type of sacrifice that is a whole burnt offering, the type Abraham was asked to make of Isaac. At a later time, it was also a type of sacrifice performed at the Temple. The word *holocaust* in reference to the Nazi extermination of the Jews was apparently used for the first time in 1942 in a British newspaper, but it did not become a common term until the late 1950s. The Hebrew terms referring to the same events are *shoah* or *hurban*, both of which mean catastrophe.[34]

The Holocaust has been, and continues to be, a turning point in the interpretation of the Akedah and one that seems to have polarized the Jewish community. A number of Jewish writers "agree in viewing the Nazi Holocaust as a reenactment of the *akedah* and the *akedah* as a prefiguration of the Holocaust" (Brown, 1982:103), but there is little agreement in the interpretation of the analogy. Some continue to admire the patriarchs, Abraham in particular, and see in his model of faith a means of preserving dignity in the face of adversity.[35] They would try to emulate his heroic courage. According to Cohen, Steinsaltz—a renowned Talmudic scholar—"tells us that if we accept the fatherhood of God, we must obey His every command. This vision is compelling enough to elicit the consent of hundreds of millions of men and women of all nations and religions who are able, on faith alone, to accept as the voice of God a command to sacrifice their sons" (Cohen, 1990:54). Significantly, Steinsaltz does not consider the relationship between the notion of fatherhood and obedience, but neither does Cohen who has an opposite response.

Cohen and a number of others are "appalled by this response to the Akedah, to the theology that underlies it and to its ethical implications" (ibid.:55). Cohen suggests that we need to change the model and theology of the Akedah and "to learn how to project our imaginations toward an all-embracing vision of cosmic peace and seek out a path to it" (ibid.:60). His conviction is based on his belief, surely not held by all, that our image of God is a human convention (ibid.:59). Because it is a human convention, or human conception, it can be changed. The Holocaust has forced many Jews to reexamine traditional theology and the models of God and faith through which it is conveyed. "Can a set of values which demands the sacrifice of life be worthy of our absolute commitment?" (ibid.:51) The answer for some is "no."

According to Michael Brown, a literary critic, authors Gilboa and Alterman "view the *akedah* and the Nazi Holocaust as enormities to be avoided by rebellion against God. Their Abrahams do not slaughter and their Isaacs are not sacrificed, not because God intervenes, but because they refuse to hear the command that Biblical Abraham heard" (Brown, 1982:105). Similarly, he claims that Agnon and Wiseman "perceive

Europe's Jews as having been bound on the altar of Jewishness by their faithful ancestors" (ibid.). Their faith, not their faithlessness, has resulted in their destruction, an interpretation that clearly draws on the medieval transformation of the meaning of punishment not as divine disfavor but as the trials of the righteous. At the same time, they make it clear that they no longer accept that view. Brown points out that in a number of contemporary Jewish sources, "Abraham and Isaac no longer serve as role models to be emulated . . . but as object lessons to be avoided" (ibid.: 111). This also seems to be the conclusion reached by Neil Gordon in his recent (1995) novel, *The Sacrifice of Isaac*. Nevertheless, there are surely also numerous Jews who find meaning and comfort in thinking of the deaths of their loved ones as sacrifices for their faith, perhaps even so that their descendants might finally have a homeland.

THE AKEDAH IN ISRAEL

The Akedah must also have been invoked to inspire people to fight for and, if necessary, sacrifice themselves for the land of Israel. Immediately after the War of Independence, "the image settled on Isaac as the young *sabra* sacrificing himself on the national altar, with the connivance of his father, Abraham" (Abramson, 1990:107). Yet, while the "post-Holocaust Israeli generation views the *Akedah* story exclusively from the point of view of the sacrificed Isaac" (ibid.), it is a model and role they reject. This rejection became even more noticeable after the Six Day War, when "soldiers explicitly refused to accept the notion of self-sacrifice represented by the *Akedah* . . . and directed their anger at the fathers who had sent them into battle" (ibid.:108). Said one: "I am not willing to be an eternal Isaac climbing onto the altar without asking why, or understanding" (T. Gid⸢on, quoted in ibid.:109).[36] The Akedah has functioned to justify sending sons off to war, and not just among Israelis. It was used during World Wars I and II and Vietnam, and its use helped to construe these wars as holy. (Construing the victims, symbolically, as sons also obliterates the numerous daughters who lost their lives fighting these wars.) According to Cohen, the Akedah has allowed "Man . . . to weasel his way out of the responsibility for eliminating war, hatred and violence of all kinds," but as far as Cohen is concerned, man "is no longer justified, in any way, to putting God's stamp of approval on his resort to arms" (Cohen, 1990:59).

There can be no question that the Akedah, as model, regardless of the interpretation, "has begun to appear again with force and frequency in Israeli writing" (Abramson, 1990:103). Indeed, as long ago as 1971, a symposium was held in Israel to ascertain "the relevance of the Akedah-tradition to Israel's struggle for survival" (Wineman, 1977:8). Even if there is no consensus about the relevance of the story or about which interpretation is most appropriate, the contemporary writers and artists demonstrate that the Akedah story/model is clearly not one that is confined only to the ancient world or to religious contexts but is a powerful myth that people and nations have lived by.

Often the model is secularized to portray problems between fathers and sons, and the lack of understanding between the beliefs and values of the older generation and the younger. Some stories attempt to take Abraham's point of view; they sympathize with a father "bewildered by his son's defection for all he, the father had done was to obey God's command, which in historical terms meant fidelity to God's law" (Abramson, 1990:112). In stories by Amos Oz and A. B. Yehoshua such a father is treated quite differently: there he is portrayed as one who "has never understood or accepted the son's own cultural development, and has tried to impose his own standards on him" (ibid.:113). That fate, of course, is hardly confined to Jews, but the cultural availability of the Akedah has given these experiences mythical as well as deep historical significance.

In Oz's poignant story entitled "The Way of the Wind," the father is "unable to tolerate a son who turns out to be something other than an extension of the father himself" (Wineman, 1977:116). Not too surprisingly, the emphasis focuses on reproduction and the lineage the father wishes to establish. He thinks of the grandsons "who will bear his image and his name." It is quite clear he is thinking of a patrilineage, as he does not countenance the possibility of a daughter and, indeed, seems to exclude women from the process altogether—he disposes of his wife as soon as she has borne him a son. His grandsons will have two fathers: "my son will be the biological father, I'll implant the spirit in them" (ibid.:117–8).[37] This is an interesting example of the psychological effects of patriarchal ideology and the notion that the father is the one who transmits both life and spirit; but in this instance, the grandfather arrogates to himself the godlike role as he relegates to his son the merely biological one normally associated with women in the reproductive process. Here the distinction between spirit and matter is divided between men. In the story, the father purposely deceives the boy's mother by signing the paper that permits the son to join the air force. The son wants to escape from the father, but he cannot escape from his father's desire that he prove himself a man and a worthy son. This internalized desire leads to his death. The sins of the fathers shall be visited upon the sons from generation unto generation. Perhaps it is true that the "Akedah has become a national symbol representing the tragedy of Israel in general and of sons in particular" (Abramson, 1990:114).

The following two poems by contemporary American Jewish women incorporate some of my thoughts about the Akedah; Ostriker's presents it as a "Gentlemen's Agreement" and alludes to the power inherent in it, whereas Wilner's suggests an alternative—a new map that entails new implications and scenarios. Even though a different choice is voiced by the mother, this need not lead to any conclusion about the essential attributes of women; rather, women in patriarchal society have come to symbolize the virtues of compassion and nurturance and have been socialized to promote them. The choice can be made by all of us, men and women alike, but it demands a rejection of the Akedah model and all that it implies. It demands a complete transformation of the model, its values, and our social arrangements. It would mean a moral revolution.

In numerous modern Jewish stories, and in the painting by Chagall, the distinction between the Akedah and the Crucifixion has become blurred. Despite the fact that in Genesis 22 Isaac is not sacrificed, psychologically it is as if the sacrifice has occurred. Abraham's willingness is the core that is left when all the other layers of interpretation are peeled away. In the next chapter I address the ways the story has shaped the Christian tradition.

The Story of Abraham
ALICIA OSTRIKER

I started by reading the banner headline
The way you read the big print at the eye doctor's.
It said I AM THE LORD GOD
ALMIGHTY AND I LOVE YOU ESPECIALLY. No problem. Very good.
One line down it said PACK UP, I'M SENDING YOU OVERSEAS. It said
YOU WILL HAVE AS MANY CHILDREN AS THERE ARE SANDS IN THE
SEA AND STARS IN THE SKY.
THEY WILL POSSESS THE LAND AND
I AM PERSONALLY GOING TO BLESS THEM.
The smaller print said: I am going
To bless them as long as they obey me.
Otherwise there may be
Certain repercussions. The even smaller
Print explained how we needed
A memorable logo for our organization
And he had just the ticket, a mark of absolute
Distinction, it would only hurt for a minute.
The print kept getting smaller and blurrier,
The instructions more bizarre.
Hold on, I interrupted. I'd like to check

Some of this out with my wife.
NO WAY. THIS IS BETWEEN US MEN.
AND IF YOU HAPPEN TO BE THINKING
ABOUT LOOPHOLES
FORGET IT, MAN. It said they preferred
Not to use strong arm techniques. It said
I'd already signed on.

Sarah's Choice
ELEANOR WILNER

A little late rain   *The testing*
the desert in the beauty of its winter   *of Sarah*
bloom, the cactus ablaze
with yellow flowers that glow
even at night in the reflected light
of moon and the shattered crystal of sand
when time was so new
that God still walked
among the tents, leaving no prints
in the sand, but a brand burned into
the heart—on such a night
it must have been, although
it is not written in the Book
how God spoke to Sarah
what he demanded of her
how many questions came of it
how a certain faith was
fractured, as a stone is split
by its own fault, a climate of extremes
and one last drastic change
in the temperature.

"Go!" said the Voice. "Take your son,
your only son, whom you love,
take him to the mountain, bind him
and make of him a burnt offering."
Now Isaac was the son of Sarah's age,
a gift, so she thought, from God. And how
could he ask her even to imagine such a thing—
to take the knife
of the butcher and thrust it
into such a trusting heart, then

light the pyre on which tomorrow burns.
What fear could be more holy than the fear of *that?*

"Go!" said the Voice. Authority's own.
And Sarah rose to her feet, stepped out
of the tent of Abraham to stand between
the desert and the distant sky, holding its stars
like tears it was too cold to shed.
Perhaps she was afraid the firmament
would shudder and give way, crushing her
like a line of ants who, watching
the ants ahead marching safe under the arch,
are suddenly smashed by the heel
they never suspected. For Sarah,
with her desert-dwelling mind, could
see the grander scale in which the heel
might simply be the underside of some Divine
intention. On such a scale, what is
a human son? So there she stood, absurd
in the cosmic scene, an old woman bent
as a question mark, a mote in the eye
of God. And then it was that Sarah spoke
in a soft voice, a speech
the canon does not record.

"No." said Sarah to the Voice.   *The*
"I will not be chosen. Nor shall my son—   *teachings*
if I can help it. You have promised Abraham,   *of Sarah*
through this boy, a great nation. So either
this sacrifice is sham, or else it is a sin.
Shame," she said, for such is the presumption
of mothers, "for thinking me a fool,
for asking such a thing. You must have known
I would choose Isaac. What use have I
for History—an arrow already bent
when it is fired from the bow?"

Saying that, Sarah went into the tent
and found her restless son awake, as if
he'd grown aware of the narrow bed in which he lay.
And Sarah spoke out of the silence
she had herself created, or that had been there
all along. "Tomorrow you will be
a man. Tonight, then, I must tell you

the little that I know. You can be chosen
or you can choose. Not both.

The voice of the prophet grows shrill.
He will read even defeat as a sign
of distinction, until pain itself
becomes holy. In that day, how shall we tell
the victims from the saints,
the torturers from the agents of God?"
"But mother," said Isaac, "if we were not God's
chosen people, what then should we be? I am afraid
of being nothing." And Sarah laughed.

Then she reached out her hand. "Isaac,   *The*
I am going now, before Abraham awakes, before   *unbinding*
the sun, to find Hagar the Egyptian and her son   *of Isaac*
whom I cast out, drunk on pride,
God's promises, the seed of Abraham
in my own late-blooming loins."

"But Ishmael," said Isaac, "how should I greet him?"
"As you greet yourself," she said, "when you bend
over the well to draw water and see your image,
not knowing it reversed. You must know your brother
now, or you will see your own face looking back
the day you're at each other's throats."

She wrapped herself in a thick dark cloak
against the desert's enmity, and tying up
her stylus, bowl, some dates, a gourd
for water—she swung her bundle on her back,
reached out once more toward Isaac.
"It's time," she said. "Choose now."

"But what will happen if we go?" the boy
Isaac asked. "I don't know," Sarah said
"But it is written   what will happen   if you stay."

Fig. 5. Andrea Mantegna, *The Sacrifice of Abraham*. Monochrome painting: imitation of relief. (c. 1490). Kunsthistorisches Museum, Vienna, Austria. Erich Lessing/Art Resource, N.Y.

CHAPTER SIX

Christian Commentary

$\mathbf{F}$OR CHRISTIANS, generally, the "sacrifice" of Isaac is thought to prefigure the Crucifixion, which they believe is the most important event in world history. In Genesis, God asks Abraham to sacrifice his son, his only son, the one whom he loves, but at the critical moment God interrupts the sacrifice. It is as if that deed, left unfinished, is finally completed when God the Father sacrifices his only begotten son for the redemption of the world.

The notion of prefigurement establishes a theological as well as psychological connection between the two events. But it also entails a conception of the world in which the Bible is presumed to record a continuous and unitary history of salvation punctuated by specific salvific events such as the Akedah (Frei, 1974:3). It is a view in which everything "that happens in the world can only be conceived as an element in this sequence; into it everything that is known about the world . . . must be fitted in as an ingredient of the divine plan" (Auerbach quoted in ibid.).[1] The notion of prefigurement is an important strategy for the Christian encompassment of Hebrew Scripture; the Hebrew Bible is no longer something separate and autonomous but is transformed into the Old Testament, into that which prefigured the New Testament.

Although the Crucifixion is thought to have superseded the Akedah, it does not erase it from Christian awareness. Christians are reminded of it in numerous ways: (1) by direct reference and allusion in the New Testament, (2) in sermons and liturgy, especially at Easter time when Genesis 22 is traditionally recited, either on Good Friday or during the Easter Vigil,[2] (3) in Sunday school and Bible study classes, (4) in noncanonical early Christian works such as "The Testament of Abraham," (5) in the writings of the Church Fathers such as Origen, Tertullian, and, of course, Augustine, (6) in medieval works—it was apparently a major theme in all the important medieval morality plays, (7) in works by the Protestant reformers, (8) in modern scholarly literature, both religiously motivated and secular, (9) in spontaneous reflections of contemporary ministers and lay people, and finally (10) in religious and secular works of art. It is one of the most common themes in Christian religious art; the Princeton Index of Medieval Art, for example, lists more than 1450 entries up to the Middle Ages alone. The story of the near sacrifice of Isaac continues to be depicted in literature, sculpture, painting, music, and film. In these many ways, it has been a constant image in Christian consciousness since the beginning, and through artistic media, especially, it has permeated the consciousness of people living in Christian cultures, whether or not they are believers.

In the way that many of us are affected by a wide range of commentaries and images—often without being aware of their provenance—I will draw on the range of sources above without overly cataloging them or trying to tie them to their original context. This book is not meant to be a compendium of references to Abraham and Isaac. Indeed, it would be impossible to encompass them all in one book and presumptuous for one person to try.

It is also difficult, though important, to keep in mind the distinction between Christian commentary on Genesis 22, as it is in the Hebrew Bible (Old Testament), and Christian commentary on the way Genesis 22 figures in the New Testament. The distinction is more conceptual than practical, as these lines are often blurred in practice.

When I spoke to people about the story, the most spontaneous response was that the Akedah prefigured the Crucifixion. A Baptist pastor was more explicit: "It is an example of the 'law of first mention'—that is, when a person or concept is first introduced in the Bible. The story of Abraham and Isaac is clearly a type of Christ and Crucifixion. . . . there is also present the theme of deliverance from death because God could have raised Isaac from the dead if Abraham had sacrificed him."[3] He did not know that such an idea was elaborated in some rabbinic commentary; instead he quoted from the New Testament book of Hebrews: "By faith, Abraham when he was tried, offered up Isaac, and he that had received the promises offered up his only begotten son. . . . Accounting that God was able to raise him up, even from the dead, from whence he also received him in a figure" (Heb. 11:17,19). This is the most explicit reference to the Akedah story in the New Testament, and it incorporates a number of themes to be discussed: faith, promises, and resurrection.

The Baptist pastor is not alone in thinking that the Akedah prefigures the Resurrection as well as the Crucifixion, as we shall see, but more common ways to illustrate prefigurement are the attempts to make superficial analogies between the two events. For example, "Isaac," said Tertullian, "when delivered up by his father for a sacrifice, himself carried the wood . . . and did at that early date set forth the death of Christ, who when surrendered as a victim by his Father carried the wood of his own passion" (Tertullian, *Against Marcion* 3:18:225; also Tertullian, *Answer to the Jews*, 13:250–1). Similar notions can be found in most of the early Church Fathers and was reproduced spontaneously by Cristos Valenti's minister in 1991 in California: "Abraham laid the wood upon Isaac just as the cross was laid upon Jesus."

Others have noted the parallels between the liminal three-day journey of Abraham and Isaac from their home to Mt. Moriah and the liminal three-day period between the Crucifixion and the Resurrection. And a few have commented that there were two other lads along with Isaac, as there were two other men crucified along with Jesus.

The ram suspended in the thicket has often been seen as an analogy for Christ hung on the Cross, and Tertullian implies that the thorny crown encircling Jesus' head recalled the brambles of that bush (Tertullian, *Answer to the Jews*, 13:251). Many, too, have noted the analogy between the male lamb sacrificed in Isaac's stead and the appellation of Jesus as "The Lamb of God" (John 1:29[4] and 1 Peter 1:19–20). That lamb "who was foreordained before the foundation of the world" recalls the ram that was created on the sixth day of Creation and had been waiting in the wings until its appointed time—to be sacrificed in Isaac's stead. To my knowledge no one has noted the similarity between the ass that accompanied Abraham and Isaac and the one that Jesus rode into Jerusalem on Palm Sunday.

Another parallel, of course, concerns the language of the "beloved son" (cf. Levenson, 1993). Still others have noted the similarity in the miracle of the conceptions of both Isaac and Jesus—in each case the conception was announced by an angel or messenger of God. Although that situation has provoked centuries of commentary about the suspicions of both Abraham and Joseph regarding paternity, no one has remarked that the *monogenes* (only begotten son), as Jesus is known, implies a "monogenetic" theory of procreation. The seed-child comes from only one source, in this case, only from God. Mary is merely the carrier and nurturer, not co-creator. A graphic example of this is illustrated in a late fifteenth century painting, The Annunciation (see fig. 6). The child (Jesus) is imagined as coming down *whole* from God; that is, Mary is impregnated with the whole child—she does not contribute to its form or identity, but contributes only the physical earthly, nurturant material. The *theory* of procreation is the same whether divine or human; the difference is whether God the Father or a human male is progenitor. The role of the mother is the same whether it is Mary or an ordinary woman (Delaney, 1986).

Prefigurement as a mode of interpretation—for example, the way the Akedah prefigures the Crucifixion—seems much closer to the spirit of the

FIG. 6. *The Annunciation* (c. 1480). Master of the Retable of the
Reyes Catolicos. Spanish. Oil on pine panel. Fine Arts Museums of San Francisco.
Gift of the Samuel H. Kress Foundation.

early Christians and to "fundamentalists" than it is to contemporary Biblical scholarship, which is concerned primarily with understanding the story in its ancient historical context. The latter is a worthwhile pursuit, but it ignores the fact that although the story is situated in the past, it continues to have emotional resonance in the present. The emphasis on historical reconstruction has helped to blur Jewish and Christian differences (of the scholars), but it also defuses the theological, cultural, and psychological significance of the story. The outcome of such a strategy is what scholar of Christian origins, Larry Wills, has called "exegesis across a chasm" (personal communication), meaning that much contemporary exegesis is directed to resurrecting the historical context with little regard to its continuing power to affect millions of people every year. Such an approach contributes to the perception that the story belongs in remote antiquity and is not a myth we live through, and by, today.

This perception may also recapitulate the experience of individual Christians, who generally first hear the story of Abraham when they are very young—that is, in their own prehistory. A number of informants told me that they first heard the Abraham story in Sunday school and that it was among the earliest Bible stories they had heard or remember hearing. Genesis is indeed the book best known to Christians. The stories of the Garden, Adam and Eve, Cain and Abel, and Abraham are as well known to Christian children as is the nativity of Jesus, probably better known than the Passion narrative and Crucifixion. Some people recalled an overwhelming feeling of fear and dread when they first heard the Abraham story—a feeling set down at a time when children have no defense or little means for discussing it with their adult teachers, who try to explain it as a story of love. There it remains, unquestioned, as part of the taken-for-granted cultural background.[5] It is, I think, a strange way to learn about love. Love, in that context, has to do with obedience in a hierarchical relationship. "By consenting to offer to God his only son, Abraham proved his perfect love, and his example became the cornerstone of the whole Jewish theology of love" (Vermes, 1973:193). This notion of fatherly love is, of course, reinforced by the idea that "God so loved the world he gave his only begotten son" (John 3:16). It is difficult to imagine that Christians would not make the connection between the two cases. It is also important to consider what the story has bequeathed about the meaning of love.

For most Christians, it is clear that the story of the sacrifice of Isaac is the prefiguration of the Crucifixion—yet what seems obvious to lay people is not so obvious to scholars. "Despite its significance, the Akedah has, until recently, not attracted much scholarly attention" (Daly, 1977: 74). And the recent debate turns on whether the story of the sacrifice of Isaac influenced the development of Christian theology or, conversely, whether the theology of the Crucifixion provoked Jewish reinterpretation of the story. Although the debate appears to focus on issues of dating of sources and the meaning of certain references, it is also fueled by religious commitments. It is extremely difficult to assign dates to much of the material from what Christians call the "intertestamental period." Christian theologians perhaps want to minimize the influence of Jewish ideas and models of what they hold as the unique event in world history. Jews, on the other hand, could easily view these maneuvers by Christians as yet another means of denying the dependence of Christianity on Judaism and of co-opting a centrally meaningful story from Jewish tradition.

All interpretations, whether divinely inspired or not, are human constructions. They do not occur in a vacuum, nor are they created ex nihilo, and they always depend on the prior context of interpretations common to the culture—even as they may be transformed. "How was it that this infamous death could so quickly become interpreted as a representative, atoning, sacrificial death and in what interpretive framework was such an understanding possible at all?" (Hengel, 1981:1). The Akedah surely seems a likely model for the interpretation of the crucifixion. Yet, because there are few explicit references in the New Testament (e.g., Hebrews, Romans, and James) and a relatively small number of possible allusions, some scholars assume it could not have served as the model. On the other hand, it could also be argued that it was so well known to the Jews who followed Jesus that even the slightest allusion would evoke the story. After all, the story was not mentioned again in the Hebrew Bible, yet its significance can hardly be debated. A number of scholars, both Jewish and Christian, feel that "by NT times the Akedah had become practically a summary of Jewish sacrificial soteriology" (Daly, 1977:74), and furthermore, "that the sacrificial soteriology of the NT can no longer be discussed without consideration of the Akedah" (ibid., 75).

Others, notably Davies and Chilton, disagree. They think that the elaboration of the Akedah was part of a rabbinic polemic against Christianity. They base their argument on the fact that the term *Akedah*, to refer to the story in Genesis 22, did not come into discourse until the late second century. When they say "the NT does not even attest the existence of the Aqedah, much less show its influence" (Davies and Chilton, 1978:515) they mean very narrowly the *aggadic* interpretation of Isaac as vicarious atonement in which he either was reduced to ashes or shed his blood.[6] Using the term *Akedah* to refer to Jewish understandings of the story before the Christian era, or to early Christian uses of the story, may be anachronistic; nevertheless, it seems extreme to assume that the story, was not influential (Segal, [1984]1987:113).

Schoeps, standing almost alone at midcentury, believed that the story served as a model for Paul's theology yet it has scarcely been noticed in the vast bibliography of Paul (Schoeps, 1946:385). "The significance of the Cross for Paul cannot be fully understood without his tacit reference to the sacrifice of Isaac: Paul's exegesis is here rabbinical" (ibid.:392). Indeed, much of the evidence Schoeps brings to bear on his point derives from (later) rabbinic commentary, which, therefore, may be somewhat anachronistic. It is also possible, of course, that such commentary reflects earlier, oral traditions. Nevertheless, as we shall see, Abraham was extremely important for Paul, and it is unlikely that he was unfamiliar with the story. Vermes asserts that the story was well known in the first century and used by Paul to interpret the death of Jesus as atonement (Vermes 1973:218).

Vermes believes that at some point before and during the period around the time of Jesus, the focus of emphasis in the story shifted from Abraham to Isaac. Rather than passive victim, Isaac became an active participant and the exemplar of the Jewish martyr. "Isaac offered *himself* to be a sacrifice for the sake of righteousness" (4 Macc. 13:12, emphasis added). This self-offering, according to Vermes, served as the "key to the doctrine of atonement or Redemption" (Vermes, 1973:193).

Although the interconnected themes of martyrdom and resurrection had been developed in pre-Christian works, "the motif of Isaac's sacrifice as the example *par excellence* of martyrdom does not appear until the first century, pre-eminently in the book of 4 Maccabees dated to the early 30s but devoid of Christian influence" (Segal, [1984]1987:117). It seems but a short step to associate Isaac as martyr with the notion of the "suffering servant" and, though Segal doesn't see that relation, Vermes and Rosenberg do. The latter, in fact, suggests that "in Jewish tradition Isaac is the prototype of the 'suffering servant' bound upon the altar" (Rosenberg, 1965:385). Because Jesus is so often associated with the Suffering Servant in Christian exegesis, this would make clear the link between Isaac and Jesus.

Rosenberg bases his conclusion, in part, on the passage in Maccabees quoted above, for the "righteous one" is how the "suffering servant" is known in Jewish tradition. If this were proved, it would be good evidence that the theology of Jesus was modeled not only on the suffering servant, as a number of Christian theologians emphasize, but also on the exegetical tradition of the time, regarding Isaac. Given the strong association between the Akedah theme and the servant motif in Judaism and, according to Vermes, in "the oldest pre-Marcan stratum of the Christian *kerygma*," he asks "whether Jesus himself was conscious of his destiny as being the fulfillment of Isaac's sacrifice" and, thus, whether "the introduction of the Akedah motif into Christianity was due, not to St. Paul, but to Jesus of Nazareth" (Vermes, 1973:223).

Rosenberg has elaborated the relation between "Jesus, Isaac and the Suffering Servant" (Rosenberg, 1965), and he also introduces another

interesting idea. Numerous scholars have noted that the story of the
sacrifice of Isaac appears in the book of Jubilees, where it is associated
with Passover. Rosenberg pushes it much further and connects Jubilees
with the Gospel of Matthew.

Jubilees, a pre-Christian Jewish book, incorporates the dating of events
and a calendar that divides history into sequences of Jubilee periods—
seven years times seven years and a major Jubilee every fifty years. A
generation is equivalent to a Jubilee. The calendar was used by the Essenes, and Rosenberg notes that there is considerable evidence that Jesus
and his disciples followed that calendar (Rosenberg, 1965:386). More
important, evidence that the Akedah served as a model for the interpretation of Jesus' death is found in the connections Rosenberg sees between
Jubilees and Matthew. Matthew 1:17 records fourteen generations from
Abraham to David, fourteen from David to the Babylonian exile, and
fourteen from the Babylonian exile to Jesus—comparable to the forty-
two Jubilees from Creation to Abraham. "The sacrifice of Jesus becomes
exactly parallel to the offering of Isaac, for the book of Jubilees (13:16;
17:15; 19:1) indicates that the offering of Isaac had taken place just prior
to the beginning of the forty-second jubilee after the Creation of the
world" (Rosenberg, 1965:387). Jesus and his disciples believed the Messiah would come during the Jubilee year in which they were living—the
eighty-fifth Jubilee after Creation—adding weight to the idea that Jesus
may have imagined himself not only as the Messiah but also as the sacrificial victim. (The tradition that the Messiah would come in the eighty-fifth
Jubilee after Creation is also preserved in Sanhedrin 97b.)

Jubilees, as one of the books that associates the Akedah with Passover,
implies, according to Segal, that the story is related not only to the liberation from Egypt but to all future liberations. Nevertheless, liberation
or redemption appears to be associated, at least in several important
places—in the Akedah, in the Passover, and in the Crucifixion—with
human sacrifice:

> In either case, however, the festival is involved with the theme of human
> sacrifice; either Isaac, who was saved from death upon the altar by the
> offering of a ram in his place, or the first born of Israel in Egypt, who were
> redeemed from death at the hand of the הַמַּשְׁחִית ("the Destroyer") by the
> blood of the paschal lambs slain in their stead. It was therefore fitting that
> Jesus, the Lamb of God, should meditate before going to his death at
> Gethsemane on the Mount of Olives, the site to the east of Jerusalem that
> in Jewish folklore was sacred to the "Destroyer." (Rosenberg, 1965:386)

If the Akedah was associated with Passover at some time or by some
groups of Jews then the strong connection between Passover and the Last
Supper/Crucifixion-Eucharist would provide a strong psychological and

theological link between the two events.[7] To deny these links seems at times to be no more than scholarly petulance.

The themes of expiation, atonement, martyrdom, and suffering, as well as the concept of the Messiah, were all present by the time of Christianity (cf. Segal, [1984]1987:122–3; Hengel, 1981:1), but whether all were tied together into a specific theology and then focused on and exemplified by the Akedah is a question. Was it an active model around the time of Christ or was it merely an ancient story recalled in certain disparate instances? During the confusion of the intertestamental period, the Temple was destroyed and the Jews were persecuted and dispersed. There was also a proliferation of millennial separatist sects (Essenes, Qumrani, Gnostics, and who knows how many others), some expressing extremes of behavior and seeking new ways, new beliefs, and rituals. Out of the turmoil emerged new religious sensibilities—both the conceptual system of Christianity, in a variety of forms, and renewed forms of Judaism. Both emerged in relation to each other; it was not the end of one and the beginning of another, as Christian theology assumes and as Christians tend to think.

Regardless of the issues of provenance—which will continue to fuel heated debates among historians, theologians, and believers—and far more important for this book is the fact that the Akedah and its associations have been part of the *common* heritage of Jews and Christians for nearly two millennia.[8] Not all of the associations and versions of the story are known to all Jews and Christians, but they are available as a common store of images, ideas, names, and objects. Yet just "because many of the motifs which dominate Christian exegesis are present in Jewish exegesis," one need not assume that "Christianity merely took them all over, effecting no transformation in the traditions as it employed them" (ibid.:122). No doubt the early Jewish-Christians, following Jesus himself, felt that they were cleansing and simplifying Judaism, but with time and the mutual resistance between this new community and other Jews, it became not another form of Judaism but a new vision, a new formulation of the world—the New Covenant. This New Covenant, however, was joined to, and dependent for its meaning on, the Old.

PROMISES OF ABRAHAM

Because Christ claimed to fulfill the "promises" adumbrated in the Old Testament, nascent Christianity had to clarify the nature of the promises and to make the case that Christians were the rightful heirs. The story of Abraham became pivotal—not only to convince other Jews to embrace the new covenant, but also, oddly enough, to convince Gentiles.

"In thy seed shall all the nations of the earth be blessed because thou
has obeyed my voice" (Gen. 22:18). The question turns on: who is the
seed of Abraham; who are the children of Abraham; who are the rightful
heirs of the promises given to him? Would *seed* refer only to the descendants of Isaac and Jacob, that is, to the Jews (the circumcised), or would
it also refer to the "many nations" including even the uncircumcised
Gentiles?

The very first sentence of the New Testament appears to answer that
question: "The book of the generations of Jesus Christ, the son of David,
the son of Abraham" (Matt. 1:1). The lineage is not traced to Noah or to
Adam, who might figure more easily as general, universal ancestors, but
specifically to Abraham, the first patriarch, the one credited with being
aware of the one God, the one with whom God made a covenant symbolized by circumcision, and the one willing to sacrifice even his son if that
were demanded by his God. The genealogical link collapses all intervening generations but David, and he was apparently included in order to
establish Jesus' claim to be the Messiah.

Paul makes the link more explicit in his letter to the Galatians, as he
also radicalizes it: "Now to Abraham and his seed were the promises
made. He saith not, And to seeds, as of many; but as of one, And to thy
seed, which is Christ" (Gal. 3:16).[9] Jesus Christ is heir to the promises
because he is figured as the true seed/son of Abraham. Paul's interpretive
strategy was momentous. With one word (*seed*) he established a direct
link between Abraham and Jesus and securely anchored Christianity in
the Jewish heritage, while simultaneously rendering the intervening period between Abraham and Jesus irrelevant. The collapsing of generations is a masterful interpretive strategy and exactly the opposite of that
of modern biblical historians. Rather than collapsing the chasm, modern
interpreters widen it by placing Abraham in his ancient context and trying to keep him there. The early Christians wanted to bring him closer,
and they foreshortened history by collapsing the distance between Abraham and Jesus. At the same time, without any mention of the Akedah, the
formulation of Jesus as the true seed/son of Abraham identifies Jesus with
Isaac, automatically evoking the Akedah story and hinting at the possibility of Jesus' own sacrifice.

The other Gospels open differently, but in all of them the figure of
Abraham is of critical importance in trying to define the new community
and legitimize its claims. Although the New Testament opens with the
Gospels, they were apparently of later composition than Paul's letters.
Incorporated into the canon, Paul's letters may provide the earliest Chris-
tian commentary about Abraham. Paul refers to Abraham nineteen times
in only three letters—more than to anyone else except Jesus. He uses
Abraham to discuss the nature of faith and the relation between Christian

and Jew. For Paul, Abraham is father of faith not only for Jews but for all believers (Rom. 4:11–8). Neither physical descent nor keeping Jewish law would be the decisive factor, however; instead, those who exhibited the kind of *faith* that Abraham did would be included in the new community, the new covenant.

Jews who merely followed the law and practices were enslaved, according to Paul; only belief in Jesus Christ would set them free. In a statement that was later incorporated into an early sermon by Augustine (Sermon 2, [c. 391 A.D] 1990:180), Paul said: "Abraham had two sons, one by a slave and one by a free woman. But the son of the slave was born according to the flesh, the son of the free woman through promise. Now this is an allegory: these women are the two Testaments" (Gal. 4:22–4). This allegory compares Jews to Ishmael, son of Abraham via Hagar, thereby illustrating the Jews' enslavement to the law. (This identification would surprise many Muslims who claim their descent from Ishmael, son of Abraham by Hagar.)

In early Christian discourse the word *law* was often used as a kind of shorthand for circumcision, which was interpreted as the sign that Jews are bound to, or enslaved by, the law. Christians were free, liberated from the yoke of slavery. Moreover, Paul's assertion that the children of Abraham through Hagar were "children of the flesh," whereas those through Sarah were "children of the promise" (Gal. 4:23), elaborates the distinction between physical and spiritual kinship and also sets the stage for much of early Christian theologizing. It could also be understood and interpreted by Jews as a ploy by Christians to steal the birthright away from the Jews.

Although Paul still included Jews as chosen by God and, therefore, in a privileged position for recognizing the divinity of Jesus, they could no longer automatically consider themselves the heirs to the promises. He demanded that they reform and believe in Jesus. Such a demand could be considered the beginning of attempts at "disinheriting the Jews,"[10] but it was even more pronounced in John. The eighth chapter of the Gospel of John, which focuses on Abraham, picks up the theme of bondage. He has the Jews answer: "We are Abraham's seed and were never in bondage; how sayest thou Ye shall be made free?" (John 8:33). Jesus appears to agree that they are children of Abraham but says that if they were, they would do the works of Abraham (John 8:39), namely exhibit his kind of faith. Because they do not, he says, "Ye are of your father the devil" (John, 8:44), in what is perhaps the first instance of the demonizing of the Jews. Almost two thousand years later Wharton asks: "Is it a necessary article of faith to *deny* that Jews are legitimate, continuing children of Abraham? For nearly 2,000 years the answer is yes" (Wharton, 1988: 385). The disinheriting of the Jews did not happen all at once but was the logical consequence of some of the early claims of the Christians. Abraham was a pivotal figure in the gradual transformation from Jewish Christian to Gentile Christian.

One early attempt can be clearly glimpsed in the work of Melito, Bishop of Sardis (c. A.D. 150–180), who was writing before there was a Christian canon, authorized tenets of faith, or regularized practices, and in a place and time when there was a well-established Jewish community. The content as well as the direction of his thought was shaped by interaction with that community. But rather than taking a defensive stance, he went on the offensive. In his Paschal Homily, for example, he viciously attacked the Jews for killing Jesus, and, even more, for not knowing whom they had murdered. In Melito's work, at least what survives from it, the Akedah becomes central in showing that the new dispensation overrides the old. Melito's three surviving fragments relating to the Akedah are "the first genuine evidence we have of the direction Christian thinking on the Akedah would take. At a later date the conflict [between Jews and Christians] would become more apparent, but the outlines of the debate are already present in Melito" (Wilken, 1976:68). Melito "attempts to rescue Isaac for the Christians" (ibid. 62), by drawing an analogy between Isaac and Christ and emphasizing that Jesus' sacrifice is the more perfect and complete because he died, whereas Isaac did not. In another fragment, the ram is the analogue of Christ; as the lamb redeemed Isaac, so too does the Lord redeem the world. In the Christological interpretation of the Akedah, the meaning of the story can be found only in Jesus. In this interpretation, Abraham becomes, in a sense, the first witness for Christ.

CHURCH FATHERS

The story of the "sacrifice" of Isaac achieves even greater prominence in the patristic writings than in the New Testament, and it becomes central in the developing Christian piety. Almost all of the early Church Fathers commented on it:

> Origen, writing in the early third century, devoted a large section of his homilies on Genesis to the figure of Abraham; Ambrose in the fourth century wrote two books on him; Gregory of Nyssa, Chrysostom, and others preached about him regularly; Cyril of Alexandria in the early fifth century discusses him extensively in a book on Genesis and in an Easter sermon; Augustine devotes a dozen chapters to him in *The City of God*, and numerous other writers hold him up as a model and example for Christians. (Wilken, 1972:724)

A complete study of the commentaries of these early Christian writers would make fascinating reading, but it would be an enormous undertaking, and it far exceeds the scope and purpose of this study.[11] Here I can give only a sampling. In one of his homilies Origen addressed the fathers in the congregation, especially those who had lost sons during the ordinary course of life. He tells them to learn from Abraham: "show that your faith in God is stronger than your human feelings. For Abraham, though he loves his son, preferred the love of God to human love" (Origen [c. A.D. 185–254] 1982, 8:7). The intent may be noble, but the implication of that way of thinking is, to my mind, perverse. Essentially it admonishes those who grieve overmuch.[12] The child is in heaven and all is well. The child is not *represented*; he or she has no voice, is silenced and obliterated. We are encouraged to focus our attention on God, or on the father, not on the child.

Irenaeus talked of Abraham as a model in Christian life, not just for Christ, but also for God!

> Righteously also do we, possessing the same faith as Abraham and taking up the cross as Isaac did the wood, follow Him. . . . For in Abraham man had learned beforehand and had been accustomed to follow the word of God. For Abraham, according to his faith, followed the command of the Word of God, and with a ready mind delivered up, as a sacrifice to God, his only begotten and beloved son, *in order that God also might be pleased to offer up for all his seed His own beloved and only-begotten Son, as a sacrifice for our redemption.* (Irenaeus [c. A.D. 120–202] 1903:467, emphasis added)

In other words, it appears that God's eventual sacrifice of His Son depended on Abraham's prior willingness. This theme was also taken up in some medieval plays; as Kolve points out, "the fulfillment *depends* upon the figure" (Kolve, 1966:74), namely, that which prefigured or foreshadowed the later event. One of the messages, surely, was that Abraham prefigured God the Father giving His own Son, but also emphasized was Isaac's obedience, his submission to his father's will, as a type of Christ figure. But regardless of exactly *how* Abraham and Isaac are portrayed, they were a prominent part of English medieval play cycles. Indeed, the story of the sacrifice occurred in all of those that included a section on the Old Testament. In four extant plays the section on Genesis ends with Genesis 22. In some cases, such as the Brome cycle, the Abraham story may have stood alone as a separate independent play.[13]

The centrality of the Abraham story for medieval English piety cannot be overlooked. Perhaps for that very reason it has continued to strike a particular resonance in the English-speaking world. But it was clearly present even earlier. Apparently three versions of the story survive in Old

FIG. 7. Filippo
Brunelleschi,
*Abraham in the
Act of Sacrificing
Isaac* Museo
Nazionale
Bargello,
Florence, Italy.
Alinari/Art
Resource, N.Y.

FIG. 8. Lorenzo,
Ghiberti, Gilded
bronze relief of the
sacrifice of Isaac
by Abraham.
Museo Nazionale
del Bargello,
Florence, Italy.
Alinari/Art
Resource, N.Y.

English and must have been written prior to Aelfric, who wrote a commentary on it.[14] Its place in the medieval play cycles may have been achieved in part because it was prominently depicted in paintings, stained glass windows, psalters, and literature. When Old Testament history was depicted at all, Genesis was often the only text included, and it usually ended with Genesis 22. It is also "at this point that the Old English poem, *Genesis*, comes to an end, and Bede's commentary on Genesis does not extend beyond this point. The propriety of this stopping place is self-evident: the effects of the Fall have by then been fully displayed and the Redemption has been fully foreshadowed" (Woolf, 1972:63–4).

The figural tendency that is so strong in these medieval works is attributed by Kolve (1966) to the emphasis on history and on the God who shows himself in time. It is very different from an allegorical tendency. The figural tendency is not a new invention but was already evident in Tertullian: "he insisted on the historical validity of Old Testament events: for him the *spiritual* sense lay in perceiving the relationship between two apparently disconnected historical happenings. In his terminology the fulfillment (or second event) is spoken of as *veritas* and the figure that announces it as *umbra* or *imago*" (Kolve, 1966:65). Regardless of when it originated, this mode of interpreting the text has been, and continues to be, a very important strand in Christian thought (cf. Daniélou, 1960; Frei, 1974; Handelman, 1982).

Because the story of the "sacrifice" of Isaac "had always been taken by Christian theologians to foreshadow the sacrifice of Christ" (Hartt, 1975: 127), it became the subject of a sculptural competition in Florence in 1401. Seven sculptors were chosen to submit plans for the panels on the doors of the Florentine Baptistery; among them were Brunelleschi and the young Ghiberti, whose plan won (see fig. 7 and 8).[15]

Who Shall Inherit?

Because Christians claimed that Jesus was the fulfillment of the law and the prophets—that the new dispensation abrogated the old—the identity of the proper descendants/heirs of God's promises to Abraham became an uppermost concern. A tension between physical and spiritual descent clearly existed. Some claimed that physical descent (being Jewish) gave them a privileged position, and others claimed that only faith in Jesus Christ mattered. The latter position was surely designed to include the Gentiles in the community. But if they were to be reckoned children of Abraham, a means other than circumcision had to be found. For the mark of being Jewish was not only following certain laws and practices, but, quintessentially, circumcision. It is not clear whether the Gentiles refused to be circumcised, whether they vehemently opposed the practice, or whether their unwillingness was simply assumed. Although the wording of the following passage from Romans is obtuse, the message Paul wants to convey seems to mean that Abraham "is the common father of Jew and Gentile alike according to faith alone" (Siker, 1991:59).

> He received the sign of circumcision, a seal of the righteousness of the faith while *he had yet* being uncircumcised: that he might be the father of all them who believe, though they be not circumcised; that righteousness might be imputed unto them also: And the father of circumcision to them who are not of the circumcision only, but who also walk in the steps of that faith of our father Abraham, which *he had* being *yet* uncircumcised. (Romans 4:11–2)

Circumcision alone, therefore, was not to allow Jews to claim Abraham as father; they also needed faith.

Oddly, Abraham, the first to be circumcised, became the vehicle for the inclusion of the uncircumcised, that is, the Gentiles. According to Paul and presumably to many early Christians, Abraham's faith was independent of the law; he was reckoned righteous before the law (Gen. 15:6), before the institution of either circumcision or later Mosaic law. The covenant established by means of circumcision was interpreted as a physical sign of his faith, which had preceded it. Therefore, neither circumcision nor all the rest of Jewish law was necessary in order to be included among God's people.

Christian critique of circumcision did not, however, extend to an investigation of the meaning and implications of its gendered specificity. Early Christian thinkers and leaders did not explain (perhaps did not need to explain) why the sign of the covenant was inscribed only on male flesh, for they, too, believed that the penis was *the* organ of generativity, fatherhood, and transmission of the line. Although they might dispense with circumcision, associations between spirituality and male generativity were metaphorically transferred and reinforced; the focus was no longer the physical line but the spiritual line, and the means of transmission not semen but the seminal word—the *logos spermatikos*.

A passage in James seems, on the surface, to contradict Paul's view when he says that "faith without works is dead" (James 2:20) and uses the Akedah as the example. But it could also be interpreted to mean that the fruit of faith is works, that they give outward expression of an inner condition; not that one is justified by following certain practices but that one's practices are the expression of faith (cf. Siker, 1991:98–9). And clearly, for James, the Akedah is the example par excellence: "Was not Abraham our father justified by works when he had offered Isaac his son upon the altar?" (James 2:21). James seems to have concluded that faith is completed by works.

Faith is the important term for Paul and for other early Christian writers. In Hebrews it occurs more than in any other book in the New Testament; in chapter 11 alone it occurs twenty-four times and begins eighteen sentences. "By faith Abraham, when he was tried, offered up Isaac: and he that had received the promises offered up his only begotten son, Of whom it was said, That in Isaac shall thy seed be called" (Heb. 11:17–8). Although others are mentioned who also have faith, it is generally felt that Abraham is the focal point. He is held up as the model for all those who believe. "The seed which was promised to Abraham seems to have been further realized in the eyes of the author of Hebrews not merely in the numerous offspring which come to Abraham through Isaac and his physical descendants as a result of the promise, but in the spiritual seed composed of all those who, like Abraham, have faith when they are tested" (Swetnam 1981:128). These individuals are chosen one-by-one by God—they are the ones who constitute the "seed" of Abraham (ibid.: 104). They are the children of the promise; they inherit the promises. "Chosenness" was no longer relegated to a specific *ethné* (group of people) but was acquired, through divine election, by specific individuals.

In addition, the promises are transformed from physical blessings to purely spiritual ones. God's promises to Abraham were seed (many descendants) and land; in Christianity these are transformed into spiritual seed (of saved souls) and the Heavenly Home. Tertullian draws attention to the difference, which he claims was prophesied in the promise to Abraham. The promise of descendants as multiple as "the sand on the seashore and the stars in heaven" was for him "an intimation of an earthly as well as a heavenly dispensation" (Tertullian, *Against Marcion*, 249). So, too, is the land spiritualized; it becomes eschatological. The citizenship of the true children of Abraham is in heaven; they will inherit that home and sit at the banquet table with their father Abraham (Matt. 8:11–2). If not at his table, then in his bosom. "Abraham's Bosom," according to Tertullian, was a kind of waiting place—neither heaven nor hell—but a place for the reception of the souls of his *sons* even from among the Gentiles (Tertullian, *Against Marcion*, 455).

Faith is intimately related to belief in the resurrection, which, according to some rabbinic midrashim, as well as Christian interpretation, was first hinted at in Genesis 22 (see chapter 5). Abraham, they say, was willing to go through with the sacrifice of Isaac because he was convinced that God would bring him back or could raise him from the dead if necessary. That interpretation could make it seem like Abraham was only going through the motions. It also gives too much specificity to

Abraham's faith and seems to vitiate other views of his faith—that it was precisely a "leap" of faith, a leap into the unknown, a leap with the confidence, no doubt, that his God knew what was best for him. One might also interpret his faith as an active stance, not merely as belief *in* something. Additionally, if his faith consisted in the belief that God would resurrect his son, his faith would have been focused more on resurrection than on God, related ideas surely but different nevertheless.

If Abraham's faith was, and continues to be, the model of faith, one could ask what theological need there is for Jesus? Yet the answer seems implicit in the question, for from a developed Christian point of view, at least, Abraham has the kind of faith in God that Christians ought to have in Jesus. Jesus is the one to whom this faith ought to be directed. From the Christian point of view, he completes what was begun with Abraham. In the Gospel of John, Abraham *is* a witness for Christ. "Jesus said unto them, Verily, verily, I say unto you, Before Abraham, I was" (John 8:58). This is a claim not only for the preexistence of Christ but primarily for his divinity.[16]

In any case, "Abraham is thus seen as the focal point for all of the OT heroes, even for those who preceded him. And the aspect of Abraham which is central is the sacrifice of Isaac. To this pole of history is opposed the death and resurrection of Christ which acts as an opposing pole" (Swetnam, 1981:129). *Opposing* here does not mean in opposition but more that Abraham and Jesus are the alpha and omega that encompass biblical faith.

That was also the position of Martin Luther, whose church at Wittenberg contains a huge triptych above the altar, one panel of which depicts the "sacrifice" of Isaac. Luther began his commentary on Genesis 22 on 27 October 1539, during a period of the plague.[17] In his struggle against Catholic orthodoxy and its increasing involvement with "works," such as acts of penance and indulgences, Luther claimed that one is saved by faith alone. And Abraham became important for his exposition. God's blessing comes only through the seed of Abraham which is Christ, he said, citing Paul's statement (see above). For Luther, Abraham was justified by faith; he must have understood the resurrection of the dead because he believed in the promise but was commanded to kill his son. "Life and death are alike for the godly," one must keep faith no matter what God does or asks (Luther, [1539–41]1964:120). Once you get a command from God you cannot do anything but obey, and you must undertake the task without hesitation or trepidation. This sounds very close to what Cristos Valenti said at his trial. Luther does not elaborate on how this command would come, and he also denounces those Catholics who boast that they have heard the voice of God: because Jesus has come there is no more need of voices, miracles, apparitions; one is saved by faith alone.

Inextricably linked with faith is obedience. Obedience was exhibited not just by Abraham but also by Isaac. Luther appears to equate Isaac with Christ in his obedience to his father's will. Referring to Isaac, Luther says: "With the exception of Christ we have no such similar example of obedience" (ibid.:114). At the same time, Luther warns that Abraham's extraordinary example should not be dragged along as a precedent to be followed. Instead we should imitate his obedience and his faith. "Because of God, Abraham is willing to give up not only his son, Sarah, his inheritance, his house and his church but even his own life" (ibid.:98). Although Abraham had twice given Sarah up (Gen. 12, 20; see Speiser, 1963), there is little evidence that he was willing to give up his inheritance, house, church, or his own life; furthermore there is a difference between giving up things and taking another person's life, a difference Luther does not address. Nor does he ask what right Abraham had to involve other people in such a unilateral decision.

He does, however, express some concern about the deception of both Sarah and Isaac. When he speculates about Sarah, he reveals what we would call "sexist presumptions": Abraham must have concealed from her what he was about to do because she was too weak to withstand the great shock it would cause (ibid.).[18] He is more concerned about the deception of the son, and he thinks Abraham must have told him he was to be the lamb but that this conversation was omitted by Moses. (This passage shows that Luther believed that the Pentateuch or Torah was written by Moses; it also shows his flexible way of reading between the lines.)

There is much more one could say about Luther's commentary and the way Abraham figures in it. But I want to draw attention to his theological use of the word *seed*. Although Abraham is important in Luther's theology, this is primarily because of Abraham's relation to Jesus, his seed. "The blessed Seed alone delivers from death" (ibid.:165). Throughout the English translation of Luther's commentary, *seed* is always capitalized; it is reified in the true sense of the word, for *the Seed is Jesus who is God*. In the King James version of the Bible, references to seed in the Old Testament are starred, as prophetic announcements of Christ. Seed is divine; it is identified with God. No wonder Luther can say: "Nowhere is there light, life or salvation except through this Seed" (ibid.:177). There is an unbroken stream, a "gushing fountain" (ibid.:151) of the divine lineage through Abraham to Christ who is also God. It is clearly a relation between father and son, whether Abraham and Isaac on the human plane, or God the Father and Christ the Son on the divine. The use of the language of procreation for theological conception has a long history, and Luther's use of it seems quite deliberate.[19] Although he uses procreative language theologically, he is unaware that he is using a *theory* of procreation.

THE "SEED" OF ABRAHAM: (KINSHIP)

Questions of what constitutes a Christian cannot be separated from who is a Christian. These questions have to do with inheritance and kinship but are framed in terms of seed (*sperma* in the Septuagint, a Greek translation of the Old Testament made sometime in the third century B.C. and usually referred to as *LXX*). Other scholars have focused on the referents of seed in Genesis 22:18 (and elsewhere, in relation to Abraham). Swetnam, in particular, has a number of sections on the meaning of *seed* in various books of the New Testament, but meaning for him is clearly referential—that is, who is being referred to. He does not ask *what* is the meaning of *seed*. My concern has been with the constitutive meaning of *seed* and with the theological and social implications.

Seed encapsulates the biblical notions of procreation as biblical scholar, Robert Alter has noted. In speaking of the importance of the divinely chosen lineage in Genesis, he says: "nothing is allowed to detract our focused attention from the primary, problematic subject of the proper channel for seed (since this is thought of both figuratively and in the most concretely physical way, I have translated it literally throughout)" (Alter, 1981:6). I wish others had done the same, for the translation of *seed* as posterity, descendants, or progeny conceals that these are a matter of seed. Although Alter recognized the symbolic importance and specificity of seed, he seemed oblivious to the gendered implications. Writing in the late twentieth century, he cannot be excused for neglecting that women, too, have "seed"; but because he did, he also lost the opportunity to challenge the theology that is so interdependent with it. That is, although most of the commentators accept the idea that *seed* means progeny and that only men produce seed, they are not self-reflexive: *they do not examine the way gender is inextricably bound up with theological conceptions.* The gendered meanings are so obvious and yet have been overlooked by all of the commentators.

The entire theology is wrapped up with the construction of masculinity as it is related to fatherhood; both circumcision (for Jews) and seed focus on, and highlight, male pro-*creative* abilities. Denaturalized, male generativity is used symbolically to describe God's creativity; conversely, God's creative power is naturalized in the notions of male generativity. The notion of masculinity (what a man is) has, in the West, been intimately involved with notions of paternity—a point Mary Daly seems to have missed in her otherwise groundbreaking critique of the gender of God, *Beyond God the Father* (1973). Despite the title, she does not really explore the meanings of fatherhood and the way paternity is a *concept* embedded in a theory of procreation. Instead she assigns fatherhood to the category of the natural, and this leads her to attribute the negative aspects of patriarchy to male nature rather than to a particular construction of it.

Just because the notion of masculinity has involved a notion of male generativity, this does not mean that any particular man has to become a father in order to exercise his power. Rather, every man is imagined as endowed with the ability to produce seed, and it is this ability that bestows maleness with life-giving, authoritative, god-like power. It has to do with notions of paternity and thus with an entire *theory* of procreation. Abraham, who receives the promises, is able to pass them down, able to transmit them to his seed and, through his seed, to him who Christians claim is Heir, to Christ himself. As the idea of procreation becomes spiritualized or, as I would prefer, metaphorized (as is done in the theological conceptions), maleness and paternity are essential features. Exceptions are often useful to point out the more general assumptions.

One passage that has perplexed commentators for some time is Hebrews 11:11: "Through faith Sarah herself received strength to conceive seed." The English translation *conceive seed* obscures the Greek connotations whereby the words "must be understood in an active sense, and in all normal Greek usage can only refer to the active operation of the male in generation" (Black quoted in Swetnam, 1981:99, n. 59). Such an understanding has raised questions about the intentions of the author of Hebrews. Did he (or she) think (a) that Sarah had become like a man, as Hannah was said to have done when she let her sons be sacrificed, (b) that the passage was evidence of a two-seed theory of procreation, or finally (c) that it implied primarily that her *faith* was so strong. "What has failed to be suggested so far is rather simple: the word . . . is being used in a spiritual sense" (Swetnam, 1981:100). Van der Horst (1990, 1992), on the other hand, thinks it reveals a glimmer of a two-seed theory of procreation. He briefly reviews material on procreation from 500 B.C. to A.D. 500, but he also notes that a two-seed theory does not necessarily imply that the female seed is generative or equal.[20] In other words, textual evidence alone is not sufficient. Perhaps it could also be interpreted to mean that in her old age Sarah was given the strength of a man to be able to conceive seed, in the sense of being able to hold onto it.[21] Men do not conceive seed, they produce it.

Despite the fact that Swetnam and Van der Horst (and no doubt others) noticed the peculiarity in that one passage, they failed to use it to question the usual interpretations—that the male is the one who produces

seed and thus pro-creates. They failed also to see the implications for and
about women and the way it has been integral to theological conceptions.
In the painting of the Annunciation we have already seen how it has been
expressed visually.

Whether fatherhood is physical or spiritual, whether Abraham or God
is father, it is still fatherhood, not motherhood, that bestows identity and
symbolizes divinity. "To speak of one's paternity reveals one's basic identity" (Siker, 1991:135), as Jesus himself appears to indicate, when he says
repeatedly in the Gospel of John that he knows *where he comes from and
where he is going*: from and to the "Father." Notions of identity cannot
be separated from notions of origin: who you are is related to where you
come from, whether conceived physically, socially, or cosmologically;
each level is gendered. Jesus can speak with the voice of the Father because, basically, Father and Son *are* one. As Isaac is the son of Abraham
in a way he is not the son of Sarah, so too is Christ the son of God the
Father in a way that he is not considered the son of Mary. Mothers are
not equal parents; there is really only one parent. Father and Son are one,
they are of the same essence (see especially John 5:18ff.); mother and son
are not. Nor are mother and daughter of the same essence because a
daughter also proceeds from the father; women, in this view, lack the
ability to pass on themselves. It is paternity, not maternity, that confers
identity; knowing who your father is legitimates you as a full person.
Although for John, and Christianity generally, physical, genetic descent is
not the determining element in whether one is a child of Abraham, paternity in the conceptual/spiritual sense is. It is important to understand why
this is so and what this implies, not just for and about women, but also
regarding the essentially gendered nature of theology.

INTERPRETIVE STRATEGIES

It is not enough merely to take a woman's or a mother's point of view, as
a number of feminist scholars working with the biblical text have done
(cf. Schüssler-Fiorenza, 1992; Trible, 1984; Bach, 1993). That assumes
the meaning of *woman* or *mother* is self-evident; such a stance may re-
dress the imbalance of attention, but it does not question the essential
premises. To resurrect women's voices, especially the cry of the mothers—Hagar, Sarah, Mary, and the Mary at the contemporary trial—is
important. But these women can only react; their reactions are predeter-
mined by the structure of power between the genders. This hierarchical
order is premised on the meaning of gender in the context of procreation
which, in turn, is connected to a wider system of meanings of coming-
into-being.

If, indeed, a monogenetic theory of procreation—in which the life-giving element, the identity, even the soul, comes from (or is transmitted by) only one (masculine) source—is correlative with the theological doctrine of monotheism, then gender and theology are inextricably entangled. For example, if the child came equally from both God and Mary, Mary would be co-Creator along with God, but she is not. Had she been so, the concept and meaning of God and of the female procreative role would be vastly different from what they are.

A feminist strategy for interpretation, in my view, must focus not on what a religious tradition has to say *about* women and men, but on the way female and male are constructed *by* the theology, and vice versa. Rather than analyzing the story from a perspective that takes the genders for granted, we need to ask, instead, how the story itself constructs and reinforces the meanings of gender so as to appear natural, inscribed in the very nature of the universe.

Such a strategy, however, is difficult for those for whom God is a constant—somehow separate from, impervious to, and unentangled in human meanings—and who also have a vested interest in preserving the religious tradition. They have a number of other options: (a) to retreat and reinforce the system as a scheme given by God and therefore not open to change, (b) to try to change some of the institutional arrangements, for instance by admitting women to the priesthood or the rabbinate, or (c) to try to change the language so as to be more inclusive. As noted earlier, however, a particular theory of language is being implemented, a theory that assumes that meaning exists separate from language and is not constituted by and through language (see note 23, chapter 1). We have already seen what gets swept under the rug when such a seemingly simple word as *seed* is changed to *children*.

Some feminists have also suggested a notion of Mother/Father God as a way to resolve the problem of male bias, but, given the argument of this book, it is clear that that would only perpetuate and reinforce the stereotypes of maternity and paternity we have been discussing. Rather than salvaging theology, we need to rethink the entire system and the structures and values that are embedded in it. But if we are to begin to construct more humane theories of human existence, it is of crucial importance to rethink these powerful religious traditions, their foundational stories, and the underlying assumptions.

Focusing on God rather than Abraham, a few feminist scholars (e.g., Brown and Parker, 1990; Brock, 1990; Kraemer, 1992) have begun to question why the sacrifice of the son should be a model of faith and the supreme example of love and absolution. Kraemer, for example, suggests that "those preoccupied with Christianity might do well to reflect on the differences between a religion whose central myth is that of the separation and ultimate reunion of mother and daughter beloved of one another, and that of a religion whose central myth is of a father who requires the painful sacrificial death of his only son" (Kraemer, 1992:208).[22] This is an attack on the central idea, the central performative act of Christianity: "God so loved the world, he gave his only begotten son." Along with Kraemer, Brown and Parker ask whether we should continue to accept such a model. "Throughout the Scriptures is the idea that Jesus died for our sins. Did he? Is there not another way for sins to be forgiven: Why an idea of original sin? Christianity has functioned to perpetuate the Fall, for without it there is no need for a savior" (Brown and Parker, 1990:2). Their concern is for the way this ideology has affected women. They argue that throughout Christian history women have more often than men been identified with Christ, have been called upon to be self-sacrificing and to suffer in silence as Jesus suffered in obedience to his father's will.

The model of the Crucifixion conveys the message that suffering is redemptive; Brown and Parker have also begun to see in it a model of abuse: "Divine child abuse is paraded as salvific and the child who suffers 'without even raising a voice' is lauded as the hope of the world" (ibid.). This is serious stuff; they are courageous for even voicing it. The model they criticize has implications not just for women but for men, and especially for children. Their critique demands a total revaluation and reordering of human society and social ethics. But it extends beyond the strictly Christian context they are working in. Except for a brief mention of Abraham in relation to the power of blood to atone for sin, they do not consider the structuring power of this story for the Christian one. Had they related their observations to the story of Abraham, they would have realized that the same theme is common to all three monotheistic religions, and they might, then, have been able to broaden their critique of Christianity to include a critique of monotheism and the notion of a Creator God.

FIG. 9. A Turkish postcard of the "Kurban."

CHAPTER SEVEN

Muslim Interpretations

MUHAMMAD'S mission was to recall the people to the monotheistic faith of Abraham, a fact about Islam of which many Westerners are unaware. Yet it is essential. Because Islam shares many figures, concepts, and practices with both Judaism and Christianity, some people assume it is a synthesized and therefore distorted version of them. The historical framework of biblical religious tradition fosters such a view—that Islam, being a relatively recent arrival on the religious scene, seeks to upstage Judaism and Christianity. Yet, because it goes back to Abraham, Islam is, in its own view, the original of which both Judaism and Christianity are distortions. For example, Muhammad attempts to persuade the People of the Book, "Why will you argue about Abraham, when the Torah and the Gospel were not revealed until *after* him?" (Qur'an 3:65 emphasis mine). For "Abraham was not a Jew, neither a Christian, but he was a pure monotheist (*hanif*) and one who submitted (*muslim*) to God; certainly he was never of the idolaters" (Qur'an 3:67).

In pre-Islamic times Abraham was known as *hanif*, a true monotheist, and he is referred to in that way even today. The term *muslim* means submission to God, and simply describes one who recognizes that everyone and everything is dependent on Him.[1] Because Muslims assume that dependence is self-evident, it is incomprehensible to them why Jews, Christians, and others reject Muhammad's teaching. Their rejection is interpreted not merely as nonbelief but as active rejection of obvious truth.

Islam, then, can best be described as a new/old religion (Firestone, 1990:157); Muhammad was the newest (and the last) in a long line of prophets, but because he was trying to restore the old, original religion of Abraham, Islam is both new and old, the alpha and omega of true religion, not *a* religion. Jews and Christians will not be convinced, but the idea is important for any understanding of Islam. A grave misunderstanding was perpetrated, for example, when Islam was referred to as Muhammadanism, for Muhammad does not have the role and function Jesus does in Christianity. And Abraham is at least as important as Muhammad for Islam.

Abraham, the "Friend of God" (al-Khalil)—an epithet that may derive from the Bible (2 Chron. 20:7; Isaiah 41:8; see Firestone, 1990:141, n.46; see also James 2:23, and the Epistle of Clement, 11:1)—is not a shadowy figure relegated to the mists of time, but absolutely central to Islam. Hardly just an ancient hook on which to hang a new prophetic mantle, his life and deeds are inextricably woven into the very fabric of Islam.

> The spiritual presence of Abraham is always felt in Arabia, as in the whole Muslim world, not only in the frequency with which his name (in its Arabic form Ibrahim) is given to children, but also in the ever-recurring remembrance, both in the Koran and in the Muslims' daily prayers, of the patriarch's role as the first conscious preacher of God's Oneness: which also explains the great importance given by Islam to the annual pilgrimage to Mecca, which since earliest times has been intimately connected with the story of Abraham (Asad, 1954:377).[2]

As we shall see, the meaning and rituals of the pilgrimage (hajj) refer to events in the life of Abraham. The Hajj culminates in the Feast of the Sacrifice (Arabic: Id al-Adha; Turkish: Kurban Bayramı), the holiest day in the Muslim calendar. That day commemorates Abraham's willingness to sacrifice his son at God's command, and, in commemoration of Abraham's deed, each male head of household slaughters a ram (or other appropriate animal substitute). In Mecca tens of thousands of animals are sacrificed on that day; it is not just in Mecca, however, that the sacrifice occurs, but throughout the Muslim world.[3]

Etched viscerally into the sentiments of all Muslims is the sight, sound, and smell of that sacrifice. Children in the village in Turkey where I lived for nearly two years used to tell me that "if God had not provided Ibrahim with a ram, fathers would still be slaughtering their children."[4] They were steeped in the notion that it is because of God's mercy that fathers no longer sacrifice their sons—a lesson that encourages both their thanks and their indebtedness to God and that reinforces the notion of patriarchal power. When children misbehaved, for example, the most common threat was "You'd better be good or I'll make a kurban out of you." Kurban (Arabic qurban) means sacrifice, but refers to and evokes Abraham's near-sacrifice of his son and his actual sacrifice of the ram.[5]

My understanding of the importance of Abraham for Islam has been conditioned by my fieldwork in Turkey. My interpretation of his significance is therefore more immediate and more ethnographically grounded than my accounts of his place in Judaism and Christianity. That may be fortunate, as his role in Islam is less familiar to most Americans and Europeans, who, I suspect, will be the readers of this book. It is first necessary to give a brief description of the sources of Muslim interpretation.

SOURCES OF MUSLIM INTERPRETATION

In addition to Muhammad himself the sources of interpretation are primarily the Qur'an, the holy book communicated to Muhammad from God through Gabriel (*Jibril*); the *hadith* or traditions of the Prophet as remembered and passed along by friends; and a vast array of medieval (eighth to fourteenth century) exegetical commentaries or "tales of the prophets."[6]

Muhammad

Muhammad was born c. A.D. 570 in Mecca to Amina; Abdullah, his father, had died while she was still pregnant. Muhammad's mother died when he was six, and he went to live with his paternal grandfather 'Abd al-Muttalib, who belonged to the tribe of the Qureysh. (An early biography of Muhammad relates that al-Muttalib made a vow to sacrifice him [Firestone, 1990:110], but this assertion does not seem to be much elaborated). Upon the death of his grandfather two years later, Muhammad was taken care of by his paternal uncle, Abu Talib. Muhammad got to see some of the world when he worked for the widow Khadija, a wealthy merchant, and she was so impressed by his trustworthiness that she proposed to him. Although she was fifteen years older (he was twenty-five and she was forty), their marriage of twenty-six years was, apparently, a happy one.[7] They had a number of children but only the girls survived infancy. After Khadija's death, Muhammad took other wives, but with them he had no children (except for a son Ibrahim by a concubine Mary; this son also died in infancy).

Muhammad used to take Khadija and the children to a cave in the mountains (Mt. Hira) for a month of meditation—the month was *Ramadan* (the "Scorcher"), which at that time meant the month of heat. In Islam it would become the month of fasting and would no longer be associated only with the summer. The Muslim calendar is a lunar one, and thus holy days and holy periods, such as Ramadan, move relative to the solar year and, vis-à-vis the solar calendar, are celebrated ten days earlier each year. Also, holidays are not fixed to a particular season, as are Christmas, Easter, Yom Kippur, or Passover, but move around the year and make a complete revolution every thirty-three years. I have suggested elsewhere (Delaney, 1991:291) that this contrapuntal rhythm helps to emphasize the separation between the things of this world and those of the spirit.

In Islam, Ramadan commemorates the month in which the Qur'an began to be revealed. Muhammad was forty at the time.[8] One night when he was asleep or "dead to the world" in meditative trance, he heard a voice call out: "Read."[9] Muhammed is said to have responded, "But I can't read." He was illiterate. The voice called out again, and Muhammad responded the same way. The third time he asked: "What can I read?" And the voice responded:

> Read: In the name of thy Lord Who createth.
> Createth man from a clot.
> Read: And it is thy Lord the Most Bountiful
> Who teacheth by the pen,
> Teacheth man that which he knew not.   (Qur'an 96:1–5)[10]

This was the first revelation, but it is not the first *sura* (chapter) in the Qur'an. Instead it is number ninety-six—a first indication of a major difference between the Qur'an and the Bible. When Muhammad shook himself awake, the words were as if inscribed upon his heart. Soon afterward he heard the voice again: "O Muhammad! Thou art Allah's messenger, and I am Gabriel." Much shaken by this experience, he was later to be assured that he had received a divine call to be the Messenger of God.

Muhammad reported what he heard to his friends; they, in turn, wrote down what he said. These written suras were dispersed among some of his followers, and a number of people committed them to memory. When some of them were killed in a battle, those remaining collected the suras and arranged them in the form the Qur'an has to this day. The accepted tradition is that all of the suras were written down while Muhammad was alive; this is a fact of which Muslims are proud. They contrast it with the Gospels, which, as Turkish villagers explained to me, are obviously distortions of the Word because there are four somewhat different versions of the same story and all were written after the Crucifixion.

Qur'an

Despite scholarly debates about the composition of the "canon," the popular as well as the theological position is clear: the Word is One, undiluted.[11] The Qur'an is not merely inspired by God, it *is* the word of God. The Qur'an is not a record of the events of His people or His interventions among them; it is an exhortation to remember that God is God.

Because the Qur'an is the word of God, the sacred words must be learned in the language in which they were communicated, namely Arabic. The Qur'an cannot really be translated; all "translations" are called *interpretations*, for clearly they are human attempts to render the word of God. In countries where Arabic is not the native language, such as Turkey, people nevertheless learn the Arabic text. Because the emphasis is on knowing the exact words, there has always been a great stress on memorization. Throughout the Muslim world there are people, including illiterate villagers, who have committed the entire Qur'an to memory. This appears to be a very different sense of learning and education than that of Western Enlightenment, which imagines education as a drawing out of truth through the process of reasoning (see Eickelman, 1978).

Although the Qur'an is a historical book in the sense that much more is known about the date and mode of its composition than about the Hebrew Bible or the New Testament, it is not a historically constructed book. By that I mean that it is not constructed chronologically, as is the Bible, which begins with Creation and proceeds to recount the history of God's people. To people accustomed to the narrative style of the Bible, the Qur'an is very disorienting. There is "very little narrated history (in fact, very little narration at all) and, in the standard order of the suras, it is a disjunctive and discontinuous book of lessons, warnings, instructions, and exhortations" (Waldman, 1986:51). The style is more poetic than narrative, a style that is more conducive to recitation and memorization.[12] The "Qur'an, despite its having a written form, presents itself as essentially an oral composition" whereas "whatever the oral qualities and the dimensions of the Hebrew Bible, it has come down to us as a written composition" (ibid.).[13]

Although many biblical figures, such as Abraham, Joseph, and Mary, are found in the Qur'an, they do not appear in the same order as in the Bible and their characters are not as fully developed, leading many Westerners to conclude that Muslims got it all wrong. But that would be to misunderstand the differences between the Bible and the Qur'an. Muhammad's task was not to tell the story of his people but to call them (back) to God, to turn them from their supposedly pagan, idolatrous ways. The familiar biblical characters are intended, it seems, to be representatives of a type, to be used for didactic purposes. The Qur'an warns Muslims about their fate if they do not heed the message, and it gives instruction about the conduct of daily life.

Hadith *and Other Traditions*

The *hadith* are collections of traditions about Muhammad—things he said and things he did—as recounted by relatives and friends and passed down over generations. There are a number of collections of *hadith;* some are more respected than others because of the *isnad* or line of transmission. That is, the authenticity of a tradition is only as good as the authenticity of the transmission. It is a lineage, even a patrilineage, and even though it is not biologically based, the stress on authenticity in this realm is comparable to the stress on authentic paternity in the biological one. Some traditions have no authentic or trustworthy line of transmission, and these have an aura of illegitimacy about them.

In addition, numerous tales and traditions are recounted in medieval commentaries such as Ibn Ishaq's *Sirah*, which is a "Life" of Muhammad set in a world-historical schema, and Al-Tabari's *History*. Newby (1989) suggests that the *hadith* and the tales are really two different kinds of biographies of Muhammad; the *hadith* are fragmented, whereas the tales try to situate the life of Muhammad in the context of the lives of other prophets. Some of these tales incorporate a great deal of pre-Islamic (Jewish, Christian, Persian, and Arab) material (cf. Firestone, 1990). Those that refer to biblical figures were not just "borrowed" from Jewish and Christian scriptures, however, nor even from direct oral transmission by Jews and Christians; instead a great many of these tales had been circulating for centuries in that area of the world, and therefore each tradition could incorporate them as it wished. The fragmentary nature of the references to biblical figures in the Qur'an and *hadith*, however, must have been a motivation for Muslim scholars to search out the biblical referents, especially Abraham, given his importance for Muhammad (cf. Newby 1989:13–4). These traditions should not be considered pale reflections of their biblical referents. Once elaborated and inserted into a new theological/historical scheme, they are really new versions.

With regard to the story of Abraham and its interpretations, I do not argue for one correct version over others; indeed, as most collections include a variety of versions, even contradictory ones, the idea of a canonical version is alien to Islam. Nor do I try to place any particular version in its specific historical or social context, except for anecdotal material from my own fieldwork. Instead, my concern is with some of the features of the myth—what has appeared to be significant about Abraham in Islam—rather than with any particular instantiation of it. No doubt some features have been more important to some groups at some times and other features to other groups at other times. I do not suggest that all features have been known by all Muslims at all times any more than I suggested that all Jews know all the various Jewish interpretations of the story. Even fewer Jews and Muslims are aware that their versions of the Abraham legend overlap a great deal, especially stories involving Abraham's astronomical knowledge (Qur'an, 6:76ff.), his iconoclasm (Qur'an 21:58ff.), and the story of Nimrod and the fiery furnace (see below). On these points the influence is not one way, that is from Jewish to Muslim, for it is also possible that Muslim elaborations of the stories influenced later rabbinic, midrashic material.

Certain individuals or groups have no doubt possessed and promoted their own interpretations, but certain features are indispensible and do not change very much. Central texts exist, central practices continue to be practiced, and both are continually taught and promulgated. This is true of the story of Abraham and the sacrifice.

The references to Abraham in the Qur'an—all two hundred forty-five of them—are scattered throughout; they do not form one coherent story situated at a chronologically appropriate place. The fullest account concerns the sacrifice story, found in Sura 37:100–13.

100. My Lord! Vouchsafe me of the righteous.
101. So We gave him tidings of a gentle son.
102. And when (his son) was old enough to walk with him, (Abraham) said: O my dear son, I have seen in a dream that I must sacrifice thee. So look, what thinkest thou? He said: O my father! Do that which thou art commanded. Allah willing, thou shalt find me of the steadfast.
103. Then, when they had both surrendered (to Allah), and he had flung him down upon his face,
104. We called unto him: O Abraham!
105. Thou hast already fulfilled the vision. Lo! thus do We reward the good.
106. Lo! that verily was a clear test.
107. Then We ransomed him with a tremendous victim.
108. And We left for him among the later folk (the salutation):
109. Peace be unto Abraham!
110. Thus do We reward the good.
111. Lo! he is one of Our believing slaves.
112. And We gave him tidings of the birth of Isaac, a Prophet of the righteous.
113. And We blessed him and Isaac. And of their seed are some who do good, and some who plainly wrong themselves.

Much in this telling of the story is familiar to readers of the Bible: the test;[14] the calling out at the last minute saying that he had fulfilled the test; the ransom by substitution of another victim, although it does not specify that it was a ram;[15] and the blessing to him and to Isaac and the mention of their seed. But much is different. Most notably, unlike the biblical version, Abraham tells his son what is to take place, and the son responds in the way that he does in some of the Jewish commentary, for example in Josephus (see chapter 5). There is no mention of the place, nor of the accoutrements of sacrifice—the fire, the wood, and the knife; these are, however, elaborated in the stories. The Qur'an specifies the position of the son and the fact that Abraham flings him down on his face (or in some versions his forehead). This is a position that deviates from the way an animal would be sacrificed (Firestone, 1990:119). The Qur'an mentions the seed of Abraham, but the blessing is not that the seed will become a great nation; rather, it is a statement that some seed will be good and some will not, perhaps an allusion to the Parable of the Sower in the Gospel of Matthew. It is clear that Abraham is a model of the righteous man, one who surrenders totally to God. And so, too, is his son.

Conflicting Legends

The meaning of the story is not contested: Abraham's great faith was proved by his obedience/submission to God—that is, by his willingness to sacrifice his son at God's command. But there are conflicting stories about when the sacrifice story and practice entered the Hajj tradition and about the details: (1) Which son is the intended victim—Ishmael or Isaac? (2) Where did the sacrifice take place—in Syria, Jerusalem, or Mecca? And much less clearly, (3) when did it take place: (a) before or after the building of the Ka'ba (the huge stone shrine in Mecca toward which Muslims pray, and which is the goal of pilgrims, see below), (b) before or after Ishmael's marriages, which would have made him more than a boy "who was old enough to walk with him," or (c) before or after the institution of the pilgrimage?

That there has been any question about such issues may come as a surprise to many Muslims who assume Ishmael was the son to be sacrificed and for whom the traditions associating Abraham with Mecca and the rituals of the Hajj appear to be rooted in immemorial custom. Indeed, the conflicting details of the stories may be of interest only to scholars; ordinary Muslims no doubt learn whatever version is told in their community. And though the contradictory, even mutually exclusive accounts, may interest Muslim scholars, the contradictions may not overly trouble them. If the goal is primarily heuristic, and Muslim interest and concern are directed to the archetypal, exemplary model in the story, rather than to an ascertaining of the accuracy of the historical details, as Crow (1986:27) and others assert, then the details may be threads to elaborate rather than to unravel. Such a method may be an indication of a very different scholarly style and motivation.

Despite the fact that he is mentioned only twelve times in the Qur'an, Ishmael, son of Abraham by Hagar, is, in Muslim tradition, considered the ancestor of the Arabs. Apparently there is no mention of either of them in pre-Islamic Arab traditions. Although there is precedent for it in Jewish (and Christian) tradition, the creation of this genealogy for Arabs was apparently the work of Muhammad.[16] By this means, Muhammad created an identity for Arabs that was at once ethnic and religious. The earliest biography of Muhammad (Ibn Ishaq) traces his lineage back to Abraham via Ishmael and then back to Adam. By placing Muhammad in the sacred lineage, he was able to give a new direction to sacred history— for the "underlying claim of the text is that there is a new dispensation and a new line of inheritance" (Newby, 1989:66). Ibn Ishaq gives him a biological genealogy as well as the more prophetic one in which the divine light is bestowed by God to the chosen ones; it is in a sense a divine genealogy.[17] Once again we see the symbolic conflation of divinity, light, and seed—a connection also pointed out by Eliade (1971), who did not, however, draw out the assumptions about, and implications for, gender.

Kisa'i, a twelfth-century scholar who wrote an engaging "Tales of the Prophets," conflates the biological and prophetic genealogy. Abraham's father heard a voice say to him: "Your wife's youth has been restored to her that she may produce the brilliant light that is in your seed" (al-Kisa'i, 1978:136). As soon as they had completed the sexual act in which Abraham was conceived, a voice proclaimed: "There is no god but God alone who hath no partner" (ibid.). This is also what Abraham is said to have proclaimed at the moment of his birth (al-Kisa'i, 1978:137).

The divine light that is transmitted in the sacred lineage, as well as the precociousness of Abraham, reappears in the stories about Muhammad's birth, especially in a long poem, the *Mevlidi Serifi* by Suleyman Celebi (d. 1421). In Turkey it is traditionally recited forty days after a death and thereafter on the anniversary of a person's death (Delaney, 1991; Tapper and Tapper, 1987). In addition, by continually drawing attention to the fact that God has no partner, especially in reference to human procreative activity, I feel that Muslim interpreters do protest too much; I take it as a sign of interest in both the differences and similarities between procreation and creation.

Although Ishmael is rarely mentioned in the Qur'an, he is, today, the one most Muslims assume was the intended sacrifice. Yet a renowned Muslim scholar of the tenth century, Al-Tabari, notes: "The earliest sages of our Prophet's nation disagree about which of Abraham's two sons it was that he was commanded to sacrifice. Some say it was Isaac, while others say it was Ishmael" (Al-Tabari, [c. 915]1987:82). And he goes on to list those who have sided with one or the other. Firestone has searched a number of traditions in addition to Al-Tabari and says that when "all the traditions are collated we find a surprisingly close count. One hundred thirty authoritative statements consider Isaac to be the intended victim; one hundred thirty-three consider it to have been Ishmael" (Firestone, 1990:135).

The difference of opinion has to do primarily with the source of a particular tradition. Although all of these stories were collected by medieval Muslim scholars, many of them obviously pre-dated the Muslim era. Crow (1986) and others suggest that the ones that focus on Sarah and Isaac are pre-Islamic and that those focused on Hagar and Ishmael are Muslim. That does not mean, however, that everywhere in the Muslim world Ishmael has supplanted Isaac in the popular imagination. Westermarck noted in 1933 that some Moroccans still believed it was Isaac (cited in Firestone, 1990:151, n. 123). Ironically, the process of homogenization and unification progresses as the diverse traditions become better known through the spread of literacy and education.

One unusual story relates that the caliph ʿUmar, in the area of Syria quite close to Haran, the traditional home of Abraham, thought his Muslim companions were mistaken to think Ishmael was the intended sacrifice. So he called in a Jewish scholar, who allegedly had converted to Islam. He also seemed to have converted his former traditions. When asked which son Abraham was commanded to sacrifice, he answered: "Ishmael . . . the Jews know that, but they are envious of you, O Arabs, because it was your father who was named in God's command and to whom God ascribed such merit for his steadfastness in obeying God's command" (Al-Tabari, [c. 915]1987:88; cf. Newby, 1989:77).

Ishmael is presumed to be the intended sacrifice in part because of his association with Abraham in the building of the Kaʿba. Although there is just the merest mention of it in the Qurʾan—"And when Abraham and Ishmael were raising the foundations of the House . . ." (Qurʾan, 2: 127)—that part of the Abraham legend is elaborated in the stories. But we must back up a bit and say a little more about some of the main features of Abraham's life as recounted in Muslim tradition, in order to see where some of the various pieces fit.

ABRAHAM'S CHARACTER

Abraham was born in Mesopotamia, specified in some versions as Kufah in what is now southern Iraq, during the reign of Nimrod of Babylon. Nimrod was given an oracle that a boy born in his time would grow up and break the idols of his religion and thus his rule. So he had all the newborn boys slaughtered—all except Abraham whose mother hid him in a cave. Similar oracle motifs, and attempts to thwart them by Pharaoh and Herod, are found in the birth narratives of Moses and Jesus.[18] Whether these motifs were transferred to Abraham or whether he was the source of them, I do not know; in any case, they can be used by Muslims to show that his birth and his trials prefigure those of Moses, Jesus, and Muhammad.

Abraham's iconoclasm is well known in both Jewish midrash and Muslim legend. His father was supposedly a maker of idols. Abraham was even thought to have peddled them, but he knew they were worthless. One day he went to the factory and smashed all but the largest, and into its hand Abraham put the ax so it would appear that the great idol had smashed the others. When questioned about the destruction he said: "Ask them," referring to the idols. The interrogators said: "But they cannot speak." Abraham made his point: "Then why do you worship them?"

Muhammad is also said to have smashed the idols—in Mecca. In pre-Islamic Arabia, this city had been a traditional pilgrimage site for the various tribes who came to worship there. Mecca was the home of numerous idols, some say as many as three hundred sixty, but the most famous were the three female deities, al-Lat, al-Uzza, and Manat, who are named in the Qur'an (53:19–20).[19] In this and in a number of other ways Muhammad is clearly being assimilated into the model and figure of Abraham. Whether Muhammad consciously modeled himself after him is impossible to know, but after his night journey (mir'aj) to heaven, where he met the other prophets, including Abraham, he is thought to have said: "I have never seen a man more like myself than Abraham" (Newby, 1989:19).[20] The elaborations of their lives in stories and legends show so many parallels and overlaps that it is often difficult to keep them apart.

Abraham's monotheism was apparently the product of deduction, crystallized when he realized that the luminaries he had worshipped—the stars, the moon, and even the sun—set. "Lo! I have turned my face toward him Who created the heavens and the earth, as one by nature upright, and I am not of the idolaters" (Qur'an 6:80). Abraham's astronomical knowledge may have been attributed to him because of the existence of an observatory at Haran (see fig. 10). As in biblical tradition, Haran is alleged to be Abraham's home or at least a major stopping place on his hijra that ultimately took him to Mecca. Hijra means emigration and is most often used in reference to Muhammad's departure from Mecca to Medina in A.D. 622. It is the date that begins the Muslim calendar. Year one A.H. (after Hijra) is not the date of either the birth or death of Muhammad but of the departure of the faithful from the city in which it had become impossible to practice their faith; thus it also represents the consolidation of the first faithful Muslim community in Medina. Hijra can be used today to legitimate a person's or people's emigration from a land of disbelief.[21]

FIG. 10. Remains of the observatory at Haran, Turkey. Photo by author.

FIG. 11. Pool near the Ibrahim *cami* in Urfa, Turkey. Photo by author.

Abraham's proclamation of the one God brought him into open conflict with Nimrod. When he was about forty, Gabriel descended to him
and told him he must fight Nimrod. Abraham was the same age as
Muhammad when the same angel, Gabriel, appeared to him. Abraham
shouted out: "O people! Say that there is no god but God and that I,
Abraham, am God's apostle" (al-Kisa'i, 1978:142). This is similar to
what is claimed for Muhammad in the confession of faith: "There is no
god but God and Muhammad is his Messenger." Nimrod attempted to
cast Abraham into the fiery furnace and so do away with him. Because of
his steadfast belief, however, God protected him. Numerous legends
place this event near Haran. These legends are still very much alive in
Urfa, a town near Haran, where people told me that the pit of fire turned
into a pool of cool water and the embers into goldfish. Today these sacred fish are still being fed in the beautiful pool near the Ibrahim *cami*
(mosque). (See figs. 11 and 12.)

Abraham married Sarah, the daughter of his paternal uncle, not his
half-sister as in the biblical account (see Firestone, 1990:29). The biblical
stories of her barrenness and of her giving Hagar, her handmaid, to Abraham are also common in Islam. So too is the story in which Abraham
casts out Hagar and Ishmael. In the biblical account the destination is
unknown, whereas in some of the best-known Muslim accounts, Abraham accompanies them to Mecca and helps to settle them there. Not only
does this feature perform a valuable exegetical function, joining the bibli-

FIG. 12. Painting depicting legends relating to Abraham. Urfa, Turkey.
Photo by author.

cal-Syrian aspect of the story with the Muslim-Mecca aspects, it also adds
a more compassionate element to Abraham's character than the one portrayed in the Genesis account. Nevertheless, Hagar and Ishmael are still
left to fend for themselves in desert country. The story of Hagar's frantic
search for water has been memorialized in a ritual of the Hajj whereby
pilgrims run between al-Safa and al-Marwah, desirous of drinking from
the well of Zamzam and taking some of it home for their relatives and
friends.

Although Abraham must return to Sarah in Syria he often visits Hagar
and Ishmael in Mecca. In some traditions, al-Kisa'i for instance, Ishmael
grows up and marries, and Hagar dies, all before the building of the
Ka'ba. One popular theme in a number of traditions is Abraham's view
of Ishmael's wife. When Abraham arrives at Ishmael's home, he is out
hunting. His wife is inhospitable to Abraham and offers him neither food
nor water. He leaves a message for his son: "Change the threshold of your
house," meaning "get rid of this woman"; the message also confirms my
belief that *threshold* or *gate* can refer to female genitals. The next time
Abraham visits, he finds a different woman. She invites him in, offers

food and water, and washes his head or, in some versions, anoints it with oil. Some suggest that while this was done he stood on a stone that was called the *Maqam Ibrahim* because his footprint became imprinted in it (cf. Firestone, 1990:77)—a tradition that, as we shall see, conflicts with the one that places the Maqam Ibrahim next to the Kaʿba. Abraham is pleased with the new wife and tells her to inform Ishmael that "his threshold is sound." On the third and last visit of Abraham to Ishmael, the al-Kisaʾi tale recounts the story of the building of the Kaʿba, after which Ishmael is said to live and prosper for one hundred thirty-seven years. Only in a later chapter is the sacrifice story told; it occurs in Syria and the son to be sacrificed is Isaac.

In the reconstructed account of Ibn Ishaq, felt to be one of the earliest collections of tales within a biography of Muhammad, the sacrifice occurs in Mecca, the intended victim is Ishmael, and the event occurs after the building of the Kaʿba and the institution of the pilgrimage. After Ishmael is redeemed by the animal sacrifice, he goes on to marry. The details may not matter much; indeed al-Tabari includes them all! What is important are the various elements—the building of the Kaʿba, the pilgrimage, and the sacrifice. No doubt the desire to transpose them to Mecca is motivated by a desire to distinguish and reinforce the specifically Muslim character of the traditions.

When Abraham visits his Meccan family, he allegedly is transported by the miraculous horse, Buraq. Much later, the same miraculous horse is said to have transported Muhammad from Mecca to Jerusalem for the night journey (*mirʾaj*). The ascension is said to have taken place on the former site of the Jewish temple, the site that, in other legends, is said to be the one where Abraham attempted to sacrifice his son.[22] This extraordinarily sacred spot for both Muslims and Jews (as well as for Christians) is now covered by the Muslim shrine, al Haram al Sharif, also known as the Dome of the Rock (see fig. 13). At the beginning of his mission, Muhammad had Muslims orient their prayers toward Jerusalem rather than Mecca. Only after rebuilding and purifying the Kaʿba was the direction changed.

ABRAHAM, MUHAMMAD, AND THE KAʿBA

When Muhammad rebuilt the Kaʿba he reenacted Abraham's deed. Abraham was ordered to build God's "house" (temple) and was shown the way by the Sakina (related to Hebrew Shekhina), a two-headed wind that could speak or, in other versions, coiled up around the spot where the first temple had been. When Abraham brushed off the sand that had covered it up, he revealed the stone of the original temple—that which Adam

FIG. 13. The Dome of the Rock (al Haram al Sharif). Jerusalem, Israel.
Photo by Sandra Razieli.

had built. Some versions claim it was where God left his print. During the
flood the Ka'ba was taken up to heaven where the angels flitted about it,
as the circumambulation by pilgrims is meant to replicate.

Upon that spot Abraham and Ishmael raised the foundations of the
Ka'ba. When Abraham got tired or had to reach too high, Ishmael
brought a stone for him to stand on; it is now known as the *Maqam Ibrahim* for the footprint Abraham left on it. In a number of the building
stories Ishmael comes off as somewhat incompetent and Abraham somewhat impatient. When Ishmael was sent to find the cornerstone, he could
not find one, or the one he found was not good enough, or he was too
late, and Abraham berated him and said, "God would not entrust such a
thing to you, my boy!"

The Black Stone, nestled in the Ka'ba, is not the *Maqam Ibrahim*; it is
said by some to be the eye of God; alternatively it is his hand, which
blesses all who touch it—reason enough that all pilgrims to Mecca en-
deavor to touch or kiss it. It is also alleged that it is the only relic to have
come down from the time of Adam, and that it was originally white and
contained the voices (souls) of all the living.[23]

One version claims that Gabriel brought a white sapphire from India, which Adam had brought down from Heaven, but the sapphire turned black, either because women menstruated over it or because of the sins of mankind (Firestone, 1990:87; for other excellent accounts of legends about the Black Stone, see Esin, 1963, and Lazarus-Yafeh, 1981). The Black Stone is today encased in a frame of silver which, to me, has the appearance of a vagina complete with labial folds. I was unaware that anyone else made this association until I spoke with several people who had recently made the Hajj and who independently told me of their associations. Whether the majority are of the same opinion I do not know. Nevertheless, the belief that it turned black because of menstrual blood supports such a view. The female symbolism of the Ka'ba has also been noted by Lazarus-Yafeh (1981:30), who cites several texts in which the Ka'ba is imaged as a bride who, on Judgment Day, will be led to her wedding; those who are able to catch hold of her covers will enter Paradise with her. The *kiswa* or covering of the Ka'ba is referred to as its veil. Extending out from the Black Stone and the Ka'ba, Mecca is felt to be the "mother of towns," the first dry ground floating upon the waters from which the rest of the earth spread out.[24]

After the Ka'ba was restored, a number of stories allege that Abraham had a vision telling him to sacrifice his son. The fact that Ishmael had helped him build it is taken by some as evidence that he was the son to be sacrificed. It is also evidence that he had reached the "time of running"— that is, of being able to help Abraham with his work. In other versions, however, and not necessarily the earliest, the vision occurs in Syria and the son is Isaac (see for example, al-Kisa'i, 1978:160–62); in still others the intended sacrifice is said to occur either in Jerusalem, perhaps at the site that, in Jewish tradition, is associated with the site of the ancient temple or, if near Jerusalem, perhaps in the vicinity of the Valley of Hinnom.[25]

As in Jewish midrash, there is also, in Muslim legend, the story of Satan trying to dissuade Abraham from his horrible deed and, as in the Jewish case, he gets nowhere. Ishmael is represented as obedient and willing—the perfect model of the perfect sacrifice. But, just as in Jewish midrash, there are hints that he was anxious:

> make my bonds fast, for if death is hard, I do not believe I will be able to endure it when I feel death's touch. Hone your knife so that you can finish me off and release me. When you lay me down to sacrifice me, lay me on my face; do not lay me on my side, for I fear that if you look at my face, you will turn soft and abandon the command of God. If you wish, *return my shirt to my mother*, for it might be a consolation to her. (Newby, 1989:78, emphasis added)

Reading that part of the story, I was reminded of the shirt Cristos Valenti gave his mother (via his lawyer) every day and of the fresh one she handed back to him.

God is said to have turned the knife to its blunt side, to have pushed it away and indicated what was to be sacrificed instead. Muslim art shows a ram being led or held by an angel, usually said to be Gabriel (Jibril).[26] The Muslim story al-Kisa'i tells replicates the Jewish midrash whereby the ram is "the ram of Abel son of Adam, which he sacrificed to his Lord and which He accepted. I have grazed in the meadows of Paradise for forty autumns" (al-Kisa'i, 1978:162).

HAJJ[27]

When Abraham had completed building the Ka'ba, he was commanded to go to the top of a nearby hill and call all humankind to the pilgrimage. His voice was said to have been amplified so that it was heard all over the earth. This may be the origin of the Muslim idea that originally all peoples had true religion but some forgot. But "Everyone who makes the Pilgrimage is today of those who answered Abraham" (Newby, 1989: 75).

Muhammad's role in establishing the pilgrimage is pretty well effaced; in this perception he has become merely the conduit for reinstating the original pilgrimage instituted by Abraham. That pilgrimage, according to Muhammad, had fallen into disuse and, over time, had been distorted by the Arab tribes who made a pilgrimage to Mecca for the purpose of worshipping their idols. Whether by divine inspiration or clever strategy, Muhammad's reinterpretation of this pilgrimage as a distortion of the ancient pilgrimage instituted by Abraham, rhetorically, at least, subsumed the Arab tribes in his plan. It did not allow for a separate and different religion; they were cast as infidels rejecting the true faith. Only after consolidating the Muslim community at Medina did Muhammad revisit Mecca. It was then that he was said to have cleansed the temple area of idols, rebuilt the Ka'ba, and declared thereafter the Hajj. Muhammad made a pilgrimage back to his home, but he never again returned there to live.

In making the Hajj, then, pilgrims not only fulfill one of the obligations of faith incumbent upon all who are financially and physically able, they also simultaneously make a journey to the center of faith (cf. Turner, 1972–73). Mecca represents an image of their ultimate home, for Mecca is the *axis mundi*, felt to be the city nearest to heaven. It is an earthly mirror reflecting their heavenly home.[28] Making the Hajj is meant to be the ultimate expression of a life of faith, regardless of the other reasons a particular person has for undertaking it and regardless of its other benefits. By following in the footsteps not just of Muhammad but also of Abraham, they signify, at least in theory, a devotion reminiscent of Abraham's.

Muhammad inscribed a number of these legendary events into the rituals of the Hajj and thereby inscribed them into the lives of Muslims. Those who actually go on the Hajj have already learned by heart the myth and the ritual: they circumambulate the Kaʿba seven times counterclockwise, as the angels are said to circulate around the Throne of God; they pray on the Maqam Ibrahim; they touch or kiss the Black Stone nestled in its corner. They run between al-Safa and al-Marwah remembering the distraught Hagar seeking water for her son. They stone three pillars in Mina to remind them of Satan's attempt to divert Abraham from his duty (others say the three pillars represent the three pre-Islamic goddesses, see above); they stand on the plain of ʿArafat from noon to sunset and praise God. Finally, at the end of the Hajj, the rituals culminate in the Feast of the Sacrifice, when each male head of household sacrifices a ram (or substitute) as Abraham did. In Mecca hundreds of thousands of animals are slaughtered; but because the sacrifice is replicated throughout the Muslim world, it becomes the mimetic means by which Muslims everywhere are joined in a community of faith as well as blood.

Abraham as Model

Abraham is the exemplary model, the quintessential model of a man of faith. Muhammad clearly drew upon (or constructed) this model to pattern his own behavior and beliefs. In stepping into the footsteps of an archetypal figure, however, Muhammad tends to merge his personality with that of Abraham, or perhaps Abraham's tends to merge with Muhammad's. What each may lose in distinctness they gain in the combined power of their mission. Although Muhammad clearly had a major part in shaping Islam, he is cast merely as the Messenger, the instrument for transmitting or revealing the original message given to Abraham. As Muhammad attempted to insert himself into the mythic pattern, the sacred precedent, so too do others attempt to model their behavior and beliefs upon the *sunna* (behavior) of the Prophet. His character and behavior, as recorded in the *hadith* and tales, are the basis for daily life as well as the law, *shariʿa*. All Muslims should be following the model laid down not just by Muhammad but by Abraham.

Yet the model is clearly a male model. Only males can legitimately step into it, and only males are participants in the sacrifice. It may be true that the ritual establishes a community of faith and blood, but that identity is performed and transmitted by men. This, I believe, is not an incidental detail but at the heart of the sacrifice. It is both similar and dissimilar to the Christian Eucharist for which, traditionally, only a male priest (or minister) could perform the ritual and transmit the sacred power. That power, it is believed, has been transmitted only in a consecrated line of males that began with the Apostles. In Christianity, sacred power is held by the few. In Islam, each and every male head of household can himself have intercourse with the sacred when he performs the sacrifice that substitutes for and symbolizes Abraham's son, an act that ritually enacts and reinforces patriarchal power.

The implications of the story and model are worked out in somewhat different ways in various Muslim communities (cf. Bowen, 1992). Perhaps nowhere is the story so elaborated as in Morocco. "For Muslims, the myth of Ibrahim is humanity's archetypal interaction with God, an awesome act involving awesome players" (Combs-Schilling, 1989:248). There an innovation has been introduced into the ritual. About three hundred years ago the monarchs of the "ʿAlawi dynasty began the practice of having the blood-descendant king sacrifice a ram on behalf of the community of believers as a whole" (ibid.:222). By means of this dramatic innovation (which for some approaches blasphemy) the "monarchs became the sacrificial link between God and nation, the means by which God could see the collectivity's faith and grant his favor. Through the performance, the Moroccan monarchs inserted themselves into the single most powerful canonical ritual in Islam and into the mythic foundations upon which it rests" (ibid.). When the king slits the throat of the ram on behalf of the people, he becomes an intervening link or mediator between the people and, through Muhammad and Abraham, ultimately, God. Conversely, he becomes the vehicle that channels creative power to earth. He places himself in the line that begins with Abraham, goes through Muhammad, and then passes down to each head of household—a patriline that transmits sacred power. The king becomes both the symbolic representative of the community and its link to transcendence. In this way the performance of the Great Sacrifice becomes "the most powerful ritual support of the Moroccan monarchy" (ibid.:223). But it does much more than that.

It also reaffirms patriarchal power by means of the metaphorical equivalence—between the highest and lowest males—established in the ritual. In the ritual, "the identity of the king is intermingled with that of the household heads. . . . For individual heads of households to undercut the authority of the overarching ruler would be to undercut their own power base" (ibid.:252).

The patriarchal power inherent in the Great Sacrifice is also reenacted and reinforced during the wedding ceremonies of a first marriage, which,

Combs-Schilling claims, is metaphorically equivalent and helps to bring out the sexual and gender-based elements in the ritual.[29] The symbolic parallels she draws accord, to a great extent, with what I observed in Turkey, and are no doubt common in much of the Muslim world.[30] In Morocco, however, the bridegroom becomes not just a generic "king for a day," he becomes symbolically the embodiment of "the Moroccan king, the blood descendant of Muhammad who reigns from Morocco's throne" (ibid.:190). The bridegroom does not embody the living ruler so much as what the ruler symbolizes: (pro-)creativity.

A similar meaning is conveyed in Turkish wedding festivities (Delaney, 1991:86, 140) and these, in turn, are connected to the symbols, ceremonies, and practices related to circumcision. Circumcision is the event that initiates the boy into manhood and symbolizes his potential to reproduce; it also simultaneously initiates him into the Muslim brotherhood. The same word, *düğün*, is used for both the circumcision and the wedding festivities. In addition, a phrase, *mürüvvet görmek* (to see the good day of your child), is said to the parents of the boy on the occasion of his circumcision as well as to the parents of the wedding couple. *Mürüvvet* means abundance, munificence, possibly also manliness, but it implies reproductive wealth, symbolized by the coins thrown at the wedding.

The innovation in the Moroccan marriage ritual may have come about during the reign of Mawlay Isma'il, for apparently his "reproductive prowess was unparalleled" (Combs-Schilling, 1989:191); he is said to have produced seven hundred sons.[31] The monarch's creative role is linked to procreative power, which, she suggests, is symbolized by the sword. When they "wish their leader good luck and hope that he is girded with a sufficiently powerful sword so that creation can begin" (ibid.:194), they are referring simultaneously to the sword that protects the people and the other "sword," or phallus, that creates them. The image of the sword figures in the sayings and songs recited during the wedding rituals. I found similar imagery, although not so pronounced, in Turkey (Delaney, 1991:138ff.).

As the previously subservient young male is transformed into the phallic king, the young woman is transformed into a passive bride. With her white gown and eyes rimmed in black, just like the sacrificial ram, she is laid on the bed where the bridegroom "enters, and in an act of some violence, he forces his way into her, causing the lifeblood to flow" (Combs-Schilling, 1989:188). The bloody sheet is often displayed after this act of intercourse. If no blood flows, it is assumed she is not a virgin, and she can be slain, in which case she would become the literal sacrifice. Although this does not happen often, it does happen.[32]

In the Moroccan wedding ceremony, the bride has come to symbolize the ram sacrificed in lieu of the son—that is, an equivalence has been established between the son, the ram, and the bride. Although the gender difference is notable, the hierarchical structure is maintained—as a man (even a king) must submit to God, and a son to his father, so should a woman to her husband. We might also recall that in the Bible, Israel is referred to both as God's firstborn son and as his bride.

In any case, the idea that the girl could be punished unto death for her transgression serves as a powerful sword held over her head. Through the spilling of the woman's blood at first intercourse, the man controls the powers of life and death; through intercourse he will produce children that will continue the "earthly community of Muslims through the regeneration of men's patrilines on earth" (ibid.:205). Procreation, Combs-Schilling claims, is for the glory of God. Before sacrificing, and at the moment of ejaculation during sexual intercourse, a man should call out the name of God, the "Bi'smi'llah." She argues that sacrifice by the knife is mimetic to sexual intercourse, with the male taking the role of the actor in each case. In turn, by modeling itself on the actions that bring about life in this world, sacrifice becomes a symbolic pathway to eternal life.

Combs-Schilling has given a rich and convincing account of the meaning of blood sacrifice in Moroccan Islam and its relation to the story of Abraham. Nevertheless, she, like Jay, assumes, rather than challenges, the meaning of paternity. Despite the plethora of evidence regarding its meaning as creativity, she does not use that to examine its constructedness within a theory of procreation and, thus, loses an opportunity to reevaluate the meanings of paternity, maternity, and (the imagined lack of) female generativity. In her book she, like Jay, assumes procreation has to do primarily with biology, with the natural, and insists on maintaining a strict distinction between the world of nature (biology) and the divine realm. But this distinction is, itself, part of the gendered conception of the world that is, I suggest, intimately related to the theory of procreation I have been discussing. In this theory, let us recall, it is the male who imparts the divine spark of life while the female represents and contributes the material nature—and this is *not* just a theory of biology.

FROM SACRED TO SECULAR

Although we tend to think about procreation primarily, if not exclusively, as a biological, natural event that has little to do with culture and even less with the divine, that context is not adequate, for it cannot explain the valuations of the roles of each gender nor their symbolic elaboration in other contexts. While certain physiological processes are universal, the way they are conceptualized varies considerably. Western cultures have elaborated an integrated system wherein creativity, imagined as masculine in character, is the connecting link between the divine and human worlds. Procreation is not just about biology and the natural, since the male's contribution (seed) has been imagined as the conduit for the divine; his is the creative role that bestows life and identity. Only women's role as providing the nurturant material has been imagined as within the realm of the natural. Creation and procreation are not separate, but are deeply interconnected.

A different way of conceptualizing procreation, therefore, demands a different way of conceptualizing both the spiritual world and the natural world—in short, a different cosmology or world view. In the monotheistic cosmology, there is only one principle of creation, symbolically masculine, and it is manifest on both human and divine planes. Monotheism and monogenesis constitute one integrated and mutually reinforcing system. And in this system, the story of Abraham is central.

Because Islam is conceptualized as a return or recall to the one, true, original religion given in the beginning to Abraham, his story may be more actively present in Islam than in either Judaism or Christianity. That is especially true when, annually, a man sacrifices an animal in commemoration of the ram sacrificed in place of his son; but it is also true as pilgrims retrace his footsteps and reenact some of the dramas of his life that have become part of the rituals of the Hajj.

In all three monotheisms, however, the story has been a primary structuring force and a powerful influence on human psychology and the dynamics of history. On the psychological level, it has figured in notions of faith and steadfastness, sacrifice and love, authority and obedience, gender and family relations. On the stage of history, it figures in conflicts over territory, cities, and shrines that continue to this day. These conflicts are as volatile and violent as they are (and can easily become more so) because they ultimately return to the question of who *is* the true seed of Abraham, who *is* the true heir and, therefore, who has the right to the patrimony. It would be a great step toward peace if these "sons" could acknowledge their joint claims and agree to work out ways to share it. But it would be a much greater step if they could recognize the assumptions about gender and procreation without which the story and all its consequences could not make sense. Then the choice becomes clearer: can we allow new stories, new social arrangements, new values to emerge, or will some continue to demand, despite the bloodshed and the inequalities, a return to these older values and structures?

In the next section I focus on one of the ways some of these values and structures have become secularized and seen as part of the human condition rather than the outcome of particular historical, theosocial systems. Freudian psychoanalysis has been another powerful mode of interpretation of human behavior and the dynamics of history, and, again, the dynamics turn on the relations of sons and fathers. Oddly, Freud did not explore or include as integral to this theory either the relation of fathers to their sons or, more important, how the meaning of *father* is partly responsible for the dynamics. In chapter 8 I will show how Freud assumed, but did not examine, a particular notion of paternity and how this systemic neglect bequeathed a distorted and incomplete vision of gender, the family, and the motive of history. In chapter 9 I critically analyze the work of some of his followers who have tried to correct his blind spot and thereby salvage his theory.

PART FOUR

The Testimony of

Psychoanalysis

CHAPTER EIGHT

Freud's Blind Spot

THE STORIES in the Bible and the Qur'an have had, and continue to have, an enormous impact on human psychology and society. They affect the way we live and what we value. In a very broad sense they are the myths we live by, whether in specifically religious contexts or as they have been transformed into secular narratives. It is all the more curious, then, that Freud—the great mythmaker of modern times—passed over a biblical story in favor of a Greek myth as the paradigm of human psychology and society, especially when he admitted that biblical stories had had a profound effect on him.[1]

Drawing on the ancient Greek myth of Oedipus, he created a modern analogue that he felt explained both individual and social dynamics. For him, it represented the foundation of society and something ever-present in the human condition. Today, it is a myth by means of which many people interpret their lives—not only through the process of psychoanalysis but also because of its diffusion into popular culture. And yet there is a glaring *scotoma* or blind spot.[2] Freud focused primarily on the son, and the son's feelings and relation to the father, and gave little attention to the father, and the father's feelings toward the son. This exclusive focus seems to have blinded him to the importance of including the father in his theoretical frame. Moreover, it prevented him from seeing that the meaning of *son* is constituted in relation to that of *father* and vice versa. Freud's neglect is systemic, not a minor oversight but a major distortion that has far-reaching implications for his theory, and ours—about the person, about religion, and about the nature of culture. In Freud's theory and practice, the father is unassailable; his absence is omnipresent but invisible, analogous to that of the father God. His absence serves to reify and reinforce patriarchy.

Although the dominant myth in Freud's work is Oedipus, toward the end of life he turned to the biblical story of Moses. In this chapter, I continue the exploration of monotheism, Abraham, and fatherhood, oddly enough, through an analysis of Freud's *Moses and Monotheism*. The question that began my investigation is really quite simple—even absurdly so. Why did Freud focus on *Moses* and monotheism rather than on Abraham? Abraham, not Moses, is traditionally the man associated with monotheism in all three monotheistic religions—Judaism, Christianity, and Islam.[3] The more I investigate *Moses and Monotheism*, the more that question cries out. Why did Freud fabricate a story out of whole cloth, as it were, about the symbolic sons killing their father instead of using and analyzing the story that is actually *in* the biblical text—that of a father willing to kill his son if God demanded? Why did he ignore the biblical text and substitute his own version? What did his substitution reveal? Although Freud may have thought the tradition was a distorting screen through which one could see only dimly the "real, true" events, his normal method would have been to analyze the manifest content as a means to arrive at the underlying, latent meaning. In this case, he changed the manifest content, the tradition.

The book is flawed historically and theoretically; it is not written in his pellucid style, and it is extremely repetitive. That, in itself, is significant, at least according to Freud, for he felt that repetitions often pointed to an unresolved issue of obsessive concern. This was Freud's last major study, as he himself seemed to be aware; it presented him with an opportunity to reflect on his life's work as well as to revise some of the more discredited ideas and concepts developed in *Totem and Taboo* on which *Moses and Monotheism* depended. Instead, he repeated and reinforced them, vigorously.

Rather than viewing *Moses and Monotheism* as an embarrassement, as evidence of Freud's advancing age, as many did when it first appeared, or as a personal, though veiled statement about his Jewishness or about his relationship with his father, as more recent scholarship proposes,[4] I suggest it is a key to his entire corpus. It is the culmination and integration of some of his major ideas—the Oedipus complex, the transmission of cultural memory, the correlation between individual and cultural development—directed in this instance to an investigation of the psychological underpinnings of the society in which he lived. It should be taken seriously if for no other reason than that Freud took it seriously.

It may never be possible to know exactly why Freud neglected the Abraham story, and this glaring oversight may ultimately relate to Freud's Jewishness or to his father complex. I am not suggesting it was purposeful; on the contrary, a blind spot is something one is not generally aware of. Nor is it my purpose to psychoanalyze Freud, even though I do occasionally speculate about his personal motivations. If, as I believe, *Moses and Monotheism* is a key to his entire corpus, it also, inadvertently, provides the key for questioning these ideas.

My investigation does not depend on searching for new, or as yet un-discovered, external evidence for some clues that will help to answer my initial question. For me, the clues are internal; they lie scattered throughout his work. Following Freud's example, I pay close attention not just to what he says but also to what he leaves unsaid, and I ask questions that he himself might easily have asked. If, as he notes in *Moses and Monotheism*, distortions in a text are like a murder,[5] what did he (try to) cover up and why? He has not covered his tracks very well, as he himself admitted (Freud, 1939:52, SE 23:43). What do the "striking omissions, disturbing repetitions, palpable contradictions" (ibid.) reveal? Where do they lead us?

The striking omission of Abraham, like Ariadne's thread, leads into the labyrinth of Freud's thought and to a major theme at the very heart of his work. Hidden away, ignored, neglected (dare I say repressed?), this theme could be considered the dark, unanalyzed side of the Oedipus complex. The Abraham story is more about the father than the son, about the father's willingness to kill the son, whereas in Freud's interpretation of the Oedipus drama, the focus is on the son and his killing of the father. Freud then uses that story as a means to talk about unconscious desires that he claims are universal. Oedipus's "destiny moves us only because it might have been ours—because the oracle laid the same curse upon us before our birth as upon him. It is the fate of all of us, perhaps, to direct our first sexual impulse towards our mother and our first hatred and our first murderous wish against our father" (Freud, SE 4:262). Does this really refer to all of us or only to males? If the latter, the complex cannot be considered universal. In addition, Oedipus did not know, at first, that it was his father he had killed (or, for that matter, that it was his mother he had married); the son's murderous wish as well as his incestuous sexual desire is Freud's idea, Freud's addition to the myth.

The first murderous wish *in* the myth belonged to the father. Anyone familiar with the Oedipus myth, and Freud surely was, for he wrote a paper on it while at the Gymnasion, knows that Laius, the father of Oedipus, first tried to get rid of his son; indeed that was the act that set the drama in motion. Laius pierced Oedipus's foot with a nail—the name *Oedipus* means swollen foot—and abandoned him or, in some versions, gave him to a servant to dispose of. Yet Freud puts the action in the passive voice (Oedipus was abandoned), concealing the father's active role.[6] Perhaps it is the father's murderous wishes that activate them in the son; at the very least, they ought to be considered relationally. But in his psychological interpretation and use of the myth, Freud did not develop a theory in which the actions and wishes of father and son are interrelated. It is not that the father is absent, he is simply not implicated or interrogated.[7] As Freud ignored the role of the father in the Greek drama so, too, did he ignore it in the Bible.

Instead of using the story of Abraham to question and perhaps revise his earlier ideas, he used his earlier ideas as the framework to construct his own version of the biblical myth. *Moses and Monotheism* was the culmination of Freud's more general theory of religion and society, the final chapter, so to speak, of the book he had written twenty-five years earlier, *Totem and Taboo*. In order to fully understand *Moses and Monotheism*, it is necessary to recapitulate the thesis of *Totem and Taboo*.[8]

Totem and Taboo (1913) was Freud's first foray into anthropology; he drew upon (certain) anthropological sources[9] and wished to make a contribution to theory about the origin of religion, morals, and social organization.[10] Freud was deeply concerned about origins and in this he was much closer to his nineteenth-century forebears than to his contemporary theorists (see chapter 1). Like them, Freud thought that a specific type of religion, in this case monotheism, would have its roots in the origin of religion itself, and that is what he set out to discover in *Totem and Taboo*. Like his nineteenth-century predecessors, he thought the origin of religion could be found in what was considered the most primitive religion known, that of the Australian aborigines, for there we might discern "a well-preserved picture of an early stage of our own development" (Freud, SE 13:1).[11]

Using texts of Darwin, Atkinson, and Robertson Smith, Freud constructed his own origin myth. Freud's equivalent of Genesis, his origin story, begins not with the Word but with the Deed and, unlike Genesis, this assertion, taken from Goethe's *Faust*, is the last line rather than the first in the book: "In the beginning was the Deed" (Freud, SE 13:161).

FREUD'S ORIGIN MYTH

The story in essence is as follows: Once upon a time there was "a violent and jealous father who keeps all the females for himself and drives away his sons as they grow up. . . . One day the brothers who had been driven out came together, killed and devoured their father, and so made an end of the patriarchal horde" (Freud, SE 13:141, and repeated in Freud, 1939:102–3 [SE 23:81]).

In order that the sons not have this overthrow repeated against themselves, they formed what Freud considered *the* social contract, in which they: (1) renounced their rights to all of the women hoarded by their father, (2) began the first communal society based on laws, (3) set up a taboo on murder, and (4) began to worship the totem surrogate for the father.[12] In this way, "The dead father became stronger than the living one had been. . . . They could attempt, in their relation to this surrogate father, to allay their burning sense of guilt, to bring about a kind of reconciliation with their father" (Freud, SE 13:143–4).

It is a good story and it makes sense, especially because acceptance has been prepared by the web of associations that Freud has built up in the preceding chapters on incest, totemism, ambivalence, and taboo. The associations and evidence begin to unravel, however, as soon as the story is subjected to an anthropological critique. Yet even then, I believe the most obvious and most important problems remain unseen, perhaps precisely because they are so transparent, so much a part of his and our common-sense assumptions—the myth we live by. An excellent summary of the anthropological response already exists, so I shall not attempt to recapitulate it here except where it becomes relevant to my critique.[13] In what follows I take up each point of his story in turn.

"*A violent and jealous father.*" Here, Freud assumes that violence, at least among males, is a primary instinct and that it is tied to male sexual jealousy. It should more appropriately be called "innate male sexual greed," for the desire to possess and hoard all the women is taken for granted as self-evident. Aggression and sexuality do combine in his notion of *libido* or active sexuality, which Freud characterized as masculine regardless of whether it was displayed by men or women. In addition, and rather surprisingly given Freud's own ideas about the polymorphous nature of human sexuality, there is an assumption of innate heterosexuality—for each of the sons "would have wished, like his father, to have all the women to himself" (ibid.:144). Perhaps Freud took heterosexuality for granted in this case because he thought it was the most "natural" society, that is, the closest to nature; still, this assumption contradicts his belief that such a society would not yet have instituted repressions necessary for the dominance of heterosexuality. Curiously, he does not consider the supposedly frustrating situation of the sons as a possible reason for the development of homosexuality.

Others such as Marx and Engels have argued that sexual jealousy is related to a desire to ensure children of undisputed paternity. Although Freud does not speak of sexual jealousy in these terms, I believe it is an unexamined assumption in his theory.

"*Who keeps all the women to himself.*" Few question Freud's silly idea that the primal male could have kept all the females to himself even if he wanted to.[14] Freud assumed that the primal father was so powerful that he could subdue the women and keep the sons at bay until he drove them away. This goes against all common sense: (a) What could have prevented the women from fleeing? Does the assumption of male power mask another, unstated assumption of primal, essential female passivity and immobility? (b) On the other hand, if the primal father had helpers in

keeping a rein on his harem, who and where were they? (c) In all proba-
bility, the sons were stronger than the father; surely, together, they could
have overpowered him—as indeed, they eventually did. (d) The sons
might also have joined forces with the women and together plotted to do
away with the tyrant. This solution would have involved women in the
deed. Greek mythology includes several well-known examples of this sce-
nario—Cronos plots with his mother to castrate the father and, later,
Zeus plots with his mother to overcome the father. Freud knew of these
examples, for he refers to them in other contexts (e.g., Freud, SE 4:256,
SE 5:619).

The sons could also have taken foreign women, as they did after the
murder. What prevented them from doing that earlier, especially given
their supposedly insatiable desire? What was so special about those particular women? If Freud presupposed the erotic attachments of the sons to
their mothers, he needed to say more about the basis of that assumption—are the attachments in this case "natural," or are they possibly provoked by the behavior of the father? Would the jealous father have permitted such erotic attachments to develop?

If the father was so threatened by the sons, and if he was so powerful,
why did he wait until the sons had grown up to drive them away? He
could simply have killed them off when they were born. This theme, too,
figures in Greek mythology. In this case, perhaps Freud thought Greek
mythology was not applicable, because the primal family was not quite
human; indeed, it was the murder of the father and its consequences that
he felt ushered in full humanity.[15] On the other hand, if fathers' murderous wishes are included in Greek mythology, why are they not also useful
for considering the mental endowments of humanity? Why is the myth of
Oedipus, alone, so considered and, even then, only the story of the son's
(not the father's) murderous wishes? If primitives were cannibals as Freud
believed, why didn't the father simply gobble up his sons as they were
born?

*"One day the brothers who had been driven out [of the horde] came
together, killed and devoured their father. . . . United they had the courage to do and succeeded in doing what would have been impossible for
them individually"* (Freud, SE 13:141). But what had prevented them
from uniting *in* the horde? Of course, getting together for a common purpose presupposes language and society, and Freud even presupposes
some cultural or technical advance that would have given them the sense
of power necessary to do the deed. Yet the deed, itself, is supposed to be
the origin of society and culture.

*"Cannibal savages as they were, it goes without saying that they de-
voured their victim as well as killing him"* (Freud, SE 13:142). Freud
simply assumes that they devoured the father because he assumes that the

most primitive peoples were cannibals, and he repeats this belief in *Moses and Monotheism* (Freud, 1939:103 [SE 23:81]). There is no evidence at all for this supposition, but the idea was, and still is, a popular belief about primitives, especially archaic ones; the idea is perpetuated in much psychoanalytic writing, for example, by psychoanalyst Martin Bergmann (1992). In any case, eating the father was, according to Freud, the origin of the totem feast; by incorporating the flesh of the father the sons became identified with him. For Freud, then, the original sacrifice was human; the animal (totem) was already a substitute.

For Freud, the sons' deed marked the end of the patriarchal horde. But the very notion of the primal horde, taken from Darwin and Atkinson, "is merely hypothetical. It is a mere guess that the earliest organization of man resembles that of the gorilla rather than that of trooping monkeys" (Kroeber, [1920]1952:302).[16] Beyond that, however, is the question of whether one can legitimately read from animal behavior to human. For is it not the case that what we read of animal behavior has already been endowed with analogies from human behavior and social organization? Once human forms have been inscribed onto animal life, we then read back what these animals tell us about ourselves (Marx in Sahlins, 1976: 53; Haraway, 1989).

Second, and for my purposes more important, how can there be a patriarchal horde without a notion of patriarch? It was essential for Freud that the primal male was the father; otherwise neither the story nor the consequences that he believed flowed from the deed would make sense.[17]

Freud presupposed a notion of father; yet therein lies a "palpable contradiction" in his theory. For it was precisely the "discovery" of paternity that, for Freud and others, marked a major advance in civilization. How then, could such an idea have been present, *ab origine*, in that most archaic society?

> A great advance was made in civilization when men decided to put their inferences upon a level with the testimony of their senses and to make the step from matriarchy to patriarchy. The pre-historic figures which show a smaller person sitting upon the head of a larger one are representations of patrilineal descent; Athena had no mother, but sprang from the head of Zeus. A witness who testifies to something before a court of law is still called "Zeuge" (literally "begetter") in German, *after the part played by the male in procreation.* (Freud, SE 10: 233, n. 1, emphasis mine)[18]

The problems with his view about paternity and the momentous shift from matriarchy to patriarchy that he and many others assume occurred have already been dealt with (chapter 1). Here, it is important to point out that the errors of these assumptions had momentous implications for his theory, and through him, for contemporary theory about gender, social organization, and the symbolization of power.

Parenthetically, it is important to note that Freud not only ignores the story, recounted in Hesiod, that Athena did have a mother by the name of Metis; he also ignores how it came about that Athena was born from the head of Zeus. Zeus was afraid of Metis because she was said to be greater than all the other gods, and so he gobbled her up when she was pregnant with Athena and then passed her daughter off as his own creation (see chapter 7, n. 18).

More relevant to our discussion, however, is that if the "discovery" of paternity represents a step forward in civilization, as Freud asserts, how can he presuppose its existence at the dawn of society? Put more forcefully: *if there was no idea of paternity, how could there have been a primal father?* There could only have been a primal male.

Without the notion of father as "begetter," as the one who engenders the sons, the killing of the male head of the horde could not possibly have had the power and meaning Freud attributed to it. It would have been simply homicide—horrible, but unfortunately, a fairly frequent event. The deed that supposedly generated religion, society, and morals would instead only tell us something about the supposed propensity of males to kill (innate male aggression); it could not have been a patricide—a crime that Freud feels is far more weighty.[19]

Without a notion of paternity or father in the primal horde, could the meaning of *son* possibly carry the same valence? And why would these "sons" feel such a "burning sense of guilt" about a man whom they hardly knew, who had treated them cruelly and banished them? Yet the remorse these "sons" allegedly felt was so profound it (a) was repressed and unconsciously projected onto an animal totem—the substitute for the father which ultimately, through a series of transformations, becomes the great Father God—and (b) left a generalized feeling of guilt that was bequeathed to all subsequent generations. These we shall take up shortly.

The killing of the father and the religion that developed from this deed could not possibly have the same meaning and relevance for women as they have for men. Freud does not consider this difference, but implies that culture is entirely male-generated. In Freud's script of the deed that sets humanity on its course, women are hardly mentioned except as passive pawns in the action that takes place between father and son.[20]

For that is finally what the origin story comes down to: "the beginnings of religion, ethics, society and art converge in the Oedipus complex. . . . [These and] the problems of social psychology are soluble on the basis of one single concrete point—a man's relation to his father" (Freud, SE 13:156-7). At the very least, why not also a father's relation to his son? I shall leave to one side Freud's idea that the origins of religion and society stem only from the relationship between fathers and sons, rather than from that between mothers and daughters, or fathers and daughters, or mothers and sons. Here I want to focus on the father-son relation.

Had Freud raised the question about a man's relation to his son in addition to that of a man's relation to his father, he might have developed a theory that implicated fathers in the problems of their sons (and daughters). Such a question might have led him to develop a theory about fatherhood and, in turn, might have prompted him to ask another, vitally important question: What is the meaning of father and upon what does that meaning depend? It is a question he could very easily have asked; he had all the answers, but he never put them together. Had he done so, I believe it would have been necessary for him to revise his conclusions about the Oedipus complex, about the nature and origin of culture, and about religion and monotheism in a way that would have resulted in a book very differerent from *Moses and Monotheism*. I will postpone the implications of this failure until after we have a better sense of what he did do, namely to repeat the thesis formulated in *Totem and Taboo* as the basis for the story he constructs in *Moses and Monotheism*.

From Totem and Taboo to
Moses and Monotheism

For Freud the origin of society rests on a murderous deed committed in primeval times. It was a deed so horrible that it made a powerful impression on the perpetrators—so powerful, in fact, that it left a permanent mark.[21] It became an acquired characteristic of the human race as the human race passed from barbarity to society. At the very end of *Totem and Taboo* Freud had the courage to ask himself whether "the mere hostile *impulse* against the father, the mere existence of a wishful *phantasy* of killing and devouring him, would have been enough to produce the moral reaction that created totemism and taboo. In this way we should avoid the necessity for deriving the origin of our cultural legacy, of which we justly feel so proud, from a hideous crime, revolting to all our feelings." (Freud, SE 13:160). Yet because of his distinction between primitives and modern neurotics, namely that the latter are inhibited, that with them thought substitutes for action whereas primitives are uninhibited, that with them "thought passes directly into action," he finally says "it may safely be assumed that 'in the beginning was the Deed'" (ibid.:161).[22] Although several years previously he had abandoned the notion of a causative *deed* in relation to the development of neuroses in individuals, he held fast to the idea of such a deed when it came to his cultural studies.

In *Moses and Monotheism*, he confesses that perhaps the story he told in *Totem and Taboo* had been too condensed, "as if what in reality took centuries to achieve, and during that long time was repeated innumerably, had happened only once"(Freud, 1939:102 [SE 23:81]). Whether there was one deed or a number of them, it (they) occurred in primeval times and the knowledge of the deed(s) was repressed. In the long period of time between the primal horde and the early history of the Jews, there was a gradual return of the repressed (ibid.:169–170 [ibid.:132ff.]).[23] In historical times, "the mental residue of those primeval times has become a heritage which, with each new generation, needs only to be awakened, not to be reacquired" (ibid.:170 [ibid.:132]). The repetition of the primal crime on the person of Moses enabled the emotional fervor attaching to the original murder and its consequences to be reawakened, reacquired, and reinforced. That is the power of the story he tells in *Moses and Monotheism*.

MOSES AND MONOTHEISM

Freud creates his own version of the story of Moses in three separate but repetitive essays—the first two published in 1937 and then together in book form with the third in 1939. In these essays Freud brings all of his work on individual psychology (the Oedipus complex) and its relation to the origin and structure of society to bear on the origins of his own society and, specifically, on the conflict between Judaism and Christianity that was threatening to shatter his world.

Freud was deeply concerned about the rise of anti-Semitism under Hitler. *Moses and Monotheism* can, at least in part, be read as Freud's attempt to answer the questions: What is it about Judaism and Jews that provokes such hatred? How to explain it, and more important, how to defuse it? (Cf. Gilman, 1993). These queries provided strong, but clearly not the only, motivations for Freud to take up the question of the origin of Judaism. Also motivating his quest was the possibility of demonstrating his conviction that "religious phenomena are to be understood only on the model of the neurotic symptoms of the individual" (ibid.:71 [ibid.:58]). Thereby, Freud could use what he learned of the latter to theorize about the former. In the development of a neurosis, he says, there is an "early trauma—defence—latency—outbreak of neurosis—partial return of the repressed material" (ibid.:101 [ibid.:80]), and this is the periodization he uses to develop his theory about the rise and power of Mosaic monotheism.

With the contributions of Meyer, Sellin, and Rank, Freud spins a web of associations and conjectures that can be quite mesmerizing. The first clues are linguistic: he argues, quite persuasively, and using evidence from Meyer and others, that the very name of Moses is Egyptian. That, however, does not mean that the man Moses *was* Egyptian, but this is the conclusion Freud draws. He notes a discrepancy between the two Biblical accounts of Moses—Moses in Egypt and Moses among the Midianites—and suggests that there has been a conflation of two quite separate traditions, each of which involved a man named Moses (ibid.:41 [ibid.:36]). But he does not see how that undermines his thesis about the name: if this second Moses acquired *his* name by borrowing it from the first, as Freud implies, why couldn't the Egyptian Moses have borrowed his name?

The second clue is the way the Moses story contravenes the standard version of the myth of "the birth of the hero," as described by Otto Rank. In the typical form of the myth a child is born of noble parents; his "conception is impeded with difficulty" and, most important, the father receives a warning—an oracle or dream—that his son will be a danger to him. In response to the oracle, the father typically exposes the infant to the elements or in some way tries to get rid of the child, who is taken in by a humble couple and then, after many adventures and trials, emerges victorious to avenge his father and claim fame and fortune for himself (ibid.:7–8 [ibid.:10–11]). This *is* the Oedipus story.

The Moses story as portrayed in the Bible, Freud says, is the reverse: Moses is born into a humble family and brought up among nobility. But rather than a reversal, it may simply represent a difference between Greek and biblical myth. In the stories of both Isaac and Jesus, for example, the children are born of humble parents and their conceptions are unusual. Nevertheless, with regard to Moses, the "reversal" is not as simple as Freud would like. Moses "is the child of Jewish Levites" (ibid.:11 [ibid.: 13]), and although Pharoah's daughter does draw him out of the water, she turns him over to a wet nurse who, it turns out, is actually his own mother (Exod. 2:9). Jewish tradition holds that the Levites were the group (class or caste) of priests: they would hardly have been of the more humble or poorer classes, although Freud might have meant that they were humbled because of their captivity. More important, how could they be Jewish Levites without Judaism? If Moses is the father of the Jewish people, as Freud says, the one who brings or gives the religion of Judaism, then how could he be from a family of Jewish Levites? Indeed, before Judaism, what could that mean? Faced with such a "palpable contradiction," Freud simply changes the tradition and claims that *that* "seems a transparent distortion of the actual state of affairs: the Levites were instead, Moses' people." He was not born *of* Levites—instead, they were the retinue he brought with him during the Exodus, "his nearest adherents, his scribes, his servants" (Freud, 1939:45 [SE 23:38]). That still does not explain their Jewishness.

Nevertheless, the reversal is significant for Freud in the same way he thinks reversals in dreams are significant; they lead to a (distorted) truth. By analogy with individual psychology, he surmised that the same phenomenon was operative in myth, the collective dreams of a people. The truth that the reversal hides, Freud conjectures, is that Moses is an Egyptian of high rank, probably associated with the court, who lived in or near the time of Ikhnaton.

Ikhnaton was originally called Amenhotep IV after his father, Amenhotep III. The *Amen* part of the name refers to the god Amon, and the *aton* in Ikhnaton refers to the god he elevated to the prime position, Aton, the Sun-God, whom he worshipped "not as a material object, but as a symbol of a divine being whose energy was manifested in his rays" (ibid.:23 [ibid.:22]). According to Freud, Ikhnaton "ascended the throne about 1375 B.C. . . . (and) undertook to force upon his subjects a new religion, one contrary to their ancient traditions and to all their familiar habits. It was a strict monotheism" (ibid.:21 [ibid.:20]), imposed with harshness and intolerance. Such "religious intolerance, which was foreign to antiquity before this and for long after, was inevitably born with the belief in one God" (ibid.).

Freud's picture of Ikhnaton is in stark contrast to the one that his friend and colleague Karl Abraham painted earlier (1912), and which Freud knew about, as we shall see. From Karl Abraham we learn that Ikhnaton was only nine when his father died and that the kingdom was ruled for a time by his mother and by regents. Ikhnaton was a frail and poetic type, interested more in the arts of leisure than in conquests and battles, and he was devoted to his beautiful wife, Nefertiti, until his death at the age of twenty-five.

Freud imagined that *his* Moses was a follower of the Aton monotheistic religion and that he had hopes of rising in the Egyptian hierarchy. With the early death of Ikhnaton and the destruction of the Aton cult, these dreams or hopes of Moses were also dashed.[24] Freud imagined that Moses had been put in charge of the Jewish people, and that, with the return to power of the enemies of Ikhnaton, there were persecutions, which provided a reason for the Exodus. Freud suggests that Moses chose these Jews as his people, successfully led them out of Egypt, and then tried to reinstitute the Aton religion. While wandering hungry in the desert, they began to "murmur" and rebel and one day rose up against him and killed him.[25]

As with the murder of the primal father recounted in *Totem and Taboo*, the guilt or remorse after this terrible deed led them to reify, if not deify, Moses and made them adhere even more strictly to his rules. The repetition of the primal crime is what gives such power to Jewish monotheism and its "child," Christianity. Freud believed the murder was repressed. But if the murder of Moses was repressed (Freud, 1939:86 [SE 23:68]), why didn't Freud consider the possibility that the literal "sacrifice" of Isaac had been repressed?

The murder, according to Freud, was repressed; only traces—distorted, displaced, and transformed—remained, and those are what he claims to have unraveled. At the same time, he leaves as many traces or clues for us to unravel.

First, Moses is not the father of those who murdered him except perhaps in a symbolic sense. This might have alerted Freud to the fact that the primary issue is authority, not biology, and that revelation might have led him to rethink his thesis in *Totem and Taboo*. Moses is not referred to as father (*avinu*) in Jewish tradition. Indeed, according to Rice, "no patriarchal qualities were ever attached to Moses" (Rice, 1990:161); Moses is referred to as teacher (*rabeynu*). The title of father is reserved for Abraham, and it is from him, not Moses, that Jews (as well as Christians and Muslims) claim their descent. In addition, Freud makes no case for the incestuous desires of these "sons" for the wife of Moses or for the women he did not, in any case, hoard. Yet these were the prime motives for the primal crime, the residual traces of which Freud believes have been deposited in every male's Oedipus complex. But if the "father" and "sons" in this case are symbolic rather than biological and the motive primarily authority and obedience, what kept Freud from using this insight to critique his earlier theories about the Oedipus complex and its social ramifications in *Totem and Taboo*?

Second, Freud attributes the rise of Egyptian monotheism, before Ikhnaton, to political, especially imperial motives: already during the time of Thothmes III "Egypt had become a world power. . . . This imperialism was reflected in religion as universality and monotheism" (Freud, 1939: 22 [SE 23:21]). In the third essay, Freud states this even more clearly: "In Egypt monotheism had grown—as far as we understand its growth—as an ancillary effect of imperialism; God was the reflection of a Pharaoh autocratically governing a great world Empire" (ibid.:80 [ibid.:65]). But if Freud assumed that, for the Egyptians, the idea of uniting under one god was a very useful means to consolidate a multicultural empire, why should the foundation of *Jewish* monotheism depend on a repetition of the primal crime, the murder of the father (see Coward, 1983:214–5)? Conversely, does he see no contradiction in his explanation of the original Egyptian monotheism? By stretching the theory a bit, Freud attributes to Ikhnaton the Oedipal tendencies that rightly needed to be applied to the earlier florescence.

Perhaps it is true that Ikhnaton substituted a God (Aton) for his father and "directed his efforts to effacing all traces of the god for whom his father and he *himself* were named" (Abraham, [1912]1935:551, my emphasis), namely Amon. If one is to interpret his deed as a wish to murder the father, then one would at the same time have to interpret it as a suicide. Instead, Ikhnaton's erasure of the names with Amon affixed seems to have been motivated more by his hatred for the god Amon than by hatred for the father he hardly knew. The "return of the repressed" god, Aton, did not involve a murder, remorse, or the deification of the murdered father but had, at least according to Karl Abraham (1912), much to do with Ikhnaton's mother and her women friends, who had been devotees of Aton.

One cannot rule out the possibility that Egyptian monotheism might have emerged in relation to a repetition of the murder of the primal father, but since Freud considered other factors such as imperialism and authority, these should have been taken into account in considering the rise of Jewish monotheism.

Third, as there are many violent and horrible deeds recorded in the Bible, particularly in Genesis and Exodus, why was the murder of Moses, alone, repressed? Why should the murder of Moses be more horrific than his order for the murder of three thousand of his compatriots because of their disobedience (Exod. 32:28)? Why should the murder of the father be more significant than the murder of the son? Finally, why didn't Freud consider the possibility that the repressed murder in the Bible was not of the "father" but of the son, Isaac?

CHRISTIANITY

If the repressed murder had been that of the son, Isaac (as even a few biblical scholars assert), Freud might have made more sense of Christianity than he did. Not only did he dismiss and distort Jewish tradition, he also did violence to Christian tradition. The murder of Jesus became for Freud not the completion of the suspended sacrifice of Isaac or its possible repetition, but the expiation of the original crime, namely the murder of the Father. He attributed it to "a growing feeling of guiltiness . . . as a precursor or the return of the repressed material" (Freud, 1939:109 [SE 23:86]). He claimed that Paul rightly traced it to its primeval source and "this he called original sin; it was a crime against God that could be expiated only through death" (ibid.). Original sin was transformed by Freud into murder (of God the Father); he ignored both Jewish and Christian religious tradition, which interpreted it as disobedience. He also failed to take into account a traditional Jewish interpretation of Abraham's deed—that his obedience to God made up for, atoned for, Adam's disobedience. Abraham's deed (willingness), we may recall, bestowed merit upon Jews that redeemed them from God's wrath. Freud might have asked why God should be so angry, why the sacrifice of a child would be the appropriate propitiatory response, or why obedience was so important, but he did not. Such an exploration might even have provided a suitable rationale for the murder of the father.

He ignored the tradition altogether and substituted his own psycho-analytic explanation of events. At least in his individual case studies, he describes the patient's story; here he dispenses with it. In his terms, Jesus' death is an expiation for the original murder; therefore, Christians are liberated from *guilt* because his death amounts to their admission that they have killed God (the Father). Christian doctrine, on the contrary, teaches that through Christ's death Christians are liberated from *sin*—his death atones for their sin. Freud does not ask why "an all powerful God can find no other way to absolve us from sin but to sacrifice his own beloved son" (Bergmann, 1988:251).

Freud's explanation changes the terms, for example from sin to guilt, and reduces the significance and meaning that Christ's death has for Christians. In fact, Freud blames Jesus for what happened. "That the Redeemer sacrifice himself as an innocent man was an obvious tendentious distortion. . . . [He] could be no one else but he who was most guilty, the leader of the brother horde who had overpowered the Father" (Freud, 1939:110 [SE 23:87]). Freud goes on to say that Christ was either "the heir of an unfulfilled wish-phantasy [or] his successor and his reincarnation" (ibid.:110–11 [ibid.:87]); in other words, he was the son who had usurped the father's place "just as in those dark times every son had longed to do" (ibid.:112 [ibid.:88]). Christianity is the triumph of the sons, the brother-band; it is, according to Freud, a son-religion, whereas Judaism remained a father religion.

Jews could not or would not join the brother-band; they obdurately refused to acknowledge the murder of the father (ibid.:114 [ibid.:90]) and, instead, compensated ever more persistently by their adherence to the strict regime required by the father.[26] This is Freud's tortuous way of explaining the terrible accusations Christians throughout the centuries have hurled at the Jews, namely that they are "Christ-killers"; no doubt such accusations were being heard again in Freud's Germany. When Christians say to Jews: "You have killed our God," Freud interprets it to mean, not Christ the son, but "the archetype of God, the primeval Father and his reincarnations" (ibid.:115 [ibid:90]), an interpretation that would probably serve only to arouse their ire as Freud, himself, seemed to be aware.

Freud's contorted explanation ignored other possibilities that resonate much better with both historical and theological traditions. First, it was Jesus' own disciple, Judas Iscariot, who betrayed him; true, he was a Jew, but so too was Jesus; the traitor was one of his own. It is not as if a Jew

killed a Christian, for there were no Christians at the time, there were
only followers of the Jew, Jesus. A disciple betrayed him and "he was
crucified under Pontius Pilate," as the Christian "Confession of Faith"
repeatedly reminds believers. Although the Gospels portray Pilate as
washing his hands of the whole affair (Matt. 27:24; Mark 15:15; Luke
23:24), he, nevertheless, did ultimately allow it to happen. Others have
noted that the Jews could not have killed Jesus because "crucifixion was
a Roman punishment for rebels, Jews would have stoned him" (Bergmann, 1988:252), or similarly, that only the Sanhedrin (the highest judi-
cial and ecclesiastical council of the ancient Jews) could have sentenced
him but that they would not have met during Passover.

Far more important, Freud ignored the theological interpretation of
the death of Jesus: that God the Father sacrificed his only begotten son.
One could easily imagine either that the Crucifixion repeated the Akedah,
and thus acknowledge what had been covered up, or that it completed a
deed that had been left unfinished; in either case, one is much closer to
tradition and perhaps to the psychological complexes it bequeathed. Psychoanalytically, Freud might then have interpreted the Crucifixion as the
repetition and coming to consciousness of the original repressed murder—that of Abraham's son. If that were too strong, he might have interpreted it as the fulfillment of an original repressed wish. In a general sense
Christians interpret their religion as the culmination of the law and the
prophets, the fulfillment of Judaism; more specifically it is the fulfillment
of the promises given to Abraham.

In a book on a biblical figure and on a story of "sons" killing the "father," it is hard to imagine that Freud could *not* have thought of the story
of Father Abraham and his willingness to kill his son. An initial question
must be whether Freud knew of the story of Abraham. The Abraham
story is one that I wager all children with even the most minimal of religious educations—in Judaism, Christianity, or Islam—eventually hear.
And, "every male child who has been exposed to the story has been affected by it because of the universality and timelessness of its theme.
Sigmund Freud was no exception" (Rice, 1990:161). I am not convinced
of the universality of its theme, but it has persisted in certain cultures for
several thousand years and its effects are felt not just by male children. It
is not clear on what Rice bases his assumptions about Freud, but it is true
that Freud had at least minimal acquaintance with Judaism and the
Bible.[27] Most scholars think Freud had more than that, that he was intimately acquainted with biblical stories. Rice, for example, thinks young
Sigmund was sent to Jewish primary school (ibid., 1990:181f.) and Yerushalmi imagines that his father may even have taught him Hebrew and

German as he told his son stories from their family bible (Yerushalmi, 1991:64).[28]

Listening to the biblical stories and peering at the family Bible—the Philippson's illustrated Bible with its full-page engraving of Moses holding the stone tablets as frontispiece (see fig. 14) and numerous illustrations of Egyptian scenes, objects, and motifs—it is not difficult to surmise that Freud's attachment to Moses and to all things Egyptian was forged in his childhood or youth.[29] Krull (1986:163) even makes the interesting suggestion that the adult Freud may have tried to replicate the Egyptian drawings with the collection of statues and figurines that filled his study in Vienna.

The Bible and its stories were, it seems, part of his childhood. His acquaintance with Greek myth and language came later, when he was a student at the Gymnasion. It was there that Freud first translated *Oedipus Rex* as part of his classical education. Freud confessed in his *Autobiography*: "My deep engrossment in the Bible story (almost as soon as I had learnt the art of reading) had, as I recognized much later, an enduring effect upon the direction of my interests" (Freud, SE 20:8).[30] Again, why did he choose a Greek myth rather than a biblical one as the human archetype?[31]

We can safely assume that Freud knew the story of Abraham. In fact, we do not really need to seek outside confirmation, as Freud himself lets us know that he was aware of it. He mentions it in his work, though only three times in his entire corpus, and then in a very offhand, casual way. On the surface it seems it did not affect him the way Rice thought it should. But the casualness and brevity of his citation could have been an indication of what he might, in others, have called an "avoidance reaction."

The first time Freud mentions Abraham is in the case study known as "Wolfman" (Freud, 1914, published in 1918). It was the child who actually mentioned it; Freud simply quoted him. "God had treated his son harshly and cruelly, but he was not better towards men; he had sacrificed his own son and had ordered Abraham to do the same" (Freud, SE 17: 65–6). The boy became terrified of God. Freud goes on to say, "The boy had some kind of inkling of the ambivalent feelings towards the father which are *an underlying factor in all religions*. . . . [H]is opposition soon turned instead directly against the figure of God" (ibid.:65, my emphasis, because this is hardly established fact). The ambivalent feelings may have arisen during the boy's initial obsession with questions about procreation and where babies come from and therefore may have been directly related to the Oedipal complex. The boy's statement may also have been a way to talk to Freud about his fear of his father and/or of cruelty experienced

Fig. 14. *Moses* etching from the Philippson Bible. *Mikra Torah Neviim
U-Khetuvim- Die Israelitische Bibel. Enthaltend den heiligen Urtext,
die deutsche Uebertragung, die allgemeine ausfurliche Erlauterung mit mehr
als 500 englischen Holzschnitten.* Leipzig: Baumgartner, 1858.
From Andover-Harvard Theological Library of Harvard
Divinity School, S.C.R. 391 Philippson.

or expected. That is, the son's ambivalent feelings may have arisen not only from his Oedipal wishes; they may have been due, in part, to behavior of the father. Freud should have been more attentive to the connections the child was drawing between notions of fatherhood, Abraham, and God.[32]

Freud mentions Abraham only two other times, both in *Moses and Monotheism*, and in neither case does he mention the sacrifice story. That seems extremely odd in a book that creates a story about "sons" killing the "father." In the first instance Freud thinks Abraham can be dispensed with because he is a legendary figure, an invention and projection of later prophets. But what an odd reason for Freud to reject him; after all, Freud uses another legend, that of Oedipus, as a way of analyzing universal complexes, so why not the story of Abraham? It has the additional merit of being a story that is repeated year after year—at Rosh Hashanah, at Easter, and during the Muslim Hajj—and generation after generation; it could, therefore, much more easily be understood as having shaped Western attitudes about the relation between fathers and sons. No society repeats the Oedipus story in a ritual context. But, for Freud, psychological complexes had to be anchored in something more solid than a notion of cultural transmission; he felt it necessary to elaborate his idea of some kind of genetic inheritance, albeit an initially acquired characteristic. Finally, if the first page of *Moses and Monotheism* is any indication, Freud seems to have regarded Moses as only relatively less legendary. For Freud, however, it was not only that Abraham was legendary: he believed he had been invented with a specific purpose, namely to displace the acts of Moses onto Abraham in order to cover up the *fact* that Moses was Egyptian.

One of the most important acts that Freud attributes to Moses, rather than Abraham, is the introduction of the custom of circumcision to the Hebrews. The Bible, he believes, covers this up: "the Biblical account, it is true, often contradicts it [and] dates the custom back to the time of the patriarchs as a sign of the covenant concluded between God and Abraham" (Freud, 1939:29 [SE 23:26]). The Bible specifically states that circumcision was first introduced by Abraham and is a sign of the covenant: "This is my covenant, which ye shall keep, between me and you and thy seed after thee; Every man child among you shall be circumcised" (Gen. 17:10). Can such an important Biblical story on which Hebrew identity and other events hinge be dismissed so easily? The practice was common among the Egyptians, and Freud takes this as further proof that Moses, too, was an Egyptian who later introduced the practice to his "chosen" people, the Hebrews. He seems never to have imagined that Abraham, during his sojourn in Egypt (Gen. 12), may have introduced circumcision to the Egyptians, and monotheism, too. In other words, we might more easily trace the genealogy of monotheism from Abraham to Ikhnaton rather than from the latter to Moses. Freud ignored this possibility, which adheres more closely to the biblical text, and instead proposed that it was Ikhnaton's monotheism that Moses attempted to revive. Freud's avoidance of Abraham appears to be overdetermined.

PERSONAL OMISSION

There is another, more personal, explanation for Freud's avoidance of Abraham that is closer to home and should not be overlooked. Although my purpose here is primarily to point out the relation betweeen the personal and the theoretical, some of my observations may contribute to the efforts of those who try to psychoanalyze Freud.

"Freud had forgotten that—as with Moses—an 'Abraham' had preceded him in Egypt" (Shengold, 1972:134). Shengold attributes Freud's omission of the biblical Abraham to a paraphraxis (a psychologically motivated slip) in relation to his associate Karl Abraham. Freud had conveniently forgotten that Karl Abraham had written an article on the Egyptian King Ikhnaton and monotheism long before Freud's *Moses and Monotheism* was even begun. Shengold thinks Freud's lapse stems from the psychologically motivated "death wishes" he harbored toward some of his own symbolic "sons," that is, his followers. Jung had been the favorite "son," chosen to succeed Freud, but after his defection, the honor was bestowed on Abraham. As we shall see, however, events precluded his succession.

Abraham's paper psychoanalyzes Amenhotep IV and, in a number of ways, anticipates Freud's theses in *Moses and Monotheism*: "Ikhnaton's doctrine not only contains the essential components of Old Testament Jewish monotheism but in many respects is in advance of it" (Abraham, [1912]1935:553).[33] For example, because Ikhnaton did not visualize his god, he "forbids any pictorial representation of the god—which command becomes a forerunner of Mosaic law" (ibid.). Further on, he notes that the intangible, invisible god would be a weakness of the religion because such a god would never appeal to the masses. This theme becomes a major point in *Moses and Monotheism* and is proffered as a reason why Christianity, with its profusion of images, became so popular. Abraham also discussed the similarity between the names Aton and Adonis, which may have prompted Freud's discussion of Aton and Adonai (ibid.:540).

Freud, who was usually so scrupulous in citing the work of others, clearly should have credited Abraham, as he did Sellin, Meyer, and Rank,

for some of the ideas in his book. The fact that Freud cited Rank, another
of his associates, does not excuse him for failing to cite Abraham's work,
as Kanzer (1972:160) proposed.[34] Abraham's paper was well known to
Freud and had been a subject not only of their correspondence but also
of a small conference of his associates. Abraham first wrote to Freud on
11 January 1912, to tell him of his new paper on a "theme that will
interest you: about Amenhotep IV and the Aton cult." He goes on to acknowledge his "first introduction to Egyptology that I enjoyed in Vienna
in December 1907" (Abraham and Freud, 1965:111–2).

Freud's answer, written three days later, begins with the exclamation:
"Just think of it, Amenhotep IV in the light of psychoanalysis. That is
surely a great advance in orientation" (ibid.:112). By 3 June 1912, Freud
writes, "I have read your Egyptian study with the pleasure that I always
derive both from your way of writing and way of thinking, and should
like to make only two criticisms or suggestions" (ibid.:118).[35] Abraham
took them into consideration, and Freud wrote again 21 October 1912,
saying: "I like your Amenhotep in its revised form much better" (ibid.:
124).

Abraham's paper was discussed at a meeting of the main members of
the psychoanalytic circle in Munich a month later, in November 1912.
Presciently, the issue of citation and attribution came up during the meeting. Jung felt that too much was being made of the erasure of Ikhnaton's
father's name.[36] Freud's testy response was that Jung had not cited *him* in
some recent work, implying that he, too, was trying to efface his "father."
When Jung began to defend himself, Freud fainted. It was the third time
he had fainted in *that* room in the Park Hotel (the other two times were
in 1906 and 1908). Jung was also present on those two occasions and
both times they had been discussing the death wishes of son to father.
Although Freud accused Jung of having death wishes toward him, he did
not appear to acknowledge his own.[37] It does seem as if Freud found it
difficult to tolerate disciples who had independent opinions and who did
not adhere strictly to his theory. He seemed to want to put his stamp on
them as had the "Great Man" (see *Moses and Monotheism*, 1939:136–42
[SE 23:107–11]). Any straying was felt as betrayal.[38]

Ten years later, Freud was again reminded of Abraham's paper, for
he made allusions to it in a letter he wrote to Abraham, 4 March 1923,
thanking him for some clippings about the discovery of Tutankhamen's
tomb (Abraham and Freud, 1965:334). Not long after that (on Christmas
Day 1925) Abraham, although twenty-one years younger than Freud,
was dead, and Freud was deprived of his chosen successor. Yet it seems
that Freud had already become ambivalent about his decision, for sadly,
during Abraham's illness, their exchange of letters had become fairly
frosty and Abraham even complained that he was beginning to feel the

brunt of Freud's hostility. Freud's reaction may partly be explained by the fact that Abraham's doctor during his illness was Fliess, the very man with whom Freud had had an intimate relation, then quarreled and broke with. Although Freud had once recommended Fliess to Abraham, he may have felt some jealousy as well as betrayal when Abraham communicated to Freud how highly he regarded Fliess. Freud had not taken Abraham's illness very seriously and had jokingly written: "I feel your illness to be a kind of unfair competition." When Abraham died so precipitously, Freud may have felt guilty; perhaps he realized, unconsciously, or could not acknowledge, that his "death-wishes" had been fulfilled. Did Freud find it significant that his chosen son had died on the day Christ was born?

Freud should have acknowledged Karl Abraham in *Moses and Monotheism*. And his name ought to have jogged a memory of the biblical Abraham (Yerushalmi, 1991:5). Indeed, when Freud first met Karl Abraham, he asked whether he was a descendent of his namesake Abraham—a way of asking whether he was Jewish yet contradicting his belief that Jewishness comes from Moses not Abraham.[39] Furthermore, the fact that Christians and Muslims also claim Abraham as their father might have led Freud to consider the foundational story that unites all three monotheisms—the story of a father willing to sacrifice his son.

Freud's avoidance of Abraham points to a much larger issue—his reluctance to hold fathers partly responsible for the problems of their children, or to consider their role and their (possibly ambivalent) feelings toward their children. Had he done so, he would have been forced to consider whether "father" and "son" refer to relationships given in nature or whether they are interrelated terms that derive their meaning from a particular theory of procreation. He might then have been led to the realization that the terms, their meanings, and the myths about them are *not universal* but relate to a particular social, historical, and cultural context. That, as we saw in chapter 1, is what the "virgin birth controversy" is all about, namely, whether the Trobriand Islanders (among others) had a *concept* of paternity and, if not, how the absence of it affected their social life and religious conceptions. Ernest Jones, a colleague of Freud and promulgator of psychoanalysis in England, became one of the interlocutors in that debate with his paper, "Mother-right and the Sexual Ignorance of Savages" (Jones, 1924). Other of his successors turned to the figure of the father in attempts to correct Freud's blind spot. However, they carefully adjusted the lens but left the frame intact. They turned their attention to the figure of the father but did not scrutinize the meaning of "father."

CHAPTER NINE

Sa(l)vaging Freud

THE ABSENCE of the father in Freud's work has not gone unnoticed by his successors, but their correctives stay within the psychoanalytic paradigm. Some even stay within the Greek mythological context and suggest, for example, a "Laius complex" to complement the "Oedipus complex" (Devereux, 1953). Others suggest a biblical context but emphasize a story other than Abraham—for example, the story of Cain and Abel (cf.Yerushalmi, 1991:92; Rieff, [1959] 1979:195) or the Garden of Eden (Mazlish, 1969)—without taking into account the foundational place of the story of Abraham in the monotheistic religious traditions. Nevertheless, a handful of psychoanalytically trained doctors and scholars have focused on the Abraham story as a corrective to Freud's emphasis both on Greek myth and on the son over the father.[1]

Their perspectives highlight a dimension that was not brought out in Freud's work, but they see it as merely additive. They are salvage attempts—the story of Abraham is interpreted as balancing or completing Freudian theory. Like their counterparts in biblical scholarship, these analysts have a vested interest in recovering the story for the tradition, in this case psychoanalytic tradition, rather than exploring the ways the story of Abraham challenges it. Fundamental to the psychoanalytic, as to the religious, interpretations is the unquestioned assumption that "father" or "paternity" means merely the social acknowledgment of a biological tie to a child rather than a social construction relative to a particular *theory* of procreation—a theory that imputes creativity and agency to the male at the expense and devaluation of the female role.

Because my interpretation of Freud's blind spot diverges widely from these psychoanalytic revisions, this chapter is not intended as an extended review and critique of their work—a tack that would take us way off course. By picking my way around them and pointing out the hidden dangers in their commonplace assumptions, I use them to chart my own course. The route may be somewhat tedious and of interest mostly to specialists, but it illuminates the depths to which Freudians have gone to salvage his theory, and it highlights the significance of my critical departure. Readers who wish to investigate these byways further should consult the references.

DEVEREUX

I begin briefly with Devereux because he was one of the first "to note that psychoanalytic theory pays exceedingly little attention to certain complexes which . . . complement the Oedipus complex" (Devereux, 1953: 132), especially what he calls the Laius complex. He attributes Freud's scotoma vis-à-vis the father both to the authoritarian structure and atmosphere of nineteenth-century families and to "the adults' deep-seated need to place all responsibility for the Oedipus complex upon the child; and to ignore, whenever possible, certain parental attitudes which actually *stimulate* the infant's Oedipal tendencies" (ibid., emphasis added). I do not know on what grounds Devereux postulates "adults' deep-seated need," but the failure to implicate fathers in their children's neuroses rests with Freud.

Freud had actually started out on that path because of the stories his female patients told about being "seduced" by the father or by a father substitute, such as another male relative. Even here, however, one can glimpse Freud's effort to excuse the father, for what was at stake was hardly seduction but incest or rape; indeed, the girl/daughter was the one labeled "seductive." When he abandoned the "seduction theory," he developed the thesis that neurotic symptoms were the fulfillments of wishes or fantasies on the part of the child (in this case the female child) rather than the inscriptions of faults of the fathers or their surrogates. Perhaps he was unwilling to believe that so many fathers, or their substitutes, could be abusing their daughters, even though in several of the cases there was corroborating evidence. It is even stranger to consider that although the patients he was dealing with were female, the theory he eventually elaborated—the Oedipus complex—focused on males, a double abandonment. In any case, his theory changed from being interpsychic to intrapsychic, from seeing psychological problems as social to locating them within the individual.[2]

This change occurred during a period of time immediately following the death of Freud's own father. Perhaps, as a number of scholars have suggested (Krull, 1986; Robert, 1976; Balmary, [1979]1982; Rice,

1990), Freud was unwilling or unable to confront his father and thus recognized that if he had left stones unturned, he would now have to deal with the consequences by himself. Perhaps he also realized that he had stepped into his father's place and was now invested with the authority to which he had aspired, and he did not want to relinquish it.[3] For me, these personal factors, however interesting, matter less than the implications they had for his theory and practice, and for what they tell us about the implicit cultural theory he produced.

By detailing the unsavory character of Laius, Devereux attempted to historicize and particularize the Oedipus complex. He suggested that Laius had brought on himself the fate he confronted at the crossroads because of his own belligerent behavior (a) by exposing the infant Oedipus, and (b) even earlier by the homosexual rape of Chrysippus, the son of King Pelops. For Devereux, at least, the Oedipus complex is activated by the desires and actions of the father at least as much as it is by those of the son.

WELLISCH

Although in agreement with the last comment, Wellisch breaks out of the Greek script for psychoanalysis with his book *Isaac and Oedipus* (1954), in which he suggests that "the Akedah motif . . . is the Biblical extension of the Oedipus complex" (Wellisch, 1954:113) and is more appropriate for the psychology of modern man. Modern psychology, he observes, is based on nonbiblical ideas, yet the Akedah is "the fundamental event on which the whole Bible stands" (ibid.:57) and is basic to the religious development of Judaism, Christianity, and Islam. It has, he asserts, been far more influential in molding family values and psyches than have the Greek tragedies. A very good point indeed.

Isaac and Oedipus is hardly a direct critique of *Moses and Monotheism*; the latter book is not mentioned at all and the few references to Moses are biblical ones. Nevertheless, because it presents the Akedah, the story of Abraham's near sacrifice of Isaac, as the complement to Freud's interpretation of Oedipus, it is relevant here.

For Wellisch, "the Akedah story describes *the resolution of the Oedipus conflict*" (ibid.:78, emphasis in the original). Unlike what might be called a Laius complex, the Akedah resolves the Oedipus complex with love, establishing thereby a new relation between parent and child (ibid.: 23). This relation transcends the solution that might be effected by the addition of a Laius complex to the Oedipus complex. For Wellisch, the addition would not be a solution but more like a balancing act "between

the opposing tendencies of the wish to possess the child completely or
even to kill him and the desire not to do so" (ibid.:4). The reconciliation
between parent and child, by which Wellisch actually means father and
son, is brought about by the father's "abandonment of his possessive,
aggressive tendencies and especially infanticidal tendencies and their re-
placement by a covenant of love" (ibid.). We shall see in a moment what
he means by *love*.

Wellisch's argument, however, rests on a few untenable, or at least
highly questionable, assumptions embedded in a theory of sociocultural
evolution popular in the nineteenth century but discredited by most twentieth-century anthropologists. One must be suspicious of a theory that
depends, as his does, on an evolutionary schema that posits a unitary,
universal cultural evolution consisting of stages: (1) primitive, (2) oedipal, and (3) Akedah.[4] On the very first page he states: "The first and most
primitive stage is characterized by intense aggression and possessiveness
of the parents. This aggression is particularly severe in the father and is
directed mainly to his sons . . . [I]t not infrequently culminated in infanticide" (ibid.:3–4). Not only does he assume an infanticidal impulse; he
projects it back to the dawn of history, which both he and Freud assumed
was mean, brutish, and cannibalistic. He gives no evidence for these as-
sertions but seems to have carried them over directly from Freud, who,
without mentioning the word infanticide, and without any explanation,
indicates that those most vulnerable to male aggression are newborn babies, menstruating and birthing women, and the dead (Freud, SE 13:33).

Correlative with the assumption of a barbaric past is Wellisch's assumption of some kind of primordial (male) aggression that automatically would be directed to a man's children, especially his sons. He claims
that infanticide has been practiced "all over the world by all races and
nations" (Wellisch, 1954:11) in *historic* times, and cites a number of
myths to support his claim. His belief in evolutionary progress leads him
to conclude that if infanticide was practiced in historic times, then it must
have been practiced even more assiduously in primeval times. Yet he
might just as easily have asserted a more Edenic past and considered that
infanticide or child sacrifice (which he does not really distinguish) may
have arisen *with* civilization. As discussed in chapter 3, all evidence for
child sacrifice is in complex, civilized societies, not simple ones, and from
times much later than the story of Abraham. Wellisch's statement is a
prime example of evolutionary reasoning: he simply assumes that earlier
means barbaric and historic means civilized—in the sense of an advance
in moral development. The historic instances of infanticide are, in this
kind of reasoning, seen as "survivals" of a more brutish past.[5] In the same
way, he simply assumes that human sacrifice preceded that of animals
(ibid.:30). These assumptions are so common that they are rarely ques-

tioned; it is difficult to persuade people that they are interpretations, not fact—interpretations that derive from a *conception* of the past, as well as of the present.[6]

Wellisch does, however, point out that "if one considers the possibility of the sons having killed the primordial father," as Freud did in both *Totem and Taboo* and *Moses and Monotheism*, then "one can infer that this was due to the father's behavior. One can assume that in the beginning was infanticide" (ibid.:10). Wellisch's statement, like Devereux's, has the merit of raising the question of why Freud did not really consider how the father's behavior provoked the sons' action and how the father, therefore, is inextricably implicated. Wellisch leads us to expect some discussion on the development of the father complex, but that does not occur. Instead he moves to religion and the idea of a higher power.

Wellisch's theory is rendered even more suspect by his examples of the new covenant between parent and child, which he calls *love*. "The readiness of the child to be sacrificed at his parent's command plays a great role in the development of filio-parental relationships. It . . . reached its noblest fulfillment in the attitude of Isaac towards Abraham" (ibid.:12). Note the singular *parent*; he really means the son's submission to the father: "By the surrender to the father's command, the son is greater than the father" (ibid.:94).

For Wellisch, the *child's* selfless love is therapeutic and brings about a more harmonious family relationship. He cites a chilling example from his clinical practice. A man who had returned from World War II began to exact military discipline from his wife and two sons. "He had very strict ideas about what is right and wrong and his ethics centred around discipline and doing what one is told. These ideas he linked with his belief in God, the Church, law and order" (ibid.:106). He was obsessed with duty and obedience and expected the same from his family. When the sons rebelled, they were punished. Wellisch does not question the destructive behavior of the father in this instance, nor the basis of the father's authority; instead he advises the family to submit to his authority and discipline because these are derived from principles rooted in religion. (The work of Philip Greven on Christian childrearing practices, cited in chapter 10, is again relevant.)

Although this solution may have calmed the tensions in that household, we must wonder what psychic violence was further perpetrated on the sons. The wife's collusion was solicited; she was encouraged to accept her husband's values and to use her influence to get the sons to accept them as well. Wellisch's theory and therapy ends, like Freud's, by supporting the father at the expense of the son. It reinforces rather than challenges the themes of authority and obedience that are so central to the Akedah.

BAKAN

David Bakan, a Canadian psychologist and professor, and a longtime
student of Freud, has also discussed the relevance of the Abraham story
for modern psychology. Like Wellisch, he assumes an "infanticidal impulse" and attributes its mitigation to the Abraham-Isaac story. "*Infanticide is, in the wider sense of the term, primitive. It would be obscuring
reality to call this trait 'instinctive.' It is not common to all mankind. Yet
it comes so near being inherent in the primeval parent-child relationship
that one is tempted to say of it: 'here, if anywhere, is a bit of behavior
natural to primitive man.'*" (Bakan, 1971:56, emphasis in the original).
Although Bakan admits that infanticide is not universal, it is close enough
for him. The attribution of such an impulse to archaic societies is purely
speculative—there can be no empirical evidence. Nor does he investigate
contemporary "primitive" societies,[7] but he theorizes that infanticide and
child abuse are related to the so-called discovery of paternity, which eventually all peoples must acquire as they ascend the evolutionary ladder.
The "discovery" of paternity is thought to evoke an impulse to infanticide
because of concern over legitimacy, that is, whether a specific child is
really a man's own, and the entailed responsibility for that child. The
Bible, he claims, is the document that depicts the crisis precipitated by this
discovery, and the Abraham story mitigates it.

Because the themes and issues Bakan and I discuss appear similar, it is
of critical importance to distinguish our very deep differences. For this
reason, I devote slightly more space to him. We agree that "Paternity is
one of the most frequent themes in both the Old and the New Testaments.
. . . [T]he authors of the Bible were extremely preoccupied with fatherhood" (Bakan, 1974:205). Where we differ is on whether the Bible reflects the *crisis* of paternity or symbolizes, instead, the establishment and
elaboration of the *notion* of paternity, the patriarchal family, and the
values that support it, making them appear as if they are rooted in the
structures of the universe rather than in a particular culture. The Akedah,
for me, could hardly represent the mitigation of an "infanticidal impulse," but it might possibly represent the beginning of an infanticidal
impulse.

Paternity, according to Bakan, has both positive and negative sides: on
the one hand the "biblical mind discovered children could be created at
will . . . [that] *men* truly became as gods in this respect" (ibid.:206, emphasis added). Although human men were not immortal as were the gods,
they saw the "possibility of achieving biological immortality by means of
the willful *creation* of offspring" (ibid.:207, emphasis added). In the preface to *Slaughter of the Innocents*, his book about child abuse, Bakan
claims that the "dawn of civilization must have been when man learned

that through planting seed, in the ground or sexually, he could create life at will" (Bakan, 1971:ix), and armed with that knowledge, men could also assume the right to take life or take control over it. But is this *knowledge* or a particular construction of procreative events? Bakan has perpetuated without question the idea that it is *men*, not women, who create children. Because he fails to use contemporary knowledge of procreation to reveal the assumptions embedded in these ancient beliefs, he has no basis from which to criticize them, and thus he reinforces them. He does not consider the possible effects on women or whether there might have been some struggle over this interpretation of creativity. Did women object to being likened to soil? Did they also desire immortality? Nor does he consider that not all cultures have been seed-planting ones, nor have all made an analogy between agriculture and procreation, between semen and seed. This view of procreation and the emphasis on the male role is a theory, a *construction*, not a "discovery." But it is here that his conflation of biological relationship and male creativity is most baldly stated.

The idea of paternity as male (pro-)creativity makes sense of the patrifiliation or identification of children with the father, but it entails other problems. Bakan believes that the "difficulties arising from men's assuming responsibility for *their* children also gave rise to a temptation to kill their children" (Bakan, 1979:15) because:

> First, the offspring might not be loyal, might not continue to provide, might not continue to obey, and might even kill their parents. Thus arises the obedience morality of the Bible. . . . Second, the simple burdensomeness of raising children under conditions of shortages of resources was itself a threat. . . . Third, the biblical mind was compromised by the possibility of lack of authentic paternity . . . (and) was especially uneasy about the first born, because the first born is ever of dubious paternity if the gestation period is not known. (ibid.:)

Although Bakan does not specify sons, that is who he is thinking about. The ambivalence toward the firstborn, he believes, is illustrated by the commandment "sanctify unto me all the firstborn," in which the firstborn sons are dedicated to God.[8] The focus on sons becomes immediately understandable if one believes that the son is, via seed, the incarnation of the father and the one who carries on his line; a father had to be sure a son was his own.

Bakan argues, quite rightly, that the emphasis on obedience is intimately related to paternity. Even if the son should not rise up and usurp the father's place violently, he keeps in front of the father the idea that he will ultimately succeed him. By demanding obedience from the son, the father can determine when that will be. It should be pointed out that obedience is required of the wife as well as the son, for upon her fidelity lies the guarantee of authentic paternity. (The obedience of wives is still part of traditional marriage vows.) Bakan asserts that the "covenant of God and Israel is of the same order as the covenant *extended* to a woman in marriage" (ibid.:163, my emphasis). Israel sometimes figures as the wife or bride of God; in this patronizing statement it is clear that there is an ascending hierarchy of obedience and the feminine is subordinate. Bakan even talks of the "effeminization" of the son in relation to the father, and of the father in relation to God (cf. Eilberg-Schwartz, 1994).

The consequence, however, of the son's submission to the father and the father's to God is that God's power and authority is channeled through males. Circumcision, the sign of the covenant given to Abraham "may be understood," according to Bakan, "as representing God's having delegated his procreative prerogative to man" (Bakan, 1979:141). Yet it is not to *man* but to men; the covenant was signed on the penis, on what was considered *the* generative organ. There was no comparable covenant with women. Bakan reinforces the patrilineal ideology when he notes that the sexual-generative ability, bestowed by God, is transferred from father to son throughout the generations.

All of these themes are exemplified in the story of Abraham, which Bakan sees as the mitigation of the infanticidal impulse. In fact, he asserts that "the essence of Judaism and Christianity is the management of the infanticidal impulse . . . and a binding of the father against acting out the impulse" (Bakan, 1974:208). The use of the term *binding* is a clear reference to the Akedah but for Bakan it is the father, not the son, who is bound.

The "infanticidal impulse" emerges with the "discovery" of paternity; its transcendence, which the Akedah supposedly symbolizes, has the result of men taking responsibility for their children. A number of additional assumptions are entailed in this interpretation, but they are merely stated, not examined. First, Bakan assumes that it is only with the "discovery" of paternity that men would be involved in child care at all. Before the discovery, he had assumed that it was women's function to "provid[e] maintenance, protection and education of the young" (Bakan, 1979:28). In this way, he gives agency to biology; biology determines social arrangements, especially the strict division of labor based on biological function. He assumes that previous to the "discovery" only women were biologically involved, thus only women would have had the responsibility of caring for children. There are grave problems with this argument; had he not dismissed anthropological evidence and theory so summarily, he might have avoided some of them. In all cultures, regardless of whether there is an ideology of biological relation at all or of paternity in particular, men participate in the rearing of children (see Introduction). All kinship systems, even matrilineal ones, have a role and function for the male vis-à-vis the children of the woman he marries or lives with. Bakan's assumption that men will assume care only for children who are biologically their own merely replicates and reinforces our own cultural ideology—it is not universal.

The logic of his argument forces him to come out in support of patriarchal religion and, by implication, patriarchal society. The Akedah represents for Bakan "the establishment of a patrilineal and patriarchal ideology" (ibid.:134) consequent on the "discovery" of paternity; at the same time, the Akedah also represents a mitigation of an infanticidal impulse brought about by this "discovery." He concludes that patriarchy is an advance because it "is associated with what is perhaps the most important step toward the *reduction* of male-female sex role difference in the history of civilization" (ibid.:166, emphasis added), namely that men take responsibility for children. His conclusion is contrary not only to anthropological evidence, but also to the evidence he brings from contemporary Western societies (Bakan, 1971) where many men have abandoned, hurt, or destroyed their children (see chapter 10). Nevertheless, the logic of his argument leads to the conclusion that we have forgotten the message of the Akedah, which, for him, mitigates the "infanticidal impulse." But it also demands the obedience and submission of the child (and the wife); the implications of his theory imply a return to patriarchal family values rather than a radical questioning of them. My argument that the story represents the construction, establishment, and naturalization of sex role *differences* makes much more sense of the evidence.

BALMARY

Marie Balmary, a French psychoanalyst, also recognized that Freud had a problem with incorporating the psychology of the father into his theory of psychoneuroses. She thought that by *Psychoanalyzing Psychoanalysis* (1979) she might be able to locate his "hidden fault." She, too, begins her investigation with the observation that Freud ignored the figure and character of Laius in his construction of the Oedipus complex. She believes that whatever patricidal and incestuous wishes Oedipus had were intimately related to the character and actions of his father. Although she focuses on the loathsome character of Laius, particularly in his betrayal of Pelops's hospitality (by the homosexual rape of his son Chrysippus), she puts very little emphasis on the fact that Laius first tried to get rid of Oedipus. Freud may not have known about the Chrysippus episode but he did know of Laius's attempt to dispose of his son.

In any case, Balmary says that the Oedipus myth is about the intimate links between father and son and asks why, then, does Freud focus on Oedipus alone. Why not a theory of the father's hidden fault (Balmary, [1979]1982:27)? She, like a number of others, notes that Freud had originally started in that direction, but then stopped rather abruptly. Again, like a number of others, she realizes that the abandonment of the "seduction theory" was intimately related to the death of Freud's father. Balmary thinks that the abrupt shift in the direction of his thought had to do with Freud's inability to confront his father about his past, particularly his relationship with the hidden woman, Rebecca.[9] Jakob Freud's secret was a sexual one—a liaison or brief marriage with a woman who then disappeared without a trace. Balmary claims that behind the sexual fault is murder or, at least, actions that led to another's death, and that this is the fault of Freud's father that neither he nor Freud could acknowledge. How "could Freud reveal the fault of his father just when his father was appearing before his judge?" (ibid.:41) that is, just at the time his father was dying. His secret went with him to his grave but its effects are transmitted from generation to generation, for "the patient does not suffer from his own faults but from those of the dominating if he cannot denounce them" (ibid.:87).[10]

Like a detective, Balmary presents detailed evidence of the three weeks in Freud's life during which he made that "great transition." In the process, the father's fault was carried to the son, and its effects are known by its absence in his theory. And, as has become clear since Freud's death, the effects have been transmitted to several generations of analysts who have continued to deny the "fault" of the fathers, a denial that has had particularly damaging effects on women patients (e.g., Herman, 1981; Lerman, 1986; Masson, 1984). Even though Balmary may have pinpointed the fault of Freud's father and Freud's reluctance to confront him with it, and outlined the way the fault was transmitted to his theory and practice, this does not explain the "faults" of numerous other fathers.

Balmary is aware of this problem and attempts to resolve it with the idea that "the origin of neurosis is not sexual desire alone nor even sexual trauma alone, but all the faults committed by the very people who present the law to the child" (Balmary, 1979:164). For her, symptoms are demands for recognition, and the cure consists in connecting the deed, or betrayal, to the one who committed it (ibid.:128), to discover the witness to what we had known alone (ibid.:162). This, surely, is an important therapeutic idea. In this work she locates the cause of neurosis externally either in the father or, in a Lacanian mode, in the law he represents. What she does not do is ask why the father represents the law or, conversely, why the law represents the father. These are questions that neither Lacan nor his numerous, even feminist, followers have satisfactorily answered. They assert that the phallus symbolizes the law of the father, but they deny that the meanings of *the phallus* are derived from the physical penis. On the contrary, I suggest, that precisely because the penis has been imagined as the primary instrument of human generativity or creativity, it can become "larger than life" as *the phallus*.

Balmary's more recent book, *Le sacrifice interdit* (The Forbidden/ Interrupted Sacrifice, 1986), is a psychoanalytically influenced reading of the story of Abraham's sacrifice. Although she retains the interpersonal aspect of her theory and focuses more on Abraham, the father, than on Isaac, the son, she does not use it as a foil for Freud's Moses nor as a complement to the Oedipus complex. She does not find fault with Abraham but instead elevates him into a modern existential hero struggling with the issue of separation and individuation, coming to autonomous selfhood free of encumbering relations.[11] This is signaled, she thinks, by God's command to Abraham, "Go forth," which she interpretes to mean something like: "Go find yourself." She believes that one cannot become a full autonomous being if one is ensnared in relationships that one is not willingly committed to. Her interpretation is conditioned by modern psychoanalytic theory and especially by the valuation of autonomy and individuation, which may not have been cultural ideals when Genesis was written and which have recently come under a great deal of feminist criticism. The ideals of autonomy and independence, in contrast to interdependence and caring, are heavily involved with social contract theory, which, as recent criticism (Pateman, 1988; Glendon, 1991; Fraser, 1989) has shown, is built on a masculine model.

Abraham *is* identified with his son, but I do not think the story mitigates that identification; instead I think it inscribes it. Balmary thinks Abraham must cut the ties that bind so that they can come together again, allied in a relationship freely chosen. These echoes of social contract theory versus patriarchalism seem particularly inappropriate and anachronistic in the case of Abraham, who is symbolically, culturally, and religiously the first patriarch.[12] According to Balmary, when Abraham responds to three calls from God, he cuts the ties that bind him—to his parents, to his wife, and to his son (Balmary, 1986:205). What he cuts in the "sacrifice" is not Isaac himself, but the *relation* that ties them, thus freeing Isaac to become his own person, not just a reproduction of his parents. But the story does not free Isaac. She seems to have forgotten that after their trial on the mountain, Abraham descends alone. Moreover, Isaac does not become much of a person in his own right after the Akedah; it is as if all life had been taken out of him. These facts have been noted by a number of biblical commentators, and a few have taken them as evidence that perhaps Isaac was really killed (see chapter 5). Balmary retreats from considering such a possibility and instead goes off in an equally speculative direction even more at variance with centuries of tradition.[13]

She also overlooks what Steinmetz (1991) and others have recognized: that the son in this story is imagined as of the same essence as the father. He is Abraham's seed—seed that will become a great nation and inherit the land. The ability to pass on this essence is given only to males—the fault line is the patriline.

She arrives at her conclusion by denying that the command was to sacrifice. She rightly says that the word for *sacrifice* is not in the text, that God asked only that Abraham *offer up* Isaac. Yet the word ʿ*olah* (burnt offering), which is in the text, signifies a sacrificial offering, and this "mistake," she says, has been inscribed in the tradition. Therefore, she thinks that Abraham was in great danger of misunderstanding God's command.[14] He had to wake up to what was meant—namely that he separate himself from his son psychologically. "You did not withold your son" means, for her, "you did not hold onto him." That might be fine for Abraham and perhaps it might free him from his attachment, but it seems to me that there might be other ways to illustrate this point without such trauma to the son.

In *Le sacrifice interdit* Balmary repeats the same fault she accuses Freud of when she claims that "the *Interpretation of Dreams* is the result of Freud's refusal to reprove the father" (Balmary, 1979:79). She does not reprove the father; her interpretation of the Abraham story is an apologetic interpretation. Like Freud, she ends by upholding and justifying the system that upholds and justifies the father.

MILLER

The only voice crying from the psychoanalytic wilderness is that of the Swiss psychoanalyst Alice Miller, in a chapter entitled "When Isaac Arises from the Sacrificial Altar" in *The Untouched Key: Tracing Childhood Trauma in Creativity and Destructiveness* (1988; English trans. 1990). When she examined a number of paintings depicting the scene of the sacrifice, she noticed that Abraham never looked directly at Isaac and "there is no pain to be seen in Abraham's face, no hesitation, no searching, no questioning, no sign that he is conscious of the tragic nature of his situation. All the artists, even Rembrandt, portray him as God's obedient instrument, whose sole concern is to function properly." She goes on to ask: "Why did they all take it for granted that the Bible passage could not be questioned?" (Miller, 1990:141).

Although astonished by their failure to doubt the received text, she attributes their lack of nerve to a "fundamental fact of our existence": that all of us have had firsthand experience of being at the mercy of our fathers, so much so that the "moral expressed in the story has almost been accorded the legitimacy of a natural law" (ibid.). Regardless of whether we have all experienced paternal abuse, paternal authority has had the status of something akin to natural law in that it has been culturally legitimated through religious texts, secular institutions, and modes of behavior. Such a moral structure demands the obedience and submission of women and children but is often symbolically rendered through sons.

Miller deplores this state of filial passivity and calls for "sons" to wake up, not to take the law into their own hands and kill the father, which would only perpetuate the problem, but to begin to question the law and its legitimacy. She constructs a dialogue between Isaac and Abraham that echoes my own childhood questions about the story as well as some of the dialogue between Cristos and his small daughter.

> Isaac will ask, "Father, why do you want to kill me?" and will be given the answer "It is God's will." "Who is God?" the son will ask. "The great and benevolent Father of us all, Whom we must obey," Abraham will answer. "Doesn't it grieve you," the son will want to know, "to have to carry out this command?" "It is not for me to take my feelings into account when God orders me to do something." "Then who are you," Isaac will ask, "if you carry out His orders without any feeling, and Who is this God, Who can demand such a thing of you?" (Miller, 1990:144)

Like the child who pointed out the obvious in the tale about the emperor's new clothes, it is about time we asked such obvious questions, especially of our sacred tales, the myths we live by. Miller's confrontation with the Abraham-Isaac story resulted in a radical questioning of psychoanalytic theory and practice, with which she had been involved for a quarter century. In her own theory and practice she has taken the side of the child and worked to expose abuse personally, theoretically, institutionally, and culturally.

BERGMANN

The latest book by a psychoanalyst on the Abraham story, that by Martin Bergmann, *In the Shadow of Moloch: The Sacrifice of Children and its Impact on Western Religions* (1992), takes no note whatsoever of his analytic colleagues Miller, Bakan, or Balmary.[15] Such an oversight makes one wonder about his research methods. It is also the latest example of what results when psychoanalysts enter into the realm of anthropology without any acquaintance with anthropological theory since Frazer and W. Robertson Smith. Bergmann does make passing reference to Levi-Strauss but turns him into a cultural particularist instead of the comparativist he is.

Bergmann first wrote about the Abraham story in 1988 and discussed it again when he played the part of the psychiatrist in Woody Allen's film *Crimes and Misdemeanors*. In the film he asks how it was that the early

Israelites conceived of a God who cares and demands that we act morally but, at the first opportunity, asks Abraham to sacrifice his son. That question is not answered in the film, but an attempt is made in Bergmann's book. He begins with the unsubstantiated assumption that ritual infanticide was a "ubiquitous custom" practiced long ago by those cannibal savages. Furthermore, he contends that "the struggle against this custom has been a driving force in the development of Western religions" (Bergmann, 1992:1). This could be a statement taken directly from Bakan, whom Bergmann does not cite. He travels down the predictable path, stating that *survivals* of this custom continue to exist in the unconscious and in certain religious rituals such as the Eucharist. He does not imagine, let alone ask, whether they might emerge relative to a specific concept of paternity and to a Father God.

With the exception of Miller, it seems that all of these theorists reached a limit—the *terminus ad quem*—beyond which they could not go. The limiting concept is the father who, for them, seems like the sun in a heliocentric universe; they revolve around it, blinded by its power.[16] In order to move beyond, they need to get a new perspective, they need a new theory, and especially they need a better anthropology.

The limit seems insurmountable, but it is not. What is needed is more attention to the meaning and definition of father. This, of course, would not prevent particular fathers from abusing their power and their children, but it would enable us to see this abuse as an extreme case of "acting out" or acting upon what is implicit in an entire system that institutionalizes, naturalizes, and legitimates paternal power.[17]

FATHERHOOD, MONOTHEISM, AND ABRAHAM

Although Freud thought that the concept of *God* was a projection of the feared and admired qualities of the human father, he also seemed to attribute godlike qualities to human fathers. He appears to have put fathers, or at least the idea of the father, on a pedestal, and he approached but seemed afraid to touch it. In fact, he noted that "the sacred is obviously something that must not be touched" (Freud, 1939:154 [SE 23: 120]), which may explain why he could not approach/reproach his father. Finally, he concluded "that what is sacred was originally nothing but the perpetuated will of the primeval father" (ibid.:156 [ibid.:121]) who was larger than life—as is every father to his small child.

The image of the father that Freud presumed we all carry around with us is an image that creates both fear of the father's authority and longing for it. This idealized image is sometimes enlarged into the "Great Man," like Moses, and ultimately into God, but it originally develops from one's own father.

The decisiveness of thought, the strength of will, the forcefulness of his deeds, belong to the picture of the father; above all other things, however, the self-reliance and independence of the great man, his divine conviction of doing the right thing, which may pass into ruthlessness. He must be admired, he may be trusted, but one cannot help also being afraid of him. We should have taken a cue from the word itself; who else but the father should in childhood have been the great man? (ibid.:140 [ibid.:109–10])

Surely not all fathers possess or are seen to possess such qualities. Or is it that, despite their individual differences, each partakes of the *imago* of the great man? Freud seems to conflate or confuse the *imago* with its real-life embodiments, which may help to explain why he appears to exonerate fathers, to let them off the hook, so to speak, for each in his own way represents the "Great Man" and each deserves a portion of the respect, both love and fear, owed to such a one. Freud's image of the father is not unlike that of a Christian theologian who stated: "there is something divine in the father, seeing that there is something fatherly in God" (Quell, 1967, vol. 5:965). Both are drawing on deep-seated cultural beliefs.

For Freud, the elevated place of the father is tied to his interrelated ideas about renunciation, paternity, and cultural advance. The very idea of father, for Freud, is bound up with the renunciation of instinctual gratification. Yet this is contradicted by his description of the primal father who indulged his instincts, both aggressive and sexual. The father may have forced renunciation on the sons, but Freud stressed that it was the brothers who imposed it on themselves after the murder. Not only did they renounce all the women of the horde, they also renounced, if not the desire, at least acting upon the desire to hoard women. Each man would have a woman for himself.

RENUNCIATION

Despite the contradiction at the heart of Freud's theory of renunciation, renunciation is, nevertheless, portrayed as a male achievement; those who renounce are men; those who are renounced are women and what they symbolize, namely, sensuality and instinctual gratification. Men's renunciation becomes identified with rationality and progress, and it is exemplified by the idea of the Great Man.[18] Moses' capacity for renunciation and the strict rules he imposed on his followers provided them with a motive to kill him; their guilt, arising from the murder, caused them to reinstate his precepts. For Freud, the stringent precepts of Judaism represent the renunciation of instinctual gratification and this is, for him, what gives Judaism its masculine character. No doubt some of his effort to construct Judaism as masculine lay in his reaction to some of his contemporaries who portrayed it as feminine (e.g., Weininger, 1903; cf. Eilberg-Schwartz, 1994; Gilman, 1993). Perhaps Freud's construction represents his own "flight from the feminine."[19]

The gendered associations are not just about men and women but are intimately connected with the notions of maternity and paternity we have been discussing. Because men were thought capable of lifting themselves out of their dependence on sense perception, "to put their inferences upon a level with the testimony of their senses," the great leap forward was made possible. Freud is referring to the so-called discovery of paternity as well as to the commonplace idea that "maternity is proved by the senses whereas paternity is a surmise and a premise." This "turning from the mother to the father . . . signifies above all a victory of spirituality over the senses—that is to say, a step forward in culture" (Freud, 1939:145–6 [SE 23:114]). Freud reiterated, without quite the same flair, what Bachofen had said eighty-five years earlier. Today, echoes of these ideas are heard behind numerous statements about gender, appropriate sex roles, and intellectual ability.

For both Bachofen and Freud, the "discovery" of paternity marked not just an intellectual advance but also a spiritual one—it had to do with men and women and notions of divinity, deity, and morality—illustrating that for them, at least, gender has ethical and cosmological implications. Marx and Engels eschewed the religious dimension, but they, too, subscribed to the belief that the "discovery" of paternity and the conjectured "overthrow of mother right" ushered in the new age of patriarchal institutions based on property, among which a man could henceforth count his children.

Freud clearly reiterated what many others assumed and continue to assume without question, namely that maternity is self-evident, a matter evident to the senses, an obvious fact of nature, rather than a term that gives a particular meaning to the fact that babies come out of the bodies of women. Paternity, he assumed, was an inference that demanded abstract thought and sophisticated rational processes. Because rational processes have been ranked higher than those of the senses, the notion of paternity marked an intellectual advance by those who made the "discovery."

Maternity-Paternity

Freud, like so many others, conflates the fact that babies come out of the bodies of women with the *concept* of maternity. What is lost in the conflation is the specific meaning of maternity: it has meant giving nurture and giving birth; it has not meant creation or co-creation. Freud assumes even more about paternity, which he describes but does not examine. In order to make the assumptions more obvious, I return to the work of Bakan because he examines paternity in somewhat more detail and unwittingly allows us to see where the problematic assumptions are. Like Freud, he believes that monotheism is intimately related to paternity and that both represent a cultural advance. The problems stem from the lack of specificity about the meaning of paternity. Bakan gives several commonplace definitions but does not pursue them. In a number of places he states something similar to: "Paternity is the biological fact that men are necessary for the birth of children" (Bakan, 1979:12). Elsewhere he recognized that "in the blush of the biological discovery, men tended to believe that the total genetic endowment was theirs. They were, of course, unaware of what we know today" (ibid.:166).

That, however, is the crux of the problem in several ways, and Bakan failed to understand any of them. He did not explain why men should assume that they provided the entire "genetic" endowment, or why women would accept that explanation. Second, the problem is not just with the ancients and their lack of knowledge. It is also that *we* fail to realize that the absence of genetic theory did not prevent the ancients from constructing a concept of paternity. They weren't just hanging around until genetic theory was invented. Nor did its absence prevent *any* human group from constructing a social role for men.

In other words, Bakan does not realize that paternity was culturally constructed, not discovered. The difference between discovery and construction is vast—it entails different conceptual frameworks for the interpretation of the past as well as the present. To discover something means "to obtain knowledge through observation" (American Heritage Dictionary); it is applicable to science and the investigation of the natural world. To construct something means to build, create, or put an interpretation upon it. Today a growing group of scholars recognizes that scientific observation is, itself, culturally mediated—that scientific knowledge proceeds from, and is relative to, the construction of meanings. The danger in not comprehending this is that cultural notions of gender (and race) often become inscribed in what is usually imagined to be the neutral area of scientific theory.[20]

Paternity is obviously a concept that includes but is not limited to a biological connection. The biological definition has blinded us to the fact that paternity has also meant the primary creative role. The meaning of *father* emerged in relation to a *theory* of procreation; the male was imagined as progenitor, the creator (with God's help) and transmitter of life, and this was encapsulated in the notion of *seed*. For Bakan, male identity was tied to the notion of *seed*, and this was a positive image for him because it conveyed "man's effort to extend the boundary of his ego to include his seed" (Bakan, 1966:202).

Although it may be beneficial for a man to extend his ego boundary, Bakan does not take into account the effect on the female ego beyond acknowledging that the notion of seed "tends to make the male even more important than the female, as seed is the determining factor of the nature of the plant, with the soil, water, and sun playing only an enabling role" (ibid.:202–3). He goes on to say that the "very concept of semen as 'seed' which is deposited in the ground is suggestive that the ego has moved to include the semen" (ibid.:202–3). He means, but does not say, that the ego is male, and ignores "what we know today," that seed is composed of both male and female elements, namely, genes.

No doubt the image of seed helped a man identify with his semen and his child, but that identification was done at the expense of women (could women have an ego?). Women became symbolically equated with the soil, with the material and therefore renewable and exchangeable aspects of existence. Bakan assumes that previously only women were identified with children and therefore only women cared for them; he assumes that only when men imagine themselves *biologically* identified with their children will they begin to care for them. The identification of a man with his seed implied, for Bakan, a "motherization" of the male (ibid.:203) and a reduction in male-female sex role polarity, and it is this image of male-female relations that, he believes, is deposited in the Bible. Rather than causing a reduction in sex-role polarity, I believe this theory of procreation exaggerates it; to me, Bakan has completely misunderstood the implications of what he has said.

I am not arguing that there is no physiological connection between a man and child, but the problem has been that we tend to conflate that understanding with the one that implies that a man, by means of his seed is *the* begetter, the creative agent, the one who has the potential to create and transmit life. The simple, natural image of seed conveys enormous power. Embedded in stories that have been told for generation upon generation, the meaning of *paternity* has been operative not just in the first blush, as Bakan imagines, but for several thousand years.

MONOTHEISM

For Freud, the genesis of monotheism depends on the murder, not the definition, of the father; indeed, he states that without the two murders, the genesis of monotheism would have been impossible (Freud, 1939: 129–30 [SE 23:101]). In his last work, Freud atavistically clung to the idea of an original deed, whereas in regard to his studies of individual psychology he had abandoned that idea long ago. The murder of Moses was the historical repetition of the primal crime, a deed that, for Freud, laid the foundation for human society and morals. What was true of religion in general must be true of what he considered the most advanced type of religion, namely, monotheism. The repetition of the original crime reinforced the pattern of guilt, reification, awe, and worship that characterized the formation of what he claimed was the original god image. At the same time it was an abstraction and condensation of the image of all fathers. So, too, is Abraham.

FREUD'S BLINDNESS—ABRAHAM

Abraham is considered the father of the three monotheistic religions and the Akedah the foundational story. It was, therefore, the obvious place to begin an investigation of monotheism. Freud's own theories as well as his identification with Moses got in his way. Instead of hypothesizing an original murder of the father by the sons, Freud might have considered the attempted sacrifice of the son by the father and speculated about what that might represent. Had he considered Abraham, he might have thought about infanticidal impulses or of a primal murder of the son by the father. And that might have led him to take into consideration the role of Laius in the fate of Oedipus, and he might, then, have given us a theory of the interrelations of father and son. But he might not have stopped there; he might have pushed further and asked about the nature or, better yet, the meaning of fatherhood. Had he done so he would have realized that the relation between father and son has to do with meaning, not just about biology and sexuality, but also about authority and obedience. Indeed, he *did* recognize that in *Moses and Monotheism* but he did not use that insight to rethink his theory of individual psychology.

When Isaac was about to be sacrificed to Abraham's God, he did not cry out; at least no cry has survived. All that remains in the text is silence—silence enough to construct theological and psychological explanations. Usually Isaac's silence is interpreted as his acquiescence—that he performed his filial duty, obeyed his father as his father obeyed God. But maybe he did cry out and maybe his cry was muffled and then obliterated in the text. After all, there was no one there but Abraham to report it.

Freud did not consider Isaac and the Akedah nor its relation to the sacrifice at the heart of Christianity. Had he done so, he might have been led to wonder why Oedipus, unlike another whose feet were pierced with a nail, failed to cry out: "Father, father, why have you forsaken me?" Through the ages, theologians and, more recently, psychoanalysts have tried to drown out that cry as over and over children are sacrificed to the will of the father(s).

PART FIVE

The Social Legacy

CHAPTER TEN

Sacrificing Our Children

TODAY we do not ritually sacrifice children to a deity (if, indeed, such a practice was ever widespread). Yet every day we open the newspaper to learn of another way in which the hopes, trust, opportunities, and lives of children have been sacrificed by the people they depend on and the social, cultural, and religious systems they are taught to have faith in. In this chapter I sketch some of the connections between patriarchal power, as epitomized in the Abraham story, and ways in which children are sacrificed today, for example, through physical and sexual abuse, poverty and the welfare system, and war. To hold the story of Abraham responsible for these contemporary sacrifices would be both ridiculous and an abdication of our own responsibility. But it has had an influence, which, though subtle, is relevant.

This story, at the foundation of the three monotheistic religions, has shaped the social, cultural, and moral climates of the societies animated by them. It provides the supreme model of faith, and it incorporates notions of procreation, paternity, the family, gender definitions and roles, authority, and obedience. It is a symbolic representation of patriarchal power, and the structure, roles, and values that support it. Once these ideas, structures, and values have been internalized psychologically, rationalized philosophically, codified legally, and embedded in institutions such as marriage and the family, the military, and the church, they become part of the reality we live. Examining the assumptions in this foundational story illuminates some of the connections between these seemingly disparate areas and enables us to glimpse the outline of the myth that has shaped our lives and the social legacy we have inherited. Only then do we have the possibility of changing it. Placing contemporary social issues in a wider theosocial context opens up new avenues for research and new ways for revisioning our world.

My purpose is not to imply that religion is essentially or primarily *about* abuse. But it is about power and authority, the abuse of which is all too common. The belief that one has the single, true, right way is easy justification for forcing others to conform or punishing those who remain outside and opposed. More than that, however, power, authority, and sacrifice of the child are embedded in some of the major symbols and stories of Judaism, Christianity, and Islam. Specifically, it returns us to the Akedah, the Crucifixion, and the Kurban—the willingness of the father to sacrifice his child, and the child's obedience and submission to the father.

The story of Abraham is about both faith and male (pro-)creativity—two aspects (sacred and profane) of patriarchal power. These two aspects are related to two different modes of the sacrifice of children: on one side, the sacrifice is morally justified; on the other an extension of paternal right. Abraham showed his love for God by his willingness to kill his son. But what about his love for his *son*? The message to humans, affirmed in all three religious traditions, is that love of God must come first. Without denying that message, something else is added in Christianity—God the Father so loved the world he gave his only begotten son. But what about his love for his *son*? Jesus' will, like that of Isaac, is portrayed as at one with the Father, a complete submission of the will of the son to that of the Father. Theological interpretations of this "at-one-ment" abound; here, I focus on the implications of this sacred model of paternal power for human behavior and morality.

This model implies that to be faithful, fathers ought to be willing to sacrifice their sons if God, or some other transcendent authority, such as the State, demands. The story has been used to justify fathers sending their sons off to war—especially when the war can be imagined as "holy." The faithful *man* is a man whose faith in an abstract, transcendent concept (God) takes precedence over his earthly, emotional tie to his child; his faith renders him invulnerable to human claims.[1] This kind of psychological detachment can be very dangerous, for it can lead to a devaluation of human life. The story also communicates something to sons: it is their duty to obey. Those who do not obey should be punished, for they threaten not just the authority of fathers but also the system that supports them. The model is thoroughly authoritarian.

The authority of the father is, however, rooted in notions of paternity. The father, imagined as the author (with God's help) of human life, as God is of life in general, is symbolically allied with divine power. The child is his, is his seed; the child belongs to him. The logical consequence is that he who creates life has, implicitly at least, the power (and the right) to take it. That *is* God's prerogative as we are constantly reminded in both the Bible and the Qur'an. It has also been men's prerogative: throughout history human males have been the ones to take life—both of animals and other humans, and, more generally, have had the power (and assumed the right) to determine and control the lives of children.[2]

Patriarchal power is what connects the sacred story of the sacrifice with the more mundane but real sacrifices of real children. Obviously, not all fathers abuse their power; this is not a critique of men as people. I do not think that male violence is necessarily inherent in masculine nature; this is not an essentialist argument. Instead, I think the problem lies with the *meanings* of "father" and the ways these meanings have been institutionalized. A man need not be a father to partake of patriarchal power. His procreative ability is part of the definition of masculinity. Nevertheless, children *are* sacrificed in the name of the father, whether that father is the child's own or a surrogate, a priest, or the "fathers of state." This is not to exempt or excuse mothers, but, overwhelmingly, abuse is at the hands of fathers or other men. When it does occur at the hands of mothers it is interpreted differently. It is also predominantly "fathers of state" who make the decisions to send their sons (and now daughters) to war. In the United States, these same fathers recently decided to sacrifice an entire generation of children by cutting off their welfare benefits, thereby depriving them a modicum of access to life, liberty, and the pursuit of happiness.

In the following sections I briefly reflect on the relation between paternal power and these contemporary sacrifices of children. I start with personal and intimate occasions in which paternal power is exerted on children, and move to wider social and global issues. Abraham is not the cause of these sacrifices, but what ties them together are the interrelated meanings of God, paternity, and authority that are given their first symbolic expression in that story. Because the three monotheistic religions that have sprung from the story have exerted enormous power over numerous societies for a very long time, the meanings have been generalized, even secularized.

Physical Abuse

Out of every ten children murdered in the world, nine lived in the United States (United Nations Children's Fund Report, see *San Francisco Chronicle*, 23 September 1993);[3] every fourteen hours it is a child under five, every five hours a youth between the ages of fifteen and nineteen (Sidel, 1992, citing Children's Defense Fund report, 1991). Every day we hear that a child has been killed or maimed. It happens all across the country and among all classes of people. It happens on a scale and with means unimaginable in what we so condescendingly call "primitive" societies. Instead, in the most modern, most advanced, most affluent country in the world:

> Children have been whipped, beaten, starved, drowned, smashed against
> walls and floors, held in ice water baths, exposed to extremes of outdoor

temperatures, burned with hot irons and steam pipes. Children have been tied and kept in upright positions for long periods. They have been systematically exposed to electric shock; forced to swallow pepper, soil, feces, urine, vinegar, alcohol, and other odious materials; buried alive; had scalding water poured over their genitals; had their limbs held in open fire; placed in roadways where automobiles would run over them; placed on roofs and fire escapes in such a manner as to fall off; bitten, knifed, and shot; had their eyes gouged out (Bakan, 1971:4).

Such appalling events would never have been predicted for late twentieth-century America, certainly not by Freud or those influenced by his thought. Freud, as we have seen, believed in evolutionary advance and in the notion of civilization as something won at great cost, mainly by men, through their ability for renunciation. Primitives were assumed to act out their aggressive impulses; in modern society these impulses are supposedly bound. Modern men can only fantasize and become neurotic. And yet an argument diametrically opposed to Freud's could be made—that civilization is the progressive unleashing of aggressive tendencies inflicted anonymously on a large scale as well as on those nearest and dearest (see also Diamond, 1974).

A common assumption is that aggression is *natural*, and thus an inherent part of human nature. This obscures both the *cultural* differences in the expression of aggression and the different *kinds* of aggression, for example, those that are activated (a) in response to direct threats to one's own life or that of one's family, (b) in relation to abstract concepts such as the enemy, the nation, or God, and (c) as a result of anger or frustration. Direct aggression against children probably falls most often under (c), but it need not be carried out in the heat of anger; some punishment is done cooly and rationally. In order to lay the blame for child abuse at the feet of particular fathers, Bakan situates it in an "infanticidal impulse" that was activated by the "discovery" of paternity. But it was not a discovery about the male's biological contribution to the formation of a child, it was a specific cultural *belief*—that by planting his "seed" he created life, like God. Nevertheless, Bakan's entire discussion is situated in the context of human evolution and human nature, rather than culture.

Bakan does not consider that not all cultures have been seed-planting ones, and that those that are do not necessarily equate semen with seed, or make the seed-soil analogy for human procreation. In Western culture, however, it has served to naturalize male power, prestige, and privilege, and it is woven into the most sacred of origin myths. Human problems are not simply reflexes of human nature, or of economic or political conditions alone, but are related to specific cultures and religious traditions, especially to the stories we tell ourselves, and come to believe, about human nature and the human condition. There is no way of knowing human nature outside of culture, outside of particular cultures.

The sacrifice and betrayal of children is, I suggest, bound up with patriarchal authority, which, in turn, is bound up with the foundation story of our culture. If Abraham was willing to sacrifice his beloved son, how much easier it is to assent to the sacrifice of children who are not loved, not claimed, not "owned." Children hurt today are often not beloved, though that is not always the case; some children are singled out precisely because they are loved, and the abuse, especially sexual abuse, is done in the name of love. Others are hurt or killed because they misbehave or are perceived to misbehave. For example, James Austin, a Pennsylvania man allowed to procure a baby by "surrogacy" despite his evident lack of preparation for parenting, killed his five-week-old son because he was not behaving properly, i.e., he was crying (*New York Times*, 9 August 1995). Other children are punished because they are disobedient, and here, too, punishment can be done in the name of love or in "the best interests of the child." A jury in Texas voted to acquit Forrest Grigg in the murder of his son; the father said, "I did it for him." The son had been smoking marijuana and drinking wine, and for the father "any drugs are dangerous." His son, allegedly, was his pride and joy, but confronted with his disobedience, the father admitted that "There wasn't any question about me killing him" (see *Chicago Tribune*, 17 January 1977).

Still other children are hurt or killed because they are no longer under the father's authority. This was true in several particularly horrible cases in 1995. In Alabama, Stanley Kidd killed his fourteen-month-old twins by strapping them into their car seats and pumping the car full of carbon monoxide. He did this to avoid child support payments and to collect their life insurance (*New York Times*, 2 August 1995). Alan Gubernat killed his three-year-old son when the mother, to whom he was not married, refused to give *his* name to the child (*New York Times*, 16 May 1995). These stories appeared in small columns and could be easily overlooked. The case that received the most media coverage and riveted national attention was of a mother who also put her two children in a car and sent it rolling into a river where they drowned. Only Susan Smith became the target for the accumulated moral outrage of the nation. Her actions were seen as unnatural. But what does the lack of attention and outrage about the crimes of the fathers imply?

Although hardly generalizable, my experience in the 1980s in Chicago, as a volunteer counselor with people accused of child abuse, made me aware of how readily the abuse was justified in terms of the patriarchal authority embodied in religion. The most noticeable characteristic of my clients' stories was the stress they placed on the *obedience* of children and the religious justifications for it, including the story of Abraham.[4] The abuse, among my clients, was most often at the hands of fathers or their surrogates—uncles, brothers, friends. Mothers were not, and are not, exempt, of course, but they are structurally in a very different position. Even though we think of mother and father as equivalent, both equally parents, the argument of this book has been that the meanings and values of the terms and the roles are not only different but hierarchically ordered, and thus, the damage they inflict, even when similar, is interpreted differently.

To my clients, punishment was justified because the parents felt that obedience was their due. Citing sermons from their preachers or the Bible, these people expected that children should be brought up to obey their parents and that they, as parents, could demand obedience. They were acting in place of God and they construed their actions as in the best interests of the child. Although not always explicitly stated, they seemed to have an idea that a child is born bad;[5] therefore it is the parent's role, in fact the parent's *duty*, to train them to be good. Training and discipline were most often accomplished with corporal punishment. And the "most enduring and influential source for the widespread practice of physical punishment, both in this country and abroad, has been the Bible" (Greven, [1990]1992:6).

While these Chicago parents may have overstepped the fine line between punishment and abuse, their views can hardly be considered aberrant since they form a continuous strand in American Christianity since the founding of the nation. Philip Greven, a historian at Rutgers University, has documented the pervasiveness of beliefs about obedience, discipline, and punishment in Christian childrearing manuals and diaries from the seventeenth century to the present in the United States. For example, Jonathan Edwards, a well-known protestant minister-theologian in seventeenth century New England, and his pious wife Sarah believed "that until a child will obey his parents, he can never be brought to obey God" (ibid.:21). And they advised parents to begin to discipline a child early, at least by the time it was six months old, or at the first sign of self-will.

The goal of such punishment is to "break the will" of a child. A child should not have a will of its own but its will should coincide with that of the parent, just as we have been taught Isaac's will coincided with that of Abraham, and Jesus' will with that of God the Father. This obsession with obedience and breaking the will of infants and children continues in a number of contemporary Christian childrearing manuals: "The only issue in rebellion is will; in other words, who is going to rule—the parent or the child. The major objective of chastisement is *forcing the child's obedience to the will of his parents*" (Fugate, 1980 cited in ibid.:67, emphasis added). Another contemporary Christian pedagogue states that the chastisement "should be painful and it should last until the child's will is broken" (Hyles, 1977, cited in ibid.). Hyles tells parents to: "Require strict obedience. This obedience should always be immediate, without question or argument. . . . Obedience is the foundation for all character. It is the foundation for the home. It is the foundation for a school. It is the foundation for a country. It is the foundation for a society. It is absolutely necessary for law and order to prevail" (Hyles, 1977, in ibid.:71).[6] This vision of a totally authoritarian system, in which the will of the father is paramount, seems hardly the foundation for an emergent democracy. Any challenge to the will of the father is felt as a threat to the entire system that supports his power and, therefore, must be dealt with swiftly and forcefully.

SEXUAL ABUSE

Sexual abuse is a more intimate example of physical abuse, in which patriarchal power is specifically but inappropriately aimed at the reproductive part of the body. It has taken us a long time to believe that such abuse was happening, in part because of the belief in the supposedly universal "incest taboo," and in part because of the legacy of Freud. This is not the place to go into lengthy discussions of either the incest taboo or of the Freudian literature about incest, except to say that although all cultures have prohibited marriage and/or sexual relations between certain people construed as relatives, the specific people vary cross-culturally, and, in any case, the prohibition has not prevented the widespread incidence of incest perpetrated primarily by the father.[7] Because of the heterosexual bias and the belief that sex is for the purpose of procreation, theorists did not immediately contemplate incest between father and son. But the "growing awareness that many more boys [than previously thought] are also sexually abused by their fathers makes it impossible to maintain the comparison between human sexual activities and the breeding behavior of animals, to regard the incest taboo as a mechanism which prevents genetic defects in offspring or ensures their evolutionary fitness" (LaFontaine, 1987: 286). In other words, homosexual incest undermines the biogenetic explanations for the incest taboo.

Furthermore, many theorists assumed that "sexual relations between parents and children would subvert parental (paternal) authority" (ibid.: 269). Not until the early 1980s and the emergence of feminist critiques of previous theories, did people begin to understand paternal incest as an *expression* of paternal power and authority (Jenkins, 1992:107ff.; McKinnon, 1995; LaFontaine, 1987). Furthermore, it "was only a mild exaggeration of normal male behavior" (Glaser and Frosh, 1988; cited in Jenkins, 1992:110). Anthropologist Susan McKinnon has observed that the most remarkable aspect in discussions of incest was "the repeated refrain of normalcy. . . . The incestuous father is virtually indistinguishable from any other man in American culture. . . . The high moral and religious profile of incestuous fathers is repeatedly mentioned" (McKinnon, 1995:28). Conventional theorists did not see pathology or perversion on the part of the fathers, but blamed, instead, the "seductive" daughters and the "collusive" mothers (ibid.:31–6).

Freud's theory that the child (usually the daughter, but see the case of Schreber in Freud, [1911]SE 12) harbored sexual fantasies directed to the father exonerated fathers. He did not explore the sexual fantasies of fathers toward their daughters (or sons), or how these may have activitated them in their children. More important, his theory "ignores the issue of power," as Judith Herman, a Boston-based psychiatrist, was one of the first to point out (Herman, 1981:27). A child is "powerless in relation to an adult, she is not free to refuse a sexual advance," and, in any case, "the parent's authority over the child is usually sufficient to compel *obedience*" (ibid., emphasis added).

Incest, of course, is only one form of sexual abuse. Most nonrelative sexual abuse is, nevertheless, committed overwhelmingly by males who are often relatives or "surrogates" for the father—uncles and friends.[8] The issue of power and authority is as pertinent in these types of sexual abuse as in incest, and it is as relevant for boys as it is for girls. This has become especially clear after the revelations of numerous cases of sexual abuse of boys (and some girls) by priests.

Roman Catholic priests, referred to as "Fathers," are the very men who represent God the Father, or at least his will, on earth. They are channels for God's power; they act in his name; they are revered, respected, trusted, and looked up to for moral guidance; the abuse of that trust is, therefore, all the more reprehensible.[9] Because of priests' position, it is perhaps not so surprising that it took so long for anyone to believe that the abuse was really happening.[10] The glacially slow reaction of the church has shown that the church's primary objective was to protect the priests (fathers) identified with the institution, not the children who were hurt and abused. "The *primary* consideration in dealing with cases like these has always been keeping the affair as quiet as possible. The parents and the victims in these cases were more or less ignored," said Rev. Doyle, speaking with amazing candor to *The Boston Globe* (24 October 1992, emphasis added) about the case of James Porter, a priest accused of numerous acts of sexual abuse in several states.

These fathers, hidden behind the legitimating systems of patriarchal authority,[11] are above suspicion, beyond question; they are protected and let off the hook. For the children, however, it is a double betrayal—first by the particular "father" who perpetrated the abuse and second by the church, which, by not believing the child and hiding the abuse, has taken the side of the priest against the child.[12]

POVERTY AND WELFARE

Although physical and sexual abuse captures the imagination and indignation of society, most maltreatment of children is not as depicted in these lurid cases. Summarizing a 1983 report by the American Humane Society, anthropologists Scheper-Hughes and Stein note: "The greatest threat to child well-being and survival in our society today is from neglect, which is broadly defined in child welfare discourse as the 'deprivation of necessities,' or, in other words, poverty" (Scheper-Hughes and Stein, 1987:352). This is reiterated by Penelope Leach, a well-known British child psychologist: "Poverty," she says, "is the single most predictive indicator of risk for children" (Leach, 1994:188) or, more dramatically, "more American children in any five-year period die from causes directly related to poverty than American soldiers during the Vietnam War" (ibid.:185; see also Edelman, 1987, and Funiciello, 1993:17, who claims that poverty is "the number one killer of children in the United States"). All point out how much easier it is to focus on and pathologize a few spectacular cases of abuse than to deal with the more pervasive social and economic problems of poverty. Although poverty does not *cause* violent, physical child abuse, its stress can exacerbate situations in which it is far more likely to occur (cf. Garfinkel, 1992).

Poverty sacrifices the potential of children by depriving them of adequate care and the necessities needed to flourish (food, shelter, clothing, health care, and education). Ironically, during the 1970s and 1980s, when the country became obsessed with child abuse, Republican presidents severely slashed welfare, food stamps, and health and education benefits (Scheper-Hughes and Stein, 1987). One analyst referred to this as a "Time of Sacrifice" (DeMause, 1984), meaning that children were being sacrificed to "Reagonomics." He could not have foreseen that this trend would reach its denouement on 22 August 1996, when President Clinton signed the *Personal Responsibility and Work Opportunity Act*. With one flick of the pen, President Clinton ended "welfare as we know it," established in 1935 as part of a widespread program of social security. His action did not put an end to the problems welfare was designed to alleviate; indeed, the "welfare wars," as Nancy Fraser named them (Fraser, 1989), are just beginning. In signing the act, President Clinton merely fired the first shot.

In order to gain some perspective on the issue of welfare, we need to ask why, in the richest country in the world, millions of children live in poverty without adequate housing, food, child care, health care, and education.[13] Many scholars agree that providing adequate support for all children in the United States is economically possible; indeed, the United States could significantly alter the welfare of all children in the world. What is lacking is the social will to do so (Katz, 1986:272; Leach, 1994: 174). A number of studies have found that the United States does less than almost any other Westernized, industrialized nation in helping to defray the costs that parents shoulder in rearing children.[14] This is a shocking indictment of the social will.

Children's poverty in the United States is increasingly associated with single motherhood and with welfare (AFDC—Aid to Families with Dependent Children). The onus for poverty is placed on the character of the mothers rather than on the abdication of the fathers. Instead of analyzing the social and economic shifts that have made it difficult even for two parents to raise a child and to what Diana Pearce (1978) called the "feminization of poverty," we scapegoat the most vulnerable. The very late and desultory attention to "deadbeat dads" has never reached the level of excoriation poured on welfare mothers. Yet nonsupport of children by fathers is the major cause of women seeking AFDC. Welfare, more accurately, should have been imagined as a *government subsidy of fathers*, instead of a handout to mothers, for it is fathers' income, not mothers' care that it is meant to compensate. That interpretation might have produced more sympathy and support for mothers and children.

We are all aware that it "takes two to tango," a sperm and an ovum to begin the process that results in a child; children of welfare mothers are not the products of "virgin births." Nor are their mothers usually among those seeking the services of new reproductive technologies, sperm banks, artificial insemination, or adoption; they are girls and women who got pregnant by the traditional method, and who, for whatever reason, have been abandoned by the fathers of the children. "A woman who leaves her newborn in the hospital and never returns for it still makes headlines. You'd need a list as thick as the New York City phone book to name the men who have no idea *where* or *how* or *who* their children are" (Pollitt, 1995:20). Most women do not abandon their children; they *are* being responsible, doing what mothers have always done (caring for children or trying to), but in the face of poverty, stigma, and public scorn. Although it may be true that children in single-parent families are at greater risk, are they at risk because there are not two parents (specifically a father) or because there is no money? A number of studies have shown that children in single-parent families do as well and, in many cases, better than those brought up in two-parent families provided there is adequate financial, social, and emotional support (Stacey, 1994; Leach, 1994; Inglis, 1978; Young, 1995). If we were really concerned with the welfare of children, the marital status of the mothers would not be at issue, and we would think of creative ways to nurture and support them.

Economics is not the issue, for many of those who oppose welfare seem willing to spend their tax dollars (1) to put children in orphanages at a cost per child of $40,000 to $60,000 a year—many times an average welfare stipend (*Newsweek*, 12 December 1994); (2) to keep a young prisoner in jail at a cost of $200 a day ($73,000 a year) (*New York Times*, 16 May 1994), but balk at giving his mother $200 a week, a grant that might be enough to help her keep him out of trouble, and, perhaps more telling, (3) to pay foster mothers three to six times what welfare mothers receive to care for their own children. Nationally, AFDC has accounted for only 1 percent of the federal budget, or about $22 billion a year (compared to $300 billion for the military, some of it for things neither necessary nor wanted), yet it receives a disproportionate amount of public attention. Clearly, something besides economics is at stake in the welfare debates.

The almost exclusive focus on welfare mothers has obscured both the physical absence of fathers and, more important, their powerful, symbolic (omni-)presence. Throughout the welfare debate we have been barraged with stereotypic images of the welfare mother—a young, black woman with several children born out of wedlock. Welfare mothers are characterized as irresponsible, lazy, dependent, and the cause of contemporary social ills such as teenage pregnancy, out-of-wedlock births, crime, drugs, and violence. In this view, welfare mothers clearly represent a serious threat to the social fabric. Despite numerous facts that contradict the stereotype, it is, nevertheless, the stereotype that informs popular opinion as well as government policy.[15] It also reduces to one type the diversity of women on welfare and the different paths that led them there—for example, death of a spouse, divorce, disabilities of partner or child, unwed motherhood, inadequate health and child care, and lack of jobs that pay a "family wage."[16]

Single mothers (whether ever married or not) are being punished in proportion to belief in another stereotype—the "traditional" family, felt to be both natural and ordained. Although the word *family* originally meant all those dependent on a male head, and although it still carries some of that meaning, today it usually refers to a nuclear family composed of a married, heterosexual father and mother biologically related to their children. Regardless of whether such a family was really traditional (and a number of studies suggest it was not), it has been resurrected by a group of mutually citing social scientists connected with the Institute for American Values who, despite their conservative rhetoric, convened to inspire the "family values" agenda of the Democratic Party (see Young, 1995; Stacey, 1996). For them, fatherless families are the problem, and their solution is to put a man back into the picture. But they have few suggestions for how to do this or how to make fathers more responsible (Blankenhorn, 1995). Instead, their portrait of the ideal family holds millions of women and children hostage to a standard against which they are measured and found wanting.

The "traditional" family, according to Barbara Dafoe Whitehead, a prominent member of the aforementioned institute, is "responsible for teaching lessons of independence, self-restraint, responsibility, and right conduct, which are essential to a free, democratic society. If the family fails in these tasks, then the entire experiment in democratic, self-rule is jeopardized" (Whitehead, 1993:84). It follows that those outside the "traditional" family cannot teach these values and, therefore, are to blame for the deterioration of society. But it is the welfare mothers, not the absent, and irresponsible fathers, who threaten democratic society; they must be eliminated, at least from public consciousness. No wonder there is a "War on Welfare Mothers."[17]

The double standard runs very deep. Because women have traditionally been held responsible for emotional relationships, they are blamed for not being able to "hold onto a man." Women have also been held responsible for birth control—either they should not have sex or they should be prepared to take the consequences.[18] Studies have shown that more than two-thirds of teenage girls are impregnated by men who are between the ages of twenty and fifty, that is, by men who are far more likely to know about the biology of reproduction and can more easily obtain contraceptive devices such as condoms. A girl might harbor romantic notions of marriage and family, but the men seducing these young women have sex, not marriage, in mind—indeed, many of them may already be married. Neverthless, there is strong resistance to penalizing the unwed dad. "The attempt to make casual sexual partners behave like fathers sends the wrong message. . . . [I]t is bad policy for the state to enforce a contract that does not exist" (Schiffren, *New York Times*, 10 August 1995). Restated: *fathers are not responsible for their children unless they are married, but mothers are.*

Out-of-wedlock births have been blamed on women, and the term *illegitimate* has been reinvigorated to refer to their children. That term is both ideological and patriarchal, for it means that a child has no man to name and claim it. But why should a child be stigmatized for the "sins" of its parents which are, however, blamed only on the mothers? Why shouldn't every child be legitimate by virtue of being born?

Men have been able to exercise their paternal power (*patria potestas*) choosing which children to acknowledge and care for. There are plenty of men who father numerous children with different women and who take care of *none* of them, yet there is far greater reluctance to infringe on men's reproductive rights, including those of sex predators, than on women's (Bordo, 1993).[19] Men seem to have an inalienable right to reproduce, women only when they are dependent on a man. I have heard of no proposals to limit the reproductive freedom of unwed fathers, but people discuss, quite complacently, the sterilization of welfare mothers, a requirement to have Norplant inserted, and the cutting off of their benefits if they have another child while on welfare.

Even women who have been married can end up on welfare, and the marriage contract does not count for much once they divorce, as the dismal record of child support attests.[20] Child support orders are generally very low to begin with—often less than a man's car payment (Yee, cited in Pearce, 1990:268; Glendon, 1987:92)—but failure to pay is as common among professional, affluent men as among poor, working class men, among white men as among black men. For women, the "average drop in income after divorce or separation is 50 percent" (Garfinkel, 1992:1), and it can drop much lower depending on a variety of circumstances. Nationally the amount of unpaid child support approaches fifty billion dollars, more than enough to offset the AFDC budget. There are, and always will be, some men who are unable to pay because of disadvantages of race, education, disability, and especially lack of jobs, but the same excuses are not extended to the mothers. They are expected to shoulder the traditional male breadwinner role in addition to the traditional mothering, housekeeping role, while men have been relieved of both.

This is the crux of the problem. Women's gender roles and expectations have changed in the past twenty-five years, but men's have not. Rather than face the problems of the family "as we know it," it has been easier to blame and punish the women who, for whatever reasons, are outside of it.

Welfare is, I believe, the fissure that exposes the deep subterranean fault of patriarchy; it is the visible sign of the decline and fall of the "traditional" (patriarchal) family and the values that sustain it. The problem facing our nation has to do with values—there *is* a crisis of values. It is not, however, the loss of "family values" that is the problem, but those values themselves, especially their gender definitions, and the way in which they structure power and authority. "Historically, stable marriage systems have rested upon coercion, overt or veiled, and on inequality" (Stacey, 1996:68). William Julius Wilson, a Harvard social theorist, agrees that "without coercion . . . divorce and single motherhood rates will remain high" (ibid.). The choice facing the nation (and numerous other societies) is whether to coerce women into the "traditional" family and prevent their full personhood, or to develop creative, supportive alternatives for nurturing children. The choice is whether to perpetuate, by force if necessary, the notions of procreation, gender, and family that have been around since the Abraham story.[21] Rather than trying to rein*force* that model, the welfare issue provides an opportunity to examine its underpinnings.

Our culture, especially the religious culture, has long extolled the virtues of motherhood; it is simultaneously a sacred calling and a natural role. It is what women were created for. Freud reinforced this idea when he said: "anatomy is destiny," meaning that women are made to be mothers and that it is in their nature to nurture. The socially important job of childrearing has been perceived as simply one of the "functions" women perform (cf. Okin, 1979:241ff.). The work they do as mothers is a labor of love; it cannot and should not be compensated, which helps explain the difference in attitudes about paying foster mothers but not biological mothers for the same work. Women's "dependency work" (Young, 1995), that is, all the caretaking work expended on children, the sick and disabled, and the elderly, has been done mostly by women, mostly in the home, and it is, therefore, mostly unpaid. *To the extent that men have been exempt from "dependency work," they are dependent on the women who do it.* Men's dependence on women's work is never seen this way, however, because that work has been imagined as an inseparable part of women's nature and role, and thus has not been theorized in either capitalist or socialist economics. Society in general and governments in particular have been getting (quite a lot of) something for nothing.

Carl Degler, a social historian at Stanford, writes: "The historic family has depended for its existence and character on women's subordination . . . [meaning] that a woman will subordinate her individual interest to those of others—the members of her family." He goes on to say that "the equality of women and the institution of the family have long been at odds with each other" (Degler, 1980: vi–vii). The family, quite simply, has depended on "traditional" gender roles, regardless of whether the wife-mother also worked outside the home. Not only was that work imagined as secondary and supplementary, the woman still generally had a "second shift" of housework to do when she got home (Hochschild and Machtung, 1989). Today, whether women work because they have to or because they wish to pursue a career, they cannot do so without a great deal of rearrangment in the family. The problem has to do with the nature of work and careers that have all along been patterned on a male model (Hochschild, 1975)—a model in which the man is relieved of all the "dependency work," free to devote himself singlemindedly to his job. Women are expected to be "like men" in the labor force, but they are not relieved of the dependency work—that is simply subsumed by their gender definition.

Women are handicapped in the labor force because: (a) they have not been raised to think they will be the sole supporters of a family and have often not acquired the skills to obtain a high-paying job, (b) there are not enough jobs, and the kinds of jobs available to women tend to have long hours, and be routine, inflexible, lower-paying, temporary, and often without benefits, and (c) there are unfair wage differentials. Women's wages continue to be lower than men's whether they are doing the same or comparable work. In addition, women must pay for child care which, not infrequently, consumes more than half of their income, despite the fact that child-care workers are often paid less than parking attendants.

Outside the "protection" of the family, a woman with a child or children is expected to fulfill *both* gender roles. Mary Jo Bane and David Ellwood, President Clinton's advisors on welfare, considered this an unreasonable demand: "One parent shouldn't be expected to do the job of two" (Bane and Ellwood, 1994:150), and they resigned when the euphemistically phrased *Personal Responsibility and Work Opportunity Act* was passed. Nevertheless, their assessment of the issues, their goals and solutions were hardly different from those who ratified it. Even though a woman's dependence on a man is considered natural in a marriage, it becomes pathological once outside of it (on the issue of dependence see Fraser, 1989; Fraser and Gordon, 1994; Kittay, 1996). Welfare mothers must be made self-sufficient and independent, and the cure, according to almost all welfare "reformers," is full-time work, thereby depriving the child of the time and attention of the one remaining parent.

Our extreme valorization of self-sufficiency and independence obscures the fact that we are all (inter)dependent—on parents, on each other, on employers, and on government subsidies and contracts. Ultimately, we are all dependent on the children, for they are the ones who will care for us, for the nation, and for the world. We sacrifice them at our peril.

WAR

Since the seventeenth century more than one hundred million people have been killed in war, over 90 percent in the twentieth century (Goldson, 1993:18), and in modern wars, the majority of deaths are of civilians, many of whom are children. "Over the past 10 years, two million children have been killed in wars," others were maimed, were starving, or ill, and still others have witnessed the murder, torture, or rape of their parents, siblings, and friends.[22] War, and preparing for war, consumes people, energy, and money. Worldwide spending on armaments in 1985 was more than $980 billion. Edward Goldson, of the Children's Hospital in Denver, cited a report by Robert Sidel calculating the effects of military spending on children's welfare. He noted that

> it would cost only 1 hour's worth of the world arms spending to eradicate smallpox, that the annual budget of the World Health Organization costs about 3 hours of arms spending, and that the cost to immunize the world's children against common infectious diseases would cost less than 1 day's expenditures on arms. He went on to report that 1 year's spending on Star Wars research could provide an elementary school education for 1.4 million Latin American children, and that the cost of one Trident submarine could fund a 5-year program for universal immunization against six major deadly diseases. (Goldson, 1993:4)

In the United States, a fraction of the $300 billion annual military budget could truly eradicate the poverty of America's children. Instead of funding life, the "military-industrial complex" is taking all of us into its vortex of death. The man alleged to have coined the phrase knew very well the relation between war, welfare, and the sacrifice of children: "Every gun that is made, every warship launched, every rocket fired signifies . . . a theft from those who hunger and are not fed, those who are cold and are not clothed. This world in arms is not spending money alone. It is spending the sweat of its laborers, the genius of its scientists, the hope of its children" (Dwight David Eisenhower 16 April 1953, cited in Edelman, 1987:95). There has been a great deal of feminist theorizing about the nature and causes of war;[23] I wish only to draw attention to the relation betweeen war and the values and structure of the Abraham story. In war, sons (and now daughters) are sacrificed for the "fatherland,"[24] even though it involves killing the sons and daughters of others. Fathers seem to have a right to determine the lives of their sons and to expect obedience or submission to their will. Women are unloyal and unpatriotic if they refuse to go along with this plan. Women's duties are to give birth to future soldiers and to encourage and support war efforts. The sacrifices incurred by war are legitimated with honorable motives and sanctified with the claim that God is on our side (the most recent example is the Gulf War when both the United States and Iraq made similar claims). The job of the sons is to carry out the will of the fathers. Those who balk at the idea or refuse to serve are disobedient and unmanly. To be a real man means to be a fighting man—witness the public debate over President Clinton's avoidance of military service during the Vietnam War.

The story of Abraham was clearly behind *Who Asked Isaac?*, Robert Herhold's 1995 dramatization of the conflict between a father and son over Vietnam. The father wanted the son to join the army and fight in

Vietnam; *his* honor seemed dependent on it. The son did not want to go, but risked losing his father's love and respect if he did not. The son said poignantly, "I thought the first job of parents is to protect their children." The father responded: "I'll love my son when he proves he's a man. How can I love a wimp?" and acknowledged that he would be proud if his son died in the army.

The duty of soldiers is to protect the nation and its patrimony, primarily its land, and this duty is presented as a great honor. War is glorified and the soldiers imagine themselves as heroes (Miedzian, 1991; see also Oliver and Steinberg, 1995, regarding similar sentiments among young Muslim martyrs).[25]

But what is it, asks Benedict Anderson, about that invention of imagination—a nation—that so many millions have been willing to die for? (Anderson, 1983:129) Although the nation-state is a modern invention, the roots of the idea return us to religion and specifically to Abraham.

> Nationalism, as a collective emotional force in our culture, makes its first appearance, with explosive impact, in the Hebrew Bible. And nationalism at this stage is altogether indistinguishable from religion; the two are one and the same thing. God chose a particular people and promised them a particular land. . . . "God said to Abraham: 'Lift up now thine eyes, and look from the place where thou art northward, and southward, and eastward, and westward. For all the land which thou seest, to thee will I give it, and to thy seed for ever.'" (O'Brien, 1988:2–3, citing Gen. 13:14–5; see also Kohn, 1960; and Schwartz, 1997).

This promise of land to Abraham's seed is repeated several times in Genesis; it is the *same* land that is being fought over today. The idea of the unity between a particular people and a particular piece of land is also part of the notion of the modern nation-state.[26] What is often not recognized are the gendered aspects of this configuration.

The land flowing with milk and honey has functioned symbolically as female; those who possess it are symbolically, and often literally, male. If the land is imagined as female, then it is not surprising that male honor can be aroused to protect her virtue and her boundaries from the defilements and penetrations of others. Because sexual metaphors are bound up with nationalism (Delaney, 1995; Mosse, 1985), they are prominent in war (Cohn, 1987; Lakoff, 1990—1; Miedzian, 1991). Sexuality used metaphorically derives from the theory of procreation in which women are likened to soil, land, fields, whereas men are those who possess it, work it, and claim the result. It is in the self interest of men to protect the land and to ensure that the sons do the same.

Sons are not allowed to question: "Theirs not to make reply, / Theirs not to reason why, / Theirs but to do or die."[27] Their duty is to follow orders of their superiors, generally older men. Obedience is perhaps the primary virtue and value in the military. This was brilliantly exposed in the film "A Few Good Men," in which, under orders from their commanding officer, but against their own desire and better judgment, two young men harassed another to death. They were acquitted of murder because the defense argued that they were being good, obedient soldiers following orders; the verdict thus upheld the authoritarian, hierarchical structure of the military.

At the very top of that structure is the president. In the midst of a democracy where the consent of the people is required by the Constitution before going to war, the Father of State, nevertheless, holds godlike power in his hands. He has the right of first strike with nuclear weapons—whose destructive power has been assimilated metaphorically, in a classic instance of "doublespeak," to birth and Creation (Cohn, 1987; Easlea, 1983). He alone can set in motion forces that could annihilate millions of people, if not the entire world.[28] Who will stay his hand? It should come as no surprise that the last chapter in the novel *Fail-Safe* (Burdick and Wheeler, 1962) is entitled "The Sacrifice of Abraham." In it, the president of the United States makes a decision to drop four nuclear bombs on New York City, thereby sacrificing millions of his own countrymen, including his wife and children, in order to honor a deal he struck with another Father of State. An honorable man, he kept his "gentlemen's agreement," legitimating his action by reference to Abraham. Like Abraham's knife held perpetually over our heads, war, and the threat of war, keeps us in submission to patriarchal power.

The Abraham story is, clearly, not just an ancient story but a vividly contemporaneous one. It has, I believe, formed a continuous substrate of moral consciousness for millennia. In times of crisis it is said to resurface to remind people of their faith and to give them courage in their trials. We must ask whether this is the model of faith and the kind of courage we want now.

Conclusion

IN order to stem the tide of sacrifice—of the hopes, trust, health, and lives of children—we need more than economic solutions, we need a revolution in values. We need a new moral vision, a new myth to live by—one that will change the course of history as profoundly as did the Abraham story. I cannot provide such a myth—no one person can do that. Myths are collective enterprises; they emerge from people's experiences of the discrepancies between their personal lives and the myths with which they try to make sense of those lives. Yet, myths, like scientific theory, do not emerge *de novo*, they are always constructed out of old ones. My task has been a critical one, but criticism is not my only goal. By illuminating the assumptions built into the Abraham myth, we can better go about the task of reconstruction.

Abraham is both the father of faith and, symbolically, the first father. His story begins the patriarchal narratives but also dramatically presents the establishment of patriarchy. It is not accidental that the story revolves around a male-imaged god, a father, and a son, rather than female characters, for it involves a new understanding of masculinity, which emerges from a theory of procreation. The story symbolizes the incorporation of the assumption that the male is the generative agent in the procreative process—that by means of his seed he transmits the divine spark of life. The concept of God as creator and male as pro-creator are two aspects of the same system; indeed, I have suggested that the concept of God is a denaturalized or reified paternity, and that of the father, a naturalized divinity. These represent the two poles of an intricately intertwined system that is at once natural and divinely ordained.

In this system, definitions of male and female partake of the order of the universe, yet we know they are mutable and can be changed. Gender roles, if not definitions, are changing, but the process has not been easy. Our theory of procreation has also changed, but the changes have not yet been incorporated religiously, culturally, or emotionally. We assume that procreation is about biology and relevant primarily in medical or scientific contexts. We have failed to see that notions of procreation (coming-into-being) are bound up with a cosmological-religious system. You cannot change one without changing the other, yet the two domains are rarely brought together.

Changes are occurring also in theology and religion. In the past twenty-five years or so, more and more women have been admitted to divinity schools and seminaries. Feminist theologians, ministers, and rabbis are challenging the texts, the concepts, the rituals, the liturgies, and the institutional structures. Others, both men and women, are exploring new forms of spirituality and are forming new religious and spiritual groups. We do not know where all this ferment is leading, but it is through just this sort of process that new myths and metaphors will be forged. There is a sense of excitement but also of crisis—the old verities have become unhinged and there is yet no sight of a new anchor.

The turn of a century, and even more so the turn of a millennium, is a time of anxiety and hope. It forces people to consider both the past and the future—where we have come from and where are we going. Not surprisingly the past few years have shown a heightened interest in the stories of Genesis—there have been several new translations, and the stories have been topics of talk shows, news articles, and television dramas. Most of this recent interpretative effort has been expended to make them relevant to contemporary life, even as they seem like episodes in a soap opera (Rothstein, 1996). Historians of religion, in contrast, attempt to place the stories in their historical context, but in so doing often ignore their ability to escape historical limits and to move from religious contexts to secular ones. Anthropologists have something to contribute here.

Anthropologists have long been aware that "Myth lies at the basis of human society," as historian William McNeill (1986:23) acknowledged. Unlike historians, however, anthropologists analyze people's myths not so much for their historical truth but for the assumptions, categories, and symbols with which people imagine themselves and their world. In addition, anthropologists' lived experiences in other cultures create an awareness that there are viable alternatives to the myths we live by. Such an awareness is related to the often critical perspective anthropologists have on their own society, but it is also liberating—the way things are is not the only possible way.

As we stand at the brink of a new era, more aware than ever that we will all flourish or perish together, we are faced with a choice—to continue along the course charted thousands of years ago, or to try to chart a new one. In contemplating this choice, I ask that people consider deeply the question that motivated this book: Why is the willingness to sacrifice the child, rather than the passionate protection of the child, at the foundation of faith? I ask that people imagine how our society would have evolved if protection of the child had been the model of faith. If I have not completely convinced you with my analysis of the Abraham story, I hope I have at least, raised a reasonable doubt.

Notes

Introduction

1. Cristos Valenti is a fictitious name, but the man is real and his story is true. It will be told in chapter 2. Anthropologists are required to disguise the identities of the people they study. I chose the name Cristos because of its similarity to Christ, which was, in fact, the real nickname of the defendant.

2. The concept of the "Abrahamic" religions was put to use at the 1992 Summer Olympics in Barcelona. An Abrahamic Religious Center was built, and Jews, Christians, and Muslims worshipped under one roof, albeit at different times. *The Wall Street Journal*, 2 August 1992.

3. In speculating about the impact of the story of Abraham, E. A. Speiser, the well-known commentator on Genesis, contemplated "whether the course of recent history would have changed much if . . . Letizia Bonaparte had given birth to a girl instead of a boy . . . the chances are that the deviation from the original course which the advent of Napoleon brought about would have righted itself in due time. But in the case of Abraham, the detour became itself the main road" (Speiser, 1964:lii).

4. Kierkegaard's *Fear and Trembling* (1843) is the prime example of this type of interpretation.

5. In Islamic tradition it is generally, but not always, believed that the child to be sacrificed is Ishmael, son of Hagar, not Isaac, Sarah's son. This will be discussed in more detail in chapter 7.

6. Another foundational text is Aristotle's *Generation of Animals*. Although it appears to be primarily a zoological text (and thus by today's standards, outdated), the zoology is encompassed by wider cosmological assumptions about "coming-into-being." I am not alone in recognizing the importance of this theory and its consequences for gender definitions. See for example: Maryanne Cline Horowitz (1976) "Aristotle and Women," in *Journal of the History of Biology* 9(2):183–213; Shadia Drury (1987) "Aristotle on the Inferiority of Women," *Women and Politics* 7(4):51–65; Lynda Lange (1983) "Woman is Not a Rational Animal: On Aristotle's Biology of Reproduction," in Sandra Harding and Merrill B. Hintikka, eds., *Discovering Reality* (Dordrecht, Holland: D. Reidel Publishing Co.); The Biology and Gender Study Group (1989) "The Importance of Feminist

Critique for Contemporary Cell Biology," in N. Tuana ed., *Feminism and Science* (Bloomington: Indiana University Press); Nancy Tuana (1989) "The Weaker Seed: The Sexist Bias of Reproductive Theory," in N. Tuana, ed., above; Anne Fausto-Sterling, *Myths of Gender: Biological Theories about Men and Women* (New York: Basic Books, 1985). These feminist scientists and philosophers have rarely addressed the wider, cosmological implications. Feminist theologians, on the other hand, have addressed the gendered images of deity, but few try to bring together these two realms (religion and reproduction) so often imagined as antithetical. For exceptions see Børrensen (1991); Buell (1995); and Hultgård (1991).

7. The man who raises the issue in the film is, in "real life," a psychiatrist who has written about the story; see chapter 9. In addition to the film, Woody Allen wrote a short story about Abraham, as did Philip Roth and numerous other modern writers of fiction. Scott Turow's comments on the story at the end of his book *The Laws of Our Fathers* (1996), closely parallel mine. I only became aware of this after my manuscript was finished, and wish to thank Thomas Slaughter for showing it to me.

8. The term *gate* is often used to refer to female genitals; if other lands or cities are intended by the phrase "thy seed shall possess the gate of his enemies," perhaps they are being figured as female—an allusion that is still very common.

CHAPTER ONE
ABRAHAM ON TRIAL: CASE FOR THE PROSECUTION

1. A variety of feminist approaches to the Bible have been proposed, e.g., Bach (1990, 1993); Bal (1986, 1987, 1988); Bird (1981); Buchmann and Spiegel (1994); Newsom and Ringe (1992); Niditch (1992); Pardes (1992); Schüssler Fiorenza (1985, 1992); Schwartz (1990, 1997); and Trible (1984). But feminist interpretations have, by and large, passed over the Abraham story (e.g., Niditch [1992]; Pardes [1992]; Buchmann and Spiegel [1994]). The latter is a case in point. In their recent edited volume of essays by twenty-eight feminist interpreters of the Bible, not one of them discusses Abraham. *The Woman's Bible*, a nineteenth-century feminist critique of the Bible, especially of Genesis, also does not discuss this story.

2. David Bakan, a psychologist whose work will be discussed more thoroughly in chapters 9 and 10, has recognized the importance of paternity for the story of Abraham, but he thinks the story represents the "discovery" of paternity rather than a particular construction put on the male role in the process of procreation. The difference between *discovery* and *construction* is vast, as will become clearer as we proceed.

3. Cf. Feldman who claims that because the "Hebrew Bible channels all its

'paternal energy'. . . into the image of the heavenly father, it leaves little room for paternal authority within its human drama" (Feldman, 1994:16). However, she does not consider the way Abraham is a channel for God's power—he is assimilated to it so that his acts (and those of other fathers) are imbued with supernatural power.

4. There is, in Jewish tradition, a strand that acknowledges a feminine *aspect* of God, referred to as *Shechinah*.

5. Leach (1961, 1969) and Dundes (1988) are among the very few who have dared to deal with Genesis; a few others have looked at Biblical themes (Douglas, 1966; Feeley-Harnik,1981; Paul, 1996). Even fewer have considered the way in which Genesis may have provided the paradigm for anthropology, albeit in secularized form. George Stocking's unpublished lecture in the Anthropology Department at the University of Chicago in the early 1980s, "Genesis: Anthropology's First Paradigm," suggested that Genesis could be imagined as the paradigm for some of anthropology's concerns, especially the early focus and concern with origins. Genesis incorporates important notions about genealogy and kinship that, I feel, have served as models for constructing genealogies of languages and of human origins, not to mention the anthropological study of kinship as practiced, for example, by Morgan, Rivers, etc. Yanagisako and I (1995) argue that these secular and scientific concepts are transformations from the biblical model.

6. It is not so surprising that it is also precisely the one that has moved in to fill the gap created by the collapse of some of the others, especially the Marxist-communist vision.

7. This idea is commonplace but the use, specifically, of *splendor* is attributed to the Babylonian Talmud, where it is found in a number of places. See Wilken (1976:69) and Spiegel (1969:117, note 148).

8. A particularly engaging and easy-to-read discussion of the parallels is Sarna's *Understanding Genesis* (1966). See also Pritchard (1950); Speiser, (1964).

9. The trials of Abraham have been elaborated primarily in Jewish midrash and will be discussed in chapter 5. There are a number of different lists, and some include material that is not in the Bible, but all of them include circumcision and the sacrifice story.

10. Scholars have argued that the patriarchs could not have been monotheists because the idea did not develop until later. That does nothing to undermine my argument because my point is that monotheism frames the entire biblical story, "In the beginning God created . . . " It was within this guiding framework that the story of Abraham was redacted and given its theological significance.

11. Nor is the story of the sacrifice of Jephthah's daughter (Judges 11:29–40) foundational (cf. Trible, 1978). A story closer in sentiment to that of the two women judged by Solomon is the story of Moses (Exodus 2) where the mother relinquishes her son, the daughter watches what becomes of him, and Pharaoh's daughter rescues him and arranges that he be nursed by his biological mother.

12. This is an example of what Spivak is trying to get at in "Can the Subaltern Speak?" (Spivak, 1988). That is, how does one go about reading texts in which certain voices do not appear? A number of feminist theologians attempt to fill in the absent voices, to reconstruct possible dialogues, or, at least, to register the way women might have reacted.

13. See Yanagisako and Delaney (1995) for an elaboration of this idea. My thinking on this matter was sparked by a lecture given by George Stocking; see note 5.

14. Following are just a few of the relevant books published in the last half of the nineteenth and early twentieth centuries, but they give an indication of the concern with origins: Darwin, *Origin of Species* (1859); Lubbock, *Origins of Civilization* (1871); Morgan, *Ancient Society* (1877); Tylor, *Researches into the Early History of Mankind* (1878); Engels, *Origin of the Family, Private Property and the State* (1884); Kohler, *Prehistory of the Family* (1897); Durkheim, *Elementary Forms of the Religious Life* (1915); and Westermarck, *Origin and Development of Moral Ideas* (1917).

15. Cultural evolution is not to be confused with biological evolution, but means instead an idea that there is some ideal trajectory for human culture to which all cultures will and must conform. It is the kind of theory that permits people to say *preliterate* rather than *nonliterate*, as if literacy were dictated as part of evolution. There are other arguments with the theories of biological evolution.

16. Non-anthropologists often conflate matrilineal with matriarchal, but the two are not equivalent. There are a number of matrilineal societies, but the notion of matriarchy is problematic, most notably because it assumes a reversal of patriarchal society in which women, not men, hold positions of power. This view does not take into account the very notions of hierarchy and power that are supposedly endemic to patriarchy. More important, however, it presumes a notion of "mother" as prior to "father" (I argue that they are simultaneously constructed within a specific theory of procreation) and falls prey to the idea that matrilineal and patrilineal are the only possibilities for thinking of descent.

17. Kinship is an enormously complicated study, and debates continue among anthropologists. For very different views the reader might consult Fox (1967), Schneider (1960, 1972, 1984), and Scheffler (1972).

18. McLennan (1896:273) was a lone voice suggesting that kin terms are merely terms of address; nevertheless, he still believed that kinship *itself* was a matter of sex and blood.

19. For background to this debate, see the bibliography in Leach's paper. Cf. Malinowski (1927); Ashley-Montagu (1937); Jones (1924); Spiro (1968); and my critique of the debate, Delaney (1986).

20. A woman in Madagascar told anthropologist Gillian Feeley-Harnik that the "penis water" is like food that feeds and strengthens a child, like vitamins (personal communication).

21. Marilyn Strathern has said something quite similar with regard to the taken-for-granted division between "nature" and "culture" (1980). Nature has meant something quite specific in the West; I would say it has meant the created universe, created by God. It has a special relationship and specific meaning in monotheistic cultures that also allowed it eventually to be treated as merely the material, physical world by scientists. In other cultures where what we call the *natural world* has different ontological status and place in an overall system, there could not possibly be the dichotomy "nature-culture" as we have come to think about it.

22. If there were alternative theories, they are all but suppressed in the text. Jay (1992) believed she discerned evidence for a matrilineal descent system, but does not speak of what the procreation theory may have been. Her analysis is flawed, however, because she too often conflates kinship with biology. Beginning with the premise that the "mother is always known," she does not ask the further question: what is meant by "mother" and do all peoples have the same concept?

23. Theorists who have been major influences for this position are Saussure (1966), Whorf (1956), Sapir (1951), Benveniste (1971), and Langer (1942). For example, Saussure used a notion of a piece of paper in which one side represented the verbal image and the other the concept, and he noted that you cannot cut one without cutting the other. Moreover, he suggested that the meaning of words emerges in relation to other words; it is not a matter of reference. More recently interest has focused on context, but that hardly excludes the linguistic environment. The work of Fernandez (1986, 1991), Friedrich (1979, 1986, 1991), and Lakoff (1980) on ways that metaphor figures in the imagination is pertinent. David Schneider's work on kinship also loosened the notion that the world we live in is the same world cross-culturally; translation is not merely a matter of changing the labels—different cultures construct different conceptual worlds. See also Handelman (1989) who contrasts rabbinic-Jewish and Hellenic-Christian modes of interpretation.

24. Shelley made that statement to her husband, Holling, on the popular television program *Northern Exposure*. The imagery of seed was further reinforced by his taking up gardening at that time and getting obsessed with the seeds he was planting.

25. Denise Buell's (1995) doctoral dissertation at Harvard is a detailed study of the theological uses of procreative imagery in Clement of Alexandria. She also refers to similar practices among a number of ancient theologians, both Jewish and Christian. Others, notably DuBois (1988), have worked on procreative imagery among Greek philosophers.

26. Another recent example of this thinking can be found in Frymer-Kensky's book *In the Wake of the Goddesses* (1992). For her, paternity means only the awareness that males had a role in procreation, and she dates this discovery to about 9,000 B.C.! She has misunderstood the meaning of *paternity* and thus its relevance to biblical structures and values.

27. Many cultures appear to be male dominant; whether they are really *patriarchal*, having to do with the power of the idea of father, needs to be examined in each case. An article by Seth Mydans in the *The New York Times* (6 May 1997) showed that although men dominated in certain areas of Papua New Guinea, there was no idea that the male was the agent in procreation or that he had any biological tie to the child. Regarding patriarchal societies, we might also consider whether the notion of the male as the primary agent in procreation swept across many cultures at roughly the same time but was incorporated somewhat differently, depending on what had been the prevailing theory among each group.

CHAPTER TWO
ABRAHAM AS ALIBI? A TRIAL IN CALIFORNIA

1. As noted in the introduction, anthropologists are required to disguise the identities of the people they study. *Cristos Valenti* is a pseudonym; it has an unspecifiable, non-Anglo-Saxon ethnic character. A discussion of ethnicity would no doubt have made this a more richly nuanced study and would have explained some of the stereotypes and feelings of the jurors, but it is not the focus of this essay, nor did it ultimately affect the verdict. Neither the deed, nor the reactions to it, are the preserve of any particular group. The specific time and place of the deed and trial have been similarly disguised.

2. An exploration of the historical, archaeological, mythological, and religious interpretations of the story formed a major part of my study at Harvard Divinity School (1973–76) and resulted in an article, "The Legacy of Abraham," in 1977. I intended to write a book on the topic at some time in the future. With this case, that time seemed to have arrived. As I was finishing this book, two similar cases came to my attention. Robert Blair, of Concord, New Hampshire, killed his son (and wife) on 25 March 1996 because "God wants me to sacrifice him to Him—like Abraham and Isaac" (*Concord Monitor* [New Hampshire] 22 October 1996). He, like Valenti, said he "walked in God's grace" because he had done the right thing. Avi Kostner, of New Jersey, killed his two children (25 June 1996) by slowly (over fourteen hours) gassing them in his car. He did it after his divorce because he feared his ex-wife would convert them to Christianity. "I killed them because I loved them and didn't want them to grow up to hate me and Judaism," he said (quoted in Israeli paper, *Yediote Ahronote*, 7 March 1997, p. 21; translation by Sandra Razieli). It was the judge, Jonathan Harris, who made the reference to the Akedah and likened Kostner's son Ryan to the angel who stayed Abraham's hand. The child had called out repeatedly pleading with his father to stop. The Judge said he "violated every commandment in Judaism, in whose name he supposedly acted, in order to justify the murder to himself." (*Yediote Ahronote* 23 May 1997, p. 41).

3. Descriptions of trials are very rare in the anthropological literature. James

Clifford's "Identity in Mashpee," in his *The Predicament of Culture* (Cambridge: Harvard University Press [1988]), is a partial exception. The anthropology of law has been more concerned with customary law in nonstate societies (Max Gluckman, *Custom and Conflict in Africa*, Glencoe, Il.: Free Press, 1959; Sally Falk Moore, *Social Facts and Fabrications: "Customary" Law on Kilimanjaro, 1880– 1980* Cambridge: Cambridge University Press [1986]); different legal systems (Lawrence Rosen, *The Anthropology of Justice: Law as culture in Islamic Society*, Cambridge: Cambridge University Press, 1989; June Starr, *Law as Metaphor: From Islamic Courts to the Palace of Justice*, Albany: State University of New York, 1992); the effects of law on differentially located groups (Laura Nader, *No Access to Law*, New York, 1980; Sally E. Merry, *Getting Justice and Getting Even: Legal Consciousness among Working-Class Americans*, Chicago: University of Chicago Press, 1990; Jane Collier, *Law and Social Change in Zinacantan*, Stanford: Stanford University Press, 1973; John Comaroff and S. A. Roberts, *Rules and Processes: The Cultural Logic of Dispute in an African Context*; Chicago: University of Chicago Press, 1981; the construction of legal facts (Clifford Geertz, "Local Knowledge: Fact and Law in Comparative Perspective," in *Local Knowledge: Further Essays in Interpretative Anthropology*, New York: Basic Books, 1983); legal language (Donald Brenneis, "Language and Disputing," *Annual Review of Anthropology* (1988) 17:221–37.); and more recently on court personnel and procedure (Barbara Yngvesson and Carol J. Greenhouse, *Law and Community in Three American Towns*, Ithaca: Cornell University Press, 1994). Truman Capote's *In Cold Blood* (New York: Random House, 1965), may be somewhat closer to what I am attempting.

4. Because ancient Israelites performed blood sacrifice, Jews are, or have been, considered—in the minds of some Christians—more primitive. This prejudice has had disastrous social effects; it has also influenced theoretical work in the history of religions. See Howard Eilberg-Schwartz (1990), for an excellent discussion of this phenomenon.

5. Regarding the sacrifice of animals, see Reynolds v. United States 98 U.S. 145 (1878) and the Massachusetts case *Commonwealth v. Rogers*, 48 Mass. (7 Metc.) 500 (1844), both of which are cited in the *Case of Guiteau*, 10 F. 161 (D. D.C. 1882). See also *State of Missouri v. Roland* 808 S.W.2d 855 (Mo. App. W.D. 1991); *State of Missouri v. Clements*, 789 S.W.2d 101 (Mo. App. S.D. 1990); *State of Oregon v. Rose*, 801 P.2d 839 (Or. 1990); and the case of the *Church of the Lukumi Babalu Aye, Inc. v. City of Hialeah*, 508 U.S. 520 (1993). For a fictionalized account to test the religion clauses, see Stephen L. Pepper, *The Case of Human Sacrifice* (23 *Arizona Legal Review* 897, 1981).

6. Her observation may have reflected some of her class and ethnic stereotypes; the jurors knew that Cristos worked a lot with his hands and did manual labor. They may have expected a dark, swarthy man with large rough hands.

7. The role of the judge is to be an arbiter of the law, that of the jury to be arbiters of the facts. The judge aids the jury on points of law to enable them to

come to a reasonable view on the basis of the evidence. The prosecuting attorney represents the State's interests, not the victim's, and the role of the defense attorney is to puncture the prosecution narrative. I am indebted to Paul Rock for clarifying these points for me (see also Rock, 1993).

8. Trends in anthropology to let the voices speak for themselves (e.g., Kevin Dwyer, *Moroccan Dialogues: Anthropology in Question*, Baltimore: Johns Hopkins Press, 1982; James Clifford, *The Predicament of Cultures: Twentieth Century Ethnography, Literature, and Art*, Cambridge, Mass.: Harvard University Press, 1988) are admirable but problematic because they must always be contextualized. The quest for accurate representation is endless, but it is also selective.

9. Such an argument has been put forth for mediums, particularly female mediums of the nineteeth century. See Alex Owen, *The Darkened Room: Women, Power and Spiritualism in Late Nineteenth-Century England* (London: Virago, 1989).

10. Although several different ethnicities were represented on the jury, there were no obvious racial differences. The three jurors who were of the same ethnicity as the accused were his harshest critics; they thought he had brought shame on the group.

11. A very nice statement of what anthropologists and theologians have noted as the double nature of the holy, and Freud would call the ambivalence of the sacred—something set apart and taboo, something sacred and blessed as well as accursed and worthy of disgust, something respected and feared. Freud (SE 23: 121–2 [1939]). See also Durkheim (1915); and Otto (1923); as well as Freud (SE 13:18–74 [1913].

12. LPS is the Lanterman Petrus Short Act, a mental health law that entitles people who exhibit signs of mental illness to a court hearing; relatives cannot just put them away.

13. The history and thought about trials by jury makes for fascinating reading. Especially colorful is Lloyd Moore ([1973]1988) *The Jury: Tool of Kings, Palladium of Liberty*, Cincinnati: Anderson Publishing Company. But see also *Trial by Jury* (1877), John Proffatt reissued by Fred B. Rothman & Co. (Littleton, Colo., 1986); and more recently, *Twelve Good Men and True: The Criminal Trial Jury in England 1200–1800*, J. S. Cockburn and Thomas A. Green eds. (Princeton: Princeton University Press, 1988); *Juries on Trial*, Paula Di Perna (New York: Dembner Books, 1984); *The Jury Under Attack*, Mark Findlay and Peter Duff eds. (London: Butterworths, or Massachusetts: Butterworth Legal Publishers, 1988); John Singleton (1989), "Trial by Jury: History and Preservation" (*Trial*, 25[7]:90[6]); John M. Mitnick, "From Neighbor-Witness to Judge of Proofs: The Transformation of the English Civil Juror" (*American Journal of Legal History*, 1988, 32[3]:201–35); Lord Griffiths, "The History and Future of the Jury" (*Cambrian Law Review*, 1987, 18: 5–13); James Russell Gordley, "Law and Religion: An Imaginary Conversation with a Medieval Jurist" (*The Journal of Law and Religion*, 1986, 4[1]:193–209); George B. Johnson, "The Development of Civil

Trial by Jury in England and the United States" (*Simon Greenleaf Law Review*. 1984, 4:69–92); James E. Rooks Jr., "In Defense of the Freedom That is Our Birthright: Sources of Trial by Jury in America" (*Trial*, 1983, 19[9]46[6]); Roger D. Groot, "The Jury in Private Criminal Prosecutions before 1215" (*American Journal of Legal History*, 1984, 28[2]:147–63); D. O'Connor, "The Transition from Inquisition to Accusation" (*Criminal Law Journal*, 1984, 8[6]: 351–72. More recently, Jeffrey Abramson, *We, the Jury: the Jury System and the Ideal of Democracy* (New York: Basic Books, 1995) and Stephen J. Adler, *The Jury: Trial and Error in the American Courtroom* (New York: Times Books, 1994). A must for the history of Western law in general is Harold Berman's masterful *Law and Revolution: The Formation of the Western Legal Tradition* (Cambridge, Mass.: Harvard University Press, 1983).

14. That was the assumption of the anonymous author of *A Guide to English Juries by a Person of Quality*, attributed to Lord Somers (London 1682). He alludes to the Bible regarding twelve jurors: the Prophets were twelve, the Apostles were twelve, the Judges were twelve (pp. 9–11). He also noted that "the process by which the 'modern' jury evolved, where jurors ceased to be witnesses [for character] and became judges of fact, began in the thirteenth century" (p. 56) and was largely completed by the end of the fourteenth. Moore (1973, see note 13) cites an account in Greek mythology in which Ares was acquitted by a tie verdict of twelve gods.

15. These dichotomies (rationality versus emotion, objectivity versus subjectivity) and notions of their validity are deeply rooted in Western culture. The classic texts are Plato's *Republic* and Aristotle's *Politics*, but similar views were expressed by Freud in his 1932 letter "Why War?" See also Lakoff (1980).

16. There is extensive theory about jury selection that lawyers learn in law school and through practice, for example, Thomas A. Mauet (1988) *Fundamentals of Trial Techniques* (Boston: Little Brown and Co.); S. S. Diamond (1990) "Scientific Jury Seleciton: What Social Scientists Know and Do Not Know" (*Judicature* 73:178–3); J. M. Van Dyke (1977) *Jury Selection Procedures: Our Uncertain Commitment to Representation Panels* (Cambridge: Ballinger). Since the defense generally has the more difficult task in a murder trial, I asked the public defender what his criteria were for choosing or disqualifying jurors. He said he looked for people who were compassionate and sympathetic and a little unorthodox and independent in their thinking, and he tried to avoid the more rigid law-and-order types.

17. Cf. S. S. Diamond, "What Jurors Think: Expectations and Reactions of Citizens Who Serve as Jurors." In R. E. Litan, ed., *Verdict: Assessing the Civil Jury System* (Washington, D.C.: Brookings Institution, 1993).

18. Cf. Douglas's definitions of *holy* and *impurity*. Dirt or impurity is matter out of place (Douglas, 1978:35) and "Holiness means keeping distinct the categories of creation" (ibid.:53). Keeping the boundaries separate and distinct is part of what the sacred is all about, not just the content.

19. The effect of the structure of space and time on court procedure has been dealt with in great detail by Paul Rock (1993).

20. Ritual has been a central concern of anthropologists. Processual theories of ritual begin with Van Gennep, *Rites of Passage* (1909), and were most elaborated by Victor Turner, *The Ritual Process: Structure and Anti-Structure* (1969), *Dramas, Fields and Metaphors: Symbolic Action in Human Society* (1974), and *From Ritual to Theatre* (1982). See also Sally Falk Moore, *Law as Process* (1978); and Rosaldo *Culture and Truth* (1989).

21. Jurors were also given a set of written instructions to help in their deliberations. Court instructions, and particularly the convoluted and confusing language of such instructions, have become the focus for recent research. See Diamond (1993), "Instructing on Death: Psychologists, Juries and Judges" (*American Psychologist*, 48[4]:423–34); I. J. Severance and E. G. Loftus (1988), "Jury Instructions: A Persistent Failure to Communicate" (*North Carolina Law Review*, 67:77–109). The goal of clarification, however, appears to be to make the outcomes of jury trials more predictable. But if the outcomes of jury trials were more predictable, what would be the purpose of a jury trial?

22. Involuntary manslaughter is also an unlawful killing of a human being. It occurs "during the commission of a misdemeanor which is inherently dangerous to human life . . . or in the commission of an act, ordinarily lawful, which involves a high degree of risk of death or great bodily harm, without due caution or circumspection" (CALJIC 8.45). This definition did not apply to the case at hand.

23. "Our collective conscience does not allow punishment where it cannot impose blame." This is a statement by Judge Bazelon in *Durham v. United States*, 214 F.2d 862 (D.C. Cir. 1954) cited in Morris, 1992:126. Was Cristos to blame for the killing? For sacrifice? For believing in God? For taking biblical stories too literally, for being insane?

24. What's in a name? Names do have psychological resonance. Did the close association of his name with Christ as well as his job as a carpenter predispose him to dwell more on religious topics than he might have otherwise?

25. Jephthah promised that if he won the war he would sacrifice "whatsoever cometh forth of the doors of my house to meet me" (Judges 11:31). It was his daughter. He might have known it would be she or his wife or thought about that when he rashly made the vow. But a sacrifice in fulfillment of a vow is, according to most interpreters of the biblical stories, different from sacrifice that proceeds from God. Jephthah had asked God's help in winning the war; it was an exchange. Such is not the case with Abraham. Although one could argue that he stood to gain everything, this is not the case made by commentators. Instead, they stress that rather than a man keeping his promise by fulfilling the vow, it is God who promises Abraham everything if he proves his faith by being willing to kill his son. The Abraham story is about faith and obedience, and about recognition

of and following a higher authority, a higher law. Cristos was not fulfilling a vow, he was obeying a higher authority.

26. From Christian Scientists who refuse to take their children to the doctor and Amish who refuse to send their children to secular, public schools to the more fanatical cults of the Jim Jones, David Koresh variety, where does one draw the line? Can it be drawn, should it? The definition of religion as belief, rather than practice, is a particularly Protestant notion of religion and conflicts not only with Jewish and Muslim practices but also with those of Native Americans (for example, the peyote trials), Rastafarians, and, more recently, the case of the *Church of the Lukumi Babulu Aye, Inc. v. City of Hialeah*, 508 U.S. 520 (1993) about a Florida group who practice ritual animal sacrifice. Clearly the "free exercise" clause of the religion statutes needs clarification.

27. A curious twist on this idea was related to me by a friend living in Thailand. She told me that the state is encouraging people, especially women, not to make sacrifices *for* their families but to sacrifice their families for the good of the country; to put the nation before their loved ones.

28. Recent cases concerning abortion rights, rights of "surrogate" mothers versus the contracts of the sperm fathers, as well as the rights of the latter in several custody cases against adoptive parents, do give one pause, for they tend to support paternal over maternal rights.

29. Cross-examination is another framing device that can be artfully exploited in trials. The focus of the questions and the way they are framed determines the kind of response one is likely to get. I am grateful to Elizabeth Traugott of the Linguistics Department at Stanford for references on cross examination: for example, James Gibbons, *Language and the Law* (1994); Roger Shuy, *Language Crimes* (1993).

30. In recent years, the public (and the legal profession) has become more interested in the rights of victims to speak at murder trials and at sentencing hearings.

31. Many men, of course, choose not to fulfill that responsibility, as the dreadful state of child support and welfare testifies. Only very recently has there been any attention focused on these "deadbeat dads." Women may not want the responsibility, either, but they do not opt out in such numbers, and they often end up caring for *and* supporting their children.

32. In cases like this the ancient system of *wergeld* makes considerable sense. Then the family of the accused, in this case his parents and siblings, would make reparations to the victim or the victim's family.

33. *M'Naughten's case*, 8 Eng. Rep. 718 (1843), sometimes cited as M'Naghten. See also *Jones v. United States*, 463 U.S. 354 (1983); *People of California v. Drew*, 583 P.2d 1318 (1978), and *People of California v. Skinner*, 704 P.2d 752 (1985). In the past few years, the insanity defense has undergone renewed scrutiny. Several states (Montana, Utah, and Idaho) have abolished the insanity

defense and others, such as Pennsylvania, allow a verdict "guilty but mentally ill." In that case, the convicted person will receive psychiatric treatment and then serve out his sentence. (*New York Times*, 4 March 1996 in relation to the trial of John Salvi who killed two receptionists at abortion clinics.)

34. Norval Morris, a professor of law at the University of Chicago has written an extraordinary book on "parables of the law" (Morris, 1992). He uses the "persona" of Eric Blair (George Orwell) and descriptions of life and legal cases during his years in Burma to construct stories that will illuminate contemporary legal issues. One chapter, entitled "Ake Dah," is clearly a reference to the *Akedah*. There is also much in it that parallels the California trial, including the issue of voices and the M'Naughten rule. Morris, himself, feels "there should be no special defence of insanity to a criminal charge. The sole issue as to the accused's mind should be: did he, with a mind that was or was not 'sick,' intend or willfully risk this killing? If yes, he is responsible for it; if no, he is not" (Morris, 1992: 124).

35. Barbara Johnson cited in Bal (1988). We should keep in mind who controls the use of language and speaking and remember that in biblical tradition, God created with the Word.

36. While the prohibitions are, apparently, listed in the Talmud, I have also been told that any activities that can be interpreted as transformative through human labor are forbidden, for on the Sabbath the Lord rested. Yet the prohibition about using pens (creation by the Word) or turning on light switches ("let there be light") seem, at least to this observer, to have more to do with imitating acts of creation than they have to do with work. In any case my notes were, of necessity, jotted down from memory when the meeting was over.

CHAPTER THREE
CHILD SACRIFICE: PRACTICE OR SYMBOL?

1. For those wishing to explore theories of sacrifice, the following provide a good beginning: Beers (1992); Frazer (1890, 1913, 1919); Girard (1977); Hubert and Mauss (1898); Jay (1992); Smith (1889); Valerio (1985); and Strensky (1996), and for totemism, the book by that title by Claude Levi-Strauss who provides all the earlier references relative to the debate.

2. The strange division of animals in Gen. 15:9–17 may be a sacrifice, but the reasons for it are very obscure, and it differs from the others in that it is not an offering nor are the animals burnt.

3. The problems with this assumption were pointed out by W. Robertson Smith in his *Lectures on the Religion of the Semites* (1889). Because his conclusion rests on the now discredited theory of totemism, it cannot be taken as fact. Yet it is important for its recognition that the common assumption is dubious at best. "When the full kinship of animals with men was no longer recognized in

ordinary life, all this became unintelligible, and was explained by the doctrine that at the altar the victim took the place of a man" (Smith, 1889:346). The assumption that the ancients were barbaric and would "naturally" practice human sacrifice is particularly noticeable among psychoanalysts, as we shall see in chapters 8 and 9. Freud, for example, thought that the beginnings of society, morals, art, and religion came about through the sacrifice of the primal father.

4. But see Wineman (1980) for a different opinion.

5. A continuous narrative has been constructed from what are considered the "J" documents, *The Book of J* (translated by David Rosenberg, interpreted by Harold Bloom, 1990). It received undue notoriety because Bloom claimed "J" was written by a woman. I heartily disagree. If it had been written by a woman, I think she would not have been so complacent about the notions of procreation, the patriline, and the emphasis on male genitals and fathers and sons.

6. Although many people have begun to use B.C.E. (before the common era) instead of B.C. (before Christ), I have chosen to retain B.C. primarily because I feel that B.C.E. is a euphemism—the commonality still turns on the birth of Christ. Furthermore, Muslims would not consider this a "common" era even though they have much in common with both Judaism and Christianity. B.C. and A.D. can also serve to point out the imperialism of the Christian West. In order to rectify the bias, we need far more drastic means of reconceptualizing time.

7. See *Gods, Graves, and Scholars: The Story of Archaeology* by C.W. Ceram ([1949]1972, N.Y.: Bantam Books) for a very readable account of the work of Schliemann and others whose archaeological discoveries and deciphering skills transformed our knowledge of ancient Greece and the Near East. For a different, and more recent, assessment of Schliemann, see David A. Traill's *Schliemann of Troy: Treasure and Deceit* (1995).

8. Silberman (1982, 1989) has explored the ideological contexts in which biblical archaeology developed.

9. That, too, was the conclusion I had reached quite independently, from speculations concerning a different kind of material, namely a theory and symbols of procreation (Delaney, 1977).

10. Although Genesis 11:31 states that they went forth from Ur of the Chaldees, scholars have debated whether this refers to the famous Ur, in modern Iraq, uncovered by Leonard Woolley between 1922 and 1934, or some other place.

11. See archaeological reports, for example, Lloyd and Brice (1951); Prag (1970).

12. In an earlier article (1977), I made the suggestion that a conflict between different notions of kinship, affiliation, and procreation occurred in Haran in the late third, early second millenium and that the Abraham story reflected the outcome. This is a fascinating topic for scholars of the ancient Near East, but my own interests have shifted from trying to unearth ancient procreation theories to demonstrating the theological significance and social implications of ideas about gender, kinship, and procreation that are expressed in the Bible.

13. Some of this may be related to the suggestion by Parrot (1968:36) that the name Sarah, or more accurately Sarai, is the equivalent of an Akkadian word for *Queen*. The notion of Sarah's possible high status has been used by feminist scholars for a number of purposes. For example, Teubal (1984) imagined her a priestess but situates her in Hebron (in Palestine) rather than in Haran, and Jay (1992) called her a matriarch. Jay may have been influenced by W. Robertson Smith (1889:52, 1903) who argued that the ancient Semites were matrilineal.

14. One might also wonder whether there was a parallel regarding Inanna, the Queen of Heaven, so important in Ur and Akkad as enshrined by Enheduanna, priestess, daughter of Sargon (King of Akkad c. 2250 B.C.) and her lament about the destruction of her temple at the hands of invaders (Hallo and van Dijk, 1968). Kramer discerned a progressive demotion of female goddesses in Sumer over the same period, see "The Goddesses and the Theologians: Reflections on Women's Rights in Ancient Sumer" (Paper presented at the 23rd International Meeting of Assyriologists, September 1974, and at the University of Chicago later that year [personal copy in author's files]).

15. Instead, the remains conveyed an image of an orderly gathering, even a party, for some of the people seemed to have been playing music, others drinking wine. It is possible that they were poisoned; perhaps they were duped but perhaps they submitted willingly. Neither case really qualifies as sacrifice. A more recent example is the mass suicide of Heaven's Gate followers, which were not sacrifices and with which there was no evidence of violence.

16. The phrase is from Harding (1991) in reference to the way mainstream Christians and Americans view "fundamentalists." It is curious, surely, that the latter hurl accusations of ritual sacrifice (including of children), excessive sexual abuse, and Satanic worship at others yet in so doing enliven the idea of these in the minds of their own children.

17. I wish here to acknowledge once again the information, erudition, and material that Professor Jo Ann Hackett of Harvard University generously shared with me.

18. In cases of triple interments, they note that two of the three children were twins (always the stillborn or newborn) without any awareness or discussion of the long-standing, widespread ambivalence, even taboo, regarding twins in a number of African societies.

19. For opposing opinions see Cartun (1975), Weinfeld (1972), Moscati (1983). Several Europeans (especially Italians and French) argue against the practice, whereas Americans argue for it. Both interpretations are ideological and incorporate implicit assumptions; much of this debate reminds me of the debate among anthropologists, discussed in chapter 1, about whether certain "primitive" peoples knew about paternity.

20. Levenson (1993) says the statement should be read ironically. Yet the distinction between murder and sacrifice is often what the exegesis regarding the Abraham story turns on; see, especially, Kierkegaard.

21. Gordon Newby informed me that the two different spellings derive from two different dialects of Phoenician, both of which were transmitted to the classical authors.

22. I do not know where the first child was buried. But if there is a special burial ground in Urfa, there would, in this case, already be infant bones with the bones of the sacrificed sheep, and if the new child also died, his or her bones would also be added.

23. JoAnn Hackett informs me, however, that many of the inscriptions appear to preclude that possibility, because they are predominately in the past tense, a kind of "do et des" or thank you for service rendered. Still, presenting it as if already rendered may have been the proper way to make such an offering. Her work-in-progress on some of these inscriptions will help clarify such matters.

24. Weinfeld claims that there is "no evidence of its existence in Phoenicia" (1972:140). But more recently Sader (1991) reports that a few stelae have been found in Tyre that she thinks resemble those at Carthage. The dates cannot be confidently assigned because the finds were the result of illicit digging. Nevertheless, she speculates that they are seventh to sixth century B.C. with one possibly from the ninth century, and she further assumes that the finds belong to a child cemetery, which she calls a *tophet*. Whether it was a sacrificial site is, of course, another question.

CHAPTER FOUR
CHILD SACRIFICE IN THE BIBLE

1. I am pleased to be able to thank a friend from my Harvard Divinity School days, Jeremy Cott, who made a list of possible examples: a man in the time of Ahab (1 Kings 16:34); by Ahaz (2 Kings 16:3); by Manasseh (2 Kings 21:6); by Jephthah (Judg. 11:31); as an example of breaking covenant (Ezek. 20:26; Jer. 7:31; 19:5; 32:35); by Mesha, king of Moab, who sacrificed his son, also in relation to war, like Jephthah (2 Kings 3.27); and to the god Molech (Jer. 18.10; 32.35).

2. I would like to thank Joan Frigole (Barcelona) for calling my attention to several contemporary practices of "passing through the fire." In parts of Greece, Spain, and Portugal, rituals to purify or cure sick children consist of passing the children through the fire, having them jump over the fire, or, in one case, putting the child in an oven (cf. Handman, 1983; Tolosana, 1979).

3. Day (1989:94) cites Cazelles (1957) and Vaux (1964), and notes that with regard to Vaux this was a development of his position since 1961, when he understood *molek* to mean merely a divine name without connection to the Punic *molk*.

4. As God generally addresses men not women, this kind of admonition could mean several things: (a) indirectly it is a warning to women; or (b) a warning to men to keep watch over "their" women; or (c) that men are symbolically put in

the position of women vis-à-vis God (see Eilberg-Schwartz, 1994, for the consequences of this position for the male psyche).

5. Traditionally, in Turkey, if you asked: "How many children do you have?"
the answer would give only the number of boys. Girls were not counted in everyday conversation nor in the census.

6. That is precisely how Levenson responded, when I asked him, after his public lecture in April 1993 at Harvard Divinity School. Not only did he take for
granted what needs to be proved or at least explored, but he assumed that social
organization can be imagined as separate and prior to its ideological and cultural
expression. Such a view presupposes something natural about gender, about family, about social organization that exists prior to or outside of culture. Ultimately,
it is a psychological point of view.

7. Some also see parallels in the Sumerian story of the courtship of Inanna and
Dumezi, in which Inanna favored the farmer but was encouraged to marry the
shepherd. Regina Schwartz sees the story as paradigmatic of the violence of
monotheism where identity is constructed in opposition to an Other who is
excluded. Her book, *The Curse of Cain: The Violent Legacy of Monotheism*
(1997) came out just as this was going to press; our critiques of monotheism are
complementary.

8. Jay (1992) is one of the first to address the issue of blood sacrifice and
gender. She argues that it is primarily men who are engaged in blood sacrifice—a
ritual, she claims, that is as powerful and evident to the senses as giving birth.
Indeed, she theorizes that it is a ritual instituted in compensation for being born
of women. Through blood sacrifice men establish a transcendent paternity and
patrilineage that cannot be impugned by the vagaries of procreation. Nevertheless, a *notion* of paternity is presupposed; she did not explore what it means but
only talked about the difference between biological and social paternity, the latter
being a symbolic form of the former. Furthermore, she assumed the biological
basis of kinship and, thus, the self-evidence of maternity (see chapter 1 for discussion of these points). Because her work is on gender and sacrifice it appears to be
very close to mine, yet the differences are significant. Her primary interest is in
sacrifice; she begins with the notion/category of sacrifice, which is, she admits,
difficult to define cross-culturally. I begin with the foundation story of the three
religions which, as I stated in chapter 3, does not have much to do with ritual
sacrifice.

9. Weinfeld (1972) argues that "sacrifice" is not intended, at least not for the
human being. Instead, he believes that the animals were sacrificed, but that the
sons were merely dedicated to priestly service. Others, such as Smith (1975:478)
strongly disagree.

10. Ezekiel 20:25–26 claims that God did the same thing with the Israelites,
but there is debate about whether this should be taken literally (cf. Vaux, 1961:
444).

11. With regard to Levitical service, Cartun (1975) suggests that after the "passover" all Israelites were devoted to the service of Yahweh because Israel itself is spoken of as the firstborn son of God. When the Levites took over the function of priestly service, other firstborn sons could be redeemed. In his view redemption of the firstborn is not redemption from sacrifice but from priestly service.

12. Even if there is blood from cutting the penis, it can mean very different things depending on culture. The penis, itself, does not have same symbolic meaning cross-culturally. For example, as Bettelheim (1962) and others have remarked regarding the customs of some Australian aboriginal tribes, the penis is purportedly subincised as symbolic of *female* organs. The blood that flowed was apparently meant to be analogous to menstruation. See also Turner (1967) and Renaat Devisch (1993); however, a discussion here of these various practices would deflect the focus of our discussion.

Chapter Five
Jewish Traditions

1. Akedah comes from the root 'aqd meaning "to bind." When the term *Akedah* came into use as the title of this story is a matter of some dispute. Davies and Chilton (1978), for example, argue that it developed in response to Christian theology. For that reason they propose the more neutral "Offering of Isaac." Jews, however, refer to it as the *Akedah*.

2. The term ʿolah in Genesis 22:13 is from the root ʿalh and means "that which goes up," but it is generally taken to refer to a whole burnt offering (see *Encyclopedia Judaica*, 1979, vol. 14, p. 600).

3. Another possibility, of course, is that the story did not assume real importance until post-biblical times and in relation to developing Christian theology. For reasons discussed in the previous chapter, here, and in subsequent chapters, I am not convinced that this is an adequate answer.

4. The classic statement about this is in Auerbach's *Mimesis* (1957), but this quality is often true of biblical narrative. See also Alter (1981).

5. For a contrary opinion see, C. W. Coats (1973). Van Seters notes that it is usually accepted that verses 15 through 18 are a later addition, but he goes on to say: "The fact that such a notion of an addition is very plausible is not enough to conclude that this is actually the case" (Van Seters, 1975:228–31).

6. If the J source is somewhat earlier than E, then Moberly's idea that these lines are a late insertion is called into question. The apparent contradiction could be resolved if one presumed that they were inserted by an editor drawing on the earlier tradition of J, and maybe that is what he intended. Curiously, the only lines from Genesis 22 mentioned in Bloom's *The Book of J* are 22–4.

7. A few midrashic commentaries suggest that the reason is that Abraham got it all wrong; he misunderstood God's command. Shari Seider, a doctoral candidate at Stanford, informed me that the orthodox Jews in Argentina with whom she worked also took this view.

8. See chapter 3, note 6, regarding use of B.C., A.D. versus B.C.E. and C.E..

9. But for a dissenting opinion see Davies and Chilton (1978). The *Genesis Apocryphon*, the earliest version of Genesis extant, was found at Qumran; unfortunately it breaks off at the announcement of the birth of Isaac.

10. There is a tradition of a parallel oral law handed down to Moses at Sinai along with the written one, as perhaps the basis for customary practice and its codification in the *halakhah*.

11. This group was known as *saboraim* and their work was continued in Babylonia until the eleventh century by those called *geonim*.

12. The same idea exists in Plato's *Symposium*, where older men are imagined to inseminate the minds of their young pupils; both mirror an ideology of procreation wherein the male is imagined as the creative, life-giving agent. See also Eilberg-Schwartz (1994); compare with discussion of ritual fellatio among the Sambia of New Guinea by Herdt (1981, 1982).

13. Jo Milgrom's *The Binding of Isaac: The Akedah* (1988) is another compilation of the earliest sources. For more scholarly work, see Swetnam (1981) and Siker (1991).

14. See, also, commentaries by Nachmanides and Rashi as well as some of the literature regarding the medieval pogroms (e.g., Mintz). The idea of testing the righteous has been used in some interpretations of the Holocaust, see below.

15. The *Encyclopedia Judaica* says that in Jewish law the firstborn is the rightful heir, and this stricture is supposed to apply in polygamous households regardless of the status of the mother. The encyclopedia notes that primogeniture was disregarded in Abraham's case. I suggest, however, that perhaps it did not exist at that time, as all the firstborn sons in Genesis were passed over. See discussion in chapter 4.

16. In Islam, boys are usually circumcised some time between the ages of eight and thirteen. The ritual not only admits them into the brotherhood of Islam but also serves as an early test of masculinity.

17. This story occurs in both Genesis Rabbah and Pseudo Jonathan. Pseudo Jonathan is considered to be later, because it includes the names of Isaac's wives, which turn out to be the same names as those of Muhammad's wives, and thus the work could not have been completed until after the Muslim conquest. Of course, these names could also have been a late insertion.

18. The ten trials are variously listed in the different sources (see Milgrom, 1988:34–45, for an excellent list of the parallels). All include the following trials: leaving the land and home of his father, circumcision, twice passing off his wife as his sister, the banishment of Hagar and Ishmael, and, of course, the Akedah. I

heard about two others while I was in Urfa (Turkey), a town near Haran that was Abraham's home before the migration to Palestine. These are extrabiblical legends involving King Nimrod (Ginzberg, 1909; Firestone, 1990). Because I heard them in a Muslim context, I recount the story in chapter 7.

19. A number of scholars (e.g., Vermes, Hengel, Daly) think that the theological ideas embedded in the Akedah had a powerful shaping influence on Christianity. Davies and Chilton (1978), in contrast, think that Christian theology predates the full development of the Akedah themes and, thus, that the term *Akedah* should not be used prior to rabbinic interpretations.

20. Spiegel notes (1969:55, n. 14) that the Akedah may have been associated among the Kabbalists with Yom Kippur.

21. Melito, a Christian writing in the second Christian century in Sardis, a town in Asia Minor (now Turkey) with a sizeable and ancient Jewish community, made the connection between the Akedah and Passover (Wilken, 1976:58, n. 25), but whether that association came from the Jewish community or whether it was his own way of theologizing the Crucifixion is not clear.

22. Vermes (1961) and others argue for close relationship; Davies and Chilton (1978) think those who assert one are "skating on thin ice"; Swetnam (1981) thinks both go to extremes and argues for a more moderate approach. In addition, "a classical midrash relates that God split the Red Sea for the Israelites departing from Egypt as a reward to Abraham, who had split the logs for his own son's sacrifice" (Brown, 1982:99; cf. Miller, 1983:38), indicating that a strong connection has been imagined for quite some time. See also Genesis Rabbah and Spiegel (1969:114) for other sources.

23. It would be of interest to know the relationship between this custom and the Christian Ash Wednesday, when, at the beginning of Lent, ashes are placed on the forehead. They symbolize the recognition that we are but ashes and to ash we shall return, and they refer to the death of carnality (on Mardi Gras) and the beginning of the life of the spirit.

24. The merit is not just for redemption of sins; it is also attributed to the safe rescue of Israel's firstborn sons through the Red Sea (see note 22, above). This is a good illustration of the idea that Abraham's deed in one place led to an effect in another (Miller, 1983:37). The merit is also thought to have saved Jerusalem, in David's time, from the Destroying Angel, to have garnered forgiveness for the apostasy represented by the Golden Calf, and, finally, to have enabled the resurrection of the dead (Vermes, 1973:206–7). Nevertheless, the notion of merit is felt by some to be in contradiction with the whole tone of the Hebrew Bible; Jews are thought to be saved because of divine patrimony, not by the deeds of a man. Yet, see statement about Abraham's obedience, above.

25. See also Levenson (1993) who includes this idea in the title of his book, *The Death and Resurrection of the Beloved Son.*

26. Some traditions assert that Isaac was seven, whereas others conclude that he had to have been about thirty-seven.

27. It should be clear that I disagree with Kierkegaard's interpretation. To analyze it fully would take up too much space. Briefly, I agree with his desire to find the meaning *in* the existential situation, not in the conclusion. But I do not agree with his eulogy to the individual person, nor with the analogy he makes between what Abraham was going to do and what a mother does in weaning her infant. In one case, the child is to be sacrificed, in the other the mother is helping the child make a transition to the food he will need to grow. Kierkegaard also makes an analogy between what Abraham was going to do and what he, Kierkegaard, did in breaking his engagement with his fiancée. He could not stand her dependence on him and decided to set her free. He needed to see what he did as sacrificing his "own dear girl," and the method he chose to "wean" her from him was to act like a scoundrel. He imagined himself as the heroic martyr. See Walter Lowie's *Kierkegaard* (London: Oxford University Press, 1938).

28. Cristos Valenti used a somewhat similar excuse when he said he wanted to take his daughter with him to AA.

29. Abraham serves as a model in another way; I have been told that when one makes an orthodox conversion, one's parents become Abraham and Sarah.

30. The most popular discussion of the persecutions is S. Spiegel's *The Last Trial* ([1950]1969). But see also S. Eidelberg, ed., *The Jews and the Crusades: The Hebrew Chronicles of the First and Second Crusades* (1977); A. Mintz, *Hurban* (1984); D. Roskies, *Against the Apocalypse* (1984); and I. Marcus, "From Politics to Martyrdom: Shifting Paradigms in the Hebrew Narratives of the 1096 Crusade Riots," in *Prooftexts* (1982, 2[1]: 40–52).

31. Mintz (1984:84–5) claims that their response was different from that of the Sephardim who, faced with similar persecutions, apparently accepted a superficial conversion. This, rather than geographical dispersion, he believes, is the cause of the cultural and moral rift between the two communities.

32. The rite was apparently practiced on the Day of Atonement or on the day before Rosh Hashanah. Dr. Jorunn Buckley has informed me that this rite was being practiced in the United States until soon after World War II. In Yiddish, the expression is something like "kippeh shlagen," which means "throwing the chicken." The rabbi whirled the hen over his head and threw it into the river—it was a "scape-bird."

33. This is not unlike a similar notion in Christian interpretation—the idea that certain events prefigure or foreshadow what is to come, what will be fulfilled. As we shall see, the Akedah is thought to prefigure the Crucifixion. Mintz does not take a stand on whether this mode of interpretation was influenced by Christianity or existed separately.

34. An interesting study might focus on the way the different terms shaped the interpretation of the event and whether, for example, the use of *Holocaust* predisposed English-speaking peoples to think of the events of World War II in relation to the Akedah. Although Israelis also make the analogy, it does not spring directly to mind from either *shoah* or *hurban*. In Turkish, *kurban*, which may be related

to *hurban*, refers specifically to Abraham's (Ibrahim's) sacrifice, and when used more generally, it always evokes that allusion.

35. Among them Wiesel, Zeitlin, Roskies (see Brown, 1982) as well as Steinsaltz (see Cohen, 1990).

36. Compare with sentiments of the young Muslim martyrs, see chapter 7, note 5.

37. A different translation reads "my son can take care of them, and I'll take care of their ideas." See Oz's *Where the Jackals Howl* (translated by Nicholas deLange and Philip Simpson, 1981:49).

CHAPTER SIX
CHRISTIAN COMMENTARY

1. This may be a sacralized theory of progress; conversely, the notion of progress could be considered a secularized version of salvation history. There are, I believe, connnections between this logic and certain forms of the theory of evolution, especially sociobiology.

2. On Easter Sunday and Monday 1994, a film entitled *Abraham* was shown on television.

3. The earliest references to Isaac as a type of Christ are found in The Epistle of Barnabas (7:3) and in the work of Melito of Sardis (cf. Wilken, 1976). It also became a theme in the works of some of the major church fathers, such as Clement of Alexandria, Irenaeus, Tertullian, and Origen. See Schoeps (1946:386).

4. Origen apparently was the first to connect "The Lamb of God" (John 1:29) with the ram of Genesis 22.

5. My own experience is probably neither unique nor particularly common. I vividly remember being punished for asking impertinent questions, such as what kind of God would demand such a thing, what kind of father would obey. And when the answers were unsatisfactory I also recall saying that I could not love that God. So I was punished.

6. See Hayward (1990) for the view that the blood of Isaac has meaning in Jewish religious life independent of any Christian influence.

7. Anthropologist Gillian Feeley-Harnik has elaborated the parallels in *The Lord's Table: Eucharist and Passover in Early Christianity* (Washington, D.C.: Smithsonian Institution Press [1981]1994). The book discussses the significance of commensality and food symbolism in both Judaism and Christianity.

8. A suggestion by Spiegel (1969) regarding provenance seems to make the most sense. He says it is not necessary to assume sequential borrowing; these ideas may have been circulating during the time of the Roman persecutions and they may have developed differently in the different communities of interpretation. Many of the ideas were also common among the Greeks; the hero tradition, whereby the sacrificial death of the hero sometimes expiated the sins of the city,

began in the classical period and continued down to the time of Aesop, who was a contemporary of Jesus. See Larry Wills (in press); Gregory Nagy (1979); Hengel (1981).

9. When I speak of Paul in this way I am referring to St. Paul, the Apostle Paul, the Jew known as Saul who converted to Christianity on the way to Damascus and who wrote a number of letters that are included in the New Testament following the Gospels. He is also credited as being *the* theologian of early Christianity.

10. For an especially thorough documentation of this process, see a book with the same title, *Disinheriting the Jews: Abraham in Early Christian Controversy*, Jeffrey Siker (1991).

11. Interested readers might begin with Daniélou (1960); Lerch (1950); and a special issue of *Cahiers Sioniens* (1952), or they might begin a search in the *Ante-Nicene Christian Library* of works by commentators such as Tertullian, Origen, and Irenaeus.

12. There was, apparently, a strong moral emphasis among the Hellenistic philosophers, particularly those partial to the Stoics; perhaps it is not too surprising to find that tendency in Origen. I am grateful to Robert Gregg, Dean of Memorial Church, Stanford University, for pointing this out to me. The bias against grieving overmuch continues today in certain kinds of "fundamentalist" thinking (see Harding, 1987). It was also implicit in the court trial, where our attention was focused on the killer and not on the mother or child. The mother's grief over the child could not become palpable or legitimately recognized.

13. Curiously, in that play, perhaps alone of all the plays, Isaac wondered whether God had really ordered the sacrifice or whether it was his father's idea. If the latter, then perhaps Abraham would go through with it at another time. (Kolve, 1966:260). Isaac was portrayed as a boy and was not privy to the voice of God.

14. See Creed (1967: 69), and S. J. Crawford, ed., *The Old English Version of the Heptateuch, Aelfric's Treatise on the Old and New Testament and His Preface to Genesis* (1922).

15. I wish to thank Judith Brown (Rice University, formerly of Stanford) for bringing this material to my attention.

16. Jesus could be imagined as waiting for the critical moment to save the world, analogous to the rabbinic idea that the lamb sacrificed in Isaac's stead had been waiting for that moment since the Creation.

17. See volume 4, pp. 81–186 in his *Lectures on Genesis* ed., Jaroslav Pelikan (St. Louis: Concordia Publishing House, 1964).

18. Philo characterizes Sarah's acquiescence to the sacrifice as an act of courage and describes her attitude as manly. See my comments chapter 5. I am indebted to Robert Gregg for pointing out to me that the Greek word *andreia* means courage and derives from *andro* meaning man.

19. See Denise Buell's 1995 Harvard doctoral dissertation on the "seminal"

use of procreative imagery in theological conceptions both Jewish and Christian. The dissertation focuses primarily on the work of Clement of Alexandria, a Christian, but comparisons are made with Philo of Alexandria, a Jew. Another doctoral student, Rachel Rasmussen, shows how these images persist into twentieth-century theology, especially in the work of Paul Tillich. She is working on a theology of birth.

20. This is the position of Galen, as opposed to Aristotle, who thought women had no seed. It is also exactly what I found to be the case during my fieldwork among contemporary village Turks (Delaney, 1986, 1991). Most talked only of the male seed, but in the few cases where someone said that women, too, have seed, they were quick to point out that it was not generative, but merely lubricative. A very strange "two-seed theory" that has been circulating since the 1920s has recently surfaced among the extreme right-wing group called the Freemen. For them the "two-seed theory" does not mean that a man and a woman each contribute a seed to the formation of a child; instead it indicates Jewish versus Christian descent. "God created white gentiles as a superior race, descended directly from Adam and Eve, but . . . Jews descended from a sexual union between Eve and Satan"; that is, the line is still established via the male, either Adam or Satan. This is what the "two-seeds" refer to (*New York Times*, 12 April 1996).

21. If men are thought to produce seed, a woman's capacity has to do with whether she can hold onto it. That is how Turkish villagers explained the roles to me; they did not know of the genetic theory of procreation.

22. Kraemer acknowledges Ann Loades for suggesting this to her. Her own study of ancient Greek religion and society prevents any illusion that there is a direct correlation between religious myth and the actual treatment of women, but the question is nevertheless important.

CHAPTER SEVEN
MUSLIM INTERPRETATIONS

1. "This day I have perfected your religion for you and completed My favor unto you, and have chosen for you as religion Al-Islam," (Qur'an 5:3). *Islam* means surrender to God.

2. I prefer to use the spelling Qur'an rather than *Koran*, but when *Koran* appears in a quoted text I shall defer to that. Similarly, except in quotations, I will use God instead of Allah, Muhammad rather than Mohammed, Muslim instead of Moslem, and for consistency, Abraham instead of Ibrahim even though he is known as the latter in Muslim tradition.

3. The meat is supposed to be eaten immediately and the rest given away or disposed of. In order to deal with both the excess of meat and the health hazards, the Saudi government has recently enabled the meat to be frozen and shipped to poorer Muslim nations, and it has also expended great effort in dealing

hygienically with the carcasses. I wonder why one central sacrifice could not symbolically stand for all, and I also wonder what some future archaeologist will
make of the burial sites of millions upon millions of (mostly) sheep bones.

4. I lived and worked in a central Anatolian village, from August 1980
through July 1982, conducting anthropological fieldwork. Prior to the fieldwork,
from September 1979 through August 1980, I spent time in Ankara. See Delaney
(1991). And I have revisited (July 1986, June 1993, and December 1997). While
there, I saw a film called *Adak* (vow) based on the true story of a man who sacrificed his child because of a vow he had made to God. This event occurred in the
late 1970s; I had hoped to obtain newspaper accounts to compare with the story
of Cristos Valenti but I was unable to.

5. The concept of *kurban* has also been used in time of war. For example,
Atatürk, the founder and first president of Turkey, encouraged his soldiers to be
willing to become a *kurban* for the country he was trying to create. Anderson
(1983) believes that such sacrifice is necessary for the establishment of a nation.
The idea is also related to the notion of martyrdom embraced by numbers of
"fundamentalist" Muslims; see Oliver and Steinberg (1995), who also point out
that the *self*-sacrifice of young boys is, nevertheless, done at the *command* of an
older leader. The rhetoric is not dissimilar to that used during the Israeli War of
Independence, and the story of Abraham is never far removed.

6. A well-known one is Al-Tabari's (d. 923) *History*, which has recently been
published in English. See also the Appendix in Firestone (1990), which lists some
of the most popular.

7. Information about Muhammad's life comes from numerous biographies
and tales. An early Life of Muhammad was written by Ibn Ishaq (d. 768); for an
account of it, see chapter 4 in F. E. Peters (1990). See also Michael Cook, *Muhammad* (Oxford: Oxford University Press, 1983); Sir John Bagot Glubb, *The Life
and Times of Muhammad* (New York: Stein and Day, 1970); Alfred Guillaume,
New Light on the Life of Muhammad (Manchester: Manchester University Press,
1960); Mohammed Rauf, *The Life and Teachings of the Prophet Muhammad*
(Kuala Lumpur: Longmans, 1964); Maxime Rodinson, *Mohammed* (New York:
Pantheon Books, 1971); Montgomery Watt, *Muhammad: Prophet and Statesman*
(London: Oxford University Press, 1964).

8. Forty is a very significant number in Islam as well as in Judaism and Christianity: forty days and nights the ark weathered the flood, Jesus was forty days in
the desert, Muhammad was forty when the Qur'an began to be revealed, and
apparently Abraham was forty when he began to do battle with Nimrod. On the
significance of forty, see Stanley Brandes (1987, *Forty: The Age and the Symbol*,
Knoxville: University of Tennessee Press). In the Turkish village where I worked,
the forty days after a marriage, birth, or death were considered auspicious as well
as dangerous; traditionally the soul "opened" or was thought to be deposited by
God forty days after conception.

9. Some versions say that the opening word was *Recite*, but he was supposed

to recite what was presented as written. Since he could not read, it comes down to the same thing.

10. Qur'anic quotations are taken from the popular English version, *The Meaning of the Glorious Koran* (translated by Mohammed Marmaduke Pickthall, published as a Mentor Book from the New American Library, undated). Compare with *The Holy Qur'an* (translated by A. Yusuf Ali, published by the Islamic Propagation Centre International, Durban, 1946).

11. Newby (1989:25 n. 7), for example, cites a number of traditions about its composition.

12. See K. Nelson's *The Art of Reciting the Qur'an* (1986) and compare with R. Alter, *The Art of Biblical Narrative* (1981).

13. See Walter Ong, S. J., *Orality and Literacy*, for an excellent account of the differences between oral and written literature.

14. But note the difference in the kinds of tests from those in the Bible. See Al-Tabari ([c.915]1987:99) for accounts of the tests. According to one, "Abraham was tested with ten Islamic practices: rinsing the mouth, cleansing the nostrils with water, trimming the mustache,* using the toothstick, plucking the armpit,* paring the nails,* washing the finger-joints, circumcision,* shaving the pubic hair,* and washing the rear and the vulva." He goes on to say that "Others have said the same, except that they said that six of the ten commands were to do with the body and four of them were to do with the cultic stations." The six concerning the body include the five starred items plus bathing on Friday, and the four cultic stations are "walking around the Ka'bah, running between al-Safa and al-Marwah, stoning the pillars, and hurrying" (ibid.:100).

15. Although the Qur'anic text does not specify a ram, this is elaborated in both story and art. Unlike the biblical account, however, the ram is portrayed being brought by an angel, specifically Gabriel (Jibril). See Schapiro ([1943]1979) for a fascinating account of the differences between Muslim and Jewish-Christian depictions.

16. Dagorn (1981); but for a contrary view see Crone and Cook (Patricia Crone and Michael Cook. (1977) *Hagarism: The Making of the Islamic World.* Cambridge: Cambridge University Press). F. E. Peters (1990:25), also notes that "the genealogy of the Arabs as descendants of Ishmael was well established, and widely disseminated, long before the coming of Islam." But he does not say whether it was accepted by Jews and Christians or among pre-Islamic Arabs themselves.

17. When the Saracens crossed the Alps in A.D. 970 and captured the Abbott of Cluny, they apparently told the medieval French that Christ had descended from Abraham through Ishmael. See Schapiro ([1943]1979:305) quoting eleventh-century Rodulfus Glaber.

18. In Greek tradition the same kind of oracle was given to Kronos, to Zeus, and to Laius. One of the myths about the baby Zeus is that he was hidden in a cave on the island of Crete. When he grew up he, too, was told that a child would be

born who would surpass him. That child was Athene and her mother was Metis, the goddess "who knew more than all the gods or mortal people. But when she was about to be delivered of the goddess, grey-eyed Athene, then Zeus . . . put her away inside his own belly . . . in order that no other everlasting God, beside Zeus should ever be given the kingly position. For it had been arranged that, from her, children surpassing in wisdom should be born" (Hesiodus, 1959:176–77). The story we remember is that Zeus gave birth to Athene by himself, from his head.

19. See Lazarus-Yafeh (1981) for a good analysis of the pre-Islamic pilgrimage and attempts to Islamize it. Sabbah (Fatna Sabbah. (1984) *Woman in the Muslim Unconscious.* Mary Jo Lakeland, trans. New York: Pergamon Press) describes these goddesses, thought to be the daughters of God, who were worshipped in Mecca before Islam. Some Muslim and Western scholars think verses indicating that Muhammad recognized them have been omitted from the Qur'an; these verses have been known as "the satanic verses"—a term revived in the title of Salman Rushdie's novel. For a more scholarly treatment of the origins of Mecca as Muslim sanctuary, see Hawting (1982).

20. Newby is quoting from Guillaume's translation of Ibn Hisham's "Life of Muhammad," which, in turn, is a recension of the earliest biography of Muham-mad, that by Ibn Ishaq. Ibn Ishaq was born in Muhammad's city of Medina about seventy-five years after Muhammad's death and thus must have been privy to numerous stories about him. It is thought that his biography was written during his time at the court of al-Mansur in Baghdad.

21. It has also been used, for example, "by Egyptian fundamentalists in the 1970s for their strategy of withdrawing from corrupt secular society until such time as the state could be overthrown" (Fischer and Abedi, 1990:159). In mystical Islam *hijra* can be the inner migration of the soul away from worldly things that are thought to foster unbelief.

22. According to Newby the rock is, in Hebrew, "the foundation stone." "God is supposed to have stood on this rock and left his footprint there when he formed the earth. In Christian legend Jesus is supposed to have ascended to heaven from this rock, and the footprint is his. In Islamic lore Muhammad stood on this rock on his way to heaven, leaving his footprint. Many Jews believe that the rock supported the Holy of Holies when the Temple stood. The Islamic shrine of the Dome of the Rock now covers this rock. It can be noted that Abraham left his footprint near the Kaʿbah in Mecca when he made his pilgrimage there, thus equating the two sites" (Newby, 1989:30, n. 89). Other stories say that Abraham left his footprint on the stone when he was building the Kaʿba.

23. I am reminded of the humming black monolith that opens and closes the film *2001.*

24. I have argued elsewhere (Delaney, 1991) that the physical, earthly ele-ments that house the divine are symbolically female, whereas the divine that is eternal and transcendent is symbolically male, and furthermore, that these sym-bolic associations reinforce meanings of human gender.

25. The disparity between the different names, times, and places reminds me

of an incident that occurred in the village in Turkey just before my arrival there and resulted in a court procedure that continued the entire two years I was there (see Delaney, 1991:226, and n. 21). There were conflicting statements about when the incident occurred (the Turkish children's holiday or May Day?), about what song was played (the "Internationale" or the Turkish national anthem?), and about who instigated it (the teachers or certain villagers?). This was a recent incident that all the villagers knew about, yet the recollections did not coincide. Why then do we assume that there should be consistency with regard to ancient stories?

26. Schapiro (1979[1943]) notes that this motif is usual in Islamic portrayals but rare in Jewish or Christian ones; nevertheless it occurs. His research on that motif in Jewish and Christian art is a fascinating piece of reconstructive history. Questions—such as, how did the ram get caught in the thicket? was he newly created in a twinkling?—pose grave theological problems for those who think God's creative activity was confined to the first six days. The ram in the thicket symbolized for Christians Christ hanging on the Cross, and the thorns symbolized the Crown of Thorns.

27. I have written about the Hajj in more detail (Delaney 1990, 1991).

28. Not unlike Augustine's notion of the *City of God*, of which the earthly city is a mere reflection.

29. I cannot here reproduce all of the details of the marriage rituals any more than I can those involved in the performance of the Great Sacrifice; for those who seek to explore this further, consult Combs-Schilling (1989).

30. John Bowen (1992) criticizes Combs-Schilling for the emphasis she gives to the patriarchal character of the ritual, and cites evidence from Indonesia and other parts of Morocco to point out alternative interpretations and the ways in which women participate. But he does not really ask why sacrifice, why this story? That is the question that concerns me and Combs-Schilling, even though our answers differ slightly.

31. Similar claims about procreative prowess and spiritual power were also made by David Koresh, Elijah Muhammad, and no doubt others.

32. In order to insure that there will be a bloody sheet, some people give a couple a chicken or a pigeon to kill so that its blood can substitute for that of the girl. They seem unaware that girls/women do not always have "intact" hymens even if they are virgins.

CHAPTER EIGHT
FREUD'S BLIND SPOT

1. In this and the next chapter I am approaching Freud as mythmaker. I recognize that there is a division in the scholarly work on Freud, and rarely is the work in one cross-referenced by the other. The first group I classify roughly as those who are concerned more with the scientific or unscientific aspects of his work,

for example, Sulloway (1979); Masson (1984); Neu (1991); Grünbaum (1993); Robinson (1993); and those interested in the relation of his work to his personal and religious beliefs, for example, Bakan (1979); Bergmann (1992); Eilberg-Schwartz (1994); Gilman (1993); Paul (1996); Rice (1990); Robert (1976); Yerushalmi (1991). I am interested in the work of the former, but the latter have been more relevant to my own work. Although gender has been an issue for a number of them, few from either group have considered the importance of a notion of paternity, and those who have, such as Bakan, have conflated it with biology and have not examined its constructedness in relation to a particular theory of procreation. Much of what follows is adapted from my unpublished master's thesis at the University of Chicago (1978), a draft of which had been completed as a term paper at Harvard Divinity School (1975).

2. *Scotoma* means an area of pathologically diminished vision within the visual field, that is, a blind spot (*American Heritage Dictionary*, 1991). The word was used by Devereux (1953) to point out Freud's omission of Laius in his theory.

3. This is not to suggest that the claim is historically accurate, for theologians and historians debate whether or not monotheism, in the sense we think of it today, could have existed for either Moses or Abraham. But it was surely the guiding theme of the redactors who put the stories together in the form we have received. Abraham *is* the first monotheist in the three monotheistic traditions.

4. Notably, Yerushalmi (1991) and Rice (1990), who even link the names of Freud and Moses in the title, but see also Gresser (1994), Geller (1993), and Paul (1996), and articles by Bergmann (1988) and Kaplan (1990).

5. Quotations from *Moses and Monotheism* are from the popular Vintage Books edition translated by Katherine Jones. The wording is somewhat more vivid than in the Standard Edition (SE), but the meaning has not been changed. I have included references to the SE in each case, and use it for all other works by Freud.

6. The passive voice is in the original: *Ich meine die Sage vom Konig Odipus und das gleichnamige Drama des Sophokles. Odipus, der Sohn des Laïos, Königs von Theben, und der Jokaste, wird als Säugling ausgesetzt, weil ein Orakel . . .* (Freud. 1972[1900] "Die Traumdeutung." *Studienausgabe*, vol. 2:265, Frankfurt am Main: S. Fischer Verlag). *Säugling* means a nursing infant and *ausgesetzt* can mean abandoned. I am grateful to Judith van Herik, who graciously checked these points for me and provided the nuanced meanings to some of the words.

7. It may be that with the abandonment of the "seduction theory" (described below), which had focused on actions of fathers against daughters, he did not pursue the role of the father vis-à-vis the son in the construction of the Oedipus complex. Perhaps it also marked his growing focus on intrapsychic as opposed to interpsychic phenomena, a shift more coordinate with his hydraulic model of psychic functioning.

8. *Totem and Taboo*, in turn, followed directly on an analysis of a case of religious delusion (the case of Schreber) in which Freud began to see a relationship

between the Oedipus complex and religion. Curiously, Schreber imagined that he had to become a woman in order to bring forth the new race of humans.

9. For a detailed analysis of the sources used by Freud, see *Freud and Anthropology* by Edwin R. Wallace, 1983.

10. Such claims would be certain to attract the attention of anthropologists. Yet no German, French, or English anthropological review of *Totem and Taboo* appeared until 1920, almost seven years after its publication. Some of this lapse may be due to fact that there were no English translations until 1918, or French until 1923, but that does not excuse the absence of a German review. Some of that lapse may also be attributed to World War I. The response of anthropologists over this century has been ambivalent, to say the least, but many of us, like Kroeber ([1939]1952:309), "though remaining unconverted, have met Freud (and) recognize the encounter as memorable." In all honesty I cannot add the final phrase, "and herewith resalute him."

11. The Australian aborigines became the ultimate "Other" for the West, and every major theorist discussed them—Durkheim, Freud, Malinowski, Lévi-Strauss, etc. See Burridge (1973) for a discussion of this phenomenon. This is not the place to enter into discussion of what defines *primitive* or whether primitive material culture can be equated with primitive social organization or conceptual schemes. In fact, especially in the case of the Australian peoples, the opposite case can be made (cf. Diamond, 1974; Spencer and Gillen, 1899; Ashley-Montagu, 1937; Bell, 1983; etc). Nevertheless, the idea that Australian aborigine religion was *the* most primitive was very popular, and it was assumed by numerous social theorists, for example Durkheim (1915).

12. See Pateman (1988) for a critique of the notion of the social contract. She argues that it is really only between males, that prior to it and behind it is what she calls *The Sexual Contract.*

13. The most important critique was that by Kroeber (1920, 1939). But see also Malinowski (1927). An important summary of the debate is Wallace (1983). My own critique leaves to one side the whole problem of totemism, which has been superbly dealt with by Lévi-Strauss (1962).

14. Freud conflates *wives* with *females* (compare Freud, [1913]1950, pp. 125 and 141). Darwin said *wives*; if that is really what he meant, however, it would presuppose culture, because marriage is a sociocultural ritual. And that would obviate Freud's point that the horde was in a state of nature.

15. Malinowski made a number of excellent points in this connection. Because the primal family was, in Freud's view, not quite human, their behavior would have more closely resembled animal behavior. If that is the case, Malinowski asks: "Why should the father have to expel the sons if they naturally and instinctively are inclined to leave the family as soon as they have no more need of parental protection?" Why would they bother to return to the paternal horde and "attempt to accomplish the cumbersome and unpleasant act of killing the old male?" (Malinowski, 1927:164). Malinowski notes that Freud burdens this

prehuman family with habits and attitudes that would have been lethal for any animal species.

16. The more recent work of Dian Fossey (1983. *Gorillas in the Mist*, Boston, Mass.: Houghton Mifflin) might also challenge some of their assumptions about gorilla behavior.

17. This oversight (or lack of understanding) helps to underscore a point, so often overlooked even by feminists, that male dominance and patriarchy are not synonymous even though they may be related phenomena (see chapter 1, n. 27). Patriarchy demands a notion of *patriarch*—that is, *father*—and *father* is a meaningful term within a specific *theory* of procreation. Paul's (1996) conflation of meaning and biology leads him to conflate *father* with *senior male* and then to naturalize his behavioral traits.

18. In English, the words *testimony* and *testament*, also meaning to bear witness, are derived from *testes*. These associations may ultimately go back to Abraham, for in Genesis a servant swears an oath by placing his hand on Abraham's testicles (Gen. 24:9). The testicles were assumed to be *the* source of human generativity, an inference that was, originally, a matter of faith and belief. Although scientific theory has confirmed the testes to be the source of sperm, it has also shown the ovum to be the other indispensible source of generativity. Even modern interpreters such as Bakan or Paul tend to ignore the role of the ovum. In law, to witness something was originally also a matter of faith, not observation.

19. Indeed, the killing of the father ought to be called *patricide* not *parricide* as so many commentators have done, as it is most definitely not just the killing of a parent, but the killing of the father. Of course, perhaps they, along with Aeschylus, Clement, Augustine, Aquinas, etc., are thinking that the father is the *true* parent. Freud also makes brief reference to the *Oresteia* in connection with the supposed shift from matriarchy to patriarchy, a reference that has become popular in such discussions: "the mother is no parent of that which is called her child, but only the nurse of the new-planted seed. . . . [T]he parent is he who mounts" (Aeschylus, [c.458 B.C.], 1953, Richmond Lattimore, trans. Chicago: University of Chicago Press, 158).

20. See Rubin (1975) and Coward (1983) for excellent critiques of this position.

21. Could Freud have been thinking about the mark of Cain? This insight was provided by Bill Maurer. Perhaps it is also relevant that Freud was, and remained, a Lamarckian to the end of his life (cf. Rieff, 1979:199ff).

22. One could read chapter 1 of *Totem and Taboo* as providing contradictory evidence. In it Freud discusses the extent of *restrictions* on sexual, especially incestuous, behavior among so-called primitives. They were inhibited, he suggests, by their great fear. Anthropologists, generally, eschew psychological motivation and view such rules as relative to the cultural categories that make up a particular sociocultural world.

23. A new twist on this theme has been given by Robert Paul (1996), a psycho-

analytically trained anthropologist. He suggests that the entire Old Testament is an allegory of the primal horde. Furthermore, he thinks Genesis is really only an overture to the main events that happened in Egypt. This is surely an imaginative reading, but it ignores the centrality of the Abraham story and the model of faith and, perhaps more surprising in the contemporary intellectual climate, does not grapple with the gendered aspects of the biblical story nor with their theological or social implications.

24. Perhaps Freud was thinking, unconsciously, of the early death of Karl Abraham—his selected successor—and the continual threats of dissolution of the analytic circle. This conjecture will become clearer as we proceed.

25. Freud does not explicitly state that they also ate him; yet if this was meant to be a repetition of the primal crime, one might conclude that they did. A suggestion has also been made that the manna in the desert symbolizes the body of Moses . . . and later is transformed into the Christian Eucharist.

26. This is related to the theme of renunciation that is so important for Freud's notion of the virile strength of Judaism. See Van Herik (1982) for a superb analysis of the meaning and role of renunciation in Freud's work.

27. His father Jakob, son of Reb Schlomo, had been brought up in a *shtetl*, a Jewish community in Tysmenitz, a town in the East European area of Galicia in which there were Orthodox and Hasidic Jews as well as a group of *maskilim*, members of the Jewish Enlightenment or Haskalah (see Krull, 1986:74–91). Freud himself says that his father "did indeed come from a Chassidic background" (ibid.: 90; *Letters of Sigmund Freud*. Tania and James Stern, trans., New York: Basic Books, 1960:394). Although Jakob Freud tried to leave some of that background behind when he moved from Tysmenitz to Freiburg, he nevertheless continued the study and practice of Jewish traditions. Only when they moved to Vienna, when Sigmund was about three, did Jakob Freud begin to drop dietary observances.

28. Robert (1976:37) argues that it was the stories, not the various social, political, and intellectual movements, that interested Freud.

29. Jakob may first have had the 1848 edition, but the 1858 edition was found in Freud's library. I have seen a copy of the 1858 edition with the engraving; I do not know whether it was included in the 1848 edition.

30. By *Bible story* Freud meant the entire story of the Jewish people as told in the Hebrew Bible. The *Autobiography* was written in 1925 and did not include the line quoted; it was inserted in 1936, no doubt because of his work on *Moses and Monotheism*.

31. The reasons Kaplan adduces for why the psychoanalytic establishment did not take more seriously Wellisch's (1954) argument for a biblical psychology may also apply to Freud: (1) the traditional split between psychology and religion, (2) Freud's own adult opinions about religion, (3) attempts by psychoanalysts to appear scientific, and (4) the general academic idealization of ancient Greek life (Kaplan, 1990:74).

32. Especially as Freud had come across something quite similar not long before, in the case of Schreber (SE 12). Schreber was fixated on the torture inflicted on him by God, even though he could not call it torture. In his illness, Schreber's descriptions of the "rays" of God's love replicated the real tortures inflicted on the child by the father in the form of mechanical devices to improve his posture, keep him from touching his penis, etc. Rather than interpreting that aspect of Schreber's illness as a body hallucination, Freud interpreted it as a defense against homoerotic impulses toward his father. Schreber's father was a famous pedagogue who had written numerous works describing punitive methods of child training, including the torturous items just noted. Freud did not make a connection between the father's intrusive methods and the son's illness; instead, he just assumed the famous father was a good man and an appropriate object of desire. For a more complete analysis see Niederland (1951, 1959a, 1959b, 1960); Schatzman (1972, 1973); and Delaney, Master's thesis, University of Chicago, 1978.

33. That paper, "Amenhotep IV (Ihknaton): A Psychoanalytic Contribution to the Understanding of His Personality and the Monotheistic Cult of Aton," was first published in *Imago* in 1912 and reprinted in the *Psychoanalytic Quarterly* (1935) and in Karl Abraham's collected papers (1955).

34. Kanzer goes on to talk about the theme of the patriarchs bestowing their blessings on one of the sons, and he relates this to Freud's ongoing concern regarding the establishment of his own successor.

35. (1) Freud did not think that Abraham was justified in calling Ihknaton neurotic, for "we all have these complexes and we must guard against calling everyone neurotic" (Abraham and Freud, 1965:118). (2) Freud felt that there was no evidence for Abraham's assertion that if the mother was an important figure, the conflict with the father would be milder. But he did not object to Abraham's assertion that she was an important figure in Ihknaton's life—he was only ten when he ascended the throne and only twenty-eight when he died (Abraham, 1935:543; others say he was twenty-five years old when he died)—nor did he object to Abraham's suggestion of her role in the invention or development of monotheism. This is particularly odd, because Freud felt that monotheism was connected to masculinity.

36. A more virulent fate awaited the images of Ihknaton upon his death.

37. Shengold suggests that he did have such feelings toward Fliess, his former colleague and intimate friend, and that he associated Munich with Fliess, concluding that all these connections brought about Freud's faint.

38. Several of his letters reveal that he also wanted to put the stamp of his ideas on his wife. Regarding betrayal, he once told Rank, in relation to his theory about birth trauma: "with an idea like that any one else would set up on his own" (Abraham and Freud, 1965:352). Rank did eventually set up on his own, as did Fliess, Jung, Stekel, Ferenczi, and others, and it was interpreted as betrayal. "All my life I have been looking for friends who would not exploit and then *betray* me" (Shengold, 1972:143, emphasis in original.) Abraham, the one he seemed to

trust most, the one with whom he felt free to discuss these betrayals, finally received some of the same accusations himself.

39. Ironically, Abraham wrote a paper on the importance of names.

CHAPTER NINE
SA(L)VAGING FREUD

1. Notably Wellisch (1954); Bakan (1971, 1974, 1979); Arietti (1981); Balmary (1979, 1986); Rice (1990); and Bergmann (1992).

2. The change may also relate to Freud's "hydraulic" view of internal psychosexual functioning. Regardless, there is still a social dimension if only because of the need to recognize an "other" and become aware of "difference."

3. In a slightly different vein, Schorske suggested some time ago (1973) that Freud overcame his father by making politics an epiphenomenon of psychic forces because his father had wanted him to have a political career.

4. A much more egregious example of evolutionary-stage thinking is found in Schlossman, (1972:47–9). Sulloway (1979) argues that Freud's thinking was suffused with evolutionary theory; it is, therefore, not so surprising that his followers perpetuated it.

5. The notion of *survivals* figured quite prominently in nineteenth-century anthropology, for example, Spencer, Tylor, Morgan, and McLennan, but it has been discredited by contemporary anthropologists.

6. Such assumptions are encountered in most of the psychoanalysts who attempt to enter the area of anthropology, perhaps none more outrageously than Schlossman, who asserts, as if it is a well-known *fact*, that "matriarchal societies and religions tended to be orgiastic, castrating and cannibalistic." Matriarchal societies, which he uses interchangeably with matrilineal socioreligious cultures, "may have have existed as a transitional stage after the Old Stone Age" (Schlossman, 1972:46). He seems to be unaware that there are a number of matrilineal societies still in existence that answer to none of these outrageous descriptions. Such is the persistence of myth.

7. Had he done so, he would have found considerable evidence that child abuse is absent in a number of "primitive" societies, even if infanticide, especially of babies with gross deformities, is a feature. This is not the kind of infanticide of girls that exists in several highly civilized societies such as China and India.

8. Schlossman makes the interesting point that a firstborn is the first besides the father to pass through the woman's genitals (1972:38–9) and could, therefore arouse a father's jealousy. Yet he needs to explain why this is important only in the case of firstborn sons, not daughters.

9. She was the third woman in Jakob Freud's life, squeezed between the two that Sigmund knew of. Jakob had been married once, before he married Sigmund's mother, and that marriage gave Freud a number of older half-siblings. Before Jakob married Freud's mother, it appears he had an affair with, or perhaps

even a secret marriage to, Rebecca. This liaison appears to have interfered with Jakob's marriage to Amalia Nathanson, as Freud's birth certificate was altered, indicating that Amalia had been pregnant at the time of her marriage. See Krull (1986); Robert (1976); and Rice (1990).

10. Elsewhere Balmary says that "what the dominating does not want to recognize the dominated cannot know"; the result is that when the dominated tries to question the dominating, to learn the truth, he or she might be told: "That's crazy," or "You're crazy." This is just what happened in the case of Dora and Schreber. For fuller analysis of these case histories, see Schatzman (1972, 1973); Niederland (1959a, b); and my Master's thesis (University of Chicago, 1978).

11. I thank Gaylord Brunolfson for help with translation and discussion of *Le sacrifice interdit*. See Arietti (1981) who calls Abraham the first modern man, proposing that he is the first to have separated spirit from matter and to have raised the issue of human choice for good or evil. Abramovitch (1994) uses a theory of developmental psychology to interpret Abraham as a "spiritual revolutionary."

12. The debate between social contract theorists and patriarchalists can best be studied in a comparison between Locke's *Second Treatise on Government* and Filmer's *Patriarcha* (1680). Yet from a feminist point of view, the debate is spurious, because both focus on, and take for granted, male dominance. Women are excluded from their theorizing. Pateman's critique (1988) is essential reading.

13. Balmary proceeds with a Lacanian discussion of "othering" and "lack" that itself lacks a theory of culture in the construction of difference. This omission becomes most noticeable in her discussion of gender, which is both essentialist and heterosexist because it is based on the essential features of sexual difference—namely, that each has what the other lacks. This is a noticeable problem with a number of the so-called French feminists, and it may be attributed only in part to the lack of distinction in French between sex and gender.

14. So, too, did Woody Allen in his brief reading of the story: When Abraham is ready to sacrifice Isaac, God calls out in a deep, resonant, well-modulated voice . . . "Do you listen to every crazy idea that comes thy way?" Abraham pleads, "But doesn't that prove my love for you?" And God responds, "It proves that some men will follow any order no matter how asinine, as long as it comes from a resonant, well-modulated voice." ("Scrolls" in Woody Allen. [1975] *Without Feathers*, New York: Random House, 26–27).

15. I will not address the work of Abramovitch (1994) in this context, as he is a social anthropologist using the psychological, not psychoanalytic, theory of adult life stages described by Levinson (see Delaney, 1996). He does not question the notion of father/paternity nor discuss *Moses and Monotheism*.

16. Freud discussed the sun in relation to God and paternity in a number of places, for instance, in the case of Schreber (SE 10:81) and in *Moses and Monotheism* (1939:147).

17. Susan McKinnon (1995), for example, argues that father-daughter incest in America is not something totally alien and pathological, but only one extreme along a continuum. See chapter 10.

18. For a much more nuanced discussion of renunciation and its relation to femininity and faith, see Van Herik (1982).

19. In the nineteenth century, genius was thought to be masculine in character; women could play supporting roles such as the muse. Otto Weininger, a psychologist contemporary with Freud, wrote an influential book called *Sex and Character*, which was translated into English in 1906. Aware of Aristotle's tripartite division of soul (and one might wonder about Freud's tripartite division of the psyche), Weininger reinterpreted it in slightly more modern terms: "A woman has an unconscious life, a man has a conscious life, but the genius has the most conscious life. . . . A female genius is a contradiction in terms, for genius is simply intensified, perfectly developed, universally conscious maleness" (Weininger, 1906:189). One can see the echoes of Aristotle's vegetative, sentient, and rational souls. Some of these ideas appear to emerge in Freud's notions of hysteria (the wandering womb) and appropriate occupations for women . . . especially that too much education was psychologically dangerous. See case of Dora, for example, and her final rebellion. (I discussed this in my Master's thesis.)

20. See Ruth Hubbard, *The Politics of Women's Biology* (New Brunswick, N.J.: Rutgers University Press,1990); Sandra Harding, *The Science Question in Feminism* (Ithaca: Cornell University Press,1986); Anne Fausto-Sterling, *Myths of Gender: Biological Theories about Men and Women* (New York: Basic Books, 1985); Emily Martin, *The Woman in the Body: A Cultural Analysis of Reproduction* (Boston: Beacon Press,1987), and "The Egg and the Sperm: How Science Has Constructed a Romance Based on Sterotypical Male-Female Roles," (*Signs* 16: 485–501, 1991); Verena Stolcke, "New Reproductive Technologies: The Old Quest for Fatherhood" (*Reproductive and Genetic Engineering* 1(1):5–19); Sarah Franklin, "Romancing the Helix: Nature and Scientific Discovery" (in *Romance Revisited*. [1995] Lynne Pearce and Jackie Stacey eds., London: Falmer Press). This dynamic becomes especially disturbing when biology is reduced to genetics (cf. Marilyn Strathern, *Reproducing the Future: Essays on Anthropology, Kinship, and the New Reproductive Technologies,* Manchester: Manchester University Press,1992; Adrienne Zihlman, "Misreading Darwin on Reproduction: Reductionism in Evolutionary Theory" in Faye D. Ginsburg and Rayna Rapp, eds., *Conceiving the New World Order*, Berkeley: University of California Press, 1995) and ultimately to "information" (Stefan Helmreich, "Anthropology Inside and Outside the Looking Glass Worlds of Artificial Life," Ph.D. dissertation, Department of Anthropology, Stanford University, 1995).

CHAPTER TEN
SACRIFICING OUR CHILDREN

1. This was expressed in the emotionless response of an Israeli father whose wife and son were killed 13 December 1996 in Hebron by a Palestinian. Just as Abraham was asked to give his son, so, too, this man imagined that he was asked

to give his son for the cause. Emotional detachment has been a mark of the spiritual man for a long time, and it is also an integral part of the model of masculinity. This is the quality Freud stresses in "Why War?" (Freud, SE 22). "More care should be taken to educate an upper stratum of men with independent minds . . . whose business it would be to give direction to the dependent masses . . . a community of men who had subordinated their instinctual life to the dictatorship of reason. . . . Nothing else could unite men so completely and tenaciously even if there were no emotional ties between them" (ibid.:212–3). Freud also applies emotional detachment to love, clearly from the male point of view: "the instinct to love, when it is directed towards an object, stands in need of some contribution from the instinct for *mastery* if it is in any way to obtain *possession* of that object" (ibid.:208, emphasis added).

2. This theme is quite pervasive in literature and film; a recent example is the 1996 film *Shine*.

3. This figure excludes death due to war, which will be discussed below. It is unclear whether the figure includes female infanticide but I presume it does not. Sidel (1996) notes that in 1992, in the United States, 5,279 children were killed by guns.

4. At that time, there were reports in the press about Christian summer camps where a number of children were punished, some unto death, for disobedience.

5. There is no concept of "original sin" in Islam; children do not begin to accumulate sin until puberty. I do not know the status of this belief or its relevance for child rearing among Black Muslims.

6. Alice Miller ([1988]1990) noticed similar patterns in her study of such beliefs in Europe. Both she and Greven discuss the influential theory and practices of the child pedagogue, Daniel Schreber; Freud's misanalysis of Schreber's son's illness; and the commentary about it. See also Delaney (1978) and Inglis (1978).

7. Those interested in the topic might begin with Herman (1981), LaFontaine (1987), and Masson (1984), and consult their references.

8. Freud's (mis)analysis (and betrayal) of Dora is an extreme but obvious example. I have reanalyzed it at length in my Master's thesis (1978). See also Lerman (1986:43–9).

9. A similar abuse of trust was also purportedly committed by nearly two thousand leaders in the Boy Scouts, an organization whose purpose is the development of both the physical and moral attributes of boys. Most of them have since have been removed on charges of molestation.

10. The Church's reaction is not unlike that of the psychiatric, especially psychoanalytic, profession in its refusal to acknowledge that the sexual abuse of children by fathers and father-surrogates was, and is, widespread.

11. The Roman Catholic Church is, of course, another primary example of an authoritarian, hierarchical, and patriarchal system. The pope can command obedience from priests and lay people alike.

12. This was also true in the abuse of children by priests and nuns at the Mont

Providence Orphanage in Quebec, among others. "By declaring the orphans mentally deficient, Quebec and the church had found a way to line their coffers," since the government "paid the church more than twice as much for caring for psychiatric patients as it did for orphans" (*New York Times* 21 May 1993). The greed of the priests who ran the institutions led them to redefine their wards as mentally retarded, a definition and stigma that would follow the children all their lives. One of those children, Hervé Bertrand, now fifty years old, recalls that schooling just stopped. No longer students, they became inmates in a mental institution. Some of them *became* retarded because of the kind of treatment and (lack of) education they received. He and numerous others have described in intimate detail the physical as well as sexual abuse that went on there (see Gill, 1991, and a 1995 television documentary).

13. According to a report prepared for the Carnegie Foundation, at least one quarter of the children in the United States live in poverty (*New York Times* 12 April 1994.) Millions more live near or just above the poverty line. The gap in income between the richest and poorest is widest in the United States and has been growing wider every year (*New York Times* 15 July 1996). In any case, AFDC grants are so low that they have often been half, or less, of what the government has considered the poverty level; in no state have benefits ever reached the official poverty level.

14. See the *New York Times* 14 August 1995 citing the Luxembourg Income Study; see also the Carnegie Report (1994); Handler (1995); Kamerman (1984); Kamerman and Kahn (1989, 1994); Katz (1986); Leach (1994); Sidel (1986, 1996). The two countries that do less than the United States are Ireland and Israel, and, in both, family policies are dominated by religious groups and ideologies.

15. Here are a few well-known facts that have done little to change the myth of the welfare mother: (1) More than half of welfare mothers have been married. (2) Most of the women are working, or have worked, but cannot support their families on their wages. (3) Of women on AFDC the percentage of white women is slightly higher than black, 38 percent versus 37 percent, respectively (Bane and Ellwood, 1994); admittedly, this represents a higher proportion, in relation to their own group, of black women on AFDC than white. (4) Of children born out of wedlock, the percentage to white women is almost 60 percent and to black women about 40 percent (Young, 1995:539, taken from *Statistical Abstracts, 1993–4*, U.S. Bureau of Census). (5) Less than 3 percent of poor families are headed by women younger than nineteen. (Women's Committee of One Hundred, *New York Times* 8 August 1995. MacCurdy and O'Brien-Stain's recent California study revealed that almost no AFDC families have ever had a teenage mother, *San Francisco Chronicle*, 11 February 1997, and *Stanford Report*, 19 February 1997.) Teenage pregnancy has actually been decreasing since the 1950s. What is different is that teens are having the babies and keeping them. (6) Most welfare recipients have one or two children, about the same as, or slightly lower than, the national average. And (7) the average time on welfare has been about

two years (see Bane and Ellwood [1994], and the Women's Committee of One Hundred, cited above).

16. Men have been the beneficiaries of the "family wage," established in the late nineteenth century to enable men to support a family (cf. Sapiro, 1990; Folbre, 1991). Because of views of women's roles, primarily as mothers, women's wages remained low relative to men's and, like their role in procreation, were imagined as secondary and supportive. In addition, women were, until quite recently, barred from many of the more lucrative professions. Since so many women are now the sole supporters of their families, a kinder, gentler solution would be to pay women the "family wage."

17. It might we worthwhile to ask what has happened between President Johnson's "War on Poverty" and the current "War on Welfare Mothers" (cover of *Time* magazine 20 June 1994). Why war? Why mothers?

18. *Metro* (a weekly paper in California's Santa Clara Valley) featured a cover story (14–16 November 1996, 12[3]), "Do Men Have A Choice?" in which men claimed "entrapment" and no legal escape from the obligations of "accidental" fatherhood. However, since none of the men cited were taking responsibility for birth control, fatherhood was hardly accidental.

19. See the *New York Times* (27 August 1996) discussing a proposal to use drugs to decrease the sexual desire of felons convicted of child molestation. The use of the term *castration* is inflammatory for it is not castration that is being proposed. The drugs are related to hormones used for female birth control and menopause. Those opposed to this procedure claim it interferes with men's *right* to procreate. Such opposition was not raised when proposals for chemical or surgical sterilization of welfare mothers was discussed.

20. Noncompliance with court-ordered child support can mean anything from zero compliance to partial and sporadic compliance. The *New York Times* reported 17 July 1997 that failure to pay court-ordered child support occurs in four out of five cases. Until quite recently the money was generally paid directly to the woman; thus, it became her responsibility to hire a lawyer and sue if she did not receive the support. Without any money, that is extremely difficult. A few states now require payments to go through the court, which enables the states to pursue fathers (and some mothers) who do not comply with the court order. But the above mentioned article noted that "Federal efforts to help states increase compliance rates have failed," and several Congress members have proposed turning collection over to the IRS. In California, a few state congress members have proposed making nonpayment a felony.

21. Margaret Atwood's *The Handmaid's Tale* is a powerful and terrifying vision of just what this might entail. Although the book is a work of fiction, Atwood has stated that she took many of the separate parts from stories in the contemporary press; that is, many of the parts already exist. Moreover, the story is grounded in biblical forms and values.

22. Anthony Lewis, *New York Times* (29 December 1996), citing a report

entitled "The Impact of Armed Conflict on Children." He also reported that in Angola alone, eight thousand children have had "limbs amputated after land-mine explosions" and notes that there "are still 10 million mines under Angolan soil." Many other children are being used as soldiers. (See also "Valentina's Nightmare," *Frontline's* report on Rwanda).

23. Generally, the theorists relate war to dominant notions of *masculinity* that encourage certain attitudes and behaviors. For a start see Cohn (1987); Enloe (1990); Elshtain and Tobias (1990); Jeffords (1989); and Miedzian (1991).

24. *Fatherland* refers more to the conceptual reality of the nation; the soil, itself, is still very much figured as symbolically female. So even when the term *motherland* is used, as in Turkey, it generally refers to the physical aspects of the nation while *father* symbolizes the state (cf. Delaney, 1995).

25. The "fathers of state" who commit their "sons" (and daughters) to war have, more often than not, never experienced the horrible day-to-day combat and trench warfare (Miedzian, 1991).

26. In Christianity, the idea was allegorized, and the Promised Land came to mean Heaven, although it also figured prominently in the imaginations of the first explorers and settlers of America.

27. Lines 13 through 15 from Alfred Lord Tennyson's 1854 poem, "The Charge of the Light Brigade," depicting a sacrificial battle ([1951] *Selected Poetry of Tennyson*, Douglas Bush, ed., New York: The Modern Library, Random House, pp. 253–4).

28. "During his own impeachment proceedings, Richard Nixon said to a group of Congressmen, 'I can go into my office and pick up the telephone and in 25 minutes 70 million people would be dead'" (Scarry, 1992:25).

Select Bibliography

Abraham, Hilda C. and Ernst L. Freud, eds. (1965) *A Psycho-Analytic Dialogue: The Letters of Sigmund Freud and Karl Abraham 1907–1926*. New York: Basic Books.

Abraham, Karl. ([1912] 1935) "Amenhotep IV (Ikhnaton). A Psychoanalytic Contribution to the Understanding of His Personality and the Monotheistic Cult of Aton." *Psychoanalytic Quarterly* 4:537–69. First published in German (1912) in *Imago* 1:334–60 and reprinted in Abraham, K. (1955), 262–90.

———. (1955) *Clinical Papers and Essays on Psycho-Analysis*. New York: Brunner/Mazel.

Abramovitch, Henry Hanoch. (1994) *The First Father. Abraham: The Psychology and Culture of a Spiritual Revolutionary*. Lanham, Md: University Press of America.

Abramson, Glenda. (1990) "The Reinterpretation of the Akedah in Modern Hebrew Poetry." *Journal of Jewish Studies* 41(1):101–14.

Albright, William. (1950) *The Biblical Period*. Pittsburgh: Biblical Colloquium.

Allegro, John M. (1970) *The Sacred Mushroom and the Cross*. New York: Doubleday.

Alter, Robert. (1981) *The Art of Biblical Narrative*. New York: Basic Books.

Anderson, Benedict. (1983) *Imagined Communities*. London: Verso.

Anderson, Bernhard. (1988) "Abraham, the Friend of God." *Interpretation*. 42(4):353–66.

Arieti, Silvano. (1981) *Abraham and the Contemporary Mind*. New York: Basic Books.

Asad, Muhammad. (1954) *The Road to Mecca*. New York: Simon and Schuster.

Ashley-Montagu, M. F. (1937) *Coming into Being among the Australian Aborigines*. London: George Routledge and Sons.

Auerbach, Erich. 1953 *Mimesis*. Willard R. Trask, trans. Princeton: Princeton University Press.

Augustine. ([c. A.D. 354–430] 1990) *The Works of St. Augustine: The Sermons on the Old Testament*, part 3, vol. 1. E. Hill, trans. New York: New City Press.

Bach, Alice, ed. (1990) *The Pleasure of Her Text: Feminist Readings of Biblical and Historical Texts*. Philadelphia: Trinity Press.

Bach, Alice. (1993) "Signs of the Flesh: Observations on Characterization in the Bible." *Semeia* 63:61–79.

Bachofen, J. J. (1973) *Myth, Religion, and Mother Right*. Ralph Manheim, trans. Princeton: Princeton University Press. (From *Das Mutterrecht*, published 1861.)

Baird, William. (1988) "Abraham in the New Testament." *Interpretation* 42(4): 367–79.

Bakan, David. (1966) *The Duality of Human Experience: Isolation and Communion in Western Man*. Boston: Beacon Press.

———. (1971) *Slaughter of the Innocents: A Study of the Battered Child Phenomenon*. Boston: Beacon Press.

———. (1974) "Paternity in the Judeo-Christian Tradition." In *Changing Perspectives in the Scientific Study of Religion*. A. Eister, ed. New York: John Wiley, 203–16.

———. (1979) *And They Took Themselves Wives: The Emergence of Patriarchy in Western Civilization*. San Francisco, Calif.: Harper & Row.

Bal, Mieke. (1988) *Death and Dissymmetry: The Politics of Coherence in the Book of Judges*. Chicago: University of Chicago Press.

Balmary, Marie. (1982) *Psychoanalyzing Psychoanalysis: Freud and the Hidden Fault of the Father*. Ned Lukacher, trans. Baltimore: Johns Hopkins University Press. (Originally published in French, 1979.)

———. (1986) *Le Sacrifice Interdit: Freud et la Bible*. Paris: B. Grasset.

Bane, Mary Jo, and David Ellwood. (1994) *Welfare Realities: From Rhetoric to Reform*. Cambridge, Mass.: Harvard University Press.

Baron, Salo. (1939) Book Review of *Moses and Monotheism*. *American Journal of Sociology* xlv(3) 471–77.

———. (1969) "A Review of Freud." in R. J. Christen and H. E. Hazelton, eds. *Monotheism and Moses*. Lexington, Mass.: D. C. Heath.

Beers, William. (1992) *Women and Sacrifice: Male Narcissim and the Psychology of Religion*. Detroit: Wayne State University Press.

Bell, Diane ([1983]1993) *Daughters of the Dreaming*. Minneapolis: University of Minnesota Press.

Benveniste, Emile. (1971) *Problems in General Linguistics*. Coral Gables, Fla.: University of Miami Press.

Bergmann, Martin. (1988) "The Transformation of Ritual Infanticide in the Jewish and Christian Religions with Reference to Anti-Semitism." In *Fantasy, Myth and Reality—Essays in Honor of Jacob A. Arlow, M.D.* H. P. Blum, Y. Kramer, A. K. Richards, A. D. Richards, eds. Madison, Conn.: International Universities Press.

———. (1992) *In the Shadow of Moloch: The Sacrifice of Children and Its Impact on Western Religions*. New York: Columbia University Press.

Berman, Harold. (1983) *Law and Revolution: The Formation of the Western Legal Tradition*. Cambridge, Mass.: Harvard University Press.

Bettelheim, Bruno. ([1954]1962) *Symbolic Wounds*. New York: Collier Books.

Bimson, J. J. (1980) *Essays on the Patriarchal Narratives*. A. R. Millard and D. J. Wiseman, eds. Leicester, England: Inter-Varsity Press.

Blankenhorn, David. (1995) *Fatherless America: Confronting Our Most Urgent Social Problem*. New York: Basic Books.

Bloom, Harold. (1990) *The Book of J*. David Rosenberg, trans. New York: Grove Weidenfeld.

Bordo, Susan. (1993) *Unbearable Weight: Feminism, Western Culture and the Body*. Berkeley: University of California Press.

Børrensen, Kari Elisabeth, ed. (1991) *Image of God and Gender Models in Judaeo-Christian Tradition*. Oslo: Solum Forlag.

Bouhdiba, Abdelwahab. (1985) *Sexuality in Islam*. Alan Sheridan, trans. London: Routledge and Kegan Paul. Originally published in French (1975).

Bowen, John. (1992) "On Scriptural Essentialism and Ritual Variation: Muslim Sacrifice in Sumatra and Morocco." *American Ethnologist* 19(4)656–71.

Bright, John. ([1959]1972) *A History of Israel*. Philadelphia: Westminster Press.

Brinner, William and Stephen D. Ricks. (1986) *Studies in Islamic and Judaic Traditions*. Atlanta: Scholars Press.

Brock, Rita Nakashima. (1990) "And a Little Child Will Lead Us: Christology and Child Abuse." In *Christianity, Patriarchy, and Abuse*. Joanne Carlson Brown and Carole R. Bohn, eds., 42–61.

Brown, Joanne Carlson and Carole R. Bohn eds. ([1989]1990). *Christianity, Patriarchy and Abuse: A Feminist Critique*. New York: The Pilgrim Press.

Brown, Joanne Carlson and Rebecca Parker. (1990) "For God So Loved the World?" In *Christianity, Patriarchy, and Abuse*. Joanne Carlson Brown and Carole R. Bohn, eds., 1–30.

Brown, Michael. (1982) "Biblical Myth and Contemporary Experience: The Akedah in Modern Jewish Literature." *Judaism* 31(1): 99–111.

Buchmann, Christina and Celina Spiegel, eds. (1994) *Out of the Garden: Women Writers on the Bible*. New York: Fawcett Columbine.

Buell, Denise Kimber. (1995) "Procreative Language in Clement of Alexandria." Ph.D. diss., Harvard University.

Burdick, Eugene and Harvey Wheeler. (1962) *Fail-Safe*. New York: McGraw Hill.

Burridge, Kenelm. (1973) *Encountering Aborigines: Anthropology and the Australian Aboriginal*. New York: Pergamon Press.

CALJIC (5th edition, 1988) [California Jury Instructions, Criminal]. St. Paul, Minn.: West Publishing Co.

Carroll, Michael. (1987) "'Moses and Monotheism' Revisited—Freud's 'Personal Myth?'" *American Imago* 44(1):15–35.

Carter, Jimmy. (1985) *The Blood of Abraham*. Boston: Houghton Mifflin.

Cartun, Mark Gregory. (1975) *Humans as Sacrificial Victims in Ancient Semitic Cultures*. Thesis. Hebrew Union College—Jewish Institute of Religion.

Caspi, Mishael. (1995) *The Binding: Akedah and its Transformation in Judaism and Islam*. Lewiston, N.Y.: Mellen Biblical Press.

Chilton, B. D. (1980) "Isaac and the Second Night: A Consideration." *Biblica* 61(1):78–88.

Coats, C. W. (1973) "Abraham's Sacrifice of Faith: A Formcritical Study of Genesis 22." *Interpretation* 27:389–400.

Cohen, Jack. (1990) "Is this the Meaning of My Life? Israelis Rethink the *Akedah*." *Conservative Judaism* vol. xliii(1), 50–60.

Cohn, Carol. (1987) "Sex and Death in the Rational World of Defense Intellectuals." *Signs* vol. 12 (4):687–719.

Combs-Schilling, M. E. (1989) *Sacred Performances: Islam, Sexuality, and Sacrifice*. New York: Columbia University Press.

Coward, Rosalind. (1983) *Patriarchal Precedents*. London: Routledge and Kegan Paul.

Creed, Robert. (1967) "The Art of the Singer: Three Old English Tellings of the Offering of Isaac." In *Old English Poetry*, Robert Creed, ed. Providence, R.I.: Brown University Press.

Cross, Frank Moore. (1973) *Canaanite Myth and Hebrew Epic*. Cambridge, Mass.: Harvard University Press.

Crow, Douglas K. (1986) "The Amplification of Abraham in Islam," In *Face to Face: an Interreligious Bulletin*. vol. xii, 21–28. (Special volume on Abraham in Judaism, Christianity and Islam).

Dagorn, R. (1981) *La Geste D'Ismael d'apres l'Onomastique et la Tradition Arabes*. Geneva: Librairie Droz.

Daly, Mary. (1973) *Beyond God the Father: Toward a Philosophy of Women's Liberation*. Boston: Beacon Press.

Daly, Robert J. (1977) "The Soteriological Significance of the Sacrifice of Isaac." *The Catholic Biblical Quarterly* 39:45–75.

Daniélou, Jean. (1960) *From Shadows to Reality: Studies in the Biblical Typology of the Fathers*. London: Burns and Oates.

Davies, P. (1979) "Passover and the Dating of the Aqedah." *Journal of Jewish Studies* 30:59–67.

Davies, P. and B. Chilton. (1978) "The Aqedah: A Revised Tradition-History." *The Catholic Biblical Quarterly* vol. 40: 514–46.

Day, John. (1989) *Molech: A God of Human Sacrifice in the Old Testament*. Cambridge: Cambridge University Press.

Degler, Carl. (1980) *At Odds: Women and the Family in America from the Revolution to the Present*. Oxford: Oxford University Press.

Delaney, Carol. (1977) "The Legacy of Abraham." In *Beyond Androcentrism*. Rita Gross, ed. Missoula, Mont.: Scholars Press.

———. (1978) "Freud and the Father: Systematic Distortion in Psychoanalytic Theory and Practice." Master's thesis, University of Chicago.

———. (1986) "The Meaning of Paternity and the Virgin Birth Debate." *Man* 21(3) 494–513.

———. (1990) "The Hajj: Sacred and Secular." *American Ethnologist* 17(3) 513–30.

———. (1991) *The Seed and the Soil: Gender and Cosmology in Turkish Village Society*. Berkeley: University of California Press.

———. (1995) "Father State, Motherland, and the Birth of Modern Turkey." In *Naturalizing Power: Essays in Feminist Cultural Analysis*. S. Yanagisako and C. Delaney, eds. New York: Routledge, 177–199.

———. (1996) Book Review of *The First Father. Abraham: The Psychology and Culture of a Spiritual Revolutionary*. Henry Hanoch Abramovitch. *American Ethnologist* 23 (1).

DeMause, Lloyd. (1984) *Reagan's America*. New York: Creative Roots.

Devereux, Georges. (1953) "Why Oedipus Killed Laius." *International Journal of Psychoanalysis* 34:134–141.

Devisch, Renaat. (1993) *Weaving the Threads of Life: the Khita Gyn-eco-logical Healing Cult among the Yaka*. Chicago: University of Chicago Press.

Diamond, Stanley. (1974) *In Search of the Primitive: A Critique of Civilization*. New Brunswick, N.J.: Transaction Books.

Diodorus of Sicily. (1954) Russel M. Geer, trans. Loeb Classical Library. Vol. x, Cambridge, Mass.: Harvard University Press.

Douglas, Mary. (1966) *Purity and Danger*. London: Routledge and Kegan Paul.

Driver, S. R. (1904) *The Book of Genesis*. London: Metheun and Co.

DuBois, Page. (1988) *Sowing the Body: Psychoanalysis and Ancient Representations of Women*. Chicago: University of Chicago Press.

Dundes, Alan. (1984) *Sacred Narratives: Readings in the Theory of Myth*. Berkeley: University of California Press.

———. (1988) *The Flood Myth*. Berkeley: University of California Press.

Durkheim, Emile. (1915) *The Elementary Forms of the Religious Life*. New York: The Free Press, Macmillan Publishing Co.

Easlea, Brian. (1983) *Fathering the Unthinkable: Masculinity, Scientists, and the Nuclear Arms Race*. London: Pluto Press.

Edelman, Marion Wright. (1987) *Families in Peril*. Cambridge: Harvard University Press.

Education for Ministry. (1979) Book 1: The Beginning; Part 2: The Patriarchs (The Abraham Saga). The School of Theology, University of the South. (Course book for teaching in Episcopalian Church Schools.)

Eickelman, Dale. (1978) "The Art of Memory, Islamic Education and its Social Reproduction." *Comparative Studies in Society and History*, 20(4) 485–516.

Eilberg-Schwartz, Howard. (1990) *The Savage in Judaism*. Bloomington: Indiana University Press.

Eilberg-Schwartz, Howard. (1994) *God's Phallus and Other Problems for Men and Monotheism*. Boston: Beacon Press.

———. (1996) "The Father, the Phallus, and the Seminal Word: Dilemmas of Patrilineality in Ancient Judaism." In *Gender, Kinship, Power*. Mary Jo Maynes, Ann Waltner, Birgitte Soland, and Ulrike Strasser, eds. New York and London: Routledge.

Eissfeldt, O. *Molk als Opferbegriffim Punischen und Hebraischen und das Ende des Gottes Moloch*. Halle.

Elshtain, Jean Bethke, and Sheila Tobias. (1990) *Women, Militarism, and War: Essays in History, Politics, and Social Theory*. Savage, Md.: Rowman and Littlefield Publishers.

Elwell, Walter A., ed. (1984) *Evangelical Dictionary of Theology*. Grand Rapids, Mich.: Baker Book House.

Encyclopaedia of Islam (1960–93), Leiden: E. J. Brill.

Encyclopedia Judaica. (1971) Jerusalem: Keter Publishing House.

Engels, Frederick. ([1884]1972) *The Origin of the Family, Private Property and the State*. New York: International Publishers.

Enloe, Cynthia. (1990) *Bananas, Beaches, and Bases*. Berkeley: University of California Press.

Esin, Emel. (1963) *Mecca, the Blessed, Madinah, the Radiant*. London: Elek Books.

Eusebius. ([c. 260–340] 1903) *Preparation for the Gospel*. Edwin H. Gifford, trans., Oxford: Oxford University Press.

Feeley-Harnik, Gillian. (1981) *The Lord's Table: Eucharist and Passover in Early Christianity*. Philadelphia: University of Pennsylvania Press.

Feldman, Yael. (1994) "And Rebecca Loved Jacob, But Freud Did Not." In *Freud and Forbidden Knowledge*. Peter L. Rudnytsky and Ellen Handler Spitz, eds. N.Y.: New York University Press, 7–25.

Fernandez, James. (1991) *Beyond Metaphor: The Theory of Tropes in Anthropology*. Stanford: Stanford University Press.

Filmer, Sir Robert. (1680) *Patriarcha or the Natural Power of Kings*. London: printed for Ric. Chiswell, Matthew Gillyflower, and William Henchman.

Firestone, Reuven. (1989) "Abraham's Son as the Intended Sacrifice (al-Dhabih, Qur'an 37:99–113): Issues in Qur'anic Exegesis," *Journal of Semitic Studies* 34:95–131.

———. (1990) *Journeys in Holy Lands: The Evolution of the Abraham-Ishmael Legends in Islamic Exegesis*. Albany: State University of New York Press.

Fischer, Michael M. J. and Mehdi Abedi. (1990) *Debating Muslims: Cultural Dialogues in Postmodernity and Tradition*. Madison: University of Wisconsin Press.

Folbre, Nancy. (1991) "The Unproductive Housewife: Her Evolution in Nineteenth Century Economic Thought." *Signs* 16(3):463–84.

Foster, Benjamin (1989) "Western Asia in the Second Millenium." In *Women's*

Earliest Records From Ancient Egypt and Western Asia. Barbara Lesko, ed., Atlanta: Scholars Press, 141–43.

Fox, Robin. (1967) *"Totem and Taboo* Reconsidered." *The Structural Study of Myth and Totemism.* Edmund Leach, ed. London: Tavistock Publications. 161–178.

Fraser, Nancy. (1989) "Women, Welfare, and the Politics of Need Interpretation." In *Unruly Practices.* Minneapolis: University of Minnesota Press.

Fraser, Nancy and Linda Gordon. (1994) "Dependency Demystified: Inscriptions of the Poor in a Keyword of the Welfare State." *Social Politics: International Studies in Gender, State, and Society* 1(1):4–31.

Frazer, Sir James George. (1890) *The Golden Bough.* London: Macmillan.

———. (1913) *The Scapegoat.* London: Macmillan.

———. (1919) *Folk-Lore in the Old Testament.* New York: Macmillan.

Frei, Hans W. (1974) *The Eclipse of Biblical Narrative.* New Haven: Yale University Press.

Friedman, Richard (1987) *Who Wrote the Bible?* New York: Harper and Row.

Friedrich, Gerhard, ed. (1967) *Theological Dictionary of the New Testament.* vol 5:965. Grand Rapids, Mich.: Wm. B. Eerdmans Publishing Company.

Friedrich, Paul. (1979) *Language, Context and the Imagination.* Stanford: Stanford University Press.

———. (1986) *The Language Parallax.* Austin: University of Texas Press.

Freud, Sigmund. (1900) *Interpretation of Dreams* vol. 4. In *The Standard Edition of the Complete Psychological Works of Sigmund Freud.* James Strachey, ed. 24 vols. London: Hogarth Press, 1953–74 (hereafter SE).

———. (1909) "Notes Upon a Case of Obsessive Neurosis." SE 10.

———. (1911) "Psycho-analytic Notes on an Autobiographical Account of a Case of Paranoia (Dementia Paranoides)." SE 12.

———. (1913) *Totem and Taboo.* SE 13.

———. ([1914]1918) "From the History of an Infantile Neurosis." SE 17.

———. (1924) "An Autobiographical Study." SE 20.

———. (1933) "Why War?" SE 22 (Einstein's letter included).

———. (1939) *Moses and Monotheism.* Katherine Jones, trans. New York: Vintage Books, and SE 23.

Frymer-Kensky, Tikva. (1992) *In the Wake of the Goddesses.* N.Y.: Free Press.

Funiciello, Theresa. (1993) *Tyranny of Kindness: Dismantling the Welfare System to End Poverty in America.* New York: The Atlantic Monthly Press.

Garfinkel, Irwin. (1992) *Assuring Child Support: An Extension of Social Security.* New York: Russell Sage Foundation.

Geertz, Clifford. (1973) *Interpretation of Cultures.* New York: Basic Books.

Geller, Jay. (1993) " "Paleontological View of Freud's Study of Religion: Unearthing the *Leitfossil* Circumcision." *Modern Judaism* 13 (1): 49–70.

Genesis Apocryphon of Qumram Cave I. (1971) Joseph Fitzmyer, SJ., trans. Rome: Biblical Institute Press.

Genesis Rabbah: The Judaic Commentary to the Book of Genesis: A New American Translation. Jacob Neusner, trans. 1985, Atlanta: Scholars Press.

Gibson, Joan. (1992) "Could Christ Have Been Born a Woman?" *Journal of Feminists Studies in Religion* 8(1) 65–82.

Gill, Pauline. (1991) *Les Enfants de Duplessis*. Montreal: Libre Expression.

Gilman, Sander L. (1993) *Freud, Race, and Gender*. Princeton, N.J.: Princeton University Press.

Ginzberg, Louis. (1909) *Legends of the Jews*. (7 vols.) Philadelphia: Jewish Publication Society of America.

Girard, Rene. (1972) *Violence and the Sacred*. Baltimore: Johns Hopkins University Press.

Glaser, Danya and Stephen Frosh. (1998) *Child Sexual Abuse*. London: Macmillan Education/British Association of Social Workers.

Glendon, Mary Ann. (1987) *Abortion and Divorce in Western Law: American Failures, European Challenges*. Cambridge, Mass.: Harvard University Press.

———. (1991) *Rights Talk*. New York: Free Press.

Glueck, Nelson. (1955) "The Age of Abraham in the Negeb." *The Biblical Archaeologist* 18:2–9.

Goldberg, Harvey (1987) "Torah and Children: Symbolic Aspects of the Reproduction of Jews and Judaism." In Harvey Goldberg, ed. *Judaism Viewed from Within and Without*. Albany: State University of New York, 107–138.

Goldson, Edward. (1993) "War Is Not Good For Children." In *The Psychological Effects of War and Violence on Children*. Lewis A. Leavitt and Nathan A. Fox, eds. Hillsdale, N.J.: Lawrence Erlbaum Associates, 3–22.

Gordon, Neil. (1995) *The Sacrifice of Isaac*. New York: Random House.

Graves, Robert and Raphael Patai. ([1963]1966) *Hebrew Myths: The Book of Genesis*. New York: McGraw Hill.

Green, Alberto R. (1975) *The Role of Human Sacrifice in the Ancient Near East*. Missoula, Mont.: Scholars Press.

Gresser, Moshe. (1994) *Dual Allegiance: Freud as a Modern Jew*. Albany: State University of New York.

Greven, Philip ([1990]1992) *Spare the Child: The Religious Roots of Punishment and the Psychological Impact of Physical Abuse*. New York: Vintage Books.

Grünbaum, Adolf. (1993) *Validation in the Clinical Theory of Psychoanalysis*. Madison, Conn.: International Universities Press.

Hackett, Jo Ann. (1987) "Women's Studies and the Hebrew Bible." In *The Future of Biblical Studies: The Hebrew Scriptures*. R. Friedman and H. Williamson, eds. Atlanta, Ga.: Scholars Press, 141–164.

Hallo, William W. and J. J. A. van Dijk. (1968) *The Exaltation of Inanna*. New Haven: Yale University Press.

Handelman, S. (1982) *The Slayers of Moses: The Emergence of Rabbinic Interpretation in Modern Literary Theory*. Albany: State University of New York Press.

Handler, Joel F. (1995) *The Poverty of Welfare Reform*. New Haven: Yale University Press.

Handman, Marie-Elisabeth. (1983) *La Violence et la Ruse. Hommes et Femmes dans un Village Grec*. La Calade, Aix-en-Provence: Edisud.

Haraway, Donna. (1989) *Primate Visions: Gender, Race, and Nature in the World of Modern Science*. New York: Routledge.

Harding, Sandra. (1990) "Starting Thought from Women's Lives: Eight Resources for Maximizing Objectivity." *Journal of Social Philosophy* 21 (2/3): 140–49.

Harding, Susan. (1987) "Convicted by the Holy Spirit: the Rhetoric of Fundamental Baptist Conversion." *American Ethnologist* 14:167–181.

———. (1991) "Representing Fundamentalism: the Problem of the Repugnant Cultural Other." *Social Research* vol. 58(2):373–393.

———. (1992) "The Afterlife of Stories: Genesis of a Man of God." In *Storied Lives*. G. C. Rosenwald and R. Ochberg, eds. New Haven: Yale University Press, 60–75.

Hartt, Frederick. (1975) *History of Italian Renaissance Art*. N.J.: Prentice Hall.

Hawkesworth, M. (1989) "Knowers, Knowing, Known: Feminist Theory and Claims of Truth," *Signs* 14(31):533–557.

Hawting, G. R. (1982) "The Origins of the Muslim Sanctuary at Mecca." In *Studies on the First Century of Islamic Society*. G. H. A. Juynbull, ed. Carbondale: Southern Illinois University Press.

Hayward, C. T. R. (1990) "The Sacrifice of Isaac and Jewish Polemic Against Christianity." *The Catholic Biblical Quarterly* 52:291–306.

Haywood, Robert. (1980) "Appendix: The Aqedah." In *Sacrifice*. W. F. C. Bourdillon and Meyer Fortes, eds. London: Academic Press.

———. (1981) "The Present State of Research into the Targumic Account of the Sacrifice of Isaac." *Journal of Jewish Studies* xxxii(2):127–150.

Hengel, Martin. (1981) *The Atonement*. Philadelphia: Fortress Press.

Herdt, Gilbert. (1981) *Guardians of the Flutes: Idioms of Masculinity*. New York: McGraw-Hill.

——— ed. (1982) *Rituals of Manhood: Male Initiation in Papua New Guinea*. Berkeley: University of California Press.

Herhold, Rev. Robert M. (1995) "Who Asked Isaac?" Unpublished play performed 27 October 1995. University Lutheran Church, Palo Alto, Calif.

Herman, Judith with Lisa Hirschman. (1981) *Father-Daughter Incest*. Cambridge, Mass.: Harvard University Press.

Hesiodus. ([8th cent. B.C.] 1959) *Works and Days, Theogony, the Shield of Herakles*. Richard Lattimore, trans. Ann Arbor: University of Michigan Press.

Hill, Dorothy. (1957) *Abraham: His Heritage and Ours*. Boston: Beacon Press.

Hocart, A. M. (1973) "Kinship Systems." In *The Life-Giving Myth*. London: Tavistock Publications.

Hochschild, Arlie. (1975) "Inside the Clockwork of Male Careers." In *Women and the Power to Change*. Florence Howe, ed. New York: McGraw Hill.

Hochschild, Arlie and Anne Machtung. (1989) *The Second Shift: Working Parents and the Revolution at Home*. New York: Viking Penguin.

Hultgård, Anders. (1991) "God and the Image of Woman in Early Jewish Religion." In *Image of God and Gender Models in Judaeo-Christian Tradition*. Kari Elisabeth Børrensen, ed. Oslo: Solum Forlag.

Inglis, Ruth. (1978) *The Sins of the Fathers: A Study of the Physical and Emotional Abuse of Children*. New York: St. Martin's Press.

The Interpreter's Bible. (1952) George Arthur Buttrick et al, eds., New York: Abingdon-Cokesbury Press.

Irenaeus. ([c. A.D. 120–202] 1903) "Against Heresies." In *The Ante-Nicene Fathers*, vol. 1, N.Y.: Charles Scribner's Sons.

Jay, Nancy. (1992) *Throughout your Generations Forever: Sacrifice, Religion and Paternity*. Chicago: University of Chicago Press.

Jeffords, Susan. (1989) *The Remasculinization of America: Gender and the Vietnam War*. Bloomington: Indiana University Press.

Jenkins, Philip. (1992) *Intimate Enemies: Moral Panics in Contemporary Great Britain*. New York: Aldine de Gruyter.

Jones, Ernest. (1924) *Essays in Applied Psychoanalysis*. London: Hogarth Press.

Josephus Flavius. ([c. A.D. 30–100] 1961) *Jewish Antiquities*, Vol. 4, Book 1:222–36. Cambridge, Mass.: Loeb Classical Library, Harvard University Press.

Kamerman, Sheila B. (1984) "Women, Children, and Poverty: Public Policy and Female-headed Families in Industrialized Countries." *Signs* 10(2):249–271.

Kamerman, Sheila B. And Alfred J. Kahn. (1989) "Single-parent, Female-headed Families in Western Europe: Social Change and Response." *International Social Security Review* 1:3–34.

———. (1994) "Family Policy and the Under-3s: Money, Services, and Time in a Policy Package." *International Social Security Review* 47(3–4):31–44.

Kanzer, Mark. (1972) "Discussion of Leonard Shengold's Paper." *American Imago* 29(1)160–64.

Kant, Immanuel. ([1798]1979) *The Conflict of the Faculties*. Mary Gregor, trans. Lincoln: University of Nebraska Press.

Kaplan, Kalman. (1990) "Isaac and Oedipus: A Re-Examination of the Father-Son Relationship." *Judaism* 39(1)73–81.

Katz, Michael. (1986) *In the Shadow of the Poorhouse: A Social History of Welfare in America*. New York: Basic Books.

Kertzer, David. (1993) *Sacrificed for Honor: Italian Infant Abandonment and the Politics of Reproductive Control*. Boston: Beacon Press.

Kierkegaard, Søren. ([1843] 1941) *Fear and Trembling*. Walter Lowrie, trans. Princeton: Princeton University Press.

al-Kisa'i, Muhammed ibn Abd Allah. ([11th cent.] 1978) *Tales of the Prophets of al-Kisa'i*. Translated from the Arabic, with notes, by W. M. Thackston, Jr. Boston: Twayne Publishers.

Kister, M. J. (1971) "Maqam Ibrahim: A Stone with an Inscription." *Le Museon* (84):477–487.

Kittay, Eva. (1996) "Human Dependency and Rawlsian Equality." In *Feminists Rethink the Self*. Diana Tietjens Meyers, ed. Colo.: Westview Press.

Kohn, H. (1960) "Hebrew and Greek Roots of Modern Nationalism." In *Conflict and Cooperation Among Nations*. Ivo Duchacek, ed. New York: Holt, Rinehart and Winston, 39–41.

Kolve, V. A. (1966) *The Play Called Corpus Christi*. Stanford: Stanford University Press.

Koran, The Meaning of the Glorious. Mohammed Marmaduke Pickthall, trans. New York: A Mentor Book, n.d.

Kraemer, Ross J. (1988) *Maenads, Martyrs, Matrons, Monastics: A Source Book on Women's Religions in the Greco-Roman World*. Philadelphia: Fortress Press.

Kritzeck, James. (1965) *Sons of Abraham: Jews, Christians and Moslems*. Baltimore: Helicon Press.

Kroeber, Alfred L. ([1920]1952) "Totem and Taboo: An Ethnologic Psychoanalysis." *The Nature of Culture*. Berkeley: University of California Press, 301–5.

———. ([1939] 1952) "Totem and Taboo in Retrospect." *The Nature of Culture*. Berkeley: University of California Press, 306–9.

Krull, Marianne. (1986) *Freud and His Father*. New York and London: W. W. Norton.

LaBarre, Weston. (1958) "The Influence of Freud on Anthropology." *American Imago* 15(3) 275–328.

LaFontaine, J. S. (1987) "Preliminary Remarks on a Study of Incest in England." In *Child Survival*, Scheper-Hughes, ed. 267–290.

LaHurd, Carol Schersten. (1990) "One God, One Father: Abraham in Judaism, Christianity and Islam." *Dialog* 29(1)17–28.

Lakoff, George. (1980) *Metaphors We Live By*. Chicago: University of Chicago Press.

———. (1990–91) "Metaphor and War." Paper circulated on computer networks, December 1990; presented at Stanford University, January 1991, during the Gulf War.

Langer, Suzanne. (1942) *Philosophy in a New Key*. Cambridge, Mass.: Harvard University Press.

Lazarus-Yafeh, Hava. (1981) *Some Religious Aspects of Islam*. Leiden: E. J. Brill.

Leach, E. (1961) "Levi-Strauss in the Garden of Eden: An Examination of Some Recent Developments in the Analysis of Myth." *Transactions of the New York Academy of Sciences* 23:386–395.

———. (1967) "Virgin Birth." In *Proceedings of the Royal Anthropological Institute, 1966–67*, 39–48.

Leach, E. (1969) *Genesis as Myth*. London: Jonathan Cape.

Leach, Penelope. (1994) *Children First: What Our Society Must Do—And Is Not Doing—For Our Children Today*. New York: Alfred A. Knopf.

Lerch, David. (1950) *Isaac's Opferung Christlich Gedeudet*. Tubingen: Verlag J. C. B. Mohr.

Lerman, Hannah. (1986) *The Mote in Freud's Eye*. New York: Springer Publishing Co.

Levenson, J. (1991) "The Good Friday-Passover Connection." *New York Times* March 3.

———. (1993) *The Death and Resurrection of the Beloved Son*. New Haven: Yale University Press.

Lévi-Strauss, Claude. ([1962]1963) *Totemism*. Rodney Needham, trans. Boston: Beacon Press.

Lewis, Chaim. (1973) "From Adam's Serpent to Abraham's Ram." *Judaism* 22(4) 392–99.

Lloyd, Seton and William Brice. (1951) "Harran." *Anatolian Studies*. 1:77–111.

Longton, Joseph. (1987) *Fils d'Abraham: Panorama des Communautes Juives, Chretiennes et Musulmanes*. Belgium: Editions Brepols.

Luther, Martin. (1539–41) *Luther's Works: Lectures on Genesis* (Chapters 21–5). Jaroslav Pelikan, ed. Saint Louis: Concordia Publishing House, 1964.

Malinowski, Bronislaw. ([1927]1985) *Sex and Repression in Savage Society*. Chicago: University of Chicago Press.

———. ([1929]1982) *Sexual Life of Savages in Northwestern Melanesia*. London: Routledge and Kegan Paul.

———. ([1948]1954) *Magic, Science and Religion*. New York: Doubleday Anchor Books.

Marcus, Ivan. (1982) "From Politics to Martyrdom: Shifting Paradigms in the Hebrew Narratives of the 1096 Crusade Riots." *Prooftexts* 2:40–52.

Masson, Jeffrey M. (1984) *The Assault on Truth: Freud's Suppression of the Seduction Theory*. New York: Farrar, Straus and Giroux.

Mazlish, Bruce. (1969) "Freud as Philosopher of History." In *Monotheism and Moses*. R. J. Christen and H. E. Hazelton, eds. Lexington, Mass.: D. C. Heath and Company.

McGrath, William. (1974) "Freud as Hannibal: Politics of the Brother Band." *Central European History* 7(1).

McKinnon, Susan. (1995) "American Kinship/American Incest: Asymmetries in a Scientific Discourse." In *Naturalizing Power: Essays in Feminist Cultural Analysis*. Sylvia Yanagisako and Carol Delaney, eds. New York: Routledge, 25–46.

McLennan, J. F. (1896) *Studies in Ancient History*. London: Macmillan and Company.

McNeill, William. (1986) *Mythistory and Other Essays*. Chicago: University of Chicago Press.

Miedzian, Myriam. (1991) *Boys Will Be Boys: Breaking the Link Between Masculinity and Violence*. New York: Doubleday.

Milgrom, Jo. (1987) "From Moriah to Sinai, From Abraham to Moses, From a Man to a People." *Moment* 12(6):37–41, 59.

———. (1988) *The Akedah: A Primary Symbol in Jewish Thought and Art*. Berkeley: The Bibal Press.

Millard, A. R. and D. J. Wiseman. (1980) *Essays on the Patriarchal Narratives*. Harmondsworth, England.: Inter-Varsity Press.

Miller, Rabbi Alan. (1983) "The Binding of Isaac." *The Jewish Spectator* Fall: 37–9.

Miller, Alice. ([1988]1990) *The Untouched Key: Tracing Childhood Trauma in Creativity and Destructiveness*. New York: Anchor Books—Doubleday.

Mintz, Allan. (1984) *Hurban*. New York: Columbia University Press.

Moberly, R. W. L. (1988) "The Earliest Commentary on the Akedah." *Vestum Testamentum*. 3(3), 302–323.

Montagu, Susan. (1983) "Trobriand Gender Identity." *Mankind* 14(1):33–45.

Morgan, Lewis Henry. (1870) *Systems of Consanguinity and Affinity of the Human Family*. Washington, D.C.: Smithsonian Contributions to Knowledge.

———. ([1877]1974) *Ancient Society: or Researches in the Lines of Human Progress from Savagery through Barbarism to Civilization*. Gloucester, Mass.: Meridian Book, The World Publishing Co.

Morris, Norval. (1992) *The Brothel Boy and Other Parables of the Law*. New York: Oxford University Press.

Mosca, Paul. (1975) *Child Sacrifice in Canaanite and Israelite Religion*. Ph.D. diss., Harvard University.

Moscati, Sabatini. (1983) *Carthage*. Milan: Jaca Book.

Mosse, George. (1985) *Nationalism and Sexuality*. New York: Howard Fertig.

Musallam, Basim. (1983) *Sex and Society in Islam: Birth Control Before the Nineteenth Century*. New York: Cambridge University Press.

Nachmanides (Moses ben Nahman; Ramban). ([c.1195–1270] 1971) *Commentary on the Torah*. Rabbi Dr. Charles B. Chavel, trans. New York: Shilo Publishing House.

Nagy, Gregory. (1979) *The Best of the Achaeans*. Baltimore: Johns Hopkins University Press.

Neu, Jerome. (1991) *The Cambridge Companion to Freud*. Cambridge: Cambridge University Press.

Newby, Gordon Darnell. (1989) *The Making of the Last Prophet: A Reconstruction of the Earliest Biography of Muhammad*. Columbia, S.C.: University of South Carolina Press.

Newsom, Carole A., and Sharon H. Ringe. (1992) *The Women's Bible Commentary*. London: Westminster; Louisville, Ky: John Knox Press.

Nicholls, David. (1993) "Addressing God as Ruler: Prayer and Petition." *British Journal of Sociology*. 44(1):125–41.

Niditch, Susan. (1992) "Genesis." In *The Women's Bible Commentary*. Carole A. Newsom and Sharon H. Ringe, eds. Louisville, Ky.: Westminster/John Knox Press.

Niederland, William G. (1951) "Three Notes on the Schreber Case." *Psychoanalytic Quarterly* 20.

———. (1959a) "The 'Miracled-up' World of Schreber's Childhood." *Psychoanalytic Study of the Child* 14. New York: International Universities Press.

———. (1959b) "Schreber: Father and Son." *Psychoanalytic Quarterly* 28.

———. (1960) "Schreber's Father." *Journal of the American Psychoanalytic Association* 8.

Noonan, John Thomas. (1965) *Contraception: A History of its Treatment by the Catholic Theologians and Canonists*. Cambridge, Mass.: Belknap Press of Harvard University Press.

Novak, Michael. (1993) "Women, Ordination, and Angels." *First Things* April.

O'Brien, Connor C. (1988) *God Land: Reflections on Religion and Nationalism*. Cambridge, Mass.: Harvard University Press.

Okin, Susan. (1979) *Women in Western Political Thought*. Princeton: Princeton University Press.

Oliver, Anne Marie and Paul Steinberg. (1995) "Embodied Imperative: the Command of Death in the Underground Media of the Intifada." Unpublished paper at Center for Middle Eastern Studies, Harvard University.

Orlinsky, Harry. (1969) "Abraham and Moses." In *Monotheism and Moses*. R. J. Christen and H. E. Hazelton, eds. Lexington, Mass.: D. C. Heath and Co.

Otto, Rudolph. (1923) *The Idea of the Holy*. Oxford: Oxford University Press.

Oz, Amos. ([1965]1973) "The Way of the Wind." *Where the Jackals Howl and Other Stories*. New York: Harcourt Brace Jovanovitch, 39–60.

Pardes, Ilana. (1992) *Countertraditions in the Bible: A Feminist Approach*. Cambridge, Mass.: Harvard Univerity Press.

Paret, Rudi. (1978) "Ibrahim" and "Ishma'il." *The Encyclopaedia of Islam*. Leiden: E. J. Brill.

Parrot, Andre. (1968) *Abraham and His Times*. James H. Farley, trans. Philadelphia: Fortress Press. (First published in French, 1962).

Patai, Raphael. (1986) *The Seed of Abraham: Jews and Arabs in Contact and Conflict*. Salt Lake City: University of Utah Press.

Pateman, Carole. (1988) *The Sexual Contract*. Stanford: Stanford University Press.

Paul, Robert. (1996) *Moses and Civilization: The Meaning Behind Freud's Myth*. New Haven: Yale University Press.

Pearce, Diana. (1978) "The Feminization of Poverty: Women, Work, and Welfare." *Urban and Social Change Review* (Winter/Spring):28–36.

———. (1990) "Welfare is NOT for Women: Why the War on Poverty Cannot Conquer the Feminization of Poverty." In *Women, the State, and Welfare* Linda Gordon, ed. Madison: University of Wisconsin Press, 265–279.

Pesikta Rabbati. (1968) William Braude, trans. New Haven: Yale University Press.

Peters, F. E. (1982) *Children of Abraham*. Princeton: Princeton University Press.

———. (1986) "The Children of Abraham and Sacred History." *Face to Face: an Interreligious Bulletin* xii:4–8. (Special volume on Abraham in Judaism, Christianity and Islam).

———. (1990) *Judaism, Christianity, and Islam*. Vol. 1. Princeton: Princeton University Press.

Philo of Alexandria. ([c. 20 B.C.–A.D. 50] 1959) *De Abrahamo*. F. H. Colson, trans. Cambridge, Mass.: Loeb Classical Library, Harvard University Press.

Phipps, William E. (1989) *Genesis and Gender: Biblical Myths of Sexuality and their Cultural Impact*. New York: Praeger Publishers.

Piske de Rabbi Eliezer. (1965) G. Friedlander, trans. New York: Hermon Press.

Plaut, W. Gunther. (1974) *The Torah: A Modern Commentary*. New York: The Union of American Hebrew Congregations.

Pollitt, Katha. (1995) "Subject to Debate." *The Nation*. January 30, 20.

Prag, Kay. (1970) "The 1959 Deep Sounding at Harran in Turkey." *Levant: Journal of the British School of Archaeology in Jerusalem*. 2:63–94.

Pritchard, J. B., ed. (1950) *Ancient Near Eastern Texts Relating to the Old Testament*. Princeton: Princeton University Press.

Quell, G. (1967) Entry on "pater" in the Old Testament. In *Theological Dictionary of the New Testament*. Geoffrey W. Bromiley, ed. Grand Rapids, Mich.: William B. Eerdmans Publishers, 807–08.

Rashi. (1929) *Pentateuch with Rashi's Commentary*. Rev. M. Rosenbaum and A. M. Silbermann, trans. London: Shapiro, Vallentine.

Reid, Stephen. (1972) "*Moses and Monotheism:* Guilt and the Murder of the Primal Father." *American Imago*. 19(1):11–34.

Rice, Emanuel. (1990) *Freud and Moses: The Long Journey Home*. Albany: State University of New York Press.

Riddle, John. (1992) *Contraception and Abortion from the Ancient World to the Renaissance*. Cambridge, Mass.: Harvard University Press.

Rieff, Philip ([1959]1979) *Freud: The Mind of the Moralist*. Chicago: University of Chicago Press.

Riskin, Shlomo. (1994) "The Akeda: A Lesson in Martyrdom." *The Jerusalem Post* October 21.

Riskin, Shlomo, Sheldon Zimmerman and Alan W. Miller. (1983) "The Binding of Isaac: Three Rabbis Study and Teach a Text." *The Jewish Spectator* Fall.

Robert, Marthe. (1976) *From Oedipus to Moses*. Garden City, N.Y.: Anchor Books.

Robinson, Paul. (1993) *Freud and His Critics*. Berkeley: University of California Press.

Rock, Paul (1993) *The Social World of an English Crown Court*. Oxford: Oxford University Press.

Rosaldo, Renato (1989) *Culture and Truth*. Boston: Beacon Press.

Rosenberg, R. (1965) "Jesus, Isaac, and the 'Suffering Servant.'" *Journal of Biblical Literature* 84:381–88.

Rosenzweig, Franz. (1971) *The Star of Redemption*. New York: Holt, Rinehart and Winston.

Roskies, David G. (1984) *Against the Apocalypse: Responses to Catastrophe in Modern Jewish Culture*. Cambridge, Mass.: Harvard University Press.

Rothstein, Edward. (1996). "A Beginning Stripped of Awe." *New York Times* December 1.

Rubin, Gayle. (1975) "The Traffic in Women: Notes on the 'Political Economy' of Sex." In *Toward an Anthropology of Women*. Rayna Reiter, ed. New York: Monthly Review Press, 157–210.

Sader, Helen. (1991) "Phoenician Stelae From Tyre." *Berytus Archaeological Studies*. Vol. xxxix:101–26.

Sahlins, Marshall. (1976) *Culture and Practical Reason*. Chicago: University of Chicago Press.

———. (1981) *Historical Metaphors and Mythical Realities*. Ann Arbor: The University of Michigan Press.

Samuel, Raphael and Paul Thompson, eds. (1990) *Myths We Live By*. London: Routledge

Sandmel, Samuel. (1956) *Philo's Place in Judaism: A Study of the Conceptions of Abraham in Jewish Literature*. Cincinnati: Hebrew Union College Press.

Sapir, Edward. (1951) *Culture, Language, and Personality*. David Mandelbaum, ed. Berkeley: University of California Press.

Sapiro, Virginia. (1990) "The Gender Bias of American Social Policy." In *Women, the State, and Welfare*. Linda Gordon, ed. Madison: University of Wisconsin Press, 36–54.

Sarna, Nahum. (1966) *Understanding Genesis*. New York: McGraw Hill.

———. ed. (1989) *The JPS Torah Commentary: Genesis*. Philadelphia: The Jewish Publication Society.

Saussure, Ferdinand de. (1966) *Course in General Linguistics* New York: McGraw Hill.

Scarry, Elanie. (1992) "The Declaration of War: Constitutional and Unconstitutional Violence." In *Law's Violence*. Austin Sarat and Tom Kearns, eds. Amherst Series in Law, Jurisprudence, and Social Thought, 23–76.

Schapiro, Meyer. ([1943]1979) "The Angel with the Ram in Abraham's Sacrifice: A Parallel in Western and Islamic Art." *Late Antique, Early Christian and Medieval Art*. New York: George Braziller, 289–318.

Schatzman, Morton. (1972) "Paranoia or Persecution: The Case of Schreber." *International Journal of Psychiatry* 10(3).

———. (1973) *Soul Murder: Persecution in the Family*. New York: Random House.

Scheffler, H. W. (1972) "Systems of Kin Classification: A Structural Typology." In *Kinship Studies in the Morgan Centennial Year*. P. Reining, ed. Washington, D.C.: American Anthropological Society.

Scheper-Hughes, Nancy, ed. (1987) *Child Survival: Anthropological Perspectives on the Treatment and Maltreatment of Children*. Dordrecht: D. Reidel Publishing Company.

Scheper-Hughes, Nancy and Howard Stein. (1987) "Child Abuse and the Unconscious in American Popular Culture." In *Child Survival*. Scheper-Hughes, ed. Dordrecht: D. Reidel Publishing Company, 339–58.

Schiffren, Lisa. (1995) "Penalize the Unwed Dad? Fat Chance." *New York Times* August 10.

Schlossman, Howard. (1972) "God the Father and His Sons." *American Imago* 29(1):35–52.

Schneider, David. (1968) *American Kinship: A Cultural Account*. Englewood Cliffs, N.J.: Prentice-Hall.

———. (1972) "What is Kinship All About?" In *Kinship Studies in the Morgan Centennial Year*. P. Reining, ed. Washington, D.C.: The Anthropological Society, 32–63.

———. (1976) "Notes Toward a Theory of Culture." In *Meaning in Anthropology*. Keith H. Basso and Henry A. Selby, eds. Albuquerque, N.M.: University of New Mexico Press, 197–220.

———. (1984) *A Critique of the Study of Kinship*. Ann Arbor: University of Michigan Press.

Schoeps, H. (1946) "The Sacrifice of Isaac in Paul's Theology." *Journal of Biblical Literature* (65) 385–92.

Schorske, Carl E. (1973) "Politics and Patricide in Freud's *Interpretation of Dreams*." *The American Historical Review* 78(2).

Schüssler-Fiorenza, Elisabeth. (1985) *In Memory of Her: A Feminist Theological Reconstruction of Christian Origins*. New York: Crossroad Publishing Co.

———. (1992) *But She Said: Feminist Practices of Biblical Interpretation*. Boston: Beacon Press.

Schwartz, Regina. (1990) "Introduction: On Biblical Criticism." In *The Book and the Text: The Bible and Literary Theory*. R. Schwartz, ed. Cambridge, England: Basil Blackwell, 1–15.

———. (1997) *The Curse of Cain: The Violent Legacy of Monotheism*. Chicago: University of Chicago Press.

Scott, James C. (1990) *Domination and the Arts of Resistance: Hidden Transcripts*. New Haven: Yale University Press.

Scudder, Lewis R. (1990) "Ishmael and Isaac and Muslim-Christian Dialogue" *Dialog*. 29(1) 29–32.

Segal, Alan F. ([1984]1987) "The Sacrifice of Isaac in Early Judaism and Christianity." *The Other Judaisms of Late Antiquity*. Atlanta, Ga.: Scholars Press.

Shariati, Ali. (1980) *Hajj*. Houston, Tex.: Free Islamic Literature Inc.

Shengold, Leonard. (1972) "A Paraphraxis of Freud's in Relation to Karl Abraham." *American Imago* 29(2):123–59.

Sheppard, Gerald. (1986) "The Presentation of Abraham in the Christian Tradition." *Face to Face: An Interreligious Bulletin*. Vol. xiii:14–20.

Shulman, David. (1993) *The Hungry God: Hindu Tales of Filicide and Devotion*. Chicago: University of Chicago Press.

Sidel, Ruth. ([1986]1992) *Women and Children Last: The Plight of Poor Women in Affluent America*. New York: Penguin Books.

———. (1996) *Keeping Women and Children Last: America's War on the Poor*. New York: Penguin Books.

Siker, Jeffrey S. (1991) *Disinheriting the Jews: Abraham in Early Christian Controversy*. Louisville, Ky.: Westminster/John Knox Press.

Silberman, Neil Asher. (1982) *Digging for God and Country: Exploration in the Holy Land, 1799–1917*. New York: Doubleday, Anchor Books.

———. (1989) *Between Past and Present: Archaeology, Ideology, and Nationalism in the Modern Middle East*. New York: Doubleday, Anchor Books.

Smith, Morton. (1975) "A Note on Burning Babies." *JAOS* 95:477–79.

Smith, W. Robertson. (1889) *Lectures on the Religion of the Semites*. New York: D. Appleton & Co.

———. (1903) *Kinship and Marriage in Early Arabia*. Boston: Beacon Press.

Soler, J. (1977) "Dietary Prohibitions of the Hebrews." Elborg Forster, trans. *New York Review of Books* 26:10 (June 14), 24–30.

Speiser, E.A. (1963) "The Wife-Sister Motif in the Patriarchal Narratives." In *Biblical and Other Studies*. A. Altmann, ed. Cambridge: Harvard University Press.

———. (1964) *Genesis*. Translation and commentary for the Anchor Bible, New York: Doubleday & Co.

Spencer, W. B. and F. J. Gillen. (1899) *The Native Tribes of Central Australia*. London: Macmillan.

Spiegel, S. ([1950]1969) *The Last Trial*. Judah Goldin, trans. New York: Schocken Books.

Spiro, Melford. (1968) "Virgin Birth, Parthenogenesis, and Physiological Paternity: An Essay in Cultural Interpretation." *Man* New Series (3):242–61.

Spivak, Gayatri. (1988) "Can the Subaltern Speak?" In *Marxism and the Interpretation of Culture*. Cary Nelson and Lawrence Grossberg, eds. Urbana: University of Illinois Press, 271–313.

Stacey, Judith. (1994) "Dan Quayle's Revenge: The New Family Values Crusaders." *The Nation*, July 25/August 1, 119–22.

——— (1996) *In the Name of the Family: Rethinking Family Values in the Postmodern Age*. Boston: Beacon Press.

Stager, Lawrence. (1982) "Carthage: A View from the Tophet." *Phönizier Im Westen*. H. G. Niemeyer, ed. Mainz am Rhein: Verlag Philipp Von Zabern.

Stager, Lawrence and Samuel R. Wolff. (1984) "Child Sacrifice at Carthage: Religious Rite or Population Control?" *Biblical Archaeology Review* 30–51.

Stanton, Elizabeth Cady, ed. ([1895]1974) *The Woman's Bible*. Seattle: Coalition Task Force on Women and Religion.

Starting Points: Meeting the Needs of Our Youngest Children. April 1994. Carnegie Corporation of New York.

Steinmetz, Devora. (1991) *From Father to Son: Kinship, Conflict, and Continuity in Genesis*. Louisville, Ky.: Westminster/John Knox Press.

Strathern, Marilyn. (1980). "No Nature, No Culture: The Hagen Case." In *Nature, Culture, and Gender*. Carol MacCormack and Marilyn Strathern, eds. Cambridge: Cambridge University Press, 174–222.

Strenski, Ivan. (1996) "Between Theory and Speciality: Sacrifice in the 90s." *Religious Studies Review* 22(1):10–20.

Sulloway, Frank J. (1979) *Freud, The Biologist of the Mind*. New York: Basic Books.

Swetnam, James. (1981) *Isaac and Jesus*. Rome: Biblical Institute Press.

Syren, Roger. (1993) *The Forsaken First-Born: A Study of a Recurrent Motif in the Patriarchal Narratives*. Sheffield, England.: Sheffield Academic Press.

al-Tabari. ([c. 915] 1987) *The History of al-Tabari: Prophets and Patriarchs*. W. Brinner trans. Albany: State University of New York Press.

Talmud, Hebrew-English Edition of the Babylonian, Yoma. (1974) Rabbi Dr. Leo Jung, trans., Rabbi Dr. I. Epstein, ed., New York, London, Jerusalem: The Soncino Press.

Tapper, Nancy and Richard Tapper. (1987) "The Birth of the Prophet: Ritual and Gender in Turkish Islam." *Man* 22(1):69–92.

Targum Neofiti. (1992) Martin McNamara, MSC, trans. Minneapolis., Minn.: Michael Glazier Book Liturgical Press.

Targum Pseudo Jonathan: Genesis. (1992) Michael Maker, MSC, trans. Minneapolis, Minn.: Michael Glazier Book Liturgical Press.

Targum Onqelos. (1988) Bernard Grossfeld, Wilmington, Del.: Michael Glazier.

Tertullian. ([c. A.D. 160–230] 1970) "An Answer to the Jews." *Ante-Nicene Christian Library*. Vol. xviii. Edinburgh: T. & T. Clark. 201–53.

———. (1972) *Adversus Marcionem*. (Books 1–5) Ernest Evans, ed. and trans. Oxford: Clarendon Press.

———. (1970) "Adversus Praxean." *Ante-Nicene Christian Library*. Vol. xv. Edinburgh: T. & T. Clark.

Teubal, Savina. (1984) *Sarah the Priestess: The First Matriarch of Genesis*. Athens, Ohio: Swallow Press.

———. (1990) *Hagar The Egyptian: The Lost Tradition of the Matriarchs*. San Francisco: Harper and Row Publishers.

Thompson, Thomas L. (1974) *The Historicity of the Patriarchal Narratives: The Quest for the Historical Abraham*. Berlin: Walter de Gruyter.

Tietjen, John. (1988) "Hebrews 11:8–12." *Interpretation* 42:4, 403–07.

Tolosana, C. Lisón. (1979) *Brujería, Estructura Social y Simbolismo en Galicia*. Madrid: Akal.

Tonkinson, Robert. (1978) "Semen vs. Spirit Child in a Western Desert Culture." In *Australian Aboriginal Concepts*. L. R. Hiatt, ed. Atlantic Highlands, N.J.: Humanities Press.

Trible, Phyllis. (1978) *God and the Rhetoric of Sexuality*. Philadelphia: Fortress Press.

———. (1984) *Texts of Terror: Literary-Feminist Readings of Biblical Narratives*. Philadelphia: Fortress Press.

Turner, Victor. (1967) *The Forest of Symbols*. Ithaca: Cornell University Press.

——— (1972–3) "The Center Out There: Pilgrim's Goal." *History of Religions* 12:191–230.

Van der Horst, P. (1990) "Sarah's Seminal Emission: Hebrews 11:11 in the Light of Ancient Embryology." In *Greeks, Romans and Christians: Essays in Honor of Abraham J. Malherbe*. Minneapolis, Minn.: Fortress Press, 287–302.

———. (1992) "Did Sarah Have A Seminal Emission?" *Bible Review* 8(1) 35–9.

Van Herik, Judith. (1982) *Freud on Femininity and Faith*. Berkeley: University of California Press.

Van Seters, John. (1975) *Abraham in History and Tradition*. New Haven: Yale University Press.

Vaux, Roland de. (1961) *Ancient Israel: Its Life and Institutions*. John McHugh, trans., New York: McGraw Hill.

Vermes, Geza. ([1961]1973) *Scripture and Tradition in Judaism*. Leiden: E. J. Brill.

Waldman, Marilyn. (1986) "New Approaches to 'Biblical' Material in the Qur'an." *Studies in Islamic and Judaic Traditions*. William Brinner and S. Ricks, eds. Atlanta, Ga.: Scholars Press, 47–64.

Wallace, E. R. (1983) *Freud and Anthropology: A History and Reappraisal*. New York: International Universities Press.

Weiner, Annette. (1976) *Women of Value, Men of Renown*. Austin, Tex.: University of Texas Press.

———. (1978). "The Reproductive Model in Trobrand Society." *Mankind* 11:175–86.

Weinfeld, M. (1972) "The Worship of Molech and of the Queen of Heaven." *Ugarit Forschungen* 4:133–54.

———. (1978) "Burning Babies in Ancient Israel: A Rejoinder to Morton Smith's Article in JAOS 95 (1975)." *Ugarit Forschungen* 411–13.

Weininger, Otto. ([1903]1906) *Sex and Character*. London: W. Heineman; New York: Putnam.

Wellisch, Erich. (1954) *Isaac and Oedipus*. London: Routledge & Kegan Paul.

Wenham, G. J. (1980) "The Religion of the Patriarchs." In *Essays on the Patriarchal Narratives*. A. R. Millard and D. J. Wiseman, eds. Leicester, England: Inter-Varsity Press, 157–88.

Westermann, Claus. (1981) "Genesis 22:1–19, Abraham's Sacrifice." S. J. Scullion, trans. In *Genesis 12–36, A Commentary*. Minneapolis, Minn.: Augsburg Publishing House, 351–65.

Wharton, James A. (1988) "On the Road Again: Abraham and Contemporary Preaching." *Interpretation*. Vol. xlii (4):381–92.

Whitehead, Barbara Dafoe. (1993) "Dan Quayle Was Right." *Atlantic Monthly* 27(4):47–84.

Whorf, Benjamin. (1956) "The Relation of Habitual Thought and Behavior to Language." In *Language, Thought and Reality*. Cambridge, Mass.: M.I.T. Press.

Wilken, R. (1972) "The Christianizing of Abraham: The Interpretation of Abraham in Early Christianity." *Concordia Theological Monthly* 43:723–31.

———. (1976) "Melito, The Jewish Community at Sardis, and the Sacrifice of Isaac." *Theological Studies* 37(1) 53–69.

Wills, Lawrence M. (in press) *The Quest of the Historical Gospel: Mark, John, and the Origin of the Gospel Genre*. New York: Routledge Press.

Wineman, Lawrence. (1977) *The Akedah-Motif in the Modern Hebrew Story*. Ph.D. diss., UCLA.

Wiseman, D. J. (1980) "Abraham Reassessed." In *Essays on the Patriarchal Narratives*. A. R. Millard and D. J. Wiseman, eds. Leicester, England: Inter-Varsity Press, 139–56.

Wolkstein, Diane, and Samuel Noah Kramer. (1983) *Inanna: Queen of Heaven and Earth*. New York: Harper and Row.

Woolf, Rosemary. (1972) *English Mystery Plays*. Berkeley: University of California Press.

Wright, G. Ernest. (1960) *Biblical Archaeology*. Philadelphia: Westminster Press.

Yanagisako, Sylvia and Carol Delaney. (1995) *Naturalizing Power: Essays on Feminist Cultural Analysis*. New York: Routledge.

Yerushalmi, Yosef. (1986) "Freud on the 'Historical Novel': From the Manuscript Draft (1934) of *Moses and Monotheism*." *International Journal of Psycho-Analysis* 70:375–95.

———. (1991) *Freud's Moses: Judaism Terminable and Interminable*. New Haven: Yale University Press.

Young, Iris. (1995) "Mothers, Citizenship, and Independence: A Critique of Pure Family Values." *Ethics* 105:535–56.

Zeligs, Dorothy. (1954) "Abraham and Monotheism." *American Imago* 11(3) 293–316.

Index

Abel, 21, 72, 94, 141, 179, 211

Abraham: as before and above the law, 68, 123; Freud's references to, 205, 207; as friend of God, 163; God's promise to seed of, 14, 20, 23, 96, 109, 113, 117–18, 132, 134, 145–48, 151, 153, 168–69, 249; as having misunderstood God, 116, 222; as heroic figure, 117, 221; lineage of, 92, 124, 146, 170; as model of faith, 7, 14, 19, 101, 104, 123, 233–34, 251, 264n.25; as model of faith, in Christian community, 5, 6, 21–22, 59, 111, 147, 153–56, 250; as model of faith, in Islamic community, 5, 6, 59, 111, 180–83; as model of faith, in Jewish community, 5, 6, 21–22, 59, 125–28; Muhammad's parallels with, 172, 174, 179; paternity concerns of, 139; as patriarch, 17, 23, 119–20, 221; as Protestant figure, 58, 154–56; as sole possessor of child to be sacrificed, 7, 18, 22–23, 32, 59–60, 108–9, 234; submissiveness of, to God, 22, 44, 111, 116, 117, 162, 169, 222, 264n.25; ten trials of, 116, 272n.18; tomb of, 20; willingness of, to sacrifice his child, 6–7, 101, 107, 118, 124, 146, 149, 163, 169, 191, 234, 237; as witness for Christ, 148, 154. *See also* Abraham story; circumcision; Hagar; Isaac; Ishmael; Sarah

Abraham (television miniseries), 9, 275n.2

Abraham, Karl, 200, 202, 208–10, 285n.24

Abraham story (Akedah): absence of women from, 17–18, 60–63, 251; in art, 10, 110, 136, 138, 140, 150, 161, 175,

222; Christian references to, 137–60; contemporary uses of, 9, 130–35; as a cultural text, 9–10, 34, 74, 141; destructive legacy of, 13–14, 20–21, 109, 184, 233–53; in fiction, 9, 130–31, 256n.7; as foundational story for Judaism, Christianity, and Islam, 5, 6, 17, 20, 21–23, 73, 90–91, 101, 107, 162–63, 190, 210, 229, 233, 237, 255n.2; Freud's ignoring of, 189–210, 229; impact of, on children, 9, 50–51, 141, 163, 204, 233–50, 275n.5; as injunction against child sacrifice, 13, 33, 71, 101, 104, 218, 219; Jewish and Muslim overlaps concerning, 167–68; in Middle Ages, 126–28, 149–51, 170–71; as most patriarchal of stories, 12; obedience as theme in, 14, 32, 85, 104, 111, 116–18, 127, 129, 132, 154–55, 215, 222, 233; paternity concept established in, 94; in *piyyut*, 127; in popular culture, 9, 10, 132–36, 138; power of, 6; as precursor of Crucifixion story, 8, 46–47, 75, 109, 118, 119, 132, 137, 138–39, 141–44, 151, 153–54; psychoanalytic views of, 211–29; rationality vs. emotionality in, 49, 117, 125, 223, 234, 289n.1; redemptive quality of, 118, 120; and resurrection, 122, 138–39, 143, 153–54, 183, 273n.24; self-sacrifice vs. child sacrifice in, 22, 116–17; separation and individuation themes in, 221–22; succession as theme in, 85, 100–101; as test of faith, 21–22, 73, 115–20, 127, 168, 279n.14; as universal, 77–78, 90; in Valenti episode, 5, 53, 56, 59; Vedic

Bible: Akedah as unique event in, 72, 101, 104, 142; archaeological discoveries relating to, 24, 75–76; as authority for punishment of children, 237–38; Christian encompassment of Hebrew, 137, 141–48; contemporary interpreters of, 17, 74, 107–8, 141–43, 146, 158, 160, 252, 256n.1; Freud's family, 205, 206; historical background of text of, 74–76; as ideological, 107; on Molech, 89; other child sacrifice examples in, 22, 58, 87–104, 269n.1; patriarchy's naturalization in, 19, 28–29, 60, 109, 124–25, 216, 221; threat of destruction in, 18, 117–18, 132. *See also* Abraham story; Book of Maccabees; Book of Jubilees; Genesis; language; Pentateuch; *specific books, characters, and commentaries on the Bible*
Black Stone (in Ka'ba), 177–78, 180
blood: of broken hymen, 182–83; differences between men's and women's, 99; and expiation, 121, 142; menstrual, 178, 271n.12; and protection of Jews, 121; and union with God, 128. *See also* blood sacrifice
blood sacrifice: and Abraham's test, 101, 104; archaeological evidence regarding, 80; and blood brotherhood, 109, 180, 182, 183, 272n.16; and circumcision, 96–98, 182; vs. fruit offerings, 94–95; among Jews, 260n.4; as men's responsibility, 9, 36, 163, 180–81, 184, 270n.8. *See also* animal sacrifice; blood; child sacrifice; circumcision; human sacrifice
Bloom, Harold, 267n.5, 271n.6
Boas, Franz, 89
Book of Jubilees, 113, 115, 119–20, 144
Book of Maccabees, 113, 125, 143
Brome cycle (of medieval morality plays), 149
Brown, Joanne Carlson, 160
Brown, Michael, 129–30
Brunelleschi, Filippo, 151
Buell, Denise, 259n.25, 276n.19
Buraq (horse), 176

Cain, 21, 93, 94, 141, 211
calendar: B.C./A.D. vs. B.C.E., 267n.6; Jewish, 119–20, 144; in Jubilees, 144; Muslim, 164–65, 172
Canaan, 81, 84–85, 88, 101
cannibalism, 192, 194–95, 224, 285n.25, 287n.6
Carter, Jimmy, 9
Carthage, 81–83, 90
Cartun, Mark Gregory, 271n.11
castration, 78, 83, 97, 194, 287n.6, 292n.19
Catholic Church: and child abuse, 240–41; 290nn. 10 and 12; nuns in, 48; obedience in, 47–48; Valenti's jury's experience with, 48; Valenti's upbringing in, 41, 47–48, 58. *See also* priests
Cave of the Patriarchs, 20
Celebi, Suleyman, 170
Chagall, Marc, 110, 132
child abuse: as Abraham story's legacy, 13, 224, 233–50; and concerns about paternity, 216; divine model for, 160; and poverty, 241
child care: costs of, 247; crisis in, 6; men's involvement in, 218–19, 228; women's responsibilities for, 8, 218, 242–43, 246. *See also* childrearing practices
child sacrifice: in Abraham story, 5, 21–22, 41, 72, 87, 90, 118, 126, 169–70; Abraham story as injunction against, 13, 33, 71, 101, 104, 218, 219; animal sacrifice as substitute for, 6, 9, 13, 71–74, 119, 126, 128, 163, 195; archaeological evidence concerning, 71–86; to avoid religious conversion, 126–27; child protection vs., 5, 14, 22, 44, 47, 118, 133–35, 159–60, 249, 252–53; current welfare policies as, 14, 233, 235, 241–47, 265n.31; of firstborns, 87, 89, 90, 97; Jesus as God the Father's, 8, 47, 59, 120, 126, 137, 141, 149, 204, 234; lack of indignation concerning, 14; other Biblical examples of, 22, 58, 87–104, 257n.11, 264n.25, 269n.1; presumed end of, 6, 104, 128; as propitiatory, 203; vs. self-sacrifice, 22, 116–17; war

Ghiberti, Lorenzo, 151
Gilboa, Amir, 129
Ginzberg, Louis, 115
Gnostics, 145
goddesses, 268n.14; Athena, 195–96,
279n.18; Demeter, 160; Inanna,
268n.14; Metis, 180, 196, 279n.18;
Persephone, 160; pre-Islamic, 172
God's voice: and Abraham, 58, 113, 123;
Luther on, 154–55; and Valenti, 38–40,
42–45, 56, 58, 123
Goldberg, Harvey, 114
The Golden Bough (Frazer), 91
Goldson, Edward, 248
Gordon, Neil, 9, 130
"Great Man." *See* father(s)
Greeks (ancient): father's right to accept or
reject child among, 100, 244; hero tradi-
tion among, 275n.8; myths of, 76, 81,
82–83, 85, 194; procreation theory of,
8. *See also* goddesses
Green, Alberto R., 80
Greven, Philip, 215, 238, 290n.6
grief, 149, 276n.12
guilt, 193, 196, 200, 202, 203, 229
Gulf War, 248

Hackett, Jo Ann, 268n.17, 269n.23
hadith, 164, 166–69
Hagar, 17, 135, 147, 169–70, 174–75; ex-
clusion of, from Abraham story, 22–23,
60
Hajj, 9, 176; and Abraham story, 163,
179–80, 207; customs involved in, 123,
175, 177, 180, 184. *See also* Feast of the
Sacrifice; Mecca
hallucinations (auditory), 39–40, 42, 43
Hannah, 157
al Haram al Sharif. *See* Dome of the Rock
Haran (or Harran: Turkey), 77–79, 81,
172–74
Hebrews (ancient), 8, 207. *See also*
Israelites
Hebrews (Biblical book), 138, 153, 157
Hebron massacre, 20
Hell. *See* Gehenna
Herhold, Robert, 248–49

Herman, Judith, 240
hero: birth of, 171, 199, 279n.18
Herod, 171
Hesiod, 196
hijra, 172
Hinnom (valley of), 88, 89, 178. *See also*
Gehenna
Holiness Code. *See* Leviticus
Holocaust, 9, 128–30, 272n.14
holy (sacred), 262n.11, 263n.18
Hultgård, Anders, 30
human sacrifice: Abraham story as end of,
in Judaism, 59, 104, 126, 128; animal
sacrifice as substitution for, 6, 13, 71–
74, 119, 126, 128, 163, 195; archaeological evidence of, 80, 83–87; in civilized, not primitive, societies, 73–74,
236; among cults, 44; to Molech, 88;
and redemption, 144, 151; as sign of
God's punishment, 95–96, 234. *See also*
blood sacrifice; child sacrifice
hurban, 129

Ibn Ishaq, 167, 170, 176, 280n.20
idols, 172, 179, 273n.24
Ikhnaton (Amenhotep IV), 200, 201–2,
208, 209
illegitimacy: concerns about, 87, 92–94,
99–100, 139, 193, 216–17, 226; stigma
of, 244–45
incest, 212, 239–41, 288n.17
infanticide, 33, 214–16, 218, 219, 224,
229, 236. *See also* child sacrifice; fa-
ther(s): desire of, to kill sons; ritual
sacrifice
"insanity" (legal definition of), 63–65
"inseminate," 31–32
"intertestamental period," 142, 145
Iphigenia, 87
Irenaeus, 149, 275n.3
Isaac: Abraham's deception of, 155; as actually sacrificed, 122, 124, 126, 132,
221; age of, at sacrifice, 122, 273n.26;
"ashes of," 122, 142; "binding" of, 33,
46, 111, 121, 138–39, 149; birth of, 96,
199; blood associated with, 120, 121,
142; early Church Fathers on, 148–49;